The "Huddled Masses" Myth

THE "HUDDLED MASSES" MYTH

IMMIGRATION AND

CIVIL RIGHTS

Kevin R. Johnson

 Temple University Press
PHILADELPHIA

KF
4819
.J64
2004

Temple University Press, Philadelphia 19122
Copyright © 2004 by Temple University
All rights reserved
Published 2004
Printed in the United States of America

⊖ The paper used in this publication meets the requirements of
the American National Standard for Information Sciences—Permanence
of Paper for Printed Library Materials, ANSI Z39.48-1984

Library of Congress Cataloging-in-Publication Data

Johnson, Kevin R.
    The "huddled masses" myth : immigration and civil rights /
Kevin R. Johnson
        p.   cm.
    Includes bibliographical references and index.
    ISBN 1-59213-205-7 (cloth : alk. paper) — ISBN 1-59213-206-5 (pbk. : alk. paper)
        1. Emigration and immigration law—United States.   2. Discrimination—United
States.   3. United States—Emigration and immigration—Government policy.   I. Title.

KF4819.J64 2004
342.73′082—dc21

                                                                2003050792

2 4 6 8 9 7 5 3 1

To my family

Virginia, Teresa, Tomás, and Elena
Kenneth and Angela

Contents

Acknowledgments

The original focus of this book was the role of race in the emergence of anti-immigrant sentiment and the immigration debate in the United States. As I became immersed in the complexities of the politics of immigration and its broader impacts on U.S. social life, however, the book evolved into a broader project about U.S. immigration law and civil rights.

Some of the ideas expressed herein have been presented in a series of law review articles published over the past decade. Chapter 2 is adapted from my article *Race, the Immigration Laws, and Domestic Race Relations: A "Magic Mirror" into the Heart of Darkness*, 73 INDIANA LAW JOURNAL 1111 (1998). Chapter 3 is adapted from my article *The Antiterrorism Act, the Immigration Reform Act, and Ideological Regulation in the Immigration Laws: Important Lessons for Citizens and Noncitizens*, 28 ST. MARY'S LAW JOURNAL 833 (1997). Some of the discussions in other chapters have also been adapted from other articles.

I am grateful for the support of many people. Over the years, correspondence and conversation with Richard Delgado helped sharpen my thinking on the overarching themes of this book. I am indebted to both Richard and Jean Stefancic for their support of my scholarship throughout my academic career. Doris Braendel, then of Temple University Press, helped me immensely through the early stages of the publication process. Janet Francendese of Temple University Press guided me through the book's completion. Many friends have offered insights and support without which the publication of this book would not have been possible. Among them are George A. Martínez, Diane Amann, Christopher David Ruiz Cameron, Arturo Gándara, Michael A. Olivas, Mary Romero, Sylvia Lazos, Rex Perschbacher, Jack Ayer, Joel Dobris, Michael Scaperlanda, Amagda Pérez, Stephen Reinhardt, Bill Ong Hing, Keith Aoki, Holly Doremus, and law professors and students too numerous to list. I am also grateful to Mary Romero, Michael Welch, and Bill Hing for their helpful comments on a draft of the book manuscript.

I have been fortunate to have had the excellent research assistance of students Rebecca Jackson (University of California at Davis, 2004), Roberta Hulit (University of California at Davis, 1999), Melissa Corral (University of California at Davis, 1998), Sushil Narayanan (University of California at Davis, 1998), and Christine Shen (University of California at Davis, 1997). The University of California, Davis, Academic Senate, Committee on Research and the School of Law provided early research funding for this project; I am especially indebted to Deans Bruce Wolk (1993–1998) and Rex Perschbacher (1998–present) for their support. I also thank Brigid Jimenez, who worked long and hard on this project and many others, for her excellent editorial assistance.

As in all my endeavors, the love and patience of my wife, Virginia, and my children, Teresa, Tomás, and Elena, provided the inspiration for this book. Though some, perhaps many, of the ideas expressed herein may not be of much consequence, my devotion to my family unquestionably is.

Immigration and Civil Rights in the United States

ne of the more overquoted poems in U.S. history is Emma
Lazarus's "The New Colossus":

> Give me your tired, your poor,
> Your huddled masses yearning to breathe free,
> The wretched refuse of your teeming shore.[1]

These famous words inscribed on the Statue of Liberty unquestionably shaped the national consciousness about immigration to the United States throughout the twentieth century.[2] At times, the nation has acted with incredible generosity
toward immigrants, in a manner entirely consistent with the
laudable ideal expressed by Lazarus. However, the U.S. immigration laws have also occasioned a darker history, one that
is painful to recall and thus frequently forgotten. This book,
in its focus on this harsher side of the nation's immigration
history, contends that the U.S. government's treatment of immigrants is inextricably linked to the efforts of domestic minorities to secure civil rights and full membership in U.S. society.

At least in broad strokes, the U.S. embrace of the "huddled masses" model of immigration has influenced the nation's immigration law and policy. The United States, for example, accepts many more immigrants than most nations,
hundreds of thousands each year. Indeed, over nine hundred

1

thousand immigrants were admitted to this country in fiscal year 1996 alone.[3] The nation accepts refugees from across the globe who have fled political, racial, religious, and other invidious persecution by governments, security forces, political insurgents, and other rogue elements. Since the U.S. Congress eliminated racial exclusions from the U.S. immigration laws in the heyday of the 1960s civil rights movement, the laws have included no race-based prerequisites for admission. Consequently, the vast majority of immigrants to the United States today are people of color. Compared with other nations, the United States requires a relatively short period of residence—five years—before most immigrants are eligible for citizenship. Moreover, in the United States, citizenship may be bestowed by birth, not only by blood and ancestry as in many countries. In fact, much of the history of the U.S. immigration and nationality laws should fill U.S citizens with pride.

Another aspect of U.S. immigration history, however, is a source of shame to those who are committed to equality under the law. A cursory review of history reveals a lack of U.S openness to and acceptance of the "huddled masses," the "tired," or the "poor." This book examines how the U.S. immigration laws and their enforcement have barred racial minorities, political dissidents, the poor, actual and alleged criminals, and homosexuals from our shores and—often pursuant to procedures that are difficult, if not impossible, to square with the notion of due process of law—have caused them to be deported from the country. In addition, the following chapters look at how women—treated as the property of their husbands or, if unmarried, as potential welfare mothers (a cruelly ironic Catch-22)—have also been the subject of discriminatory practices under the immigration and nationality laws over the course of this nation's history.

As intuition would suggest, the United States has sought to exclude those categories of immigrants who share common characteristics with groups that are disfavored in this country. Despite the nation's egalitarian pronouncements, many notable episodes in U.S. history demonstrate harsh treatment of its minority citizens. The segregation of black and white children in schools, the genocide of Native American peoples, the internment of Japanese Americans during World War II, and the deportation of Mexican American citizens during the Great Depression are a few well-known examples. Such actions have flown in the face of the legal rights afforded to all U.S. citizens by the U.S. Constitution and, especially, the Bill of Rights.

At times, although certainly not always, the law has intervened to protect subordinated groups of U.S. citizens. The U.S. Supreme Court's decision in *Brown v. Board of Education*,[4] which held that segregation in the public schools failed to constitute "equal protection of the laws," is perhaps the most cherished example. The monumental decision in that case formally vindicated the legal rights of African American citizens and helped launch a major change in the U.S. civil rights landscape. Although we have yet to fully realize the integration of U.S. society, *Brown* transformed integration into a legally sanctioned and socially acceptable goal.

The U.S. government's treatment of citizens differs from its treatment of "aliens"—those who are not U.S. citizens. Claiming to exercise inherent rights as a sovereign nation, the United States has often refused to welcome people of color, political dissidents, the poor, criminals, women, and lesbians and gay men who seek to immigrate. Unlike the participation of the courts in the struggle for the rights of citizens, judicial review of the constitutionality of laws that provide for the exclusion and deportation of immigrants has been negligible. As long as noncitizens are afforded minimal procedural safeguards, the courts have afforded Congress free reign with respect to exclusion and deportation of noncitizens. Because of the unpopularity of—even hatred toward—foreigners among the general population in times of crisis and social unrest, a meaningful political check on the unfair treatment of immigrants does not exist. As a result, both Congress and the president have the ability to direct the most extreme action toward noncitizens with little fear of provoking a judicial response.

Immigration law is thus an especially illuminating resource for studying the place of domestic groups in the U.S. social hierarchy. Under traditional immigration law, the government is afforded free reign to treat noncitizens, denominated "aliens," as it sees fit. In contrast, U.S. citizens who are members of minority groups enjoy rights under the U.S. Constitution and other laws. Although these rights may be expanded or constrained depending on the political winds or the judicial philosophy of a particular era, they generally cannot lawfully be revoked for any U.S. citizen.

Consider the treatment of "undesirable" immigrants in U.S. immigration history. Consistently unwilling to intervene on behalf of noncitizens, the courts have emphasized the "plenary power" of Congress, based on notions of national sovereignty over the substantive admission and deportation provisions of the immigration laws. As philosophers have put it, government may conduct affairs as if it were in the "state of nature," able to strike out at the unpopular "aliens" who are deemed to threaten the well-being of the nation.[5] The dominant society's treatment of noncitizens gives us a view of its potential treatment of U.S. citizens who share similar characteristics if all legal constraints were lifted. What does the nation's deep commitment to the exclusion of poor immigrants, for example, tell us about society's attitudes toward the nation's poor? Similar questions are raised by virtually every ground under the U.S. immigration laws on which a noncitizen can be barred from entering the country or deported.

This book examines the U.S. immigration laws in terms of what they reveal about the dominant society's views toward the civil rights of subordinated groups in the United States. The categories of people that the nation seeks to exclude reflect society's attitude toward both citizens and legal immigrants residing in the United States who fall into these categories. To a certain extent, the law protects against such discrimination toward citizen minorities. No such moderating influence exists to protect noncitizens, however. The wholesale prohibition of the immigration of members of the Chinese working class to the United States in the late 1800s, for example, reflects the dominant white population's view of Chinese Americans and the status of Chinese American civil rights. Anti-Chinese sentiment, widespread discrimination, and violence, particularly on the West Coast, were rampant. Efforts to repatriate Mexican citizens to reduce the welfare rolls during the 1930s and to deport undocumented Mexican immigrants in the 1990s reveals how society viewed Mexican Americans in its midst. Not long after the repatriation campaigns of the 1930s, U.S. servicemen attacked and beat Mexican American youths on the streets of Los Angeles as police watched, in the famous Zoot Suit riots during World War II.[6] In short, the law has permitted a history of exclusion of the least valued citizens in U.S. society, citizens who might well be banished themselves if the law permitted.

The laws that protect the rights of all citizens moderate efforts to discriminate against minority citizens. In addition, harsh policies directed at domestic minorities have been known to cause international repercussions.[7] Indeed, some commentators go so far as to claim that *Brown v. Board of Education* and its call for desegregation was necessitated by the U.S. government's Cold War foreign policy concerns.[8] Modern civil rights sensibilities make harsh treatment of domestic minorities politically unpalatable. Domestic minorities wield a certain amount of political influence. Politicians ignore at their peril African American, Asian American, and Latina/o voters, who have been the subject of increasing political competition among Democrats and Republicans in recent years. Consequently, to a certain extent, not only legal but political constraints moderate the majority's treatment of domestic minorities.

Such constraints, however, generally do not affect the treatment of persons outside U.S. borders. Brutal treatment of foreigners has often found support among the public at large. A relatively recent example was the absence of strong objection to Haitian interdiction and repatriation in the 1990s. The Supreme Court upheld the policy, demonstrating once again that the law offers limited protection to noncitizens, particularly those who seek to enter the country.[9] After the tragedy of September 11, 2001, the public strongly supported harsh actions against Muslim and Arab noncitizens, and the federal government aggressively pursued such policies. Other nations, with domestic pressures and concerns similar to those of the United States, often accept the notion that the United States has sovereign prerogative over its borders. Thus, international law has offered few protections to noncitizens who seek entry into or resist deportation from the United States.

Occasionally, the international community pressures the United States to moderate its treatment of foreign migrants. For example, Mexico's President Vicente Fox has pressed for regularization of the immigration status of Mexican nationals in this country and for the establishment of freer migration between the United States and Mexico. Such pressures are limited, however, and if strong domestic political pressures push in another direction, they are easy for the U.S. government to ignore. Because of the relative absence of constraints in curtailing the rights of noncitizens in the political community, the United States has experienced repeated episodes of highly volatile xenophobic attacks on politically unpopular "aliens" of a particular era.

Exacerbating the relative powerlessness of noncitizens is their lack of any direct input into the political process; they must rely on the votes of people who are less directly affected by immigration law and policy. Latina/o and Asian American citizens have at times been vigilant in advocating for the rights of immigrants. In part, this stems from a desire to protect immigrant members of their own communities who suffer the brunt of the enforcement of the immigration laws. In part, it is a response to the belief that anti-immigrant sentiment reveals negative views toward their community as a whole. California's Proposition 187, which aimed to reduce public benefits to undocumented immigrants, and the strife over language regulation in the state exemplify the battles over the status of racial groups in U.S. society that laws can come to represent. Whereas Anglos supported Proposition 187 two to one, Latinas/os opposed it by an even larger margin.

As this discussion suggests, the differential treatment of citizens and noncitizens is rationalized in part by a legal fiction. The "alien" is a category of persons created entirely by the law. Much has been written about how notions of race are social constructions that serve to help justify racial subordination.[10] Beliefs in racial inferiority rationalize racial hierarchy. Historically, the negative treatment of different U.S. "racial" groups, such as the Irish and southern and eastern Europeans, that are today considered to be white is a powerful demonstration of race as a social rather than a biological construction.[11] Immigrant status, even more clearly than race, is also a social construction. It is not immutable, and it is not fixed by biology. The law creates "aliens" as outsiders who are allocated few political and legal rights. Moreover, the legal construction of "aliens" not only affects the general public's view of noncitizens but also contributes to their harsh treatment.

Given the modern sensibilities about civil rights, the unsympathetic treatment of noncitizens can be more easily rationalized than can attacks on minority citizens. As this justification goes, we support fair treatment of citizens of Mexican ancestry but simply want to halt the immigration of "aliens," especially "illegal aliens," who cause social, economic, and political problems. We are not "racist," even though the enforcement measures that we endorse fall disproportionately on people of color; we simply want to promote an immigration policy that serves all U.S. citizens.

This rationalization is unpersuasive. In the modern United States, race and immigrant status neatly, albeit loosely, coincide. The immigrants who are adversely affected by a restrictionist measure are, more likely than not, racial minorities. The vast majority of today's immigrants to the United States—as many as 80 to 90 percent each year—are people of color. Consequently, an attack on immigrants disproportionately affects people of color. This impact is a predictable, if not an intentional, consequence of many restrictionist measures in modern times. In certain circumstances, restrictionist laws and policies may, in fact, amount to an attack on people of color, with immigration status used as a proxy for race. The use of proxies to discriminate obscures the true inequality of the law and allows for the plausible denial of a discriminatory intent while ensuring discriminatory results.

In their analysis of the history of immigration laws, the chapters that follow conclude that, taken as a whole, the laws reflect the dominant sentiment about subordinated groups in the United States. As John Higham's classic study of nativism in the United States has documented,[12] this nation has historically exhibited a great intolerance for immigrants who deviate from the perceived Anglo-Saxon norm. The harsh treatment that has undeniably been meted out to disfavored groups of U.S. citizens, does not compare to the nation's harsh treatment of "aliens"—by definition outsiders to the community—who share the same characteristics as the disfavored groups of citizens. This phenomenon is evident in recent immigration milestones: the reduction of public benefits to immigrants as part of welfare reform combined with punitive immigration reform legislation in 1996; the militarization of the U.S. border with Mexico in the 1990s that resulted in hundreds of deaths of Mexican citizens; the unconscionable treatment of Haitians (poor, black, and culturally different) fleeing political and economic turmoil; the crackdown on "criminal aliens," which resulted in record levels of deportations of Mexican citizens; and the targeting of Arabs and Muslims by means of special reporting requirements, arrests, interrogations, and detention after the September 11, 2001, attacks.

These lessons hold true for most subordinated peoples in the United States. The history of racial exclusions in the immigration laws is perhaps one of the most well-known examples. Beginning in the 1800s, the race and class of Chinese immigrants prompted their exclusion under the U.S. immigration laws. Racial fears toward southern and eastern Europeans culminated in the Immigration Act of 1924 and the national origins quota system. Although the Immigration Act of 1965 eliminated the most glaring grounds for racial exclusion, the immigration laws in operation today continue to have distinctly racial impacts.

The poor, considered likely to become "public charges," have also been subjected to exclusion and deportation under the immigration laws. One of the oldest features of the federal immigration laws, the public charge provisions, adversely affects the largest numbers of potential immigrants. Today, the public charge exclusion bars thousands of immigrants from developing nations that are populated by people of color from coming to the United States each year. Political undesirables, such as anarchists, communists, and (in current parlance) "terrorists," have been marked for adverse treatment as well. In the aftermath of the Red Scare following World War I and the years dominated by Senator Joseph McCarthy's search for communists in our midst, the federal government's vigorous application of the ideological provisions of the immigration laws resulted in extreme impacts on immigrants who had lived peacefully in this country for many years.

In addition to racial, political, and class litmus tests in the U.S. immigration laws, the chapters that follow consider the treatment of "criminal aliens" and women under immigration law. "Criminal aliens," most of whom, as the laws are applied, turn out to be immigrants of color, have long been demonized. Popular "tough on crime" measures, which picked up steam in the United States in the 1990s, translated into draconian punishment of "criminal aliens," including congressional efforts to eliminate judicial review (one of the fundamental protections against bureaucratic tyranny) of their deportation orders. Immigrant women have often been denied entry into the United States as presumptive public charges or prostitutes or as members of the same undesirable groups (based, for example, on race or national origin) as their spouses. At the same time, women have been liberally admitted as immigrant spouses of male U.S. citizens. The conditions of such admission, however, have at times opened the doors to domestic violence and abuse, as exemplified most vividly in the Immigration Marriage Fraud Amendments of 1986. As the problems that face immigrant women are ignored, this group is increasingly exploited in the garment industry and other job sectors, in the burgeoning mail-order bride industry, and in the sex trade.

Lesbians and gay men were first officially marked for exclusion and deportation under the Immigration and Nationality Act of 1952 (INA), which was passed by Congress at the height of the Cold War. Premised on the view of homosexuals as deviants who were prone to communism and, because of their "secret" sexual orientation, vulnerable to blackmail, the law provided for their exclusion from the United States. The desire to exclude and deport lesbians and gay men from the United States began to wane with the nation's changing social attitudes toward these groups. But the double penalization of gay men and lesbians—as immigrants and as sexual minorities—exemplifies the double-edged sword experienced by socially unpopular groups through the nation's immigration laws.

The U.S. government's response to the tragedy of September 11, demonstrates the impact of disadvantaging characteristics that overlap. Arab and Muslim men, already racially, culturally, and religiously different from the Anglo-Saxon norm, are now being profiled as potential terrorists and political enemies of the United States as well. Similarly, the historical exclusion of political dissidents often implicated issues of race and class. The nation viewed "new" southern and eastern European immigrants of the early twentieth century as racially inferior, poor, and inclined toward anarchism, communism, and other anti-American political ideologies. Congressional concern about the commitment to democracy and self-government of the southern and eastern European "races," in part motivated the national origins quota system in the Immigration Act of 1924, which drastically reduced immigration from those nations.

Why does the United States treat its immigrants so harshly, even as it purports to embrace the world's "huddled masses" and to dedicate its efforts to improving the status of the world's disadvantaged? Why does the United States as a nation treat "outsiders" in the country harshly and noncitizens outside the country even more so? It is clear that a relationship exists between the treatment of immigrants and minority citizens. African Americans, for example, suffer many more hardships in modern social life than do whites.[13] Consider the example of U.S. policies toward black persons seeking refuge from violent political and economic upheaval in Haiti. In the 1970s, the U.S. government pursued a policy of detaining Haitians once they had landed in the United States. This was followed by the 1980s interdiction of boats from Haiti on the high seas and half-hearted attempts to identify bona fide refugees. In the 1990s, the government devised the most extreme of all measures: interdiction and immediate repatriation of all Haitians whether or not they had a credible fear of persecution, a policy that, by most accounts, violates international law. The U.S. Supreme Court refused to intervene. Moreover, this has occurred at a time when, although some might debate the degree of change, racial sensibilities toward African Americans have improved significantly over the previous one hundred years.

The cynic might argue that the case of the Haitians is exceptional. The nation feared a flood of thousands of people; we cannot, after all, accept all the poor people in the world who want to come to this "land of opportunity." This line of argument, however, disregards the obvious: that popular opinion was undoubtedly shaped by the fact that the Haitians in question were poor, black, and culturally different from most of the citizens of the United States. A mass migration of poor, black people who practiced the religion Santería and might carry the HIV virus prompted much fear. When the U.S. government returned thousands of Haitians to the violence and desperation of their homeland, objections from U.S. citizens were negligible.

Historically, women too have been marginalized and systematically disadvantaged by the U.S. immigration laws. For example, early in the twentieth century, women who married immigrants lost their citizenship under the premise that women were mere extensions of their husbands. In 1986, congressional efforts to stem sham marriages for immigration benefits created strong incentives for immigrant women to remain in violent and abusive relationships and eventually prompted a series of legislative efforts at reform.

The exclusionary aspects of the U.S. immigration laws remain intact in the modern era. The nation has become somewhat more tolerant of political dissent since the 1950s grip of McCarthyism. But even before the September 11 attacks, the U.S. government deported immigrants for their political views (sometimes after hearings in which the alleged "terrorist" was denied the opportunity to review the government's evidence) and for tenuous links to Arab and Muslim "terrorists." Legal constraints soften the treatment of poor citizens in our cities. But few constraints limit governmental power to bar the poor—the archetypal "huddled masses"—from immigrating to the United States, severely limit the eligibility of poor immigrants to public benefits, and deport those immigrants who utilize such benefits and services, all features of the modern immigration laws. Although perhaps narrowed by the U.S. Supreme Court during Chief Justice William Rehnquist's leadership, constitutional protections exist for citizen criminals; in contrast, the political process has subjected the deeply unpopular "criminal aliens" to increasingly harsh measures. Until 1990, homosexuals could be banned from entering the United States as "psychopathic personalities." At the time of the removal of that bar from the immigration laws, there was a growing recognition in this country that lesbians and gay men had rights against discrimination.

The chapters that follow explore the differential treatment of noncitizens and of citizens who share characteristics in common with noncitizens. In an era marked by intense anti-immigrant sentiment in the United States, and perhaps the world, it is especially important to understand the dynamic relationship between immigration and the civil rights of minorities. This book's examination of the relationship between the treatment of noncitizen minorities and domestic minorities offers insights into how dominant society views subordinated groups, including people of color, political dissidents, the poor, criminals, women, and homosexuals. The harsh treatment of "alien" minorities under the immigration laws is a reflection of U.S. society's potential treatment of domestic minorities, even U.S. citizens, in the absence of legal and other constraints. The history of exclusion and deportation of noncitizens under the U.S. immigration laws give us a view of the very soul of America, and what we learn is disturbing.

Without boundaries demarcated by law, the nation could well act out its true desires with respect to disfavored minority groups. Could that time ever come? The possibility may not be as far-fetched as some might believe. As part of the war on terrorism that followed September 11, 2001, the federal government aggressively acted against Arab and Muslim noncitizens, arresting, interrogating, and detaining hundreds with no evidence of individual wrongdoing and later carried out some of the same actions against U.S. citizens. Consider the case of a U.S. citizen, born Jose Padilla, who converted to Islam and changed his name to Abdullah Al-Muhajir.[14] Arrested and detained in the United States for alleged involvement in the early stages of an Al Qaeda terrorist plan to construct and detonate a "dirty bomb" in this country, he has been labeled an "enemy combatant" by the U.S. government and was denied access to an attorney. The federal government, moreover, has announced that it plans to hold al-Muhajir in a military jail indefinitely without charging him with a crime. In this precedent-setting case, the U.S. government has, by means of presidential fiat, denied a U.S. citizen protections guaranteed by the Bill of Rights. This example reveals what is at stake for citizens and noncitizens as the war on terrorism continues. It suggests that the U.S. government's treatment of noncitizens is inextricably linked to its treatment of citizens. Denial of rights to noncitizens lays the groundwork for the denial of rights to citizens. Clearly, those who are truly committed to racial justice in the United States cannot ignore the treatment of immigrants.

2

Exclusion and Deportation of Racial Minorities

he treatment of "aliens," particularly those of color, under the U.S. immigration laws parallels domestic race relations in this nation. A complex, often volatile, relationship exists between racism against citizens and racism against noncitizens. Peter Brimelow's best-selling anti-immigrant book, *Alien Nation: Common Sense About America's Immigration Disaster*,[1] exemplifies this relationship. *Alien Nation* ostensibly criticizes the state of U.S. immigration law; in fact, however, the book attacks affirmative action, "Hispanics," multiculturalism, bilingual education, and virtually any program designed to remedy discrimination in the United States.

As the legacy of chattel slavery and forced migration from Africa would have it, the United States has a long history of treating its racial minorities harshly, at times savagely. Noncitizen racial minorities, who are considered to be outside the national community, generally have been subjected not only to similar cruelties but also to such actions as deportation and indefinite detention. The differential treatment is permitted, if not encouraged, by the disparate bundles of legal rights afforded to citizen and noncitizen minorities.

The so-called "plenary power" doctrine of U.S. immigration law has historically shielded substantive immigration judgments made by the political branches of government from meaningful judicial review. This legal doctrine, born in an era when Congress aggressively acted to exclude Chinese immigrants from this nation's shores, bestows great discretion on the U.S. government in the establishment of rules that regulate the admission of noncitizens into the country. Although the Supreme Court has perhaps narrowed its scope, the plenary power doctrine remains the law of the land today.[2] Moreover, the Court has invoked the doctrine to permit the federal government, and at times the states, to discriminate against immigrants who have the lawful right to remain permanently in this country.[3]

Among other legal protections afforded to racial minorities who are citizens, they may rely on the Equal Protection Clause of the Fourteenth Amendment to challenge discriminatory governmental action[4] and the Civil Rights Act of 1964[5] to fight racism in the workplace. Although the close of the twentieth century marked a number of rollbacks in legal protections,[6] the law, at least in theory, serves to protect discrete and insular minorities from the excesses of the political process.[7]

More than just a peculiar feature of U.S. public law, the differential treatment of citizens and noncitizens is a "magic mirror" that reveals how dominant society might treat domestic minorities if legal constraints were lifted. Indeed, the harsh treatment of noncitizens of color reveals the terrifying realities of society's view of citizens of color. For example, the era of exclusion of Chinese immigrants in the 1800s occurred almost simultaneously with punitive, often violent, action against the Chinese on the West Coast. Efforts to exclude and deport Mexican citizens from the United States, which accelerated over the course of the twentieth century, similarly reflect society's general view of Mexican American citizens, just as the extraordinarily harsh policies directed toward poor, black Haitians seeking refuge from violent political and economic turmoil leave little room for doubt—if there ever was any—about how this society as a whole views its own poor black citizens. Moreover, the U.S. government's "war on terrorism" elucidates the status of all Arabs and Muslims in the United States, citizens and noncitizens alike. As suspected terrorists, their civil rights can be—and have been—sacrificed in the name of national security.

Even while attacks on immigrants of color pervade the national consciousness, some informed observers claim that racism is a historical artifact in the United States or at least has greatly diminished as a driving force behind policy making at the turn of the twenty-first century.[8] Based in part on this premise, political forces attack affirmative action,[9] multiculturalism,[10] and ameliorative programs created in response to the civil rights struggles of the 1960s. At the same historical moment, Congress, with minimal resistance, has passed increasingly restrictive immigration laws, in the name of fighting a range of social ills from welfare fraud to crime to terrorism to "illegal" immigration.[11] This chapter contends that the simultaneous anti-immigrant sentiment and antiminority backlash of the 1990s in this country was no coincidence.

With the transformation of racial sensibilities in modern times, the subordination of Asian immigrants and the use of quotas to exclude racialized peoples,[12] combined with other devices, evolved into more subtle forms of exclusion. It is no idle concern that without the Constitution and other legal protections, domestic minorities could expect no better treatment than their foreign brothers and sisters. The U.S. Supreme Court once declared that African Americans "had no rights which the white man was bound to respect."[13] In the "war on terrorism" following September 11, 2001, the U.S. government has denied two U.S. citizens their constitutional rights merely by labeling them "enemy combatants." Even with the change in racial sensibilities, this nation has at times denied rights to racial minorities. To avoid a repetition of this history, those who value civil rights must consider the exclusionary aspects of the U.S. immigration laws.

Beyond simply summarizing how racism has infected immigration law and policy in the United States, this chapter demonstrates the ways that harsh treatment of noncitizens reveals society's view of citizens of color. As psychological theory would suggest, the virulent attacks on noncitizens represent transference and displacement of animosity for racial minorities in general. Because direct attacks on minorities with respect to their race is today off-limits, discrimination is displaced to foreign minorities. A war on noncitizens of color that focuses on their immigration status rather than their race, as conscious or subconscious cover, serves to vent social frustration. Hatred for domestic minorities is transferred to a more publicly palatable target for antipathy. Such psychological devices help U.S. society reconcile its view of itself as non-racist with its harsh treatment of noncitizens of color. Noncitizens, so the rationalization goes, deserve this treatment because of their immigration status, not because of their race.

Psychological theory also helps explain some historical oddities about U.S. society's seemingly contradictory treatment of various minority groups (notably African Americans) and groups historically viewed as "foreign" (such as Asian Americans and Latinas/os). Congress passed the anti-Chinese exclusionary laws in the 1800s on the heels of the abolition of slavery and the ratification of the Reconstruction Amendments, ostensibly intended to eliminate all vestiges of this nation's "peculiar institution."[14] What legal rights the country formally extended to blacks, it ruthlessly denied Chinese immigrants. Similarly, *Brown v. Board of Education*[15] and its rejection of the "separate but equal" doctrine, a landmark achievement for African Americans, was decided the same year that the U.S. government commenced Operation Wetback, a massive campaign that resulted in the deportation of tens of thousands of both Mexican immigrants and U.S. citizens of Mexican ancestry. Both examples reflect the appearance of fair treatment of African Americans, on one hand, and a crackdown against "foreigners" on the other. When law constrained attacks on domestic minorities, animosity was displaced to foreign minorities in our midst and at our borders. Maintenance of the racial status quo serves as the unifying theme to explain these historical phenomena.[16]

In the end, we peer into a heart of darkness, where we see that the deepest fears held by racial minorities—that a majority of society desires and has consistently strived for Anglo-Saxon homogeneity and hegemony—are demonstrated to be more than justified. We are left to ponder the frailties of the human condition; what we constitute as a society; and the possibilities, if any, for racial harmony in the twenty-first century.

The History of Racial Exclusion in the U.S. Immigration Laws

Racism, along with nativism—the "intense opposition to an internal minority on the ground of its foreign (i.e., 'un-American') connections"[17]—and economic and other social forces, has unquestionably influenced the evolution of immigration law and policy in the United States. Far from existing in a social and historical vacuum, foreign and domestic racial subordination find themselves inextricably linked.

In untangling this history, critical differences between traditional immigration law and ordinary public law prove important. Although the Equal Protection Clause generally requires "strict scrutiny" of racial classifications in the law and has frequently invalidated them,[18] long ago, the U.S. Supreme Court—in a decision undisturbed to this day—upheld discrimination on the basis of race and national origin with respect to the admission of noncitizens into the country.[19] Similarly, even though in modern times discrimination on the basis of immigration status may mask an intent to discriminate against racial minorities,[20] the Court ordinarily defers to "alienage" classifications made by Congress.[21] Because the substantive provisions of the immigration laws have historically been immune from legal constraint, the political process allows the majority to have its way with noncitizens.[22]

The shameful treatment of Chinese immigrants by federal, state, and local governments (as well as by the public at large) in the 1800s represents a bitter underside to U.S. history.[23] Culminating the federalization of immigration regulation,[24] Congress passed the infamous Chinese exclusion laws that barred virtually all immigration of persons of Chinese ancestry and severely punished Chinese immigrants who violated the harsh laws.[25] Often rooted in class conflict as well as racist sympathies, discrimination and violence directed at Chinese immigrants already in the United States, particularly in California, fueled passage of the laws.[26] The efforts to exclude Chinese immigrants from our shores were clearly linked to the deeply negative attitude toward Chinese persons already in the country.

The Supreme Court emphasized national sovereignty as the rationale for not disturbing the laws that excluded the "obnoxious Chinese"[27] from the United States. In the famous *Chinese Exclusion Case*, the Court stated that "[t]he power of exclusion of foreigners [is] an incident of sovereignty belonging to the government of the United States, as a part of sovereign powers delegated by the Constitution."[28] Similarly, in *Fong Yue Ting v. United States*, the Court reasoned that "[t]he right of a nation to expel or deport foreigners . . . is as absolute and unqualified as the right to prohibit and prevent their entrance into the country."[29]

Congress later extended the Chinese exclusion laws to bar immigration from other Asian nations and to prohibit the immigration of persons of Asian ancestry from any nation.[30] The so-called Gentleman's Agreement between the U.S. and Japanese governments in 1907–1908 greatly restricted immigration from Japan.[31] The Immigration Act of 1917 expanded Chinese exclusion to prohibit immigration from the "Asiatic barred zone."[32] And a 1924 law, best known for creating the discriminatory national origins quota system, allowed for the exclusion of noncitizens "ineligible to citizenship" thus affecting Asian immigrants who, as nonwhites, were prohibited from naturalizing.[33] As one observer summarized, "Racism unquestionably influenced the anti-Asian exclusion in the immigration laws. The national climate of opinion, pervaded by racism and a burgeoning feeling of ethnic superiority or what [has been] called the 'Anglo-Saxon complex,' certainly contributed not just to the violence but also to the virtual unanimity with which the white majority put its seal of approval on anti-Chinese ends if not means."[34]

Other aspects of the immigration and nationality laws reinforced the anti-Asian sentiment reflected in the exclusion laws. For example, the Supreme Court interpreted the naturalization law, which allowed "white" immigrants as well as (after the Civil War) persons of African ancestry to naturalize, as barring Asians from naturalizing.[35] In *United States v. Thind*,[36] the Court held that an immigrant from India was not "white" and was therefore ineligible for naturalization. Similarly, in *Ozawa v. United States*,[37] the Court held that, as a nonwhite, a Japanese immigrant could not naturalize. This manipulation of the citizenship rights of racial minorities harkens back to *Dred Scott v. Sandford*,[38] in which, for the purpose of invoking the jurisdiction of the federal courts, the Court held that a freed black man was not a citizen.

Incorporating the racial discrimination encoded in federal naturalization law, state laws buttressed the racial hierarchy. Early in the twentieth century, a number of states, most notably California, passed "alien land laws," which barred the ownership of certain real property by noncitizens "ineligible to citizenship."[39] Employing legal code to mask a discriminatory intent, the measures were directed at Japanese immigrants, who, as nonwhites barred from naturalization, were "ineligible to citizenship." The political and social milieu in which these laws were passed demonstrates their racial animus. Anti-Japanese hatred dominated the campaign that culminated in passage of the alien land law by California voters.[40] Despite the obvious racial overtones, the Court rejected challenges to the land laws.

Congress passed the first wave of discriminatory immigration laws not long after the Fourteenth Amendment to the Constitution, which bars states from denying any person equal protection of the law, and other Reconstruction amendments went into effect. With the harshest treatment generally reserved for African Americans formally declared unlawful, the nation transferred animosity to another discrete and insular racial minority—one whose immigration status, race, and perceived impact on the fortunes of white workers made the treatment more socially acceptable and legally defensible. This issue surfaced in the congressional debates over ratification of the Fourteenth Amendment, when a member of Congress declared that Chinese persons could be treated less favorably than African Americans because "[the Chinese] are foreigners and the Negro is a native."[41]

Even though pre–Civil War state laws that regulated the migration of slaves served as precursors to the Chinese exclusion laws, the relationship between Chinese exclusion and the revolutionary improvements for African Americans during Reconstruction often goes ignored.[42] Congress enacted the national exclusion laws with the support of both southerners interested in rejuvenating a racial caste system and self-interested Anglos from California.[43]

It was no coincidence that greater legal freedoms for African Americans were tied to Chinese misfortunes. As one historian observed, "With Negro slavery a dead issue after 1865, greater attention was focused" on immigration from China.[44] Political forces quickly reacted to fill the racial void in the political arena. In the post–Civil War period in California, partisan political concerns, along with labor unionism, figured prominently in the anti-Chinese movement: "In 1867 [the year after the Fourteenth Amendment went into effect] California Democrats launched their offensive against the Chinese. The result . . . was a bonanza. The party laid hands on an issue of enormous potential in its own right—a new issue, uncontaminated by the sad history of the civil war, yet evocative of that entire syndrome of hatreds and loyalties which still could not quite openly be declared."[45]

The relationship between the treatment of African Americans and other racial minorities can be seen in a constitutional landmark of the nineteenth century. Justice John Marshall Harlan's dissent in *Plessy v. Ferguson*, often lauded for its grand pronouncement that "[o]ur Constitution is color-blind," noted the irony that the "separate but equal" doctrine applied to blacks, who unquestionably were part of the political community, but not to Chinese immigrants, "a race so different from our own that we do not permit those belonging to it to become citizens of the United States" and who were generally excluded from entering the country. Seeking to protect blacks by denigrating the Chinese, Justice Harlan left no doubt about his sympathies on the question of racial superiority: "The white race deems itself to be the dominant race in this country. And so it is, in prestige, in achievements, in education, in wealth and in power. So, I doubt not, it will continue to be for all time, if it remains true to its great heritage and holds fast to the principles of constitutional liberty."[46]

Some might contend that this analysis fails to recognize that the courts at various times invoked the law to protect Chinese immigrants. A most prominent example is *Yick Wo v. Hopkins*, in which the Supreme Court held in 1886 that discriminatory enforcement of a local laundry ordinance against "aliens and subjects of the Emperor of China" violated the Equal Protection Clause of the Fourteenth Amendment.[47] The decision is often cited for the proposition that a facially neutral law enforced in a racially discriminatory manner violates the Constitution;[48] however, instead of representing a commitment to racial equality, it represented an early Supreme Court foray into invalidation of economic regulation, which reached its peak during the *Lochner* era.[49] In any event, as the Court's treatment of the exclusion laws reveals, *Yick Wo* is far from representative of the prevailing judicial attitude toward the rights of persons of Chinese ancestry during the late 1800s.

Japanese Internment and Brown v. Board of Education

The historical context of the infamous decision to intern Japanese Americans and Japanese immigrants during World War II sheds light on the interrelationship between society's treatment of different minority groups. The Supreme Court ruling in *Korematsu v. United States*[50] demonstrates treatment of disfavored racial minority citizens, absent the law. In that case, the Court allowed U.S. citizens of Japanese ancestry, including some born in this country, to be detained in internment camps— a decision that reveals the difficulties inherent in drawing fine legal distinctions between noncitizens and citizens who share a common ancestry. Refusing to distinguish between noncitizens who immigrated from Japan and citizens of Japanese ancestry, the U.S. government classified all persons of Japanese ancestry, regardless of their immigration status, as "foreign" dangers to national security. Lumped together as the monolithic "Japanese" enemy, all were interned.

As the Japanese suffered from internment during World War II, African Americans, in large part because of an increased labor demand during the war, experienced improved employment opportunities and diminished discrimination.[51] As in the nineteenth century, Asian American exclusion from the national community and improved conditions for African Americans went hand in hand.

The timing of the Supreme Court's decision in *Korematsu*, one of the most well-known equal protection cases of the twentieth century, should not be ignored. The infamous decision in *Korematsu* (1944) came less than a decade before the much-revered decision in *Brown v. Board of Education*[52] (1954), which vindicated the rights of African Americans. Despite the brief time span, these cases represent the very best and worst of U.S. constitutional law. While persons of Japanese ancestry were rebuilding the remnants of their lives after the turmoil of legally sanctioned internment,[53] African Americans were seeing hope in the demise of "separate but equal" as the law of the land.

Ultimately, some of the harshest aspects of the anti-Asian laws were relaxed. Pressures to end exclusion of Chinese immigrants to the United States grew during World War II as China became a valued ally in the war effort. Japanese propaganda efforts during World War II highlighted the Chinese exclusion laws.[54] By 1943, foreign policy, rather than humanitarian, concerns prompted Congress to allow a minimum quota of Chinese immigrant visas and naturalization for Chinese immigrants.[55] In this end, the United States relaxed the Chinese exclusion laws for foreign policy reasons similar to those that inspired *Brown v. Board of Education*.[56]

The Vietnam War also reveals a relationship between Asian subordination and improvements for African Americans. As the civil rights movement of the 1960s gained rights for African Americans, the escalation of the war in Vietnam increased racism toward the Vietnamese people, which lingers to this day.[57] Aware of the racial roots of the war, as well as the impact on domestic people of color, Martin Luther King Jr. and Malcolm X, two of the most prominent African American leaders of their generation, both opposed U.S. involvement in Vietnam.[58]

As this sad history demonstrates, Asian Americans—whatever their immigration status and however long their own or their ancestors' residence in the United States—have historically been treated as foreigners in this land.[59] Some observers claim that U.S. immigration laws discriminate against Asians to this day.[60] In addition to suffering from efforts to exclude them from the national community, Asian Americans have stood accused of the high crime against the American "melting pot" mythology of refusing to assimilate.[61] Ironically, the law itself prevented full assimilation and equal citizenship. Because they were barred from naturalization, for example, immigrants from Asia (as nonwhites) were disenfranchised and prohibited from exercising political power as citizens, thus hindering Asian American political involvement in the long run.[62] Excluded from the political community, Asian Americans were first denied the opportunity to assimilate into the mainstream and then criticized for failing to do so.

The National Origins Quota System

In 1924, Congress established the much-reviled national origins quota system, a formulaic device designed to ensure stability in the ethnic composition of the United States.[63] Initially, it permitted annual immigration of up to 2 percent of the number of foreign-born persons of a particular nationality in the United States as set forth in the 1890 census.[64] In operation, the quota system "materially favored immigrants from Northern and Western Europe because the great waves from Southern and Eastern Europe did not arrive until after 1890."[65] Congress enacted the quota system in the wake of its passage of the literacy test in 1917; the test excluded from the country "[a]ll aliens over sixteen years of age, physically capable of reading, who [could] not read the English language, or some other language or dialect, including Hebrew or Yiddish."[66] As intended, the test restricted the immigration of non-English speakers, including Italians, Russians, Poles, Hungarians, Greeks, and Asians.[67]

A House report offers a clear articulation of the purposes of the national origins quota system:

> With full recognition of the material progress which we owe to the races from southern and eastern Europe, we are conscious that the continued arrival of great numbers tends to upset our balance of population, to depress our standard of living, and to unduly charge our institutions for the care of the socially inadequate. If immigration from southern and eastern Europe may enter the United States on a basis of substantial equality with that admitted from the older sources of supply, it is clear that if any appreciable number of immigrants are to be allowed to land upon our shores the balance of racial preponderance must in time pass to those elements of the population who reproduce more rapidly on a lower standard of living than those possessing other ideals. . . .
>
> . . . *[The quota system] is used in an effort to preserve, as nearly as possible, the racial status quo in the United States. It is hoped to guarantee, as best we can at this late date, racial homogeneity.*[68]

As one commentator remarked approvingly in 1924, the national origins quota system was "a scientific plan for keeping America American."[69] Implicit in such rationale, of course, was the view that persons of northern European stock were superior to members of other groups. Similarly, the conventional wisdom was that "[t]he real assimilation of aliens depends to a very large extent upon their associates after entering—'we can easily assimilate' them 'if their origins resemble the origins of the people they find when they get here.'"[70]

The racial hierarchy endorsed by proponents of the national origins quota system was entirely consistent with the academic literature of the day, which viewed the "races" of southern and eastern Europe as inferior to those of northern Europe.[71] In effect, southern and eastern European immigrants, commonly thought of today as white, were at that time "racialized" as nonwhite and therefore unworthy of joining the national community. Society constructed southern and eastern Europeans as belonging to "another race" and treated them accordingly.

A heavy dose of anti-Semitism fueled the demand for the national origins quota system; proponents hoped to limit the immigration of Jewish persons to the United States.[72] This anti-Semitism mirrored the discrimination suffered by the nation's Jewish Americans.[73] One of the great tragedies of the twentieth century was that, during World War II, anti-Semitism, enforced and reinforced by the quota system, influenced the U.S. government's refusal to accept many Jewish refugees who fled the Holocaust.[74]

Other "races" were also affected by the quota system. Asian Americans were excluded from immigrating to the United States well before 1924, but often overlooked is the fact that the quota system discouraged immigration from Africa, historically the source of precious little U.S. immigration.[75] This exclusion is entirely consistent with African American subordination within the nation and the later refusal to accept refugees who fled political turmoil in Haiti (a country populated primarily by persons of African descent).

Despite persistent criticisms, including claims that the Anglo-Saxon, northern European preference in the immigration laws adversely affected U.S. foreign policy interests,[76] the laws remained intact until 1965. Although Congress tinkered somewhat with the overall system, it maintained the quotas in the Immigration and Nationality Act of 1952 (INA), the comprehensive immigration law that (as frequently amended) remains in place today.[77] President Harry Truman vetoed the INA (a veto that Congress overrode) because it carried forward the discriminatory quota system.[78] In defending the INA's version of the quota system, one contemporary commentator claimed that the nation's ethnic composition should not be changed and that, because some known communists opposed the law, opponents should be circumspect before joining the fray.[79] A Senate report concluded that the national origins quota system "preserve[d] the sociological and cultural balance in the United States," which was justifiable because northern and western Europeans "had made the greatest contribution to the development of [the] country." The report further stated that the nation should "admit immigrants considered to be more readily assimilable because of the similarity of their cultural background to those of the principal components of our population."[80]

In sum, the national origins quota system reflects this nation's preoccupation with its racial and ethnic balance. The system was based on the desire to limit the immigration of inferior "races" from southern and eastern Europe. Domestic discrimination accompanied the exclusion in the laws. Long-standing anti-Semitism, as well as prejudice against other immigrant groups,[81] persisted in the United States.

The life of the national origins quota system spanned a period when domestic racial minorities gained formal rights under the law. As they did so, however, noncitizens at best retained their rightless place in U.S. society. In fact, the INA—which in addition to maintaining the quota system included draconian provisions (see Chapter 3) that punished noncitizen political minorities in the name of fighting communism—withdrew some rights for noncitizens.

Modern Racial Exclusion

In the wake of the Civil Rights Act of 1964,[82] Congress passed the Immigration Act of 1965.[83] This new law abolished the national origins quota system[84] and barred racial considerations from expressly entering into decisions about immigrant visas.[85] In addition, for the first time, it imposed a ceiling (120,000) on migration from the Western Hemisphere.[86] Immigration from the Western Hemisphere—specifically Latin America—had previously been restricted not through quotas but through vigorous enforcement of the exclusion and deportation grounds. The limitation on Western Hemisphere immigration was part of a compromise to those who feared a drastic upswing in Latin American immigration.[87] The blue ribbon U.S. Select Commission on Immigration and Refugee Policy summarized the history: "The United States was . . . far from free of prejudice . . . and one part of the 1965 law reflected change in policy that was in part due to antiforeign sentiments. Prejudice against dark-skinned people . . . remained strong. In the years after World War II, as the proportion of Spanish-speaking residents increased, much of the lingering nativism in the United States was directed against those from Mexico and Central and South America. . . . *Giving in to . . . pressures as a price to be paid for abolishing the national origins system, Congress put into the 1965 amendments a ceiling [on Western Hemisphere immigration] to close the last remaining open door of U.S. policy.*"[88] In effect, Congress coupled more generous treatment of those outside the Western Hemisphere with less generous treatment of Latin Americans. With the demise of the quota system, the racial demographics of the immigration stream changed significantly. Increasing numbers of immigrants of color came to the United States.[89] Not coincidentally, concern about immigration, particularly the race of the immigrants, grew over the decades that followed.[90]

It is important to note that although the abolition of the national origins quota system removed blatant discrimination from the immigration laws, it failed to eliminate racism. Various characteristics of the modern immigration laws, although facially neutral, disparately impact noncitizens of color from developing nations. The 1965 Act, for example, replaced the national origins quotas with across-the-board annual numerical limits of immigrants from each nation.[91] In operation, this ceiling creates exceedingly long lines for immigrants from developing nations, such as Mexico, the Philippines, and India, in comparison with those for people from most other nations. For example, as of March 1998, fourth-preference immigrant visas (brothers and sisters of adult citizens)[92] were being granted to Philippine nationals who applied in April 1978, compared to those who applied in October 1987 from virtually all other nations.[93] For third-preference immigrant visas (married sons and daughters of citizens),[94] the applications of Mexican citizens filed in May 1989 were being processed in March 1998, compared to September 1994 for applicants from almost every other nation.[95] Thus, similarly situated persons (e.g., siblings and children of U.S. citizens) face radically different waiting times for a visa only because of their country of origin, with accompanying racial impacts.[96]

Other changes to the immigration laws reflect racial concerns. Many commentators have lauded the Refugee Act of 1980,[97] which for the first time allowed noncitizens who flee political and related persecution in their homelands the general right to apply for asylum in the United States.[98] However, the act was motivated in part by a desire to limit U.S. acceptance of Vietnamese refugees, whom the president had allowed liberal admission after the 1975 fall of Saigon.[99] In the hope of preventing future mass migrations, the law established numerical limits on, and generally restricted the power of the president with respect to, refugee admissions. Years after Congress passed the law, Vietnamese citizens brought suit against the U.S. government, charging discrimination based on nationality in the processing of visa applications.[100] (Similarly, the immigration laws allow for the exclusion of persons likely to become public charges,[101] an inadmissibility ground given more strength in 1996 immigration reforms. As Chapter 4 demonstrates, the public charge exclusion has a disproportionate effect on noncitizens of color from developing nations.)

Passed before the heated immigration debates of the 1990s, the Immigration Act of 1990 reflects congressional concerns about the racial composition of the immigrant stream.[102] The law created a new immigrant visa program that effectively represents affirmative action for white immigrants, a group that benefited from preferential treatment under the national origins quota system until 1965.[103] In an ironic twist of political jargon, Congress established the facially neutral "diversity" visa program, which in fact prefers immigrants from nations populated primarily by white people.[104] As congressional proponents had envisioned, many Irish immigrants came to the United States under the program. Indeed, a transitional diversity program required that 40 percent of the visas would be issued to Irish immigrants.[105] In fiscal year 1995, the leading source of immigrants under the permanent diversity visa program was Poland. In 1999, despite the much greater immigration demand from Africa and Asia, as many Europeans received diversity visas as Africans and Asians combined.[106]

In short, the modern immigration laws produce disparate racial impacts. As one commentator has observed along similar lines, "Nativism . . . is not merely a shameful feature of our past. . . . Nativism afflicts our politics today, posing a clear and present danger of new anti-immigrant legislation."[107] The statement, made before September 11, 2001, later proved to be visionary, as the federal government reacted to the events of that day. The same can be said for racial discrimination in the immigration laws, as further examples demonstrate.

The War on "Illegal Aliens," aka Mexican Immigrants

The current debate over undocumented immigration in the United States cannot be fully appreciated without understanding how it fits into a long immigration history. Especially in the Southwest, the immigration laws have helped to ensure a disposable labor force.[108] During the

Great Depression, when the supply of unskilled labor dwarfed demand, both Mexican immigrants and citizens of Mexican ancestry were "repatriated" to Mexico at the behest of governmental authorities.[109] Later, under the Bracero Program in the 1940s and 1950s, the U.S. government admitted an estimated one million Mexican workers into the country as agricultural workers.[110]

At times, the call for immigration restrictions has been expressly anti-Mexican. For example, in 1956, Duke Law School's *Law and Contemporary Problems* published an article titled "A Critical Analysis of the Wetback Problem." The article referred to the 1950s as the "wetback decade" and blamed undocumented immigration from Mexico for "displacement of American workers, depressed wages, increased racial discrimination toward Americans of Mexican ancestry, illiteracy, disease, and lawlessness."[111] Although the term "wetbacks" has been replaced by "illegal aliens" in today's parlance, the modern restrictionist movement plays on remarkably similar themes.[112]

Despite the fact that undocumented persons come from nations all over the world, the nearly exclusive focus of governmental and public attention at the tail end of the twentieth century was undocumented immigration from Mexico.[113] The racial impact of the recent push to crack down on "illegal aliens" is unmistakable. Well-publicized border enforcement operations in El Paso, Texas (Operation Blockade, later renamed Operation Hold the Line because of protests from the Mexican government), and San Diego, California (Operation Gatekeeper), which differ little from military operations, have been aimed at sealing the U.S.-Mexican border and keeping undocumented Mexican citizens from entering the United States.[114] Indeed, U.S. military forces have assisted the Immigration and Naturalization Service (INS) in policing the border.[115] At the same time, reports of human rights abuses along the border abound.[116] For example, in 1997, a U.S. Marine shot and killed Esequiel Hernández Jr., a teenager and U.S. citizen with no criminal record, who was herding his family's goats near the border. Hundreds of migrants have been killed by the elements in desolate mountains and deserts, as they have tried to avoid the buildup of enforcement in major border hubs, such as El Paso and San Diego. The U.S. General Accounting Office found that, despite the redoubling of border en-

forcement, evidence of the strategy's effectiveness at reducing undocumented immigration was inconclusive.[117] A 2002 study concluded unequivocally that "there is *no* evidence that the border enforcement
build-up . . . has substantially reduced unauthorized border crossings"
and that "despite large increases in spending and Border Patrol resources
over the past nine years, the number of unauthorized immigrants increased to levels higher than those" before 1986.[118] In other words, after
causing hundreds of deaths, the new border enforcement has not proved
itself effective in reducing undocumented immigration.

Public concern about undocumented Mexican immigration heightened with a significant increase in the population of persons of Mexican ancestry in the United States.[119] In return, Mexican American resistance to anti-immigrant sentiment and restrictionist proposals, like
the heated debates over bilingual education and crime, are but another
battlefield in the struggle for status in the U.S. social hierarchy.[120]

Mexican Americans, and Latinas/os more generally, have a self-interest
in fighting overzealous border enforcement. In the fervor to locate and
deport undocumented Mexican citizens, Mexican Americans, often
stereotyped as "foreigners" by the national community, can fall into the
enforcement net.[121] In the infamous 1954 deportation campaign known
as Operation Wetback, for example, "the Mexican American community
was affected because the campaign was aimed at only one racial group,
which meant that the burden of proving one's citizenship fell totally
upon people of Mexican descent. Those unable to present such proof
were arrested and returned to Mexico."[122] Similarly, evidence suggests
that the immigration law provisions that allow for sanctions against those
who employ undocumented persons have resulted in "a serious pattern
of discrimination" on the part of employers against persons of Latin
American and persons of Asian ancestry.[123]

The historical relationship between subordination of Mexican Americans, viewed as a "foreign" minority, and African Americans, viewed as
a domestic minority, is telling. During the New Deal, while the government scrambled to provide public benefits to citizens who satisfied
eligibility requirements,[124] both Mexican American citizens and Mexican immigrants were effectively deported to Mexico. In 1954, the same
year that the Supreme Court handed down the much-lauded *Brown v.*

Board of Education[125] decision, the U.S. government commenced Operation Wetback, the mass deportation campaign directed at undocumented Mexicans. Ironically, the war on Mexican immigrants and Mexican American citizens coincided with the recognition of formal legal rights for African Americans. At that time, it was far from clear that the Equal Protection Clause of the Fourteenth Amendment on which *Brown* rested offered any protection to Mexican Americans.[126] During a period when the law promised (although perhaps failed to deliver) new legal protections to African Americans, a legally sanctioned deportation campaign struck with a vengeance at persons of Mexican ancestry.

With race remaining central to modern immigration enforcement, persons of Mexican ancestry have experienced its detrimental impacts. Although racial profiling by police has been criticized from many corners, it is part and parcel of the enforcement of the immigration laws. In 1975, applying the Fourth Amendment reasonable suspicion standard applicable to an investigatory stop in *United States v. Brignoni-Ponce*, the Supreme Court held that Border Patrol officers on roving patrols may stop persons "only if . . . aware of specific articulable facts together with rational inferences from these facts, that reasonably warrant suspicion that the vehicles contain aliens who may be illegally in the country." In so doing, the Court found that the stop in question violated the Fourth Amendment because Border Patrol officers relied *exclusively* on "the apparent Mexican ancestry" of the occupants of an automobile. The Court further stated, however, that "*the likelihood that any given person of Mexican ancestry is an alien is high enough to make Mexican appearance a relevant factor*, but standing alone does not justify stopping all Mexican-Americans to ask if they are aliens."[127]

Brignoni-Ponce has greatly shaped immigration enforcement in the United States since 1975. In an important deviation from ordinary Fourth Amendment doctrine, the Court in *Brignoni-Ponce* authorized the Border Patrol to rely on "Mexican appearance" even if no individual, much less one who "appears Mexican," has been specifically identified as having violated the immigration laws. This authorization is premised on nothing more than the statistical probability that persons of "Mexican appearance" are undocumented. In support of its reasoning, the Court recounted the federal government's estimation that 85 percent of the undocumented immigrants in the United States came from Mexico.[128]

The Court's authorization of Border Patrol consideration of "Mexican appearance" in *Brignoni-Ponce* conflicts with its recognition that "[l]arge numbers of native-born and naturalized citizens have the physical characteristics identified with Mexican ancestry, and even in the border area a relatively small proportion of them are aliens,"[129] which acknowledges the overly inclusive nature of the Border Patrol's racial classification. Even assuming that statistical probabilities might justify stopping persons of "Mexican appearance," the Court's allegation that a high percentage of the total undocumented population consists of Mexicans fails to square with the best information currently available. More important, the Court's legal analysis failed to give sufficient weight to the undisputed fact that a relatively small percentage of people of Mexican ancestry in the United States are undocumented. The indignities of the immigration stops deprive U.S. citizens and lawful immigrants who "look Mexican" of their civil rights.

Building on *Brignoni-Ponce*, the Supreme Court subsequently afforded even greater leeway to Border Patrol officers who stop drivers at permanent checkpoints located many miles from the international border with Mexico. Classifying the intrusion as "sufficiently minimal," in *United States v. Martinez-Fuerte*, the Court held that referrals to secondary inspection at permanent checkpoints "made largely on the basis of apparent Mexican ancestry"[130] do not run afoul of the Constitution. The Court emphasized the Border Patrol's need for flexibility and, as it had in *Brignoni-Ponce*, repeated the government's assertion that 85 percent of the undocumented population in the United States is of Mexican origin.

Although *Brignoni-Ponce* might be praised for invalidating a stop predicated exclusively on "Mexican appearance," by stating that race may properly contribute to the decision to stop a person, the Court opened the door to the Border Patrol's reliance on race combined with little more than a hunch about lack of documentation. Concerns about racial discrimination are heightened by the fact that "Border Patrol officers may use racial stereotypes as a proxy for illegal conduct without being subjectively aware of doing so."[131] Current INS practices differ little, if at all, from INS practices before the Court's decision in *Brignoni-Ponce*. However, the Border Patrol officers' expansion of the Court's endorsement of the use of "Mexican appearance" to the broader category of "Hispanic appearance" is important. This accommodation is a response to the significant increase in Central American immigration to the United States through Mexico since the 1980s.

The INS admittedly employs crude undocumented immigrant profiles, with race as the touchstone. In many cases, Border Patrol officers expressly rely upon a person's "Hispanic appearance" as a factor in making an immigration stop.[132] (In one case in which plaintiffs alleged that the INS engaged in a pattern and practice of exclusively race-based stops, INS officials testified that an officer may properly rely on not only Hispanic appearance but also a "hungry look," a "dirty, unkempt" appearance, or the use of "work clothing.")[133] In effect, the INS defense in some cases amounts to the claim that, because most alleged "illegal aliens" are Hispanic, statistical probabilities justify the stop.[134] Although courts occasionally find that stops fail to satisfy the Supreme Court's minimal requirements,[135] race-based enforcement generally continues unabated, unreported, and unremedied.

As this discussion suggests, the Border Patrol's undocumented immigrant profile contains elements of class as well as race.[136] Poor and working-class persons of stereotypical "Hispanic appearance" bear the brunt of Border Patrol enforcement efforts. However, other Latinas/os have been subjected to stops as well. For example, the *New York Times* reported that two Mexican American judges had been repeatedly stopped and questioned by the Border Patrol in south Texas.[137] Border Patrol agents once pulled over the conservative law-and-order mayor of a Los Angeles, California, suburb to verify his citizenship status. According to the Border Patrol agents, the mayor, a third-generation Mexican American who was driving a pick-up truck, fit the undocumented immigrant "profile"; the mayor's explanation: "[Y]ou get stopped if you are Mexican. Period."[138]

Contending that the U.S. government regularly violates the wide latitude it is afforded by the Supreme Court, plaintiffs in many lawsuits have alleged that the Border Patrol relies almost exclusively on race in making immigration stops.[139] For example, in 1992, U.S. citizens of Hispanic descent, including students, graduates, faculty, and staff at a high school in El Paso, Texas, contended that Border Patrol officers engaged in a pattern and practice of interrogating Mexican American citizens about their immigration status and that officers on occasion physically assaulted those who asserted their legal rights.[140] Similarly, in *Hodgers-Durgin v. de la Vina*,[141] the INS stood accused of stopping Arizona motorists of Latina/o descent without the reasonable suspicion required by law.

Contrary to popular belief, race-based immigration enforcement extends far from the border and into every region of the United States. Heightened immigration enforcement and civil rights complaints accompanied increased Mexican and Central American migration to the South and Pacific Northwest.[142] Latinas/os have long leveled legal challenges against alleged immigration enforcement excesses in the Midwest.[143] Ohio law enforcement officers, for example, were accused of stopping and detaining Hispanic motorists based on race or national origin to interrogate them about their immigration status.[144]

State and local governments, at times with federal support, have engaged in egregious race-based immigration enforcement against Latinas/os.[145] During and after the violence that followed the May 1992 acquittal of police officers charged in the beating of Rodney King in Los Angeles, local law enforcement officers, with the cooperation of the INS, arrested and deported numerous undocumented Latina/o immigrants.[146] In July 1997, local police in Chandler, a suburb of Phoenix, Arizona, in cooperation with the Border Patrol, engaged in an operation that involved stopping cars with drivers or passengers of "Mexican appearance" to check their immigration status in the name of community redevelopment. Police officers stopped "[n]umerous American citizens and legal residents . . . on multiple occasions . . . for no other reason than their skin color or Mexican appearance or use of the Spanish language."[147]

The fact that claims of discriminatory enforcement of the immigration laws continue should be no surprise. By bestowing the Border Patrol with vast discretion, the Supreme Court has invited race to dominate immigration enforcement. As one ground-level study of immigration enforcement concludes, Border Patrol "[o]fficers can easily strengthen their reasonable suspicion for an interrogation *after* they have begun talking to an individual. . . . *It is easy to come up with the necessary articulable facts after the fact*"; this is commonly known within the Border Patrol as "*'canned p.c.'* (probable cause)."[148] Moreover, officers may falsely believe that they can identify an undocumented person to a near certainty.[149]

This formula is tailor-made for a pattern of stops based primarily on "Hispanic appearance" and legally defensible rationales concocted after the fact. One federal judge went so far as to contend that the law has evolved to include an exception to the Fourth Amendment for the Border Patrol acting in the border region: "[H]istory is likely to judge the judiciary's evisceration of the Fourth Amendment in the vicinity of the Mexican border as yet another jurisprudential nadir, joining Korematsu [v. United States (1944) (upholding Japanese internment)], Dred Scott [v. Sandford, (1856) (ruling that freed blacks were not U.S. citizens)], and even Plessy [v. Ferguson, (1896) (approving the separate, but equal doctrine)] on the list of our most shameful failures to discharge our duty of defending constitutional civil liberties against the popular hue and cry that would have us abridge them."[150]

The sanctioning of the use of race by the Supreme Court in *Brignoni-Ponce* has influenced other modes of immigration enforcement. No doubt encouraged by the Court's reasoning, the INS relies on "Hispanic appearance" in selecting workplaces for enforcement operations in the search for undocumented workers.[151] During these raids, which the Supreme Court refused to classify as "seizures" subject to the constraints of the Fourth Amendment,[152] the INS has focused on persons of apparent Latin American ancestry for interrogation.[153]

By driving the national economic status of undocumented Latin Americans farther underground, race profiling in immigration enforcement facilitates the exploitation of the undocumented by employers, who can play on their fears of apprehension. Employers can remain confident that undocumented workers, conditioned as they are to having Hispanic appearance place their immigration status instantly in question, are unlikely to report workplace violations to the authorities, given that the courts are unlikely to remedy any wrongs.[154]

No device in place effectively deters excessive reliance on race by the INS in the enforcement of the immigration laws. Legal challenges to misconduct, such as class actions, run into formidable legal barriers.[155]

Commentators routinely criticize internal INS complaint procedures as ineffective.[156] The Supreme Court has held that the exclusionary rule generally does not cover civil removal proceedings, so that the findings from an unlawful stop ordinarily remain admissible.[157] Although the Court emphasized that it was not dealing "with egregious violations of Fourth Amendment or other liberties that might transgress notions of fundamental fairness and undermine the probative value of the evidence obtained,"[158] proving such extreme conduct is difficult.[159] Because race is considered a proper factor among many for consideration in an immigration stop, it is difficult to establish, as the current state of the law requires, that race was the *exclusive* reason for the stop.

One observer summarized the status of border enforcement in 1985 in words that continue to ring true: "Immigration authorities can still effectively stop and interrogate anyone they meet . . . providing only that the [person] looks foreign. While they cannot in theory question people on the basis of racial or ethnic appearance alone, they in fact do so consistently, and no one familiar with the realities of immigration enforcement would suggest the contrary."[160]

It is important to recall that the Supreme Court relied on incorrect statistical data in sanctioning racial profiling by the INS. In vesting the Border Patrol with discretion to consider "Mexican appearance" in immigration stops, the Court relied on the government's assertion that 85 percent of the undocumented population in the United States was of Mexican ancestry. Assuming that this figure is relevant to the inquiry, it is as far off the mark today as it was in all likelihood in 1975.[161] In 1981, the final report of the U.S. Select Commission on Immigration and Refugee Policy summarized U.S. Bureau of the Census data to the effect that "Mexican nationals probably account *for less than half* of the undocumented/illegal population."[162] According to recent INS estimates, Mexican citizens constitute only little more than half the undocumented population,[163] a far cry from the unsubstantiated government estimate provided to the Supreme Court in 1975.

In addition, as of October 1996, over 40 percent of undocumented persons had entered the country legally, with the requisite papers, but then violated the terms of their visas.[164] Visa violations are generally unaffected by heightened border security measures, which by their nature focus on unlawful entry. "About 16 percent of the Mexican undocumented population are [nonimmigrant] overstays, compared to . . . 91 percent from all other countries."[165] Thus, increased border enforcement focuses disproportionately on the Mexican component of the undocumented population in the United States.

In any event, instead of considering the percentage of undocumented persons of Mexican ancestry in the country, the Supreme Court would have done better to consider the percentage of the total Hispanic population in the United States that is *not* undocumented. This number represents the population subjected to the injuries inflicted by racial profiling in immigration enforcement, injuries to which the Court in *Brignoni-Ponce* paid no serious heed. The population of persons of "Hispanic appearance" *lawfully* in the United States and vulnerable to race-based immigration stops is significant, having grown substantially since 1975.[166] In 1997, nearly thirty million people of Hispanic ancestry, over 11 percent of the total U.S. population, lived in the United States.[167] This was an increase from 6.5 percent of the population, or 14.6 million people, in 1980.[168] As of October 1996, however, only a little more than three million undocumented Mexican and Central American immigrants lived in the United States.[169] A rough estimate from these figures reveals that the vast majority (over 90 percent) of the Hispanics in the United States are lawful immigrants or citizens.

Much-publicized population projections show growing numbers of Hispanics in this country. The Bureau of the Census estimates that, by 2050, Hispanics will constitute nearly 25 percent of the U.S. population.[170] Hundreds of thousands of lawful immigrants of Latin American ancestry reside in this country. In fiscal year 1997 alone, the United States admitted more than 146,000 lawful permanent residents from Mexico.[171] More than 640,000 Mexican immigrants lawfully immigrated to the United States between 1971 and 1980, about 1.7 million between 1981and 1990, and more than 1.8 million between 1991 and 1997.[172] In fiscal years 1988 to 1997, nearly 600,000 Mexican immigrants became naturalized U.S. citizens.[173]

In 1990, Hispanics in California, whose southern border is one of the focal points of U.S. immigration enforcement, constituted *more than one-*

quarter of the state's population.[174] In 1998, more than ten million Hispanics lived in the Golden State.[175] Hispanics constitute a large percentage, sometimes even a majority, of the population in many localities on or near California's border with Mexico.[176] For example, in
Imperial County, California, an important site of border enforcement,
Hispanics constitute over 70 percent of the population.[177]

Because of the dramatic growth of the Latina/o community, which is
projected to continue, the number of persons vulnerable to and the percentage of the total population potentially injured by race-based immigration stops has increased significantly since the Supreme Court's 1975
decision in *Brignoni-Ponce*. Given the millions of Latinas/os who lawfully reside in the United States, "Hispanic appearance" holds little probative value in determining whether a person lacks proper immigration
documentation; in equal protection terms, the classification is overinclusive. Like the proverbial "dragnet," it punishes "the innocent by-
stander, the hapless victim of circumstance or association. . . . [S]uch
classifications fly squarely in the face of our traditional antipathy to as-
sertions of mass guilt and guilt by association."[178]

Although stops and documentation interrogations may appear to be
minimal intrusions to persons who are unlikely targets, for those who are
repeatedly targeted, such enforcement practices contribute to a diminished sense of belonging to U.S. society. Especially in the Southwest,
immigration enforcement regularly subjects Mexican American citizens
and lawful immigrants to indignities to which Anglos are rarely subjected. The net is cast so wide that large numbers of Latinas/os in some
regions remain under constant suspicion and are subjected to repeated
stops and interrogations by Border Patrol officers. In the small border
town of El Cenizo, Texas, which is 80 percent Spanish-speaking, for example, increased border enforcement has been accompanied by numerous allegations of Border Patrol harassment of U.S. citizens and lawful immigrants of Mexican ancestry.[179] "Border Patrol officers who stop
cars based in substantial part on whether the occupants 'look Mexican'
infringe on the freedom of movement of Latinos who are permanent
resident aliens and citizens as well as those who are undocumented."[180]
As a federal judge dissenting in a case that upheld a Border Patrol stop

observed, "How is this practice distinguishable from the former practice of Southern peace officers who randomly stopped black pedestrians to inquire, 'hey, boy, what are you doin' in this neighborhood?'"[181]

The Border Patrol's targeting of persons of "Hispanic appearance" contributes to the fact that in recent years, although Mexican and Latin American citizens constitute only slightly more than half of the total undocumented population in the United States, they have been subjected to *close to 90 percent* of the deportations.[182] This targeting, of course, closely resembles the racial profiling of African Americans in criminal law enforcement, which has resulted in a disproportionate number of African Americans in U.S. prisons. Similarly, race-based enforcement has reportedly led to the unlawful arrest, and sometimes even the deportation, of U.S. citizens of Mexican ancestry.[183]

Border Patrol reliance on race also reinforces negative stereotypes about "Latina/o appearance." Phenotype varies dramatically among persons of Latin American ancestry.[184] "Most [persons of Mexican ancestry, for example,] are of dark complexion with black hair. . . . *But many are blond, blue-eyed and 'white,' while others have red hair and hazel eyes.*"[185] The stereotype of the dark-haired, brown-skinned (often linked to a "dirty" appearance)[186] "Mexican" disregards the rich diversity of physical appearances among Latinas/os. Racially discriminatory immigration enforcement may bear some responsibility for the damaging personal consequences that can occur when Latinas/os change their physical appearance in an attempt to "pass" as Spanish or white.[187] The diversity among Latinas/os suggests that significant room for error exists when Border Patrol officers seek to detect undocumented persons by focusing on stereotypical Hispanic appearance. In this respect, the classification is underinclusive as well as overinclusive.

Just as racial profiling breeds cynicism about the criminal justice system in minority communities, it foments distrust of immigration officials and other government authorities and discourages lawful permanent residents from Mexico from fully embracing a U.S. national identity. This distrust may well contribute to the historically low naturalization rates of Mexican immigrants.[188] Similarly, by placing a cloud over the citizenship status of virtually all Latinas/os, race-based enforcement serves to limit Latina/o social integration into the mainstream. Disregarding this limitation, or perhaps even twisting it against Latinas/os, some commentators have claimed that because of Latinas/os failure to assimilate, immigration from Latin America should be curtailed.

Asylum, Haitian Interdiction, and the Politics of Race

U.S. law and policy toward noncitizens who have fled civil war, political and other persecution, and genocide in their native lands have historically been influenced by nativism and racism. Unfortunately, for example, domestic anti-Semitism contributed to the Roosevelt administration's decision to turn its back on Jewish refugees who fled the Holocaust. In addition, Congress's passage of the Refugee Act of 1980 counted among its more humanitarian purposes the hope of reducing the number of refugees admitted from Vietnam.

Race alone, however, has not influenced U.S. refugee and asylum policy. In the latter half of the twentieth century, for example, immigrants from China and Cuba received generous treatment from the U.S. government in no small part because of foreign policy concerns; because the U.S. government was at odds with the communist governments of Cuba and the People's Republic of China, admitting refugees from these countries was viewed as an implicit condemnation of their governments.[189] The United States routinely denied asylum to Central Americans who fled regimes that, despite their abominable human rights records, were considered allies, but often the United States granted asylum to Poles who fled a harsh communist government at odds with our own.[190]

Policy conflicts occasionally resulted in confused and inconsistent U.S. policies. For example, the treatment of Chinese refugees, including many who claimed persecution because of resistance to China's one-child rule, was erratic at best.[191] While foreign policy interests favored liberal admissions (and thus implicitly condemned China's communist government), domestic fears militated in favor of numerical limits. The U.S. government initially showed sympathy for Chinese refugees.[192] In the 1990s, however, fearing a mass migration from China, the executive branch began to detain all Chinese migrants who came to the United

States on ships (such as the much-publicized example of the Golden Venture in 1993) and to interdict Chinese ships outside U.S. territorial waters to prevent them from reaching the mainland.[193]

The fluctuations in policy aside, the U.S. government commonly went to extraordinary lengths to halt feared mass migrations of people of color. It implemented special detention policies directed at Central Americans and made concerted efforts to encourage potential asylum applicants to forgo their claims and "voluntarily" leave the country.[194] However, few U.S. policies—with the possible exception of the nation's rejection of Jewish refugees who fled the Holocaust—approached the government's shameful treatment of black persons who fled the political violence in Haiti. Often unrecognized is the fact that by stigmatizing African American citizens, "U.S. immigration policy toward Haiti may harm a historically disadvantaged group—namely, black Americans."[195]

For much of recent history, the U.S. government has generally supported the Haitian government, in large part because the various regimes have been stridently anticommunist.[196] In stark contrast, however, both Democratic and Republican administrations have been at odds with Cuba, Haiti's neighbor, since Fidel Castro came to power in 1959. Foreign policy has visibly influenced asylum policy toward persons who fled the two nations: Cubans have generally received much more favorable treatment than Haitians.[197]

In the late 1970s, an increasing number of Haitians sailed to south Florida in makeshift boats. In 1981, to diminish the flow of refugees and to deter others from following, the Reagan administration initiated a program in which the U.S. Coast Guard interdicted Haitian boats and allowed INS officers to screen applicants to determine whether they had plausible claims for asylum and the withholding of deportation.[198] Between 1981 and 1991, the Coast Guard interdicted some twenty-five thousand Haitians.

After a military coup toppled the democratically elected Haitian government in September 1991, the Bush administration imposed economic sanctions on Haiti and suspended interdiction; in November 1991, interdiction recommenced. As a result of the coup, in the Court's words, "'hundreds of Haitians [were] killed, tortured, detained without a warrant, or subjected to violence and the destruction of their property because of their political beliefs. Thousands [were] forced into hiding.'"[199] In the six months following October 1991, the Coast Guard intercepted more than thirty-four thousand Haitians on the high seas, exceeding the number interdicted during the previous ten years. In May 1992, President George H. Bush attempted to stop the flow of refugees by repatriating all Haitians without screening to determine their eligibility to remain in the United States.[200] Despite campaign promises to the contrary, President Bill Clinton continued Haitian interdiction and repatriation and forcefully defended the policy against legal challenge.[201]

The Supreme Court ultimately upheld the executive branch's unprecedented Haitian repatriation policy.[202] The Court did so without squarely addressing the friend-of-the-court brief claim of the National Association for the Advancement of Colored People (NAACP), TransAfrica, and the Congressional Black Caucus that the policy was discriminatory and that the Haitians were being subjected to "separate and unequal" treatment.[203] This claim reemerged in 2002 as south Florida saw a new influx of Haitian migrants who were subjected to detention and other harsh treatment to which their Cuban counterparts were not.

African American activist groups were not alone in condemning the executive branch's harsh policies toward the Haitians as race-based.[204] Indeed, people of color from Haiti constituted the first group of refugees ever singled out by the U.S. armed forces for interdiction on the high seas. Still, the issue is complex. Cubans, who have historically received much more favorable treatment than Haitians, are also considered people of color by U.S. social standards. In addition to concerns of race and mass migration, the executive branch's foreign policy goals may explain the disparate treatment between Haitians and Cubans. In the late 1990s, Cubans were subjected to interdiction when a mass migration threatened south Florida. Interestingly, many in this particular immigrant cohort were poorer than past Cuban migrants had been and were more likely to be Afro-Cuban. Subtle racism inevitably reduced the potential for significant resistance to an interdiction program directed exclusively at Haitian refugees. As law professor Steve Legomsky declared, "'The public would never [have stood] for this if the boat people were Europeans.'"[205] The race, class, language, and culture of the Haitians, as well as the popular belief that many were infected with the HIV virus, un-questionably contributed to the domestic resistance to their admission.[206]

In the end, asylum seekers from Haiti, one of the few nations near the United States with a large black population, suffered some of the harshest treatment imaginable at the hands of the U.S. government. The Supreme Court's sanctioning of that treatment occurred in the aftermath of the 1992 violence in Los Angeles in response to the Rodney King verdict. At the same historical moment when the nation focused its attention on building racial harmony with African Americans at home, it was excluding black people from abroad.

Proposition 187 and Race

One of the racial milestones of the 1990s in the United States was the passage of California's Proposition 187, whose goal was to deny public benefits, including a public education, to undocumented immigrants. To bolster a sagging reelection campaign, California Governor Pete Wilson capitalized on public dissatisfaction with immigration by staunchly supporting the initiative. Television advertisements that emphasized Wilson's unqualified support for Proposition 187 showed shadowy Mexicans crossing the border in large numbers.[207] As the initiative's "Save Our State" moniker suggests, supporters blamed undocumented Mexicans for state economic woes that were more likely attributable to drastic reductions in federal defense spending brought on by the end of the Cold War and the demise of the Soviet Union.[208] The campaign steered clear of the fact that Proposition 187 placed in jeopardy $15 billion in federal funding, an amount that dwarfed any potential savings,[209] suggesting that factors other than economics were at work.

Nativist and racist themes inflamed the bitter Proposition 187 campaign. In a textbook example of nativist sentiment, one initiative sponsor boldly asserted, "'Illegal aliens are killing us in California. . . . Those who support illegal immigration are, in effect, anti-American.'" In a pamphlet distributed to registered voters, an argument that favored the measure proclaimed, "Proposition 187 will be the first giant stride in ultimately ending the ILLEGAL ALIEN invasion."[210] One leader in the pro-187 campaign even played on fears that, unless citizens took steps like the initiative, Mexico might ultimately annex California.[211]

The public statements of the drafters of Proposition 187 left the unmistakable imprint of racial animus. One initiative leader, Ron Prince, conjured up disturbing imagery of lynching, a device historically used to terrorize African Americans in the United States: "'You are the posse . . . and [Proposition 187] is the rope.'"[212] In addition to suggesting that Proposition 187 opponents were "anti-American," Prince linked "illegal aliens" with criminals: "'The . . . mindset on the part of illegal aliens, is to commit crimes. The first law they break is to be here illegally. The attitude from then on is, I don't have to obey your laws.'"[213] Harold Ezell, a high-ranking INS official during Ronald Reagan's presidency, who was infamous for his derogatory comments about "illegal aliens,"[214] attributed Proposition 187's widespread support to the fact that "'people are tired of watching their state run wild and become a third world country.'"[215]

Richard Mountjoy, a member of the California legislature, had consistently proposed bills directed at punishing immigrants.[216] According to Mountjoy, undocumented mothers "come here for that birth certificate. They come here to get on the California dole."[217] "[I]f you want to stop the flow of illegal aliens to our hospitals, stop the benefits. . . . *Having a child at our expense is not an emergency.*"[218] Mountjoy opined, "The people of California are subsidizing the illegal [alien] invasion to the tune of somewhere around $5 billion a year," and "[w]hen you have a flood of immigration . . . there's not long until this life boat sinks."[219]

Barbara Kiley, mayor of a town in Orange County, reportedly described the children of undocumented immigrants as "'those little f—kers.'"[220] Her husband, Richard Kiley, the political consultant for the initiative campaign, observed that the mass public protests against Proposition 187 had been counterproductive because "'[o]n TV there was nothing but Mexican flags and brown faces.'"[221] Richard Kiley reportedly stated, "'I don't mean to be inhumane, but this [undocumented] woman [seeking medical care] is a perfect example of why we need Prop. 187. . . . She has already had two children here and now she's on her third, and she doesn't even belong here. All I can say is, these people are going to have to go back home. We're paying for her care while Americans are homeless and starving in the streets.'"[222]

Barbara Coe, a Proposition 187 supporter, expressed fear of the "'militant arm of the pro-illegal activists, who have vowed to take over first California, then the Western states and then the rest of the nation.'"[223] To Coe, "illegal aliens" and crime are inextricably linked: "'You get illegal alien children, Third World children, out of our schools, and you will reduce the violence. That is a fact. . . . You're not dealing with a lot of shiny face, little kiddies. . . . You're dealing with Third World cultures who come in, they shoot, they beat, they stab and they spread their drugs around in our school system. And we're paying them to do it.'"[224]

As the racially tinged campaign demonstrated, Proposition 187, although facially neutral, was race based at its core. The fact that undocumented persons in the United States come from many nations other than Mexico never figured prominently in the debate over the initiative. The measure as proposed would have disparately impacted particular minority communities, notably undocumented Mexicans; Mexican American citizens; and citizens of other minority groups viewed as foreign, including Asian Americans.[225] Not surprisingly, voters were polarized along racial lines. White voters supported Proposition 187 by a two-to-one margin; Latinas/os opposed it by a three-to-one margin.[226]

Some of the anti-Mexican undertones of Proposition 187 were acted out after the election.[227] Some Latinas/os reported harassment, including the use of racial epithets and demands that they go back to Mexico.[228] National Public Radio broadcast a tape recording of a call received by an immigrants' rights group after the passage of Proposition 187: "Hasta la vista, you [expletive deleted] Mexicans. You're gettin' out of the [expletive deleted] damned country once and for all. We're sick and tired of your [expletive deleted] damned Spanish speaking [expletive deleted]. If we go to your country, we couldn't become a [expletive deleted] damned citizen. You son of a [expletive deleted] think you run this [expletive deleted] country. I got news for you. You're outta here, wetback. Adios, mother."[229] A founder of a group in Arizona seeking to place a Proposition 187–type initiative on the ballot in that state denied that it was a racial issue: "'My friends have never heard a racist word out of me. *I just don't like wetbacks.*'"[230]

Proposition 187's requirement that state and local agencies report undocumented persons to federal authorities would almost certainly have disproportionately impacted Latina/o and Asian citizens and immigrants, as well as other groups with characteristics perceived as "foreign." A lobbyist for the California Organization of Police and Sheriffs expressed this concern with respect to the law enforcement provisions of Proposition 187: "'There are many people who speak with accents. A police officer would have to spend hours every time he makes an arrest of somebody who doesn't speak perfect English or who is dark-skinned or Asian, trying to check out that status with the INS. I don't think the INS would be available from midnight to 9 a.m. So there are high costs to police officers on the job. . . . It would discourage people of ethnic backgrounds . . . from reporting crimes, [and] it would discourage witnesses and anybody who would be involved in any kind of crime situation.'"[231] The verification and notification requirements would be likely to have similar consequences with respect to health and social services and education.

Perceived foreignness could lead state and local officers to suspect lack of documentation.[232] Concerns over discriminatory enforcement, presumably unlawful, were heightened by the fact that Proposition 187 lacked any explanation about how its verification requirements would be implemented.[233] Ethnic minorities voiced concern about the spillover effects the measure might have on minority citizens.[234]

A court enjoined the implementation of most of Proposition 187, and it never went into effect.[235] Nonetheless, the law triggered national action. In 1996, Congress enacted welfare reform that restricted benefits to both lawful and unlawful immigrants. (See Chapter 4 for a discussion of the impact of welfare reform on poor immigrants.) As with the Chinese exclusion laws, California blazed a regrettable trail for the nation.

Whether Proposition 187 might properly be classified as "racist," however, is a complex question. Some of its support may result from concerns over the fiscal consequences of undocumented immigration. Some voters undoubtedly feared a loss of control of their culture, society, and lives.[236] Some were motivated by a desire to halt the flow of undocumented Mexican immigrants to the United States and to hasten their return to Mexico. Others were unabashedly anti-Mexican, immigration status notwithstanding. The passage of Proposition 187 may have also resulted, in part, from sheer frustration with the changes brought about by immigration. Even so, it is clear that racial bias played an important role in the passage of Proposition 187.

Proposition 187 was about much more than immigration. The initiative represented the electorate's general frustration with changing racial demographics. Whereas an effort to attack domestic racial minorities with full force is politically unsavory, an all-out war against noncitizens, with the attack focused on immigration status rather than race, can be more readily pursued. Proposition 187's reflection of racial tensions is similar to that of the English-only laws, which link language and national origin. The facially netural designation of English as "official language" directly affects the Latina/o community.[237] It is therefore no surprise that the national origins quota system of 1924 came on the heels of the 1917 addition of the English literacy requirement to the immigration laws. Both constituted parts of an overall package to limit immigration and penalize immigrants.

Lessons from the Immigration Laws: A Gauge for Domestic Minorities

Immigration law offers a helpful gauge for measuring this nation's racial sensibilities. The plenary power doctrine, a judicially created immunity for substantive immigration decisions that has long been a fixture of immigration law, gives the legislative and executive branches of the U.S. government "plenary power" over immigration matters, with little if any room for judicial review. Although consistently criticized, and arguably narrowed by the Supreme Court, the doctrine continues to represent the law of the land.[238] In this important way, immigration law has been, and remains to some extent, estranged from traditional public law, where the Constitution operates in full force.[239]

Academic attacks on the plenary power doctrine, coming from many different angles, are legion.[240] Few, if any, modern defenders of the plenary power doctrine can be found in the legal academy. Federal plenary power over immigration contrasts sharply with the Supreme Court's occasional strict scrutiny of state "alienage" classifications. In *Graham v. Richardson*, which invalidated a state welfare regulation, the Court recognized that "[a]liens as a class are a prime example of a 'discrete and insular' minority . . . for whom heightened judicial solicitude is appropriate."[241] This reasoning would seem to apply with full force to federal regulation.[242] However, the Court has consistently given federal "alienage" classifications deferential treatment, just as it has with Congress's judgments regarding substantive immigration admissions criteria. For example, in *Mathews v. Diaz*,[243] the Court invoked the plenary power doctrine and upheld limits on immigrant eligibility for a federal benefit program.

Fortunately, the plenary power doctrine has not been invoked in recent years to shield anything as contrary to this nation's modern constitutional sensibilities as the infamous Chinese exclusion laws. Express racial and national origin exclusions, which would squarely contradict such icons of the law as *Brown v. Board of Education*,[244] rarely arise in modern immigration law and policy. As we have seen, however, the facially neutral immigration laws of the modern era have distinctively racial impacts, if not motivations.

Assuming that, under the plenary power doctrine, noncitizens possess few, if any, constitutional protections with respect to entering the country, the implications of racial and national origin exclusions on citizens must be considered. Because the Constitution unquestionably protects the rights of citizens, citizens who claim injury have a better chance of successfully challenging the immigration laws than noncitizens directly affected by their operation. Courts have recognized that citizens in certain circumstances may challenge the lawfulness of immigration laws because of the impact on their rights.[245]

Gerald Rosberg focuses on the damage to U.S. citizens who share the race or national origin of groups barred from joining the national community: "[A racial or national origin] classification would . . . require strict scrutiny, not because of the injury to the aliens denied admission, but rather because of the injury to American citizens of the same race or national origin who are stigmatized by the classification. When Con-

gress declares that aliens of Chinese or Irish or Polish origin are excludable on the grounds of ancestry alone, it fixes a badge of opprobrium
on citizens of the same ancestry. . . . Except when necessary to protect
a compelling interest, Congress cannot implement a policy that has the
effect of labeling some group of citizens as inferior to others because of
their race or national origin."[246]

Others have also observed the impacts of racial and national origin exclusions on citizens. In unsuccessfully vetoing the INA, President Truman observed that the national origins quota system was "founded on
the idea that Americans with English or Irish names were better people
and better citizens than Americans with Italian or Greek or Polish
names. It was thought that people of West European origin made better citizens than Rumanians or Yugoslavs or Ukrainians or Hungarians
or Balts or Austrians. Such a concept . . . violates the great political doctrine of the Declaration of Independence that 'all men are created
equal.'"[247] Similarly, in arguing for the abolition of the quota system,
Secretary of State Dean Rusk recognized that excluding certain noncitizens suggested that "'we think . . . less well of our own citizens of
those national origins, than of other citizens.'"[248]

Brown v. Board of Education suggests that racial and national origin exclusions in the immigration laws adversely affect domestic minorities.
In that case, the Supreme Court relied on social science studies that
documented the fact that segregation of African Americans "generates
a feeling of inferiority as to their status in the community that may affect their hearts and minds in a way unlikely to be undone."[249] Similarly,
excluding immigrants of color from the country may well generate feelings of inferiority of domestic minorities who share a similar racial and
national origin background.

Racial exclusion of noncitizens under the immigration laws, be they
overt or covert, reveals to domestic minorities how they are viewed by
society. The unprecedented efforts to seal the U.S.-Mexican border
combined with the increased efforts to deport undocumented Mexicans, for example, reflect how a majority of society views Mexican Americans and suggest to what lengths society might go, if permitted under
color of law, to rid itself of domestic Mexican Americans. Recall that, during the New Deal, both Mexican American citizens and Mexican im-

migrants were "repatriated" to Mexico. It is therefore no surprise that despite perceived competition with immigrants in the job market,[250] the organized Mexican American community consistently resists the harsh attacks on immigration and immigrants.[251]

For similar reasons, African American activist organizations protested the U.S. government's ruthless actions toward impoverished Haitian refugees who faced extreme political violence in Haiti. Asian activist groups criticized not only the treatment of Chinese immigrants in the 1990s but also anti-immigrant sentiment and welfare reforms that adversely affected the Asian immigrant community. These minority groups understand the implicit connection between racial exclusions and their own place in the racial hierarchy in the United States. Their shared common ancestry allows for the understanding that animosity toward members of immigrant minority communities is not just limited to immigrants. Immigration has thus become a battlefield for status among Anglos and people of color in the United States.

The concerns of minority activists find support in psychological theory, which suggests that people generally view those of national origin ancestries different from their own as fungible. Put differently, in-groups tend to define out-groups as homogeneous.[252] The out-group homogeneity theory helps explain the persistence of racial stereotypes.[253] Many have experienced the homogenizing of racial minorities in crude and obviously false statements about how all members of certain racial minority groups "look alike."[254] The theory supports the idea that society generally classifies all persons of Mexican ancestry, for example, as the same and fails to make fine legal distinctions between them based on such factors as immigration status.

In the end, we must understand that racially exclusionary immigration laws do more than just stigmatize domestic minorities. Such laws reinforce domestic subordination of the same racial minority groups that are excluded. By barring admission of the outsider group that is subordinated domestically, society rationalizes the disparate treatment of the domestic racial minority group in question and reinforces that group's inferiority. Exclusion in the immigration laws must be viewed as an integral part of a larger mosaic of racial discrimination in U.S. society.

Lessons from Psychological Theory:
Why Immigrants of Color Are Society's Scapegoats

The historical dynamic identified here cannot be marginalized as simply an "immigration" issue. Indeed, immigration law sounds the alarm for racial minorities in the United States. Efforts to exclude noncitizen minorities from the country under the immigration laws threaten citizen minorities. One obvious threat is that, if for whatever reason—narrow interpretation by the Supreme Court, for example—the protections of the Constitution are limited or eviscerated, domestic minorities have much to fear. The harsh treatment of noncitizens of color suggests just how, in the absence of legal protections, society might behave toward domestic minorities of color. A stark example is *Korematsu*, in which the Court sanctioned the internment of both citizens and noncitizens of Japanese ancestry in the name of national security.[255]

In turn, there exists a relationship between society's treatment of domestic minorities and noncitizens of color. Congress passed the Chinese exclusion laws not long after ratification of the revolutionary Reconstruction Amendments designed to protect the rights of African Americans. *Korematsu* and Operation Wetback took place in the same general time frame as *Brown v. Board of Education*. Haitian repatriation continued almost simultaneously with the Rebuild L.A. campaign in the wake of the Rodney King violence in Los Angeles. The recurring nature of such closely timed contrasting events suggests that they should be considered part and parcel of a complex pattern of racial subordination in the United States.

Psychological theory at times has served as a tool for analyzing the legal implications of racial discrimination.[256] In some ways, the reaction to immigrants of color can be explained by the psychological construction known as transference "in which feelings toward one person are refocused on another."[257] Transference ordinarily occurs unconsciously in the individual.[258] The general public, in light of modern sensibilities, is often deterred from direct public attacks on minority citizens. Society can, however, more easily lash out with full force at noncitizens of color. In so doing, they often contend that the attacks are not racially motivated, citing other facially neutral factors as animating restrictionist goals. Such attacks amount to transference of frustration from domestic minorities to immigrants of color.

The related psychological construction of displacement also helps us understand the phenomenon.[259] "Displacement" is "[a] defense mechanism in which a drive or feeling is shifted upon a substitute object, one that is psychologically more available. For example, aggressive impulses may be displaced, as in 'scapegoating,' upon people (or even inanimate objects) who are not sources of frustration but are safer to attack."[260] Psychological studies show how displaced frustration may unconsciously result in the development of racial prejudice.[261] For example, one famous study of displaced aggression found that negative attitudes toward persons of Japanese and Mexican ancestry increased after a tedious testing session that caused children to miss a trip to the movies. Animosity was displaced from the test givers, immune from attack because of their positions of authority, to defenseless racial minorities.[262]

Such examples square with the history of scapegoating immigrants for the social problems of the day.[263] For example, when the U.S. economy plunged in the 1880s, the frustration was displaced from diffuse economic causes to Chinese immigrants. Gordon Allport offered a most apt example: "Most Germans did not see the connection between their humiliating defeat in World War I and their subsequent anti-Semitism."[264] Frustration was displaced from complex real-world causes to a simple—and defenseless—solution.

Transference and displacement serve to hide racial animosity toward all people of color, not just immigrants of color. An unsatisfied appetite for homogeneity knows no border between immigrants and citizens. Both minority citizens and minority noncitizens remain a distinct racial minority whatever the fine legal distinctions made with respect to immigration status. The popular perception that Latinas/os and Asian Americans are "foreigners" in the United States supports this notion.

Cognitive dissonance theory, under which the human mind attempts to reconcile conflicting ideas, helps explain how dominant society pits subordinated peoples against one another.[265] Generous behavior toward one racial minority allows facially neutral rationalization of harsh behavior toward other minorities, such as the group's failure to assimilate, its deficient work ethic, its use of a foreign language, or the entrance of some of its members into the country in violation of the immigration laws. As Cass Sunstein observed, "The beneficiaries of the status quo tend to . . . conclud[e] that the victims deserve their fate, that they are responsible for it, or that the current situation is part of the intractable, given, or natural order. . . . [P]eople who behave cruelly change their attitudes toward the objects of their cruelty and thus devalue them. Observers of cruelty and violence tend to do the same. The phenomenon of blaming the victim has clear cognitive and motivational foundations. The notion that the world is just, and that existing inequalities are deserved or desired, plays a large role in forming preferences and beliefs. All these phenomena played an enormous part in the history of racial and sexual discrimination."[266]

A number of other psychological and sociological theories offer some explanation for the relationship between domestic and foreign subordination. Although these and many other theories of race relations differ in important ways, each considers the whole of social relations instead of focusing on the particular misfortune of one minority group at a time. This lesson should not be lost on those who analyze anti-immigrant sentiment and domestic race relations.

This chapter has traced the historical relationship between subordination of domestic minorities and noncitizen minorities. Those who are serious about social change would do well to engage and contend with these complex interrelationships to gain a better understanding of the operation of subordination in the United States. Racial subordination is part of a cohesive whole that cannot be fully appreciated by focusing on one aspect as separate and apart from the dynamic social context.

If change is not forthcoming, what can we extrapolate from the past to predict the future? We can expect crackdowns on immigrant minorities at times when domestic racial minorities experience minimal improvements. Foreigners, like sacrifices to the gods, are the price for domestic minorities to achieve marginal gains. The psychological dynamics work together to buttress the status quo and ensure maintenance of the racial hierarchy in the United States.

For better or worse, the history of national origin and racial exclusion in U.S. immigration laws serves as a window into this nation's soul. By considering the nationalities and racial minorities that a society seeks to exclude from the national community, we can better understand how that society views citizens who share characteristics in common with the excluded group. This phenomenon is not limited to racial minorities; it applies with equal force to other groups who have been excluded from our shores under the immigration laws, including political minorities, the poor, criminals, homosexuals, and women. "Disadvantaged" in the United States means "multiply disadvantaged" under the immigration laws.

The transference of hate and the displacement of frustration from one racial minority to another explain much about the heated racial dynamics of the United States. Cognitive dissonance theory explains how the nation's use of a psychological device allows it to treat noncitizens of color harshly as it claims that racism in America is dead. Unfortunately, as immigration continues to change the complexion of U.S. society, we can expect more of the same. As racial diversity in the United States increases and the Anglo-Saxon ideal becomes less a possibility and more a distant and, for some, nostalgic memory, we can only wonder what our constant striving for homogeneity holds in store for the future.

Conclusion

This chapter has focused attention on racial restrictions in the U.S. immigration laws and their enforcement as it has pointed out the overlap between the exclusion and deportation of racial minorities and the exclusion of other categories of persons from the country. The Immigration Act of 1924, for example, limited immigration of the "inferior races" of southern and eastern Europeans in part because their alleged inferiority included a failed commitment to democracy and inability to self-govern. Restrictionist Madison Grant expressed similar reservations about Mexican immigrants around this time: "What the Melting Pot actually does in practice can be seen in Mexico, where the absorption of the blood of the original Spanish conquerors by the native Indian population has produced the racial mixture which we call Mexican and which is now engaged in demonstrating its incapacity for self-government."[267]

Efforts to remove supporters of Arab and Muslim political causes in the name of fighting "terrorism" also has a racial component. As Chapter 3 demonstrates, Arabs and Muslims have been the targets of unfavorable treatment under ideological exclusion and deportation provisions of the immigration laws in no small part because of their race and religion. Similarly, the exclusion and deportation of the poor and of criminals have racial impacts readily apparent in the modern United States. Immigrants from Mexico are the most likely group to face removal from the United States based on criminal convictions; moreover, the harshest criminal deportation provisions were added to the immigration laws as it was becoming evident that Mexican citizens constituted the largest group of immigrants in the country. Labeled as potential public charges, people of color from developing nations are the most likely group to be excluded from the United States.

In short, although the chapters that follow treat the exclusion and removal of various groups independently, each category is inextricably linked to the others. As a pattern emerges from the study, we will see which groups are most disadvantaged under the U.S. immigration laws and their enforcement. As intersectionality analysis teaches us in analyzing domestic civil rights concerns,[268] immigrants who have multiple subordinating characteristics (for example, poor immigrant women of color) face many more hardships than those who are disadvantaged in fewer ways.

3

Exclusion and Deportation of Political Undesirables

From its early days, the United States sought to limit the number of politically undesirable persons coming to this country from foreign lands. The infamous Alien and Sedition Acts of the 1790s represent one of the first examples of these efforts.[1] Over the next two centuries, Congress passed laws that penalized "alien" anarchists, communists, and other politically unpopular persons. During the twentieth century, the federal government enforced these laws with vigor in times of crisis. The hunt for political dissidents took on new meaning and urgency after September 11, 2001. The highest levels of the federal government have engaged in a concerted effort to uncover political dissent among Arab and Muslim noncitizens and to question, detain, and remove them from the country.[2]

The efforts to exclude or deport political undesirables have almost invariably been linked to domestic tensions. Indeed, ideological exclusions in the immigration laws "mask their true purpose: protection of particular social and economic values that are promoted by the American political system."[3] For example, through the Alien and Sedition Acts, the Federalists sought not only to cut off the burgeoning political support that immigrants offered to the Republicans but also to respond to tensions with the new radical French government and fear of the spread of radicalism in the United States.[4] In later turbulent times, the primary concern was that "foreigners" might infect the domestic populace with the disease of subversion, thereby causing labor turmoil and possibly even a radical takeover.[5]

In that vein, the U.S. government has traditionally employed the immigration laws, particularly the provisions that pertain to the exclusion and deportation of noncitizens, to attack perceived threats to the social order. Both labor strife and the 1901 assassination of President William McKinley by an anarchist who, although he had a foreign-sounding name, was in fact a U.S. citizen culminated in congressional passage of a 1903 law that provided for the exclusion of anarchists. Not long after the nationalist frenzy of World War I and the Bolshevik rise to power in the fledgling Soviet Union, U.S. Attorney General Alexander Mitchell Palmer commenced the infamous Palmer Raids as part of his war on the Industrial Workers of the World, which resulted in the much-publicized deportation of noncitizen activists in the labor movement. The U.S. government later employed the immigration law's ideological provisions to promote domestic ends in a relentless three-decade effort to deport labor leader Harry Bridges.

Studies often gloss over a critical facet of history: the correlation between the severe treatment that politically subversive U.S. citizens received and the constriction of the immigration laws. For example, during McCarthyism's reign in the 1950s, when citizens labeled as communists suffered blacklisting,[6] the burdens fell even more heavily on noncitizens. Some, including many who had lived in the United States for years and had enduring ties to this nation, were deported.[7] Because political and judicial restraints were not in place to prevent mistreatment, the antipathy toward communists could be fully acted upon with respect to noncitizens. In the war on communism, citizens were blacklisted from jobs, but noncitizens were banished from the country.

As the war on communism subsided, the persecution of *citizens* for their political views waned. Although ideological scrutiny in the immigration laws has lessened to some degree, noncitizens are still subjected to politically motivated immigration enforcement. Until 1990, the law expressly allowed the U.S. government to exclude noncitizens, even as temporary visitors, based on nothing more than their political beliefs.

Although Congress significantly narrowed the ideological exclusion and deportation grounds in 1990, some of these grounds exist to this day. For example, noncitizens who do no more than provide financial support for the peaceful activities of certain political organizations have been subjected to vigorous deportation efforts by the U.S. government. The efforts to stamp out terrorism and the expansion of the definition of "terrorist activity" continued with the USA PATRIOT (Uniting and Strengthening America by Providing Appropriate Tools Required to Intercept and Obstruct Terrorism) Act,[8] the initial congressional response to September 11, 2001.

In sum, the U.S. government has historically employed the immigration laws in an effort to protect the established political and social order, whether from domestic unrest or from foreign threat. As John Scanlan explains it:

> Aliens, in their persons and in their conception of society, threaten the existing social order. Such a conception of the social order requires that the national government maintain broad restrictionist powers so that it can contain the external threat aliens pose. The alien threat can be either physical, ideological, or both. It can involve the advent of "vast hordes" of people ready to wrest away American wealth and jobs, or the actual or potential dissemination of suspect or dangerous ideas about such matters as marriage, religion, or politics. In either case, those inside have the right to protect themselves against outsiders. This general right of self-protection endows the government with the particular right to restrict the political speech of aliens by barring their entry or enjoining their continued residence.[9]

As this analysis suggests, U.S. foreign relations concerns have domestic consequences. For example, nativism toward noncitizens at the end of the nineteenth century coexisted comfortably with U.S. jingoism during the Spanish-American War.[10] Tension between the U.S. and Iranian governments in the 1970s resulted in the imposition of special requirements for reporting on Iranian students in the United States.[11] September 11, 2001, resulted in similar treatment of Arab and Muslim noncitizens in the United States. These episodes demonstrate how the hostility toward foreigners *outside* our borders influences hostility toward "foreigners" *inside* our borders.

In protecting the status quo, political elites generally define the "social order" that deserves protection and identify those noncitizens from whom protection is necessary.[12] With a wealth of enforcement discretion under the immigration laws,[13] the federal government has shaped public opinion with respect to the exclusion and deportation of politically undesirable noncitizens. Throughout U.S. history, anarchists, communists, and supporters of certain foreign political organizations have been politically unpopular. Today, it is the supporters of certain foreign political organizations, such as those who advocate the rights of Palestinians in the Middle East, who suffer the consequences of being labeled as suspected terrorists. With popular public support, the U.S. government may pursue without impediment efforts to exclude or deport political subversives.

Against this historical backdrop, we can better appreciate the Antiterrorism and Effective Death Penalty Act of 1996 (Antiterrorism Act)[14] and the Illegal Immigration Reform and Immigrant Responsibility Act of 1996 (Immigration Reform Act),[15] the twin immigration reform laws passed by Congress in 1996. Although the Antiterrorism Act's name suggests concerns about combating terrorism, the genesis of the law illustrates that it is a political response to deeper uncertainty in the U.S. political order. After the much-publicized bombing of the federal building in Oklahoma City in 1995, the media reports described the suspects as having a Middle Eastern appearance and suggested the possibility that international terrorists were responsible for the attack.[16] Increased tension between the United States and various Middle East countries caused by the Gulf War, the indictment and ultimate conviction of Middle Eastern immigrants for the 1993 World Trade Center bombing in New York City,[17] and various terrorist incidents abroad made this suspicion plausible, if not probable, to the U.S. public. In signing the Antiterrorism Act into law, President Clinton acknowledged that the law was enacted in response to the Oklahoma City bombing and emphasized the part that it would play in combating international terrorism.[18] This recognition, however, disregards the fact that members of a homegrown group of bona fide U.S. citizens, including a former U.S. Army officer, were convicted of the bombing.[19] The immigration provisions of the Antiterrorism Act sweep far afield of the goal of fighting terrorism: They permit the deportation of many documented permanent residents who have family and friends in the United States and who can in no way be conceived of as terrorists, on the grounds that they have been convicted of certain criminal offenses. The collateral damage of the 1996 Anti-terrorism Act on "criminal aliens" who have nothing whatever to do with terrorism has been severe (see Chapter 5). The USA PATRIOT Act promises more of the same.

We are left to ponder why Congress would pass such draconian immigration laws in response to an act of domestic terrorism attributable to U.S. citizens. Legal and political limits exist on the government's ability to suppress domestic dissent, whether from right-wing white supremacist groups and private militia or from left-wing environmental groups. The First Amendment of the Constitution offers cherished protections to citizens who advocate unpopular political views.[20] Moreover, citizens cannot be forcibly ejected from the country for any reason, including for engaging in constitutionally protected political expression. Indeed, the very idea of deporting citizens is unthinkable in the established legal order. At the same time, restrictions on free expression and the deportation of noncitizens are both sanctioned by law.

In contrast with the concrete protections that the laws guarantee to citizens, the courts have generally been unwilling to guarantee noncitizens any protection of their political rights. For example, the courts have permitted the deportation of immigrants for political expression that would have been constitutionally protected if carried out by a U.S. citizen. Limited judicial oversight embodied in the much-maligned plenary power doctrine shields congressional action, thereby giving it freer reign to stifle the free expression of noncitizens and allowing political forces to lash out at noncitizens with ferocity.

The 1996 immigration reforms reflect a larger historical dynamic that reveals much about the relationship between domestic subordination and immigration law. Congress has acted repeatedly to penalize foreign "subversives," in no small part because the Constitution imposes limits on the government's power to punish citizens on the political fringes. As long as the constitutional safeguards for political expression of noncitizens and citizens differ drastically, we can expect recurring examples of such punitive legislation as the Antiterrorism Act and the Immigration Reform Act. The USA PATRIOT Act, passed by Congress within months of September 11, 2001, fits this mold. The lack of con-

· stitutional protections for noncitizens helps to explain such recent measures as the arrest, detention, interrogation, and special reporting requirements directed at Arab and Muslim noncitizens.

This dynamic further demonstrates the importance of the constitutional safeguards for U.S. citizens. The harsh treatment of noncitizens is a window to the extreme measures that the government might take to suppress domestic political dissent by U.S. citizens if the Constitution did not offer them protection or if the courts minimized or limited these protections through constitutional interpretation. More generally, as we have noted, the U.S. government's treatment of noncitizens reflects society's views toward citizens who share characteristics in common with noncitizens who are being punished by the government under color of law.

A History of Exclusion and Deportation of Political Undesirables

Many people in the United States justifiably take pride in the First Amendment's protection of free expression. As Justice Louis Brandeis eloquently stated, the framers of the Constitution "believed that freedom to think as you will and to speak as you think are means indispensable to the discovery and spread of political truth; that without free speech and assembly discussion would be futile; that with them, discussion affords ordinarily adequate protection against the dissemination of noxious doctrine; that the greatest menace to freedom is an inert people; that public discussion is a political duty; and that this should be a fundamental principle of the American government."[21] In a similar vein, Justice Oliver Wendell Holmes defended free speech on the grounds that "the best test of truth is the power of the thought to get itself accepted in the competition of the market."[22] Indeed, even those who advocate a narrow view of First Amendment protections would shield "political" speech from regulation.[23]

Oddly enough, for a nation that trumpets its deep commitment to political freedom, the United States has a long history of excluding and deporting political subversives.[24] In the earliest days of the republic, Congress, for partisan political reasons, passed two laws of dubious constitutionality: the Alien Enemy Act, which allowed the president to deport "alien enemies" and other noncitizens who were "natives, citizens, denizens, or subjects of a hostile nation or government,"[25] and the Alien Act, which authorized the president to deport "aliens" reasonably suspected of "treasonable or secret machinations against the government."[26] Although the acts were rarely invoked, the laws nevertheless may well have resulted in "the mass exodus of frightened foreigners."[27] These acts marked the beginning of a pattern in which domestic political tensions provoked responses directed at "foreigners."

In the late nineteenth century, the U.S. Supreme Court facilitated the passage of laws that permitted the exclusion and deportation of political undesirables by embracing the plenary power doctrine (see Chapter 2). This judicial hands-off approach to the federal immigration laws may well have encouraged, and at the very least did not discourage, Congress from passing later laws that permitted the exclusion and deportation of noncitizens of particular political persuasions, including anarchists, labor leaders, and anyone remotely affiliated with the Communist Party.[28]

The Haymarket Riots

In the 1880s, organized labor made the radical demand for an eight-hour work day. In support of that end, speakers, including some self-proclaimed anarchists, advocated labor solidarity at a rally in Chicago's Haymarket Square in 1886.[29] When police sought to disburse the crowd, a bomb exploded and the police fired on the protesters. The Supreme Court upheld the convictions of several anarchists, including two foreign-born individuals who were sentenced to death, for their involvement in the bombing.[30]

After the Haymarket incident, fears of foreign-fomented anarchy grew.[31] The assassination of President McKinley in 1901 by anarchist Leon Czolgosz, a native-born U.S. citizen assumed by many to be an immigrant because of his surname, triggered congressional action.[32] The Immigration Act of 1903 permitted the exclusion of "anarchists, or persons who believe in or advocate the overthrow by force or violence of the Government of the United States or of all government or of all forms of law, or the assassination of public officials."[33] The new law "reflected broader national concerns about radicals in the labor movement. A growing belief that the new immigrants from Eastern and Central Europe held political values that threatened the existing social and political status quo helped fuel the attack on anarchism."[34]

Beginning a pattern that prevailed for most of the twentieth century, in the landmark case of *United States ex rel. John Turner v. Williams*,[35] the Supreme Court rejected a challenge to the application of the Immigration Act of 1903. The following is an excerpt from one of John Turner's speeches that resulted in his deportation: "If no work was being done, if it were Sunday for a week or a fortnight, life in New York would be impossible, and the workers, gaining audacity, would refuse to recognize the authority of their employers and eventually take to themselves the handling of the industries. . . . All over Europe they are preparing for a general strike, which will spread over the entire industrial world. Everywhere the employers are organizing, and to me, at any rate, as an anarchist, as one who believes that the people should emancipate themselves, I look forward to this struggle as an opportunity for the workers to assert the power that is really theirs."[36] Finding that the law permitted Turner's deportation, the Supreme Court emphasized that "as long as human governments endure they cannot be denied the power of self-preservation."[37]

The Immigration Act upheld in *Turner* represented an overreaction to the violent Haymarket Riots. Mere belief in anarchism by immigrants did not cause the bombing in Chicago. Anarchistic immigrants did not cause a U.S. citizen to assassinate President McKinley. In important ways, the historical context that surrounds the Immigration Act of 1903 resembles the historical context that surrounds congressional response to later acts of violence.

The Wobblies and the Palmer Raids

The rise and fall of the Industrial Workers of the World (IWW), popularly known as the Wobblies, represents an infamous episode of U.S. history.[38] In the early twentieth century, the IWW aggressively organized the industrial workers, who had, for the most part, been ignored by the craft unions of the American Federation of Labor. "In nearly every state in the Union, Wobblies were clubbed, tarred and feathered, deported, shot, tortured, maimed, occasionally lynched, and universally despised."[39] The U.S. government, blaming foreign agitators for domestic labor unrest, began an all-out war on the IWW.[40] The impetus for this campaign was bolstered by World War I, which "gave to . . . employers and to others opposed to the IWW a golden opportunity to associate the syndicalist philosophy and militant tactics of the Wobblies with violence, terrorism, lack of patriotism, pro-Germanism and, later, with radicalism and all the violent characteristics attributed to the Bolshevik Revolution."[41] During the same general time frame, antiforeigner, antianarchist sentiment was inflamed by the notorious murder trial of two Italian immigrant anarchists, Nicola Sacco and Bartolomeo Vanzetti.[42]

In the Anarchist Act of 1918,[43] Congress clarified any doubts about the intent of the Immigration Act of 1903. The Immigration Act permitted the exclusion or deportation of "aliens who *believe in* or advocate the overthrow by force or violence of the Government of the United States or of all forms of law."[44] By clarifying ambiguities concerning which noncitizens were deportable or excludable, Congress hoped to avoid "long and hurtful delays on appeal to the courts."[45] As we shall see, in 1996, similar concerns motivated the Congress to pass immigration reform laws that significantly limited judicial review of removal orders for noncitizens.

The end of World War I failed to quell the concerns. The stated purpose of Attorney General Palmer's notorious Palmer Raids was to locate subversives responsible for a series of bombings.[46] In 1919 and 1920, the federal government rounded up, interrogated, and detained (often for lengthy periods) suspected anarchists. The government deported many immigrants, including many Wobblies, and the courts generally upheld the deportations.[47] For example, under the watchful eye of Federal Bureau of Investigation (FBI) Director J. Edgar Hoover, a famous leftist rabble-rouser named Emma Goldman was deported to the Soviet Union on a ship dubbed the Soviet Ark.[48]

Leading legal luminaries of the day, including Harvard Law School professors Zechariah Chafee Jr., Felix Frankfurter, and Roscoe Pound, denounced the Palmer Raids.[49] In the scathing *Report upon the Illegal*

Practices of the United States Department of Justice, they recognized that "[p]unishments of the utmost cruelty, and heretofore unthinkable in America, have become usual. Great numbers of persons arrested, *both aliens and citizens,* have been threatened, beaten with blackjacks, struck with fists, jailed under abominable conditions, or actually tortured."[50] The damning conclusion of the report speaks for itself: "Since these illegal acts have been committed by the highest legal powers in the United States, there is no final appeal from them except to the conscience and condemnation of the American people. American institutions have not in fact been protected by the Attorney General's ruthless suppression. On the contrary, those institutions have been seriously undermined. . . . *No organizations of radicals acting through propaganda over the last six months could have created as much revolutionary sentiment in America as has been created by the acts of the Department of Justice itself.*"[51]

Such stinging indictments had little impact on the political process. In 1920, Congress amended the Anarchist Act of 1918 to expand the ideological grounds on which noncitizens could be excluded and deported.[52] The legislative history of the Anarchist Act of 1920 makes it clear that the executive branch promoted the amendment to facilitate the deportation of noncitizens, particularly IWW members.[53]

As it did with the Immigration Act of 1903, the Supreme Court upheld congressional efforts to penalize noncitizen anarchists in the 1918 and 1920 laws. In the 1924 case of *United States ex rel. Tisi v. Tod,*[54] the Court affirmed a deportation order based on Catoni Tisi's distribution of material in English that called for the overthrow of the government even though he understood neither English nor the nature of the leaflets.

During this period, the U.S. government was ready and willing to suppress "radical" labor by cracking down on both citizens and (especially) noncitizens. Repression of citizens occurred in schemes such as the Palmer Raids; however, under the law, more extreme measures, as the mass deportations on the Soviet Ark demonstrate, could be and were taken against noncitizens accused of the crime of radicalism. Political concerns about noncitizens surfaced in other areas as well. For example, states, which had long extended suffrage to certain noncitizens, began the disfranchisement of noncitizens that remains the norm today.[55]

It is important to note that fewer than 1,250 immigrants were deported between 1911 and 1940 as a result of being labeled subversives or anarchists,[56] and fewer than 50 were formally excluded on ideological grounds.[57] However, State Department consular officers may have excluded many more noncitizens who sought visas from within their native countries.[58] In any event, raw numbers cannot measure to what extent the law might have deterred citizens and noncitizens from engaging in political activity.

The "Communist Threat"

The treatment of citizens accused of communism during the McCarthy era was unconscionable; yet it paled in comparison with the treatment of similarly accused noncitizens, as several stories demonstrate.

Congressional response to one notable exception to the courts' frequent deference to the immigration decisions of Congress provides an example: the U.S. Supreme Court's decision in *Kessler v. Strecker*[59] a case decided in 1939, well before the nation's full-blown war on communism. Joseph Strecker was born an Austrian subject, immigrated to the United States in 1912, and later joined the Communist Party. By the time the U.S. government instituted deportation proceedings against Strecker, he was no longer a party member. Holding that there was no indication that Congress intended for the deportation of *former* members of the Communist Party, the Court reversed the deportation order. In response, Congress enacted the Alien Registration Act of 1940, which, among its other provisions, allowed for the deportation of former party members;[60] it provided for the deportation of any immigrant convicted of a crime under the act, including distributing literature that advocated the overthrow of the government or knowingly belonging to a group that advocated this aim.[61]

During the McCarthy era, the U.S. government vigorously enforced the ideological exclusion and deportation grounds in the immigration laws.[62] Indeed, mere suspicion about a noncitizen's loyalties could affect whether there would even be a hearing on the matter. Landmark Supreme Court decisions of that period, such as *United States ex rel. Knauff v. Shaughnessy*[63] and *Shaughnessy v. United States ex rel. Mezei*,[64] demonstrate the harsh treatment of noncitizens allowed under the U.S. Constitution.

In *Knauff*, the Supreme Court upheld as permitted by certain wartime laws and regulations the government's exclusion of Ellen Knauff, the noncitizen wife of a U.S. citizen, without a hearing. Knauff's exclusion, which was based on confidential information, had been decided on the ground that her admission would be prejudicial to the national security of the United States.[65] The Court emphasized that the "[t]he exclusion of aliens is a fundamental act of sovereignty. The right to do so stems not from legislative power alone but is inherent in the executive power to control the foreign affairs of the nation."[66]

Mezei is perhaps an even more egregious example. Ignatz Mezei lawfully immigrated to the United States and lived in this country without incident from 1923 to 1948.[67] On his return from a trip to visit his Italian mother in Romania, the U.S. government detained him on Ellis Island and denied him reentry without a hearing. Like Knauff's exclusion, Mezei's was based on confidential information and was decided on the ground that his admission to the country would have been prejudicial to the national security, but it was also based on the ground that so much as revealing the confidential information would prejudice national security. Because no other nation would accept Mezei once the United States classified him as an undesirable, he faced the prospect of indefinite detention. Nonplussed by this possibility, the Supreme Court upheld the exclusion, emphasizing the importance of U.S. sovereignty: "Courts have long recognized the power to expel or exclude aliens as a fundamental sovereign attribute exercised by the Government's political departments largely immune from judicial control."[68]

Hearings for Knauff and Mezei ultimately revealed the weakness of the government's cases against them.[69] As a result of public support and a private bill pending in Congress, the attorney general held a hearing for Knauff.[70] Rejecting the government's claims, the Board of Immigration Appeals found no substantial evidence that Knauff gave secret information to foreign authorities or that she would engage in subversive activities if admitted into the United States.[71] The attorney general also granted Mezei an exclusion hearing. The hearing revealed that he was a former member of the Hungarian Working Sick Benefit and Education Society in New York City,[72] a group that later became the Hungarian Lodge of the International Workers Order, which the U.S. government classified as a communist organization. Although he was a former secretary and president of the lodge, Mezei denied having ever been a member of the Communist Party. The Board of Special Inquiry found Mezei excludable from the United States but, because of his minor role in the Communist Party, recommended to the attorney general that Mezei be paroled into the country.

Other noncitizens charged with communist sympathies were not nearly as fortunate as Knauff and Mezei. In *Harisiades v. Shaughnessy*,[73] the Supreme Court upheld the deportation of three former Communist Party members under the Alien Registration Act of 1940. In so doing, the Court elaborated on its fears and the need for a limited judicial role in reviewing the laws attacking communism that had been passed by Congress: "Congress received evidence that the Communist movement here has been heavily laden with aliens and that Soviet control of the American Communist Party has been largely through alien Communists. . . . [W]e have an Act of one Congress which, for a decade, subsequent Congresses have never repealed but have strengthened and extended. We, in our private opinions, need not concur in Congress'[s] policies to hold its enactments constitutional. Judicially we must tolerate what personally we may regard as legislative mistake."[74] In a concurring opinion, Justice Felix Frankfurter put an exclamation point on the Court's statement about limited judicial review: "[W]hether immigration laws have been crude and cruel, whether they may have reflected xenophobia in general or anti-Semitism or anti-Catholicism, the responsibility belongs to Congress."[75]

With the Cold War escalating, Congress passed the Internal Security Act of 1950, which listed Communist Party members and affiliates as persons who could be excluded and deported.[76] In describing the necessity for the legislation, Congress stated, *"The Communist network in the United States is inspired and controlled in large part by foreign agents. . . .* There are, under our present immigration laws, numerous aliens who have been found to be deportable, many of who[m] are free to roam the country at will. . . . One device for infiltration by Communists is by procuring naturalization for disloyal aliens who use their citizenship as a badge for admission into the fabric of our society."[77]

In *Galvan v. Press*,[78] the Supreme Court upheld, under section 22 of the Internal Security Act, the deportation of Robert Galvan, an immigrant from Mexico who had entered the United States in 1918. Galvan had been a member and officer of the Spanish Speaking Club, which the U.S. government classified as a Communist Party organization.[79] The Court reiterated the rationale for limited judicial oversight: "[A]ny policy toward aliens is vitally and intricately interwoven with contemporaneous policies in regard to the conduct of foreign relations, the war power, and the maintenance of a republican form of government, and such matters are so exclusively entrusted to the political branches of government as to be largely immune from judicial inquiry or interference."[80] The harshness of the result is apparent from Justice Black's dissent:

> Petitioner has lived in this country thirty-six years, having come here from Mexico in 1918 when only seven years of age. He has an American wife to whom he has been married for twenty years, four children all born here, and a stepson who served his country as a paratrooper. Since 1940 petitioner has been a laborer at the Van Camp Sea Food Company in San Diego, California. In 1944 petitioner became a member of the Communist Party. Deciding that he no longer wanted to belong to that party, he got out sometime around 1946 or 1947. . . . [D]uring this period of his membership the Communist Party functioned "as a distinct and active political organization." . . . Party candidates appeared on California election ballots, and no Federal law then frowned on Communist Party political activities. Now in 1954, however, petitioner is to be deported from this country solely for his lawful membership in that party. . . . [T]here is strong evidence that he was a good, law-abiding man, a steady worker and a devoted husband and father loyal to this country and its form of Government.[81]

The McCarran-Walter Act, also known as the Immigration and Nationality Act of 1952 (INA), carried forward many provisions of the Internal Security Act.[82] The trend of judicial deference toward ideological regulation continued in *Jay v. Boyd*,[83] in which, under the INA and based on confidential information, the Supreme Court upheld the deportation of a sixty-five-year-old noncitizen who had entered the United States in 1921 and had been a member of the Communist Party from

1935 through 1940, *before* membership could serve as the basis for deportation. For reasons similar to those stated in *Galvan v. Press*—that is, that Communist Party membership was entirely legal at the time of Cecil Jay's membership—Justice Hugo Black dissented, observing, "This is a strange case in a country dedicated by its founders to the maintenance of liberty under law."[84]

As this case law suggests, the ideological exclusion and deportation grounds were at their zenith during the Cold War. About 230 noncitizens were deported on ideological grounds from 1951 to 1960; this number fell precipitously to 15 from 1961 to 1970.[85] Many more political undesirables were excluded, nearly 1,100 from 1951 to 1960, before the number fell to 128 between 1961 and 1970.[86] These figures do not include the presumably larger number of noncitizens denied visas by consular officers outside the United States.

The McCarthy era is infamous for the suffering that it caused citizens who were accused of communist sympathies,[87] but the suffering that it caused noncitizens who held similar political beliefs is rarely highlighted. Citizens were blacklisted; noncitizens were subjected to banishment from a country where they had developed deep and lasting ties.[88] Noncitizens had the added disadvantage of immigrant status. The underlying theory of the Supreme Court decisions about "communist sympathizers" during this period, like the decisions about their anarchist antecedents, is that "foreign propaganda will overtake native resolve. . . . [S]ubversive aliens pose a danger that does not derive from any acts of espionage, terrorism, or revolution. Instead, the danger lies in their propensity to foment civil disorder through misrepresentations and lies, and in our propensity to be misled."[89]

The War Against Harry Bridges

The ordeal of Harry Bridges, which spanned the three decades from the New Deal through the Cold War, exemplifies not only the measures the U.S. government will take to deport alleged subversives but also how domestic political concerns shape immigration law and enforcement.

Bridges, who immigrated to the United States from Australia in 1920, "was a colorful labor leader whose accomplishments on behalf of his followers were enormous. Under his leadership, the West Coast long-shoremen rose from near-peonage to a respectable level of working conditions and wages."[90] Responding to political pressures from shipping interests and their allies, the U.S. government instituted deportation proceedings against him in 1938 on the ground that he had been a member of, or was affiliated with, the Communist Party.[91] The hearing examiner, Dean James Landis of Harvard Law School, found that red-baiting was not equivalent to proof of membership in the Communist Party and concluded that the evidence failed to support the charge.[92]

In 1940, Congress amended the immigration laws to allow the deportation of an immigrant who was *at any time* a member of or affiliated with the Communist Party. Bolstered by this congressional action, the United States again sought to deport Bridges. This time, the hearing officer found that the Marine Workers' Industrial Union was affiliated with the Communist Party and that Bridges had been a member of both organizations.[93] Rejecting that finding, the Board of Immigration Appeals ruled that Bridges had not belonged to or been affiliated with the Communist Party. However, the attorney general disagreed and ordered Bridges deported.

In a refreshing divergence from earlier and later decisions, the Supreme Court reversed the order. Recognizing that Bridges had been active in union work, the Court acknowledged that although the Marine Workers' Industrial Union had the "illegitimate objective of overthrowing the government by force," it also had "the [legitimate] objective of improving the lot of its members in the normal trade union sense."[94] The Court emphasized, *"It is clear that Congress desired to have the country rid of those aliens who embraced the political faith of force and violence. But* we cannot believe that Congress intended to cast so wide a net as to reach those whose ideas and program, though coinciding with the legitimate aims of such groups, nevertheless fell far short of overthrowing the government by force and violence. *Freedom of speech and of press is accorded aliens residing in this country."*[95] Note the inconsistency between the first and last sentences of the quotation; this can be explained, at least in part, by the limited protections extended to politically unpopular speech during this period.

In a surprisingly candid concurring opinion, Justice Frank Murphy captured the essence of the government's persistent efforts to deport Bridges: "The record in this case will stand forever as a monument to man's intolerance of man. *Seldom if ever in the history of this nation has there been such a concentrated and relentless crusade to deport an individual because he dared to exercise the freedom that . . . is guaranteed to him by the Constitution. . . . For more than a decade powerful economic and social forces have combined with public and private agencies to seek the deportation of Harry Bridges.*"[96]

Despite this setback, the United States pursued further deportation proceedings against Bridges, still without success, and later fought vehemently to defeat his petition for naturalization.[97] Later the government successfully prosecuted Bridges for conspiring to secure naturalization fraudulently, based on his statement that he had never been a member of the Communist Party, but this conviction was subsequently reversed.[98] The government's relentless pursuit subsequently included an unsuccessful attempt to denaturalize Bridges because of his alleged Communist Party membership.[99] Perhaps the government would have launched such attacks against Bridges even if he had been a citizen. However, his noncitizen status availed the government of every weapon provided by the immigration and nationality laws in its attempt to banish and otherwise castigate him.

Modern Efforts to Monitor Political Ideology

Governmental efforts to exclude subversives continue today;[100] however, the focal point is no longer the so-called communist threat. Changes to the immigration laws reflect today's emphasis on the "terrorist" threat.

Though Congress temporarily suspended the ideological exclusions in the late 1980s,[101] they remained part and parcel of the laws until 1990. Under those laws, the U.S. government excluded many foreign nationals seeking to visit the United States,[102] including Hortensia Allende, widow of the former Chilean president;[103] a member of the Palestine Liberation Organization;[104] and a high-ranking member of Nicaragua's Sandinista government.[105] As two observers have noted, "[T]he list of those excluded [under these laws] . . . reads like an intellectual and cultural honor role, including Pablo Neruda, Carlos Fuentes, Gabriel Garcia Marquez, Regis Debray, Ernst Mandel, Dario Fo, and even Pierre Trudeau [former prime minister of Canada]."[106]

The Supreme Court has characteristically upheld these ideological restrictions. For example, in *Kleindienst v. Mandel*,[107] the Supreme Court refused to overrule the attorney general's decision to exclude the Belgian editor of a socialist weekly who sought to enter the United States to speak at an academic conference.

Even so, the number of noncitizens who were formally barred from admission to the United States on ideological grounds slowly declined from more than thirty in the 1970s to a handful in the early 1980s.[108] Similarly, the number of deportations on ideological grounds decreased sharply between 1971 and 1980, and so few occurred thereafter that the INS stopped reporting the data.[109] The decline in exclusion and deportation on these grounds unquestionably represented progress. Meanwhile, however, the government has retained the power to attack noncitizens it deems ideologically unfit to remain in the United States.

The 1990 Act: Limits on and Opportunities for Censorship

Ultimately, persuasive criticism of the ideological exclusions and their incompatibility with the Constitution convinced Congress to narrow them drastically.[110] The Immigration Act of 1990 modernized the exclusion grounds for membership in a totalitarian party, eliminated the exclusion for nonimmigrants, and put further limitations on the ideological exclusion grounds.[111] It is important to note that noncitizens who were involuntary members of groups in question or who had terminated membership in a totalitarian party before they applied for a visa or admission could not be excluded as long as they were not otherwise deemed a threat to the security of the United States.[112] As amended, the law states that "an alien . . . shall not be excludable . . . because of the alien's past, current, or expected beliefs, statements, or associations, if such beliefs, statements, or associations would be lawful within the United States."[113] Such exclusions are permissible, however, if "the Secretary of State personally determines that the alien's admission would compromise a compelling United States foreign policy interest."[114]

Despite the modifications to the laws, the government maintains the power to exclude immigrants who seek to enter in order to engage in "espionage or sabotage," "any other unlawful activity," or "any activity [in opposition to the U.S. government] by force, violence, or other unlawful means."[115] The government may also exclude (1) "aliens engaged in a terrorist activity" (which, as broadly defined, allows exclusion of immigrants who provide financial support to "terrorist organizations" and which was substantially expanded in both the 1996 immigration reform laws and the USA PATRIOT Act),[116] (2) immigrants whose admission would have "potentially serious adverse foreign policy consequences for the United States,"[117] and (3) participants in Nazi persecution or genocide.[118] The Antiterrorism Act later expanded the ideological exclusions by deeming excludable any immigrant who "is a representative of a foreign terrorist organization" or "is a member of a foreign terrorist organization."[119] Under the law, the secretary of state designates a "foreign terrorist organization" after finding that the foreign organization engages in "terrorist activity" that threatens U.S. national security or the security of U.S. nationals.[120] There might thus be reasonable cause for concern that foreign policy and other political considerations might influence the State Department's designation. As one State Department official stated, "One man's terrorist is another man's freedom fighter."[121]

The 1990 act also restricted the ideological grounds for deportation, eliminating membership in a totalitarian party as a ground for deportation. As with exclusion, the act focused on "terrorist activities" or actions with serious foreign policy consequences.[122] Although the modifications made to the 1990 act represent progress, the political views of noncitizens remain relevant to a number of other immigration and nationality decisions. For example, "[a]lthough the 1990 Immigration Act cut back sharply on ideological grounds for exclusion and deportation from the United States, it maintained the McCarthy-era ideological qualifications for naturalization."[123] The naturalization laws have long required that a noncitizen be "attached to constitutional principles." This requirement has been invoked to bar naturalization of lawful permanent residents who are conscientious objectors to military service[124] and lawful per-

manent residents who are Jehovah's Witnesses because they object to
voting, participating in politics, and serving on juries.[125] Anarchists,
Communist Party members or advocates of world communism, advocates of the forceful overthrow of the U.S. government or of the assault
or assassination of government officers, and anyone who knowingly
writes or circulates publications that advocate any of these ideas are also
barred from naturalization.[126] In the past, the government has attempted
to bar naturalization of noncitizens involved in the International Workers Order, arguing that, as members of the Communist Party, they lacked
attachment to constitutional principles.[127]

The ideological restrictions on naturalization take on greater importance in light of the ever-expanding grounds for deportation. A noncitizen who is barred from naturalization runs the risk of deportation
through an act or omission, such as a crime. Such deportation is an indirect (perhaps even unintended) consequence of the ideological prerequisites in the naturalization laws.

The Los Angeles Eight

Government concerns about political subversives, often framed in terms
of combating terrorism, were revived in the early 1990s in the wake of
a number of much-publicized events, including the unsuccessful New
York World Trade Center bombing in 1993. However, concerns about
terrorism predate these events. Beginning in the 1980s, for example,
the U.S. government attempted to deport certain members or affiliates
of the Popular Front for the Liberation of Palestine (PFLP).[128] In 1987,
the government commenced deportation and exclusion proceedings
against eight members of the PFLP who became known as the Los Angeles Eight.[129] All eight were charged as deportable and excludable on
ideological and nonideological grounds.[130] However, in testimony to
Congress, the former director of the FBI and the regional counsel for the
INS made it clear that the government's efforts were based on the
group's PFLP membership.[131] The FBI apparently targeted the Los
Angeles Eight because of the leadership potential of some of the group's
members and because of their anti–United States speeches and pam-
phlets.

After the Immigration Act of 1990 narrowed the ideological exclusions, the INS instituted new proceedings that sought to deport the Los Angeles Eight under the terrorist activity provisions that were added to the INA. These render deportable "[a]ny alien who has engaged, is engaged, or at any time after entry engages in terrorist activity."[132] Terrorist activity is defined broadly as "to commit, in an individual capacity or as a member of an organization, an act of terrorist activity or an act which the actor knows, or reasonably should know, *affords material support to any individual, organization, or government in conducting a terrorist activity at any time.*"[133] This interpretation allows the INS "to deport individual aliens who have ever supported the lawful and legitimate activities of organizations that are themselves deemed to have engaged in terrorist activity. For example, an immigrant can be deported for 'raising money for a hospital, clinic, daycare center run by groups like the Salvadoran FMLN [a leftist political group]' or the African National Congress, even 'without any allegation that the alien supported any unlawful or terrorist acts of the organization.'"[134]

The government's case against the Los Angeles Eight centered on fund-raising and related political activities that would have been constitutionally protected if engaged in by citizens.[135] The group resisted deportation and filed suit alleging selective enforcement of the immigration laws for engaging in constitutionally protected activity. Uncharacteristically, the court of appeals ruled that noncitizens in deportation proceedings are entitled to First Amendment protections and remanded the case to the district court.[136] The government later moved to dismiss the case based on limitations to judicial review included in the 1996 immigration reform laws. The U.S. Supreme Court ruled that a section of the Illegal Immigration Reform and Immigrant Responsibility Act of 1996 barred the action by the Los Angeles Eight.[137]

Congress passed the provisions in the 1996 laws as part of a larger effort to remove the courts from reviewing immigration matters. Provisions of the Antiterrorism Act and the Immigration Reform Act represent a response to the legal challenges to deportation mounted by the Los Angeles Eight.[138] The legislative history to the Antiterrorism Act states that "alien terrorists . . . are able to exploit many of the substantive and procedural provisions available to deportable aliens in order to delay their removal from the U.S." and that the reforms target "the statutory and administrative protections given to such aliens . . . that enable alien terrorists to delay their removal from the U.S."[139] It further states that "alien terrorists, including representatives and members of terrorist organizations, often are able to enter the U.S. under a legitimate guise, despite the fact that their entry is inimical to the national interests. . . . In several noteworthy cases, the Department of Justice has consumed years of time and hundreds of thousands (if not millions) of dollars seeking to secure the removal of such aliens from the U.S."[140]

To avoid such delays, the Antiterrorism Act created special removal procedures for "alien terrorists."[141] The procedures include a removal court that would expeditiously consider removal of a noncitizen who is physically present in the country if the attorney general certified the person as an "alien terrorist" and removal through ordinary deportation procedures would pose a risk to the national security.[142] Reminiscent of the laws applied in the notorious cases of *Knauff* and *Mezei*, the act provides that the removal court may consider, without full disclosure to the noncitizen, classified information that in the government's judgment might endanger national security if disclosed.[143]

In its efforts to deport alleged terrorists, the U.S. government has not employed the special tribunals, which understandably include procedural safeguards for alleged terrorists. Rather, under old regulations, the government employs secret evidence proceedings that lack procedural protections. Of the twenty-five such secret evidence hearings that were pending in 1999, all involved Arabs and Muslims.[144]

The Los Angeles Eight case shows the relationship between political, religious, and racial difference, which are often inextricably linked in popular thinking about immigration. All work together to create a unique "other" made up of Arab and Muslim "terrorists" who do not deserve the protections of law. With political views outside the U.S. mainstream, Arabs and Muslims are viewed as threats to the political status quo. The religious traditions and beliefs of these "terrorists" differ from those of Christians. Moreover, Arabs and Muslims are often seen as racially different and dangerous.

The government's extreme efforts to deport the Los Angeles Eight do not constitute an isolated incident. In summary proceedings, the INS sought to exclude a lawful permanent resident originally from Jordan, based on confidential information alleging that he was a high-ranking member of the PFLP.[145] There have been similar efforts to return non-citizens to their native countries for foreign policy reasons. For example, for years, the U.S. government vigorously employed both extradition and deportation procedures to ensure that members of the Provisional Irish Republican Army (PIRA) would be returned to the United Kingdom.[146] Although the British government claims that many of the PIRA members were criminals, the political dimension to their alleged crimes cannot be ignored.

The federal government's efforts to deport "terrorists" hit new levels after the September 11, 2001, attacks. In the new removal campaigns implemented in the name of the "war on terrorism," courts and legal proceedings are being sidestepped at every turn.

September 11, 2001

By all indications, September 11, 2001, promises to be a watershed in U.S. history. After the hijacking of three commercial U.S. airliners for use as weapons of destruction against the American people, the United States went to "war" on many fronts. As expected, heightened security and an all-out criminal investigation followed. Unfortunately, blatant racial profiling of Muslims and those viewed as having an "Arab appearance" followed as well. Airlines deplaned Arab and Muslim passengers, including (in the name of keeping the flight crew from feeling "uncomfortable)" a Secret Service agent assigned to protect President George W. Bush.[147] Hate crimes against Arab Americans rose precipitously.[148] In Arizona, a U.S. citizen claiming vengeance for his country killed a Sikh immigrant from India because he mistakenly believed that the man was "Arab."[149]

Not long after the federal government instituted heightened security measures following the September 11 attacks, supporters and critics alike began to view the measures as aggressively "pushing the envelope" in their restriction of civil liberties. The government's response to September 11 exemplifies the close relationship between U.S. immigration law and civil rights. The minimal protection afforded to noncitizens has not only made them vulnerable to civil rights deprivations but also perhaps even encouraged extreme governmental conduct.

The current backlash against Arabs and Muslims in the United States
fits comfortably into a long nativist history, including the Alien and Sedition Act of the 1790s, the Palmer Raids and the Red Scare that followed
World War I, and other concerted efforts by the U.S. government to stifle political dissent. This historical moment, which is reminiscent of the
Japanese internment during World War II,[150] is especially troubling in
that perceived racial, religious, and other difference has amplified animosity toward Arabs and Muslims.[151]

In sum, a complex matrix of "otherness" based on race, national origin, religion, and political ideology contributes to the current usurpation
of the civil rights of Arabs and Muslims in the United States.[152] As the
past has shown, the ripple effects of national security measures against
Arabs and Muslims in the name of the war on terrorism may come to adversely affect the legal rights of *all* noncitizens and eventually even *citizens* as well.

The federal government responded with ferocity to the events of
September 11. Hundreds of Arabs and Muslims, many of them immigrants, were rounded up as "material witnesses" in the ongoing investigation of the terrorist attacks or were detained on relatively minor immigration violations. In 2003, the Justice Department's inspector general
concluded that the rights of many of the detainees had been flagrantly
violated.[153] The dragnet was criticized as a poor law enforcement technique and, more important, a major intrusion on fundamental civil liberties. Congress responded by passing the USA PATRIOT Act, which
allowed the government to detain suspected noncitizen "terrorists" for
up to a week without filing charges and bolstered federal law enforcement surveillance powers over both immigrants and citizens associated
with "terrorism."[154] President Bush issued a controversial military order
that limits the rights of alleged noncitizen terrorists, including those arrested in the United States, by allowing the federal government to try
them in military courts.[155]

Heightened security measures have been the first order of the day
and Arab and Muslim immigrants have been treated as threats to public safety. Within a matter of weeks, the U.S. government arrested and
detained about one thousand Arab and Muslim noncitizens.[156] This
dragnet—which brought in men from many nations, the largest numbers

from Pakistan and Egypt—apparently failed to produce *any* direct links to the terrorist acts of September 11. About one hundred of the detainees were charged with minor crimes, and another five hundred were kept in custody on minor immigration-related charges.[157]

The nature and conditions of the initial wave of mass arrests and detentions warrant consideration. Arab and Muslim detainees were held for weeks without having any charges filed against them and without being told why federal authorities continued to hold them.[158] For example, the U.S. government held Dr. Al-Bdr Al-Hazmi—a radiologist who had lived in San Antonio with his family as a lawful permanent resident for years—for two weeks, in large part because he had the same common Saudi Arabian last name as two of the September 11 hijackers.[159] The U.S. government arrested, interrogated, threatened, and held a Yemeni immigrant without charge for two months.[160] One Muslim student was arrested for visa problems and held in a local Mississippi jail, where police allegedly watched while he was beaten by other prisoners for being a terrorist.[161] A Muslim student was wrongfully indicted for lying to federal agents when he denied ownership of an airplane radio found in a hotel; it was later discovered that the radio belonged to a U.S. citizen.[162] Not surprisingly, given the tenor of the times, there was virtually no public outcry about the mass arrests. Indeed, in testimony before the U.S. Senate Judiciary Committee in December 2001, Attorney General John Ashcroft lambasted critics of the Bush administration's antiterrorism policies as aiding the terrorist cause.[163]

The dragnet did not end quickly. The Justice Department sought to interview about five thousand mostly Arab and Muslim men between the ages of eighteen and thirty-three who had arrived on nonimmigrant visas in the United States since January 1, 2000.[164] There was *no* evidence that any of the thousands had been involved in terrorist activities. Although technically "voluntary," the interviews with law enforcement authorities undoubtedly felt compulsory to many. Arab and Muslim fears of detention and deportation were reinforced by the November 2001 arrest and deportation of Mazen Al-Najjar, who had previously been held on secret evidence and released before September 11 after an immigration judge concluded that the government had failed to provide any evidence that Al-Najjar was engaged in terrorist activity.[165] This time, he was deported to Lebanon; Al-Najjar has been pressured to leave that country, and, as a stateless Palestinian, he remains in search of a country willing to accept him.

Because the questioning of Arabs and Muslims suggests that they are not loyal to the United States, it can be expected to alienate those who are interviewed. A memorandum from the Office of the U.S. Deputy Attorney General, which offered detailed instructions on information to be solicited by state and local police, mentioned that the U.S. government should be informed if an interviewee was suspected of being in violation of U.S. immigration laws.[166] This instruction reveals an effort to remove Arab and Muslim noncitizens from the country based on immigration violations that are wholly unrelated to terrorism.[167]

Considering the fact that, by most accounts, Muslims were the perpetrators of the terrorist acts of September 11, it is reasonable to suppose that a few Muslim noncitizens might have information about terrorist networks. The dragnet directed at all Arabs and Muslims, however, runs afoul of fundamental notions of equality and the individualized suspicion ordinarily required for an individual to be stopped under the Fourth Amendment.[168] It exemplifies the excessive reliance on race in the criminal investigation[169] and shows how, once race (at least with respect to nonwhites) enters the process, it can come to predominate over all else. The national targeting of a minority group for questioning is clearly overinclusive. The more than one million persons of Arab ancestry in the United States,[170] all of whom might understandably feel threatened and under suspicion, cannot miss the glaring message being sent by the federal government.

In a number of important ways, the September 11 dragnet employed by the federal government resembles the Japanese internment during World War II. As before, statistical probabilities, not individualized suspicion, resulted in action directed at a discrete and insular minority classified as an "alien enemy."[171] National identity and loyalty are defined in part by "foreignness."[172] In some ways, the current treatment of Muslims is more extralegal than was the Japanese internment. Unlike in *Korematsu*, there is no executive order at issue in this case. Moreover, nationality, which tends to be objective, is not the criterion being employed by the federal government. Rather, the government is basing its security measures on race and religion, both of which are more subjective and error prone than nationality.

The law affords considerable support for the federal government to practice selective treatment of noncitizens based on nationality. In a similar time of national crisis, when U.S. citizens were held hostage in Iran, a court of appeals in *Narenji v. Civiletti*[173] upheld a regulation that required that only Iranian students on nonimmigrant visas report to the Immigration and Naturalization Service (INS) to provide information about residence and evidence of school enrollment. The court held that the regulation had a "rational basis" and emphasized that "it is not the business of courts to pass judgment on the decisions of the President in the field of foreign policy."[174] Other courts, reviewing other regulations directed at Iranian citizens, refused to disturb the judgment of the executive branch.[175] However, the nationality-based classifications in these cases differ from the race and religious classifications employed by the federal government in response to the events of September 11.

Recent Supreme Court precedent suggests that it will be difficult, although not impossible, to prevail on any claim that the federal government is selectively enforcing the immigration laws by, for example, seeking to remove Arabs and Muslims for immigration violations unrelated to terrorism.[176] In the *American-Arab Anti-discrimination Committee* decision, addressing the Los Angeles Eight case, Justice Antonin Scalia expressed disfavor of such claims: "The Executive should not have to disclose its 'real' reasons for deeming nationals of a particular country a special threat—or indeed for simply wishing to antagonize a particular foreign country by focusing on that country's nationals—and even if it did disclose them a court would be ill equipped to determine their authenticity and utterly unable to assess their adequacy."[177] The Court, however, offered a narrow window for selective enforcement claims, acknowledging "the possibility of a rare case in which the alleged basis of discrimination is so outrageous" that a claim might rest.[178] This exception might be triggered if the U.S. government's action, instead of being closely tied to nationality, was based on race or religion, arguably the case with the policies directed at Arabs and Muslims after September 11.[179]

Judicial deference to government response to the Iranian hostage crisis has been criticized in ways that apply equally to the reaction to the events of September 11:

> *Narenji* is troublesome because an executive classification based on nationality in a foreign affairs crisis poses the danger that *the Executive will overvalue the government interest and undervalue the individual constitutional interest. In a severe crisis, the political and psychological pressures on the Executive are extreme. In this situation, executive measures may be motivated by frustration or desperation rather than an assessment of their actual usefulness, or they may reflect little more than a desire to appear stern and decisive. Conversely, in times of crisis the individual interests of persons selected for special burdens may be grossly undervalued.* Indeed, the virulence of popular feeling against Iranian nationals during the hostage crisis raises the possibility that the Executive, in imposing special burdens on Iranian students, may have been reflecting to some extent a constitutionally *impermissible hostility based on national origin.* The atmosphere during the hostage crisis was marked by a hostility directed at citizens of Iran that resembled to some extent the hostility that is frequently directed toward citizens of an enemy nation during a war.[180]

In the aftermath of September 11, the U.S. government may well have overreacted. Clearly, it placed little value on the liberty interests of Arabs and Muslims. The response may have been motivated in part by "impermissible hostility" based on race and religion. Arabs and Muslims have long suffered discrimination in the United States,[181] with hate crimes against and animosity toward Arabs and Muslims increasing greatly after September 11, 2001. With few legal constraints, the federal government adopted extreme action, perhaps for a primarily symbolic purpose.

Moreover, the dragnet may well prove to be a poor law enforcement technique. Racial profiling in criminal law enforcement has been criticized for alienating minority communities and thus increasing the difficulty of securing their cooperation.[182] At a time when Arabs and Muslims might have assisted greatly in the investigation of terrorism, they were being rounded up, humiliated, and discouraged from cooperation by threats of arrest, detention, and deportation from the United States.

This mass dragnet inevitably suggested to Muslims and all persons of Arab ancestry in the United States, including U.S. citizens, that they are considered less than full members of U.S. society. The actions of the U.S. government, even while its officials denounced discrimination against Arabs and Muslims, have marginalized persons of Arab ancestry and the Muslim religion in U.S. society and reinforced such negative stereotypes as inherent "foreignness" and suspected disloyalty to the U.S. government.

The fact that most of the hijackers involved in the September 11 attacks appear to have entered the country on student nonimmigrant visas provoked an array of federal responses. Understandably, visa monitoring concerns increased exponentially when it was learned that two suspected terrorists were granted visa renewals several months *after their deaths* in the September 11 attacks. With a mass arrest in December 2001, the INS announced its crackdown on noncitizens who violated the terms of their student visas. Arrests focused exclusively on students from nations with alleged terrorist links: Iran, Iraq, Sudan, Pakistan, Libya, Saudi Arabia, Afghanistan, and Yemen.[183] Similarly, in Januray 2002, the Justice Department announced that its Operation Absconder would focus removal efforts on six thousand young men from the Middle East who had ignored deportation orders.[184] In May 2002, Congress passed the Enhanced Border Security and Visa Entry Reform Act to improve the monitoring of noncitizens in the United States on student and other visas.[185] In June 2002, Attorney General Ashcroft announced a new National Security Entry-Exit Registration System, which will impose special registration requirements on noncitizens who (as determined by the federal government) pose national security risks.[186] Specifically, fingerprinting, photographing, and added registration requirements were imposed on nationals of Iran, Iraq, Libya, Sudan, and Syria and on any other noncitizens as determined by the attorney general,[187] who has exclusive discretion to designate noncitizens as "national security risks."

The dragnet in the wake of September 11 came after consideration of even more extreme options, some of which would have previously been virtually unthinkable. Far beyond the conventional law enforcement techniques of arrest, detention, and interrogation, torture to extract information or the threat of deportation to a country that engaged in torture was discussed as a policy option. Torture was contemplated in response to the fact that many of the "material witnesses" arrested and detained did not provide the U.S. government with the information it sought. Given the indiscriminate nature of the arrests, most of the detainees did not in all likelihood have any relevant information to provide. Support for torture came from across the political spectrum, including from some well-known advocates of civil liberties.[188] The consideration of extreme measures reflects the popular perception of Arabs and Muslims as "terrorists," a classification that taps into a long history of nativism and a view of foreigners as presumptively disloyal and dangerous to the security of the United States. The mere fact that torture was discussed in "polite company" in the wake of September 11 demonstrates the monumental shift in public opinion about the place of civil liberties in a democracy. At a minimum, the serious discussion of torture broadened the spectrum of policy options for fighting terrorism.

The federal government's reaction to the events of September 11 promises to have deep and enduring civil rights impacts. As the not-so-distant past demonstrates, immigration reforms and executive action, which have the appearance of responding to the acts of terrorism, in all likelihood will continue to adversely affect the rights of all immigrants and many citizens. Immigration reforms, such as regularization of the immigration status of many undocumented immigrants and the repeal of special secret evidence procedures, which were under serious discussion before September 11, may well go by the wayside, thus maintaining the uncertain legal status, and accompanying vulnerability, of undocumented immigrants who live on the periphery of U.S. society.[189]

Moreover, the focus on "Arab appearance" and Muslim identity has revived debate about the propriety of race profiling in law enforcement, an enduring problem for racial minorities in the United States. Before September 11, the U.S. public and policy makers had come a long way in a relatively short time in critically scrutinizing the use of race and perceived racial appearance in criminal and immigration law enforcement. One day promised to change all that.

The leeway afforded to the federal government in immigration matters allows the political branches to take swift aggressive actions, which appear to offer a "quick fix" to deeply complex problems. Immigration reform is likely to be one of the repercussions of September 11. Recent history, including the response to the 1995 Oklahoma City bombing, offers helpful, if not disconcerting, lessons in this regard. Public opinion polls suggest that voters may support immigration, civil rights, and other restrictions aimed at Arabs, including U.S. citizens.[190] If immigration reform results, the reforms will almost unquestionably adversely affect immigrants other than Arabs and Muslims as well.

Congress has already taken an initial cut at the immigration laws. Section 411 of the USA PATRIOT Act expands the definition of "terrorist activity" that may be used to justify finding an immigrant inadmissible so that it now includes a threat to use, or the use of, "any dangerous device, with intent to endanger, directly or indirectly, the safety of one or more individuals or to cause substantial damage to property." This change is likely to result in an additional removal ground for immigrants convicted of assault and similar crimes not ordinarily considered "terrorist" in nature.[191] The act further provides that a spouse or child of a "terrorist" is inadmissible.[192] A noncitizen may also be deemed inadmissible for "associat[ion] with a terrorist organization," whose broad terms seem to build on the principle of "guilt by association."[193] In addition, the act provides for retroactive application of the changes.[194] Although there was no evidence that the alleged terrorists evaded inspection at the national borders, Congress also included appropriations for increased border enforcement.[195]

In addition, the Aviation and Transportation Security Act,[196] which placed airport security in the hands of the federal government, made U.S. citizenship a qualification for airport security positions. Although arguably constitutional,[197] this stipulation adversely affects many lawful immigrants who formerly held these low-wage jobs.[198] Somewhat ironically, while immigrants can be conscripted into the military[199] and can be employed as commercial airline pilots, they cannot serve in airport security positions.

In short, the federal government responded quickly to the events of September 11, but the law enforcement tactics it employed were based on group probabilities, not individualized suspicion of wrongdoing or knowledge of wrongdoing. With negligible negative public reaction toward, and widespread public support for, the U.S. government's response, a discrete and insular minority of Arabs and Muslims in the United States has suffered the consequences.

The Dynamic at Work and Its Implications

As Gerald Neuman succinctly observed, noncitizens have been "strangers to the Constitution" because immigration laws and their application have generally been immune from constitutional review.[200] A great deal of commentary has focused on the demise, dilution, or continued vitality of the primary culprit for this phenomenon: the plenary power doctrine.[201] Although perhaps not as potent as in days past, the plenary power doctrine survives to this day and resurfaces sporadically in Supreme Court[202] and lower court[203] decisions.

In recent years, the courts have applied the plenary power doctrine in a variety of forms. In *Sale v. Haitian Centers Council, Inc.*,[204] the Supreme Court obliquely relied on a version of the doctrine in upholding the interdiction and repatriation of Haitians who sought refuge from violence in their native land. In *Reno v. Flores*, the Court emphasized the narrow judicial role in reviewing immigration law and policy: "For reasons long recognized as valid, the responsibility for regulating the relationship between the United States and our alien visitors has been committed to the political branches of the Federal Government." . . . "'[O]ver no conceivable subject is the legislative power of Congress more complete.'" . . . Thus, "in the exercise of its broad power over immigration and naturalization, 'Congress regularly makes rules that would be unacceptable if applied to citizens.'"[205] Lower courts have echoed *Flores*'s invocation of the plenary power doctrine.[206] In 2003, invoking the plenary power doctrine, the Supreme Court held that noncitizens convicted of certain crimes could be held without bail pending a deportation hearing.[207]

As recent Supreme Court decisions demonstrate, the legal protections for noncitizens and citizens differ greatly. Unlike lawful permanent residents, even those who have significant ties with the country, citizens enjoy full political and civil rights. The law affords lawful permanent residents only "partial membership" in the community.[208] For the most part, citizens are free to pursue their own beliefs as long as they refrain from committing criminal acts. In contrast, noncitizens may be subjected to exclusion or deportation for holding certain beliefs and for engaging in expressive conduct that citizens would have the constitutional right to pursue.

As the case law reveals, noncitizens have been the easiest targets for the most drastic actions of the political process.[209] Unlike politically unpopular citizens, who enjoy constitutional protection against penalization for their beliefs or political affiliation, noncitizens face deportation and exclusion if they fail the federal government's political litmus tests.

Lacking the constitutional protections afforded to citizens, noncitizens have suffered the government's harsh attempts to stifle political dissent. The cyclical nature of this dynamic reflects recurring, yet changing, national tensions. In the late 1800s and early 1900s, the economic and social tensions that accompanied industrialization and labor organization created significant turmoil. Fueled by World Wars I and II and the fear of anarchy, nationalism prompted harsh changes in the immigration laws. Although the precise nature of the social tensions has varied, public pressure has consistently prompted action by the political branches.[210] The public demanded answers to the pressing social questions of the day, and the government was pressured to take action to relieve public anxiety. By means of unfortunate, and at times shameful, government actions, laws were passed and enforced with a vengeance.

The 1996 immigration reforms and the USA PATRIOT Act, which facilitate the deportation of noncitizens, even some who cannot even colorably be classified as "terrorists," reflect Congress's understanding of the minimal judicial review afforded to immigration legislation.[211] Nor is there any real judicial check on the immigration policy of the executive branch. Indeed, Congress felt free to attempt to eliminate completely the judicial review of certain decisions made in the immigration reform legislation of 1996,[212] only to be rebuffed by a conservative U.S. Supreme Court.[213]

Politics Pure and Simple

History reveals that, generation after generation, the United States has turned to the cure-all of blaming the "foreigner" for domestic troubles. The particular "foreigner" feared has changed with the times, but the cyclical nature of the general phenomenon has remained constant. Members of Congress could not resist voting for the USA PATRIOT Act at a time of patriotic fervor, public anger, and fear in the wake of the attacks of September 11, for example. In an election year, they could not risk voting against the Antiterrorism and Effective Death Penalty Act of 1996, or the Illegal Immigration Reform Act of 1996—regardless of the fact that the laws penalize many noncitizens who have played no part in terrorism.

The immigration reforms of the past decade are simply the latest examples of a long historical dynamic. Ostensibly a reaction to the threat of terrorism, the Antiterrorism Act in fact severely penalizes immigrants who have been convicted of crimes, without taking into consideration how long they have been in the country, their ties with the nation, or any other equities in their favor.[214] President Clinton candidly acknowledged the overinclusiveness of the Antiterrorism Act, stating that it *"makes a number of major, ill-advised changes in our immigration laws having nothing to do with fighting terrorism. These provisions eliminate most remedial relief for long-term legal residents and restrict a key protection for battered spouses and children."*[215] Similarly, the USA PATRIOT Act vastly expands the surveillance powers of the federal government over both citizens and noncitizens and represents an overbroad response to the terrorist acts of September 11. Nevertheless, the president signed the bills into law.

Particularly in times of national crisis, the judiciary's hands-off approach to the review of immigration legislation encourages such extreme responses as the USA PATRIOT Act, the Antiterrorism Act, and the Immigrant Reform Act from the political branches of government in dealing with unpopular noncitizens. The absence of dialogue between Congress and the courts contributes to the extremity of the policy choices. The political vulnerability of noncitizens allows the political branches to act on their worst fears, with minimal risk of political repercussion or meaningful judicial review.

The Implications for Noncitizens and Citizens

The historical dynamic of the immigration laws' treatment of *noncitizens* sketched in this chapter points to the importance of constitutional protections for *citizens*. Without legal protections, politically undesirable citizens might be subjected to treatment similar to that suffered by politically undesirable noncitizens. Consider the McCarthy era. As constitutional protections for citizens reached a low ebb, the government attacked citizen and noncitizen "Reds" with great vigor.

The relationship between the treatment of citizens and noncitizens who share certain characteristics is evident in a number of areas. The slow deterioration of criminal rights and the implementation of increasingly harsh penalties on *citizen* criminals—such as the ever-popular Three Strikes laws and the Prison Litigation Reform Act,[216] which hindered prisoners' pursuit of civil rights claims—have made way for even harsher treatment of criminal noncitizens. The immigration reform acts of 1996, which together greatly expand criminal deportation grounds and significantly narrow relief from deportation for immigrants convicted of a crime, are illustrative.

Immigration law is a vista of the potential political and social horizon for domestic minorities, offering a glimpse at society's view of racial minorities, political undesirables, the poor, criminals, gay men, lesbians, women, and other minority groups. The series of laws designed to exclude the Chinese from entering the United States in the 1800s (see Chapter 2) and late-twentieth-century efforts to halt the flow of Haitians to our shores and to implement extreme measures against undocumented Mexicans reflect society's views of persons of Chinese descent, blacks, poor people, and citizens of Mexican ancestry in this country at various moments in time. Efforts to exclude noncitizens deemed likely to become "public charges" (see Chapter 4) similarly reflect the nation's collective consciousness about the domestic poor. It is no coincidence that 1996 welfare "reform," which reduced benefits to citizens and lawful immigrants, was passed by the same Congress that bulked up the "public charge" grounds for denial of entry to noncitizens. By the same token, the longtime classification of homosexuals as "psychopathic personalities" and therefore excludable mirrors mainstream U.S. views about lesbians and gay men (see Chapter 7).

Conclusion

U.S. immigration history reveals how our nation sees itself. For citizens, suppression of foreign ideas is limited by the First Amendment of the Constitution. The Supreme Court has consistently held, however, that few substantive constitutional protections apply to noncitizens. Because the government's hands are (at least in relative terms) tied against attacks on citizen domestic subversives, its harshest attacks have been directed at noncitizens who hold unpopular political views.

Admittedly, Congress has removed some of the more onerous litmus tests from the immigration laws. As notions of free speech have expanded with the times, constitutional protections for citizens have been broadened and grounds for excluding and deporting noncitizens based on their political views have been narrowed. In spite of these advances, however, persons outside the political mainstream, particularly noncitizens, remain disfavored generally. The USA PATRIOT Act, the Antiterrorism and Effective Death Penalty Act, and the Illegal Immigration Reform and Immigrant Responsibility Act of 1996 are the latest chapters in this history. As long as noncitizens are denied the constitutional protections afforded to citizens, the political process will penalize them. Because, unlike other discrete and insular minorities, noncitizens lack the vigilant oversight of the judiciary, they are the first victims in the war on political dissent.

Unfortunately, the lessons from the exclusion and deportation of political minorities are more far-reaching than might appear at first glance. Historically, the U.S. immigration laws, favoring immigrants who are not poor, who are not members of racial or ethnic minorities, and who are not homosexual, have reflected our efforts toward national homogeneity. When the immigrants of the day have differed from the mainstream in the United States, a majority of the public has responded negatively and sometimes ferociously. This is clearly a frightening reflection of U.S. consciousness about domestic and foreign minorities.

4

Exclusion and Deportation of the Poor

The Statue of Liberty's inscription "Give me your tired, your poor" warmly invites those in need to the proverbial land of opportunity. But the U.S. immigration laws have never welcomed the poor. In fact, from the first comprehensive federal immigration law, the laws have been designed and enforced to keep poor people out of the country. Poor and working-class immigrants have long been excluded from the United States under the public charge provisions, one of the constants of a frequently amended set of immigration laws.

The effort to bar poor people from our shores reflects a concern about what benefits or costs immigrants will confer on the country. In the absence of careful regulation, many fear that "floods" of poor people will immigrate to this country, fleeing the poverty of their native lands. These unskilled immigrants will then work for "inhuman" wages, thus driving down the pay scale for hard-working "Americans." Moreover, there is concern that poor immigrants will abuse U.S. public benefit programs, which—although less comprehensive than programs in other Western nations—grew significantly over the course of the twentieth century. Immigration perennially raises the specter of filled poorhouses and bankrupt government coffers.

Many of the thirteen British colonies, and later the states, barred immigration of "paupers" into their jurisdiction. The earliest federal immigration laws precluded the immigration of "paupers" and persons likely to become public charges. Deportation of noncitizens who become "public charges" after entering the United States has long been a feature of the federal immigration laws. Thus, simply becoming poor can subject a noncitizen to deportation.

As with other exclusion and deportation grounds, a racial dimension lurks behind the public charge grounds. Efforts to exclude and deport Chinese, Japanese, and southern and eastern European immigrants as public charges in the late nineteenth and early twentieth centuries had racial impacts. (Recall from Chapter 2 that southern and eastern Europeans were viewed as racially inferior to northern Europeans.) Today's public charge exclusion also has racial overtones, if not plainly stated racist intentions. In modern times, with many poor and working-class prospective immigrants from nations populated by people of color, public charge grounds moderate changes to the racial demographics of the United States and disparately impact these groups of noncitizens.

In addition to the public charge exclusion and deportation grounds, class biases are endemic to the modern immigration laws. Wealth and job skills clearly facilitate immigration to the United States. The employment-based visa system, for example, favors immigrants whose skills will benefit the nation's economy. An extreme example of an effort to benefit the U.S. economy through immigration is the "million dollar visa," available to those willing to invest one million dollars in the United States. The visa has been challenged as amounting to purchased entry.[1] (In some ways, this is a moot point, since the visa is undersubscribed; less-expensive ways exist for well-heeled individuals to immigrate to the United States.) Some commentators contend that the immigration laws should focus more on the national good. Today's immigrant population, they argue, is skewed in favor of the less skilled and less well educated, in no small part because the foundation for most immigrant visas is family unity.[2]

The historical concerns about immigrant consumption of public benefits have modern-day relevance. The evidence shows that immigrants come to the United States to work and to rejoin family, but as the twenty-first century neared, politicians and commentators expressed concern that public benefits served as a "magnet," attracting both legal and illegal immigrants. California's Proposition 187, which was tinged by anti-Mexican sentiment (see Chapter 2), promised to eliminate the few public benefits for which undocumented immigrants were eligible and to bar undocumented children from the public schools. The voters overwhelmingly endorsed this measure, which was later invalidated by the courts.

The federal government received Proposition 187's message about public dissatisfaction with immigrant receipt of benefits. In 1996, Congress enacted welfare reform that, in President Clinton's words, changed "welfare as we know it."[3] It eliminated immigrant eligibility for many federal benefit programs, including many public benefits funded by taxes paid by immigrants. As the clamor for welfare reform reverberated throughout the United States in the 1990s, the changes had the most painful impacts on immigrant communities. Indeed, most of the welfare reform savings came from the elimination of benefits for immigrants. The reduction of public benefits for immigrants dramatically affected people of color who had immigrated to the United States from developing nations. As a recession hit the U.S. economy after the year 2000, Congress was pressured to restore some of the public benefits that it had eliminated.

As we have noted, the treatment of the poor through the immigration laws mirrors society's view of the poor in the United States. This chapter contrasts the relationship between the marginalization of poor and working-class people under the immigration laws and the treatment of the domestic poor in the United States. As exemplified by California's Proposition 187, an immigration milestone that had national reverberations, poor immigrants already in the United States have been subjected to severe restrictions with respect to a wide array of public benefits. Historically, the poor have been disfavored, with the immigrant poor—who can, without legal constraint, be denied benefits or be excluded or removed from the country—suffering the greatest impact.

The History of Excluding and Deporting the Immigrant Poor

The modern concern about immigrant overconsumption of public benefits has a lengthy historical heritage. From the early days of this nation's history, restrictions were imposed for the purpose of limiting the immigration of potential benefit recipients. Before the federal government began significant restriction of immigration in the latter part of the nineteenth century, state and local governments sought to limit the immigration of "paupers" into their jurisdiction.[4]

The colonies and, after the American Revolution, the states, disfavored the migration of paupers into their territories. As summarized by Gerald Neuman, "The high incidence of 'pauperism' among immigrants raised concern and hostility. Many Americans viewed their country as a place where the honest, industrious, and able-bodied poor could improve their economic standing, free from the overcrowding and rigid social structure that blocked advancement in Europe. Failure to become self-supporting was seen as evidence of personal defects. Many feared that European states were sending their lazy and intemperate subjects, as well as the mentally and physically disabled, to burden America. . . . State and local efforts to avoid these burdens had very limited results. The states were more successful in raising money to defray the expense of supporting impoverished immigrants than in preventing their landing."[5] The U.S. Supreme Court addressed a number of the states' efforts to limit migration of the poor, such as bond requirements imposed on common carriers for passengers.[6] The states' purpose was clear: to avert an influx of poor migrants who threatened to fill the poorhouses and who offered no economic benefit to the community. Such efforts initially met with federal resistance.

Later federal regulation of immigration reflected similar concerns about the quality of new immigrants coming to the United States. In 1882, in one of the first comprehensive federal immigration laws, Congress barred entry to "any person unable to take care of himself or herself without becoming a public charge."[7] A few years later, Congress passed a law typical of the era, which reveals some of the categories of people popularly equated with the poor: "[T]he following classes of aliens shall be excluded from admission into the United States . . . *[a]ll idiots, insane persons, paupers, or persons likely to become a public charge, persons suffering from a loathsome or a dangerous contagious disease, persons who have been convicted of a felony or other infamous crime or misdemeanor involving moral turpitude, polygamists.*"[8]

Early federal immigration laws thus lumped together immigrants likely to become public charges and a litany of other undesirables in their exclusion provisions.[9] Much of this legislation was concerned with immigration of the poor to the United States, including unskilled laborers who drove the wage scale down for natives.[10] Workers in the United States pushed for restrictionist, anti-Chinese immigration legislation based on the claim that Chinese workers would accept wages and working conditions that no American would tolerate. Labor unions and workers relentlessly attacked "coolie labor."[11]

Through a series of amendments early in the early twentieth century, the public charge exclusion was consistently expanded in scope to allow for deportation.[12] Section 20 of the Immigration Act of 1907 provided that immigrants who "become public charges from causes existing prior to landing" may be deported "within three years after the date of entry."[13] Section 19(a) of the Immigration Act of 1917 provided for the deportation of "any alien who within five years after entry becomes a public charge from causes not affirmatively shown to have arisen subsequent to landing."[14] Both amendments allowed some forgiveness for those who suffered setbacks after they came to the United States. Still, the federal government continued to deport noncitizens under the public charge provisions.[15]

The racial dimension to the public charge cases was clear in many of the early cases that arose in the era of Asian exclusion.[16] For example, in 1903, in *The Japanese Immigrant Case*, the Supreme Court upheld the exclusion of a Japanese immigrant on the ground that she was a pauper and likely to become a public charge. Showing little sympathy for the difficulties that faced immigrants, the Court reasoned that she had not been denied the opportunity to be heard: "If the appellant's want of knowledge of the English language put her at some disadvantage in the investigation conducted by that officer, that was her misfortune, and constitutes no reason, under the Acts of Congress, or under any rule of law, for the intervention of the court."[17] Earlier, in the 1892 case of *Nishimura Ekiu v. United States*,[18] the Court upheld the exclusion of another Japanese immigrant woman under the public charge provision. (Gender dimensions to the public charge cases are discussed in Chapter 6.)

At times, race more expressly factored into the courts' public charge analysis. Early in the twentieth century, various California groups pressured the federal government to have immigration inspectors bar Asian Indians from entering the country. "Indians in San Francisco thereafter were subject to 'higher scrutiny.' Inspectors investigated all Indians thoroughly, searching for *any reason* to exclude them."[19] In a case that challenged the legality of this practice, the immigration commissioner found that an Asian Indian citizen was likely to become a public charge because there was little demand for the labor of the immigrant's race of people ("Hindoos") in the United States, a decision that, the court found, was not subject to judicial review.[20]

The state of the national economy has historically played a role in popular sentiments about immigration. Generally speaking, the immigration laws have tightened during a severe economic downturn and a diminished demand for labor and have loosened during times of prosperity and an increased demand for labor. Chinese exclusion crystallized during a severe economic downturn in the 1880s. The public charge provision has experienced this fluctuation, with the greatest concern about jobs and potential benefit abuses materializing in tight economic times. For example, in one case that made its way to the U.S. Supreme Court, an immigration commissioner sought to exclude an immigrant because of an overstocked labor market.[21]

During the Great Depression, the federal immigration laws did not sufficiently relieve the pressures of civil unrest. State and local governments in California sought to reduce the welfare rolls by repatriating persons of Mexican ancestry—citizens as well as immigrants.[22] With so many people out of work, the focus of relief efforts during the New Deal was the domestic poor.[23] The conventional wisdom was that immigrants deserved less from government. This view prevailed even though many immigrants had come to work in this country during the years of World War I and the 1920s when their labor was in high demand. No moral concerns about expelling a once-valuable labor force deterred the removal campaign.

Efforts to deport the poor often had ripple effects on U.S. citizens. In one case decided in the 1930s, a district court refused to deport a Mexican immigrant with three U.S. citizen children to Mexico because it would be unfair to the citizen children.[24] The court of appeals found that the secretary of labor's decision was final and reversed the decision of the district court,[25] thus allowing for the deportation of U.S. citizen children. Today U.S. citizen children continue to be deported with noncitizen parents.[26]

The Modern Public Charge Provisions and Regulation of the Immigrant Poor

Far from being a discarded relic of a bygone era, the public charge exclusion remains an integral part of the immigration laws to this day.[27] The Immigration and Nationality Act of 1952 (INA), whose provisions have been criticized from the outset, carried forward the public charge exclusion and deportation grounds from previous laws.[28] The public charge exclusion ground currently provides that "[a]ny alien who, in the opinion of the consular officer at the time of application for a visa, or in the opinion of the Attorney General at the time of application for admission or adjustment of status, is likely at any time to become a public charge is excludable." The INA requires the consideration of age, health, family status, assets, resources, financial status, education, and skills in determining whether a prospective immigrant is likely to become a public charge.[29]

Consular officials frequently rely on the public charge exclusion to deny immigrant and nonimmigrant visas to persons who seek to come to the United States.[30] In 1998, the public charge exclusion accounted for almost 90 percent of all initial substantive State Department exclusion decisions denying an immigrant visa.[31] In the 1990s, the U.S. government vigorously applied the public charge exclusion to elderly Asian lawful permanent residents—who had previously received benefits to which they were eligible under programs for the elderly and disabled—as they returned to the United States from visits to their native countries.[32]

In addition to barring entry to persons likely to become public charges, the INA provides that "[a]ny alien who, within five years after the date of entry, has become a public charge from causes not affirmatively shown to have arisen since entry is deportable."[33] In contrast to the public charge exclusion provision, this deportation ground is rarely invoked; few lawful permanent residents are deported for receipt of public benefits.[34] Its mere presence in the immigration laws, however, serves to deter immigrants from seeking public assistance for which they are eligible. Moreover, in the recent past, receipt of public assistance has served as the basis for denial of immigrants' requests to regularize their status in the United States.[35]

In the 1990s, the fear was, as it had been historically, that, because most of the world was poor, we must limit immigration or risk being overrun.[36] Commentators also expressed concern that low-skilled immigrant labor would flood the labor market and injure, among others, domestic minorities.[37] More generally, the fear of immigrant abuse of the public benefit systems continues to this day. Although immigrants are eligible for few public benefits, welfare receipt remains an argument for limiting immigration.[38] Consequently, putative immigrants and temporary visitors from developing nations are subjected to particularly close scrutiny. Indeed, a court found that the State Department wrongfully terminated a consular officer stationed at the U.S. consulate in Brazil who refused to engage in racial and economic stereotyping.[39]

Beyond the public charge provisions of the INA, Congress has restricted immigrants' access to major assistance programs. Most important, before the welfare reform of 1996, many federal benefit programs limited noncitizen eligibility to those "permanently residing in the United States under color of law"; the meaning of this provision has been debated, but it did not generally include undocumented persons.[40]

Congressional fear of immigrant benefit consumption has at times prompted Congress to add qualifications to immigration laws with generous provisions. For example, although before 1996 Congress granted certain noncitizens the privilege of immigrating to the United States, it effectively barred lawful permanent residents from receiving most cash assistance by considering their sponsors' income as their own in the determination of benefit eligibility.[41] Similarly, in the Immigration Act of 1990, as Congress exhibited humanitarianism in its creation of a new "temporary protected status" in the United States for persons who were fleeing armed conflict or natural disaster in their homelands, it prohibited them from participating in most federal benefit programs.[42]

Illustrating the popular concern about immigrant benefit receipt, the 1986 amnesty law was chock-full of public assistance provisions. In creating the Immigration Reform and Control Act of 1986 (IRCA) program that allowed "legalization" of undocumented immigrants who had lived and worked in the country for years, Congress generally barred immigrants who were temporary residents from receiving certain public welfare assistance for a period of five years.[43] Congress further provided that "[a]n alien is not ineligible [as a public charge] if the alien demonstrates a history of employment in the United States evidencing self-support *without receipt of public cash assistance.*"[44] These provisions penalized potential legalization applicants who had received cash assistance in the past, restricted access for the immediate future, and sent a signal to the immigrant community that lawful use of available public benefit programs presented a risk.[45] There have been sporadic reports that INS officials view current receipt of public assistance negatively in assessing the moral character of an immigrant who has petitioned for naturalization.[46] The INS has also employed the public charge ground to bar temporary visitors from becoming lawful immigrants.[47]

Generally, although not always,[48] the courts have left congressional restrictions on immigrants' receipt of benefits undisturbed. As we have seen in other areas, the courts have, instead, deferred to the political branches of federal government. For example, in rejecting constitutional challenges to Congress's decision to limit the availability of federal medical insurance to lawful permanent residents, the Supreme Court in *Mathews v. Diaz* emphasized that

> the fact that Congress has provided some welfare benefits for citizens does not require it to provide like benefits for all aliens. Neither the overnight visitor, the unfriendly agent of a hostile foreign power, the resident diplomat, nor the illegal entrant, can advance even a colorable constitutional claim to a share in *the bounty that a conscientious sovereign makes available to its own citizens and some of its guests. The decision to share that bounty with our guests may take into account the character of the relationship between the alien and this country; Congress may decide that as the alien's ties grow stronger, so does the strength of his claim to an equal share of that munificence.*[49]

Similarly, the courts deferred to the executive branch's decision to deny asylum applicants eligibility for welfare benefits, even though, in certain cases, the denial hinders pursuit of an asylum claim.[50]

The courts' deference to Congress on the provision of public assistance to immigrants is consistent with their more general long-standing lack of interference with the immigration judgments of the legislative and executive branches. Although any foreign policy rationale for this deference is less convincing with respect to benefits than with respect to immigration generally,[51] the courts appear to have eagerly adopted this approach. Judiciary deference to the other branches of government may serve to encourage extremes in policy making.[52]

Until recently, the federal courts have been more willing to review state-imposed limitations on immigrants' receipt of benefits. In *Graham v. Richardson*,[53] the Supreme Court invalidated state laws that limited public benefits to lawful immigrants. Similarly, in the litigation that challenged Proposition 187, the court found that because the bulk of the provisions that limited benefits to undocumented immigrants intruded on the federal government's authority to regulate immigration, the measure was unconstitutional.[54] In 1996, however, Congress authorized the states to reduce benefits to lawful immigrants, and the plenary power doctrine immunized the federally sanctioned cutbacks from judicial review.

California's Proposition 187

Long before California's Proposition 187 and the welfare reform of 1996, undocumented immigrants were eligible for few of the major public assistance programs generally available to the poor in the United States.[55] Moreover, serious disincentives exist for undocumented persons with respect to application for and receipt of the few public benefits and social services for which they are eligible, including the fear that seeking benefits may increase their risk of deportation or exclusion.[56]

In keeping with the many restrictions on benefit receipt, it has long been the case that "*except for refugees*, immigrants who arrived in the past decade receive public assistance at significantly *lower* rates than native-born Americans. Moreover, when refugees are excluded, immigrant use of public benefits actually *decreased* during the 1980s. Welfare use among working-age (15 to 64 years), non-refugee immigrants is very low."[57] Still, the popular misconception remains that immigrants as a group overuse public benefits and services.

Consider for a moment the circumstances that surround the admission of refugees—noncitizens who have fled political and other forms of persecution in their native countries. A refugee is a person who has been persecuted or can establish "a well-founded fear of persecution on account of race, religion, nationality, membership in a particular social group, [or] political opinion."[58] Precisely because of the circumstances of their immigration, refugees are eligible for many forms of public benefits upon admission to the United States. The United States admits refugees through the overseas refugee admission program,[59] which requires application to the U.S. government for admission from outside the country. Refugees should be distinguished from "asylees," persons fleeing persecution who successfully apply for asylum after they come to this country. A person who *applies* for asylum in this country is generally ineligible for most public benefits and, in fact, is not entitled to work authorization for up to six months while his or her claim is being adjudicated by the agency.[60] The admission of refugees by the United States has historically been highly politicized, with foreign policy considerations a critical determinant.[61] Refugees have used public benefits;[62] indeed, refugees hand-picked by the U.S. government are the only groups with high rates of public benefit usage.

In any event, although the costs of services for which undocumented persons are eligible—public education and emergency health care—are not *de minimis*, these immigrants are ineligible for the major, and the most costly, public assistance programs. Consequently, the public outcry about immigrants on welfare is, to a large extent, misplaced. Considering that perceptions differ so greatly from the facts, one might wonder whether something other than dollars-and-cents considerations has fueled the backlash against immigrants. Though precise factors are difficult to isolate, concerns may result from economic and other uncertainties and a generalized discomfort over the changes brought by immigration and immigrants and the overall unpopularity of welfare programs in the United States.

Whatever the causes, the public acted on these perceptions. In 1994, the California electorate passed an initiative known popularly as Proposition 187, created to limit public benefit eligibility to lawful immigrants to the United States. It was a precursor to congressional welfare reform in 1996. The strong feelings of support for Proposition 187 illustrate that the measure touched a raw nerve in the California electorate. Not infrequently, supporters endorsed it as they disavowed its express provisions, emphasizing that the measure would "send a message" to the federal government that illegal immigration had to be stopped. The strength and depth of this sentiment outweighed legitimate criticisms such as the fact that the costs of Proposition 187's provisions might well outweigh any benefits.[63]

The fact that Proposition 187 threatened to cost the state of California more than it promised to save suggests that fiscal concerns were not the primary motivator for its passage. California's nonpartisan legislative analyst projected that annual savings of costs of benefits and services provided to undocumented persons might be as great as $1.2 billion for education and $200 million in benefits and services.[64] The potential costs, however, greatly outweighed these savings. The annual costs to public schools and social service agencies for verifying citizenship and immigration status were estimated "in the tens of millions of dollars" with start-up costs potentially in excess of $100 million.[65] More significant still, the legislative analyst estimated that, taking into consideration the interaction of several federal laws and regulations that govern federal programs run by the states, the state stood to lose as much as $15 billion in federal funding each year upon implementation of Proposition 187.[66] With the state in the midst of a long-running budget crisis in 1994,[67] a potential $15 billion loss in federal funds was substantial to say the least. Other potential costs went ignored as well. For example, California had used state funds for prenatal care for undocumented women, while counties provided basic medical services to poor residents who lacked insurance.[68] Proposition 187's bar to the provision of such nonemergency services threatened to increase the costs of emergency services mandated by federal law.[69] The denial of prenatal care, for example, probably would have increased the costs of providing emergency care for infants, who if born in the United States would be U.S. citizens and therefore entitled to the public benefits available to all citizens.[70]

Although the Proposition 187 pamphlet distributed to registered voters included the legislative analyst's cost/benefit analysis,[71] and opponents in the election campaign attempted to highlight the measure's potential fiscal downside,[72] this argument never touched the hearts and minds of the electorate. Fiscal rationality was obviously not a primary determinant of the voters' endorsement of Proposition 187. Rather, the issue had become a general referendum about the propriety of illegal immigration.

Concerned about immigration generally, the electorate approved Proposition 187, with the campaign that culminated in its passage vilifying "illegal aliens." They were blamed for crime and for California's fiscal problems, and, many claimed, they were used as scapegoats for other state problems. Prominent national Republicans Bill Bennett and Jack Kemp expressed opposition to Proposition 187, stating that "'[f]or some, immigrants have become a popular political and social scapegoat.'" [73] The unpopularity, insularity, and lack of political power of the immigrant community unquestionably contributed to the passage of Proposition 187. Fiscal concerns appeared to be secondary. There was a deep racial undercurrent to the campaign (see Chapter 2), a characteristic consistent with the place of race in any discussion of immigration and public benefits.

If Proposition 187's provisions had gone into effect, undocumented women would have been (as with ineligibility for other benefit programs) disparately affected. The loss of prenatal care and battered spouse services, coupled with unreported spousal abuse because of a general reluctance to report crimes to police, highlight the detrimental impact that implemetntaiton of the measue would have had on undocumented women.

U.S.-citizen children of undocumented parents, children born in the United States, also stood to be negatively affected. [74] Families with mixed immigration status (e.g., citizen children with undocumented parents or vice versa) are not uncommon. Nonetheless, Proposition 187 required that schools verify the immigration status of each student's parents, even citizen students. Concern about their own potential deportation threatened to make undocumented parents reluctant to send even citizen children to school. Moreover, given the disproportionate number of female-headed households, undocumented women stood to be disparately affect by the operation of these provisions.

Welfare Reform

In 1996, in the wake of Proposition 187, Congress passed "welfare reform" in the form of the Personal Responsibility and Work Opportunity Reconciliation Act of 1996. [75] President Clinton had promised to "change welfare as we know it," and the new law unquestionably did just that. It extended Proposition 187's denial of benefits, which had targeted undocumented immigrants, to lawful immigrants as well, including those who had contributed a lifetime of taxes to support the programs. This is a point worth emphasizing—the 1996 welfare reform allowed for the denial of most benefits to *lawful* immigrants, *even the many who have resided in the United States and paid taxes for years and years.*

Welfare reform "alters the previous welfare regime for legal immigrants in two fundamental ways. First, the law grants states the authority to deny many federal and state welfare benefits to legal immigrants. . . . Second, [it] bars legal immigrants from participating in certain federal programs to which they previously had access," such as Supplemental Security Income and food stamps.[76] Welfare reform provoked a wealth of criticism from advocates of the poor and advocates of immigrants.[77] Most of the money saved through welfare reform came from eliminating immigrants from eligibility.[78] Women of color, including immigrant women of color, were especially affected.[79]

The debate over welfare reform was based on the perception that immigrants abused the public benefit system. As we have seen, however, only refugees, hand-picked by the executive branch, use benefits at rates higher than the general population. The concern about benefits also fails to factor into the equation the economic benefits of immigrant labor—both legal and undocumented—to the U.S. economy.[80]

In addition to fear of the economic consequences of benefit abuse, there was a racial overtone to the controversy. Alleged abuse by Latina/o and Asian immigrants significantly influenced welfare reform.[81] The debate over welfare in the United States has long been marred by a racial undercurrent. Welfare users are often stereotyped as black women in dysfunctional family situations living in a "culture of poverty." The so-called "welfare queen" is African American.[82] Similarly, the concern about immigrant benefit abuse has a racial element. Latinas/os and Asians are viewed as particularly prone to welfare abuse. Governor Pete Wilson of California, for example, complained about the fertile Mexican mother who immigrated unlawfully to give birth in the United States, thus providing the benefits of citizenship and the social welfare system to her child.

In tandem with welfare reform, in 1996, Congress passed the Immigration Reform and Immigrant Responsibility Act, which tightened the public charge exclusion ground by making "affidavits of support" submitted by sponsors of immigrants legally enforceable, so that state providers of public benefits may sue sponsors to recover the costs of any benefits paid to immigrants. The sponsor must agree "to provide support to maintain the sponsored alien at an annual income that is not less than 125 percent of the Federal poverty line."[83] This requirement greatly hinders the ability of U.S. citizens and lawful immigrants of moderate means to bring family members to the United States on family immigrant visas.

The 1996 amendments that tighten the affidavit of support requirements and welfare reform responded to concerns about immigrants' overuse of the public benefit system. Some expressed concern that elderly Asian immigrants abused the U.S. social security system. Computer science professor Norman Matloff, for example, testified before Congress that elderly Chinese abused the public benefit system, adding that this was a part of their "culture."[84] This pattern fits into the prevailing wisdom in the United States that public benefits are for citizens, not immigrants. Legal challenges have been brought to welfare reform and the denial of benefits to immigrants. To date, however, none has prevailed at challenging the provisions that adversely affect the immigration community.[85]

The wrath of the political process in enacting Proposition 187 and welfare reform struck fear in the immigrant community, prompting an unforseen consequence. Welfare reform and other events of the 1990s encouraged naturalization of lawful immigrants so that they could maintain or restore their eligibility for benefits. Naturalization rates spiked in the late 1990s.

This is consistent with past efforts to resist unjust immigration laws. Through legal and political means, for example, the Chinese community resisted the infamous Chinese exclusion laws and society's discrimination against Chinese people.[86] Now that the racial bars on citizenship have been removed, immigrants can—and have—naturalized in greater numbers. However, naturalization in the 1990s may have been fueled by the hope of ensuring access to public benefits rather than by a desire to participate in community governance, loyalty to the nation, and other such laudable motivations. Time will tell whether the nation's newly naturalized citizens will choose to participate in our nation's political process.

Presumed Public Charges: The Disabled

One category of noncitizens who have been subjected to the public charge exclusion deserves separate treatment: Disabled people have been excluded from the United States based on the fear of their becoming public charges and consuming precious public benefits.[87] Like race, disability is, to a certain extent, a social construction.[88] Immigration laws and agencies that enforce the laws define who is by law disabled and thus barred from entry into the United States.

Early efforts to keep "idiots" and the "feeble-minded" out of the country reflected the fear that immigrants would be unable to secure employment and would therefore end up on the public dole. These efforts also reflected the eugenics scare that inferior people would migrate to the United States and adversely affect the nation's gene pool. Before Congress passed comprehensive immigration regulation in the late nineteenth century, various states acted to restrict immigration of the poor and disabled.[89] Early in the nation's history, "[m]any feared that European states were sending their lazy and intemperate subjects, as well as the mentally and physically disabled, to burden America."[90] In 1849, the Supreme Court reviewed the constitutionality of a Massachusetts law that required compensation by ships disembarking any passenger who was a "lunatic, idiot, maimed, aged, or infirm."[91] Later, the Court ruled that the federal government could lawfully impose fines on transportation companies that brought noncitizens with "loathsome" and "contagious diseases" to the United States.[92]

Over the history of the U.S. immigration laws, mental retardation, insanity, epilepsy, and psychopathic personality have all been grounds for exclusion.[93] An 1882 immigration act barred "any convict, lunatic, idiot, or any person unable to take care of himself or herself without becoming a public charge."[94] Physical disability, such as having a hearing loss or missing an arm, could result in exclusion.[95]

Early in the twentieth century, eugenics dominated national policy discussion, profoundly influencing the immigration laws.[96] The Immigration Act of 1917 provided "[t]hat the following classes of aliens shall be excluded from admission into the United States: All idiots, imbeciles, feeble-minded persons, epileptics, insane persons; persons who have had one or more attacks of insanity at any time previously; persons of constitutional psychopathic inferiority."[97]

The Immigration Act of 1924 and its national origins quota system addressed many of the concerns about the physical and mental disabilities of immigrants by strictly limiting immigration of "inferior" races.[98] Previously, the literacy test enacted by Congress in 1917 was designed to screen for persons of a certain intellect and to limit the immigration of poor and working-class immigrants as inferior "races."[99]

During this era, in addition to the national origins quota system's focus on limiting the immigration of disfavored groups from southern and eastern Europe, great attention was placed on immigrants' health, intelligence, and able-bodiedness. Henry Goddard, famous for his study of intelligence and development of intelligence testing, participated in screening immigrants on Ellis Island for low intelligence and feeble-mindedness.[100] Part of racial inferiority was reflected, so the theory went, in physical and mental inferiority. The INA continued to bar the mentally disabled from the country, whether or not they posed any safety risk to persons in the United States. It provided for the exclusion of "aliens afflicted with psychopathic personality, epilepsy or a mental defect."[101]

Changing societal views toward disability have ultimately, though slowly, influenced the laws. In 1990, Congress passed the Americans with Disabilities Act, which limited discrimination against the disabled.[102] That same year, Congress amended the health exclusion grounds to ensure that only persons who posed a risk of injury to others could be excluded from the country.[103] Similarly, in 1994, Congress allowed immigrants with disabilities an exemption for the naturalization requirements of English fluency and knowledge of U.S. history and civics.[104] Because disabled persons are subjected to inhumane treatment in some nations, it has been argued that such treatment in extreme circumstances should consititute eligibility for asylum in the United States.[105] These liberalizations in the immigration and nationality laws are consistent with society's changing view of disability generally, as reflected in the evolution of domestic laws.[106] As we have seen in other areas, the immigration laws often mirror domestic attitudes.

Nevertheless, disabled immigrants can be barred from entering the country under the public charge exclusion. In addition, although treatment of the disabled has improved, the Supreme Court has, in recent years, restrictively interpreted the protections of Americans with Disabilities Act. In 1996, disabled immigrants lost access to many federal public benefits.[107] "Anti-immigrant activists depicted even old and poor or disabled permanent residents as 'undeserving' since they appeared to immigrate solely to benefit from the U.S. welfare system. . . . The rise in immigrant beneficiaries was attributed to the increasing immigration of older aliens—the parents of recently naturalized citizens—who came to 'retire on U.S. welfare benefits.'"[108]

Conclusion

Flying in the face of the Statue of Liberty's open invitation, the United States has long excluded and deported poor immigrants. During times when the poor have been subjected to reduced benefits, the immigrant poor have been particularly hard hit. During times (such as the Great Depression) when public benefits have been provided to the domestic poor, the immigrant poor have not only been denied benefits but have sometimes even been excluded and deported from the country. The fervor with which the United States has attacked poor noncitizens suggests that, if given similar latitude, the government would rid the country of its domestic poor as well.

5

Exclusion and Deportation of Criminals

The U.S. immigration laws have a long history of exclusion and deportation of criminals. As with other groups targeted by the immigration laws, the criminal provisions have ebbed and flowed with the immigration winds of the day. The general direction with respect to "criminal aliens," however, has been toward increasingly harsh treatment.

Of course, in some respects, the unpopularity of "criminal aliens" is understandable, perhaps even deserved in some instances. If nation-states exercise the power to restrict immigration into their territories, noncitizens convicted of crimes would seem the most likely to pose a risk to the community and therefore the least worthy of admission. Similarly, if deportation of noncitizens from a country is deemed permissible, noncitizens who commit crimes within that jurisdiction seem to be natural candidates for removal. For long-term residents of the United States who have close family and social ties in the community, however, deportation is a harsh remedy. As the Supreme Court has acknowledged, "[D]eportation may result in the loss 'of all that makes life worth living.'"[1] Consequently, the life and liberty decision of deportation should take into consideration, on a case-by-case basis, family and community ties, the length of time in the country, the severity of the crime, and other such equities.

To the contrary, at the end of the twentieth century, the U.S. immigration laws increasingly resorted to hard-line rules that make the intricacies of an individual immigration case legally irrelevant to the decision to deport noncitizens convicted of crimes. Moreover, Congress has sought to prevent the courts from reviewing the immigration bureaucracy's decisions on these important matters.

As we have seen with respect to other exclusion and deportation grounds, the belief that both the poor and certain racial groups—with the particular "race" that is targeted changing according to the latest wave of undesirable immigrants—have a propensity for criminal conduct has greatly influenced the evolution of the law. Race-based theories of criminal propensity have generally fallen into disfavor in modern times. The undercurrent of race and class, however, persists in the controversy over the legal treatment of "criminal aliens." This stems in part from the fact that the vast majority of prospective immigrants are people of color from developing nations. The criminal deportation grounds, as well as the creation of immigration crimes (such as the relatively new crime of illegal reentry into the country), disparately impact immigrants from Mexico and Central America. Just as "terrorist" has become popular shorthand for persons of Arab and Muslim ancestry, "criminal aliens" is often code for Mexican, Central American, and, to a certain extent, Asian immigrants.

The general attitude of the public and policy makers toward crime and criminals in the United States influences the treatment of "criminal aliens" under the immigration laws. From prostitution early in the twentieth century to drug offenses today, the U.S. immigration laws have reflected the law enforcement priorities of the day. This dynamic was especially evident in the later part of the twentieth century. The immigration laws became increasingly punitive toward "criminal aliens" at the same time that the death penalty made a national revival and "tough on crime" measures and the "war on drugs" soared in popularity among politicians across the political spectrum. In 1996, Congress passed immigration reforms that not only expanded in unprecedented ways the scope of crimes that can lead to removal of long-term immigrants from the country but also sought to limit, if not completely foreclose, judicial review of the removal orders of immigrants convicted of certain crimes.

As immigrants became more unpopular in the 1990s, "criminal aliens" were demonized as a serious threat to the nation.

In the legislatures and before the courts, immigrants' rights advocates have long experienced great difficulty protecting the rights of "criminal aliens." Often the most punished and perhaps the most politically vulnerable immigrant group, they have been the least able to resist punitive laws in the legislative process. "Criminal aliens" have often suffered misfortunes similar to those of domestic criminals, especially in a time of zealous criminal law enforcement, with few defenders and fewer legal protections. Unlike domestic criminals, they are vulnerable to removal from the country and, at least until September 11, 2001, had increasingly become the focal point of the federal government's immigration enforcement efforts. Consequently, as the laws became more punitive and the "criminal alien" evolved into the number one immigration enforcement priority, noncitizens, including lawful permanent residents who had lived in the United States for many years, were deported in record numbers on criminal grounds. Indeed, the removal of noncitizens on criminal grounds increased to more than 55,000 in fiscal year 1998; Mexico (seconded by El Salvador) had more of its citizens deported from the United States (42,789) than any other nation.[2]

The Anticriminal History of the U.S. Immigration Laws

From colonial times to the present, noncitizens convicted of crimes have shared the unpopularity of criminals generally in the United States. At one time, the migration of convict labor to the colonies was relatively common. By the time of the American Revolution, however, Great Britain had acted to eliminate convicts' migration to America, in part because they were being recruited as soldiers to fight the King.[3] Nonetheless, in 1751, Benjamin Franklin complained that England was sending its criminals and other undesirables to Pennsylvania and suggested in jest that rattlesnakes be sent back in return.[4]

Before Congress passed the first comprehensive federal immigration laws, several states sought to restrict the migration of convicts into their respective jurisdictions from other states and from abroad.[5] The states, however, generally did not provide for the deportation of persons convicted of crimes *after* entry.[6] Criminals instead were subjected to exclusion only upon seeking to enter the country. The first federal immigration laws marked noncitizens convicted of crimes for exclusion from the country. Later acts of Congress allowed for the deportation of immigrants convicted of crimes in this country. The modern immigration laws include vastly expanded provisions for the exclusion and removal of "criminal aliens."

In the Act of March 3, 1875, Congress excluded convicts and prostitutes from immigrating to the United States.[7] In 1882, Congress enacted immigration legislation that precluded convicts and Chinese immigrants (who were thought to be prone to criminality) from entering the country.[8] Later laws barred prostitutes from immigrating to the United States and subjected them to deportation.[9] Chapter 6 looks at the disparate impact on immigrant women, as well as the racially disparate impact on Chinese women, which resulted from the prostitution provisions of the immigration laws. Consistent with prevailing domestic concerns about prostitution in the United States at the time, prostitution was the top crime priority of the first series of federal immigration laws.

The 1917 Immigration Act officially reigned in the era of deportation of immigrants convicted of crimes on U.S. soil. Section 19 provided in relevant part that, in addition to those who have any connection whatsoever with prostitution, the following immigrants could be deported from the country: "any alien who is hereafter sentenced to imprisonment for a term of one year or more because of conviction in this country of a crime involving moral turpitude, committed within five years after the entry of the alien to the United States, or who is hereafter sentenced more than once to such a term of imprisonment because of conviction in this country of any crime involving moral turpitude, committed at any time after entry; . . . any alien who was convicted, or who admits the commission, prior to entry, of a felony or other crime of misdemeanor involving moral turpitude."[10]

The rationale for the deportation of immigrants for crimes committed after immigrating to the United States is relatively straightforward: If immigrants violate the nation's rules, they should be subject to deportation. Their presence in this country was thus a sort of revocable privilege, conditional upon their refraining from running afoul of the law. The courts upheld deportation orders based on crimes committed after immigration to the United States.[11] The 1917 act has had a lasting impact on the immigration laws, with "crimes involving moral turpitude" continuing to give rise to deportation. This elastic language has been interpreted to include crimes that involve fraud, aggravated (but not simple) forms of assault, murder, and manslaughter.[12]

As we saw in Chapter 2, 1924 was a watershed year in U.S. immigration history. The national origins quota system in the Immigration Act of 1924 hoped, in significant part, to curtail the immigration of criminals to the United States.[13] As part of forty-one volumes of restrictionist analysis, the Dillingham Commission, which thoroughly studied immigration and made recommendations for congressional action, concluded that certain national origin groups were more prone to crime than was the Anglo Saxon core of the nation.[14] Italian and Jewish immigrants were singled out as having a particular propensity for criminality. To reduce the influx of criminal immigrants, the 1924 law limited the immigration of certain racial groups deemed prone to crime. Congress considered the national origins quota system, with its racial and other foundations, to be the solution to the "criminal alien" problem.

As the events that culminated in the 1924 immigration act demonstrate, crime and immigration, with a racial undercurrent, have long been a theme in restrictionist analysis. Criminality offered a rationale for Chinese exclusion and for quotas on southern and eastern European immigrants. In a 1929 book provocatively titled *Crime, Degeneracy and Immigration: Their Interrelations and Interactions*, one lawyer proclaimed:

> Crime and degeneracy . . . became unduly manifest and continued to increase both in volume and flagrancy contemporaneously with and in direct ratio to the immigration of low grade southern and eastern Europeans. . . .
>
> By the intermixture, both racially and socially, of the disharmonic and intellectually inferior element referred to with the old American stock, the racial bloodstream of the latter has been corrupted and degeneracy in varying degrees has supervened. [15]

The Immigration Act of 1924 thus addressed a myriad of concerns all rolled into one. Immigrants of different races threatened the well-being of the United States: In addition to threatening the nation's racial composition, political stability, and economy, immigrants from southern and eastern Europe raised the specter of crime and lawlessness. Congress enacted racial, political, class, and criminal exclusions in the immigration laws to combat the criminal threat.

The goal of facilitating the deportation of criminal noncitizens animated later U.S. immigration laws. In the early 1950s, after much-publicized hearings, the Special Committee to Investigate Organized Crime in Interstate Commerce, chaired by Senator Estes Kefauver, issued a series of reports analyzing foreign organized crime in the United States.[16] The reports shaped the tough provisions of the Immigration and Nationality Act of 1952 (INA), many of which are discussed in previous chapters. Then in 1961, in response to the notorious delay and manipulation of the deportation process by reputed racketeer Carlos Marcello,[17] Congress significantly narrowed the judicial review provisions of the INA.[18] The truth of the matter, however, was that "the magnitude of the delay in Marcello's case was hardly typical, and at any rate the bulk of that delay resulted from other countries' refusals to receive him rather than from defects in the United States review system."[19]

Modern Criminal Immigration Law Provisions

The criminal exclusion and deportation grounds of the modern immigration laws grew increasingly complex and unyielding toward the end of the twentieth century. The INA, as amended, provides a detailed list of criminal exclusion and deportation grounds.[20] Although waivers and other forms of relief from exclusion and deportation generally exist, they have been drastically narrowed for convicted criminals in recent years.

A brief summary of the evolution of the criminal immigration provisions provides a fuller understanding of their generation. The emerging "war on drugs" greatly affected the development of the criminal immigration provisions. In 1988, Congress passed the Anti–Drug Abuse Act, which added the "aggravated felony" section of the INA, with a focus on facilitating the deportation of immigrants convicted of drug trafficking crimes.[21] In the 1996 immigration reform measures, Congress added significantly to the number of crimes that constituted an aggravated felony. The bulk of the expansion occurred in the 1990s, when "criminal aliens"—and criminals generally—were especially disfavored in the political arena.[22]

Reforms in 1996 contributed greatly to the immigration hazards for "criminal aliens." Throughout the early 1990s, the government had been called upon to tighten the borders to exclude criminal immigrants and to deport "criminal aliens" from the country. Efforts at punishing "criminal aliens" found popular support.[23] Proposition 187, for example, which passed by a landslide among California voters, included provisions designed to facilitate the removal of "criminal aliens" from the United States. Offering a rationale for the initiative, sponsor Barbara Coe growled, "Violent crime is rampant. Illegal-alien gangs roam our streets, dealing drugs and searching for innocent victims to rob, rape and, in many cases, murder those who dare violate their 'turf.' . . . [N]early 90 percent of all illicit drugs are brought here by illegals."[24]

Restrictionist groups similarly clamored for the removal of "criminal aliens," contending that they were the cause of the crime problem in the United States.[25] These pleas echo those that surrounded the passage of the 1924 act, yet the evidence was to the contrary. As one influential observer summarized it, "[L]egal immigrants do not appear to commit any more crime than demographically similar Americans; they may even commit less, and that crime may be less serious."[26]

Proposition 187 and the "Criminal Alien"

Heightened concern about public benefits has resulted in immigrant public benefit recipients and "criminal aliens" being lumped together as one and the same. Like immigrant welfare users, "criminal aliens" have been the subject of particular scorn in the political process. The parallel between "criminal aliens" and "illegal aliens" is particularly strong because undocumented immigrants are often characterized as lawbreakers.[27] Public alarm about "criminal aliens" grew in the early 1990s when immigrants were implicated in two well-publicized criminal episodes, the 1993 attempt to destroy the World Trade Center and a shooting outside the Central Intelligence Agency headquarters.[28]

Finding it no easy task to protect ordinary noncitizens, immigrants' rights activists faced intractable difficulties in attempting to shield "criminal aliens" from the avalanche of political efforts to penalize them. The Immigration Act of 1990[29] and the 1994 Crime Bill,[30] both of which included provisions that limited the relief available to "criminal aliens" and attempted to expedite their deportation, aptly illustrate the harsh treatment accorded them in the political process. During this time, the president, the attorney general, and the INS expressed the desire to step up the apprehension and deportation of "criminal aliens."[31]

A common public concern with respect to immigrants who receive benefits and immigrants convicted of a crime is cost. Politicians and the press frequently reported that noncitizens constituted a significant portion of the prison population.[32] Some states regularly complained about the substantial costs of incarcerating noncitizens.[33] A few high-immigration states, such as California, New York, Texas, Florida, New Jersey, Illinois, and Arizona, have large foreign-born state prison populations. California and Florida in particular registered strong disapproval over the lack of federal support for the immigrant population in prison. State fiscal concerns contributed to the national attention focused on immigrants convicted of crimes.

In light of the similarity in fiscal impact, it is not surprising that efforts to crack down on "criminal aliens" mirror efforts to abolish immigrant benefit receipt. In the same breath, restrictionists often characterize "illegal aliens" as both welfare abusers and criminals. As the Mexican ambassador to the United States observed at the height of the 1994 public debate on immigration and Proposition 187, "There is an equation now in California that goes: Illegal immigrants equal to Mexicans, equal to criminals, equal to someone who wants social services."[34] This synopsis reveals a racial element to the concern about immigrant crime and benefits receipt.

There are, of course, other reasons for the focus on "criminal aliens" in the United States. Regardless of the costs of incarceration, public antipathy toward criminals generally applies with even greater force to criminal immigrants. Like immigrants deemed to be likely public charges, "criminal aliens" have long been viewed as unworthy of joining, or continuing to be a part of, the U.S. community. The image of the predatory "criminal alien" is a powerful one.[35] Consequently, as with laws that limit the entry of potential public charges, there is a long a history of laws that exclude criminals from immigrating to the United States, and these restrictions have been stiffened substantially in the past decade.

"Criminal aliens" and immigrant benefit recipients are marginalized on multiple grounds. The political dialogue emphasizes how these "outsiders" (read: minorities) harm the "community" (read: citizens). Both categories of noncitizens, not surprisingly, share similarly vulnerable positions in the political process.

After California's voters passed Proposition 187, state and federal governments pledged to facilitate the deportation of "criminal aliens." For his part, President Clinton, who had taken an aggressive pro–law enforcement stance at odds with the traditional stance taken by Democrats, promised that his administration would expedite the removal of "criminal aliens."[36] He signed into law two major pieces of legislation that had devastating consequences for the immigrant community: the Antiterrorism and Effective Death Penalty Act (AEDPA) and the Illegal Immigration Reform and Immigrant Responsibility Act (IIRIRA).[37] As two commentators observed, "In truth, IIRIRA may be the harshest, most procrustean immigration control measure in [the twentieth] century."[38] Both laws included significant measures directed at "criminal aliens" and criminalized violations of the immigration laws.[39]

As in the past, the modern concern about "criminal aliens" contains a racial dimension. Peter Brimelow expressed it most bluntly: "Inevitably, . . . certain ethnic cultures are more crime prone than others."[40] Crime today is often associated with Mexican, Chinese, Russian, and other groups of immigrants. Europe has seen similar debates over race and immigrant criminality in recent times.[41] As with law enforcement generally, it is difficult to separate legitimate concerns from unlawful racial concerns.[42]

Currently, a wide variety of crimes can result in an immigrant's deportation from the United States. Crimes of moral turpitude, crimes that involve controlled substances (including mere drug abuser or addict status), certain firearms offenses, domestic violence, among others, subject an immigrant to possible deportation.[43] As greatly expanded by Congress (the provision is more than twenty paragraphs long in the statute books), the term "aggravated felony" runs the gamut from serious crimes, such as murder, to certain misdemeanor convictions.[44] In 1996,

Congress limited judicial review of the removal orders for aggravated felons and eliminated their eligibility for most forms of relief from deportation.[45]

With considerable pressure from Congress, the INS enforced the "criminal alien" provisions of the 1996 reform measures with great vigor. As one commentator acknowledged, "[T]he INS has adopted a take-no-prisoners approach with regard to the deportation of criminal aliens. . . . *Overall, the INS's approach to enforcement suggests an agency mentality in which the principal goal is to demonstrate increased numbers of criminal alien deportations. Indeed, the INS Commissioner's reports to Congress express pride over the high numbers of criminal aliens who have been deported. In this atmosphere, there is little attention paid to the human casualties of the new deportation regime.*"[46]

The enforcement of the criminal provisions of the U.S. immigration laws, as amended in 1996, has had a harsh effect on long-term lawful permanent residents, who face possible deportation and thus separation from family, friends, and community. For example, under the immigration reforms, certain convictions for driving while intoxicated are now classified as aggravated felonies.[47] The INS's mass arrests of convicted drunk drivers in Texas seem unlikely to decrease the national crime rate significantly.[48] As "aggravated felonies," many relatively minor narcotics violations, including possession of a controlled substance,[49] and firearms convictions currently subject a noncitizen to removal.[50] Indeed, even shoplifting can lead to deportation.[51] As a result, the harsh consequences of the 1996 immigration legislation's anti–"criminal alien" provisions have been the subject of sustained criticism.[52]

Consider the case of Jesus Collado, who immigrated to the United States from the Dominican Republic in 1972. As a teen, he had a sexual relationship with his girlfriend, a minor, and her mother turned him in to the authorities. Collado pleaded guilty to a crime of sexual abuse in the second degree, which was not a deportable offense at the time and for which he did not serve time in jail. Collado went on living a productive life, married and had children, held a responsible job, and committed no further crimes. In 1997, more than twenty years later, he returned from a trip to the Dominican Republic only to be detained by the INS and placed in removal proceedings under the mandatory detention provisions added by the 1996 immigration reform laws.[53] The INS's efforts to deport Collado were thwarted by a series of Anthony Lewis editorials in the *New York Times*. In the wake of the public attention brought to the case, the INS relented, releasing Collado from custody and allowing him to remain in the United States.[54]

The conclusion to this extraordinary case is, of course, an exception. The INS continues to deport "criminal aliens" in record numbers. In fiscal year 1998, the INS removed more than fifty-five thousand criminals from the country, more than 77 percent from Mexico. El Salvador, Guatemala, Honduras, and the Dominican Republic followed Mexico in numbers of immigrants deported from the United States.[55] Disparities in the rates of deportation may be caused by race- and class-biased U.S. law enforcement, a long-standing problem for African Americans, Latinas/os, and other minority groups.

The harsh provisions of the 1996 legislation are exemplified by congressional efforts to limit a much-cherished safeguard against bureaucratic tyranny: judicial review. Both AEDPA and IIRIRA greatly restricted judicial review of removal decisions.[56] Congress's limitation on judicial review came despite the fact that empirical studies reveal a high error rate for agencies involved in removal decisions; consequently, federal courts reverse a relatively high percentage of these decisions.[57] In 2001, the Supreme Court ruled that habeas corpus review remained intact despite provisions in the immigration laws that restrict judicial review for immigrants convicted of "aggravated felonies."[58] The executive branch had aggressively opposed judicial review of decisions to deport immigrants for drug convictions, for which they were eligible for relief under pre-1996 law.

In addition to deportation, many "criminal aliens" are now subject to mandatory detention, since the 1996 immigration reforms greatly increased the circumstances under which it is implemented. The federal government has increasingly detained "criminal aliens."[59] Resolving a split among the lower courts, the Supreme Court upheld the mandatory detention of "aggravated felons" pending their deportation hearings.[60]

One particular detention problem has involved noncitizens who were convicted of crimes, who then served their full sentences, but whose countries of origin (e.g., Cuba and several Southeast Asian nations) have not allowed the return of their citizens. The U.S. government responded by subjecting those noncitizens to indefinite detention and vigorously defended this practice in the courts. For example, in the decision of the court of appeals in *Barrera-Echavarria v. Rison*,[61] the INS detained a Cuban national who came to the United States in 1980 on the Mariel boatlift and was ordered to be returned to Cuba after convictions in the United States for burglary and armed robbery. Because the Cuban government refused to accept Barrera-Echavarria, he faced the prospect of indefinite detention, which, the court found, was not in violation of the law. Indefinite detention of a U.S. citizen, in contrast, would be patently unconstitutional.

By 2001, the INS held nearly thirty-five hundred immigrants like Barrera-Echavarria from nations including Vietnam, Cuba, Laos, and Cambodia in indefinite detention.[62] Not until 2001 did the Supreme Court intervene, concluding that Congress had, in fact, never authorized indefinite detention.[63] The INS had defended the policy—and detained noncitizens under it—for close to two decades.

Another aspect of the laws adversely affects noncitizens by criminalizing violations of the immigration laws. As amended in 1988, the federal criminal laws were changed to criminalize reentry by noncitizens after a previous deportation order.[64] This change has had a significant impact on the criminal justice system in the U.S.-Mexican border region, where large numbers of Mexican citizens have been prosecuted for illegal entry; claims of selective prosecution have been made.[65] Because federal court dockets, particularly in courts in the greater border region, have become clogged with "illegal reentry" cases, the addition of federal judges to the courts in this region has been necessary. The creation of this new crime fits the nation's history of punishing immigrants under the criminal laws for unlawful presence in the country. In the 1896 case of *Wong Wing v. United States*,[66] for example, the Supreme Court invalidated a criminal conviction based on a law that subjected Chinese immigrants who were in this country unlawfully to imprisonment at "hard labor." Although the current law does not name Mexicans, the impact of enforcement of the "crime" falls disproportionately on Mexican immigrants.

Near the turn of the century, various reform measures aimed at soft-ening the 1996 legislation's effect on "criminal aliens" were proposed. Because the anti-immigrant climate had subsided somewhat by the year 2000, immigrants' rights advocates were optimistic that the "Fix '96" reform might have a chance of prevailing in Congress. The events of September 11, 2001, however, dramatically changed the politics that surround immigration and effectively ended any short-term hopes of re-laxing the harsh provisions of the 1996 laws.

State and federal governments have begun to work more closely to ensure the deportation of "criminal aliens." After September 11, the U.S. Department of Justice solicited the assistance of local police de-partments in immigration enforcement in the "war on terrorism." This action threatened efforts by state and local police to encourage immi-grants to report crimes and cooperate with law enforcement officials without fear of deportation. Indeed, the Los Angeles Police Depart-ment, among others, prohibited officers from inquiring about the im-migration status of suspects, witnesses, and other individuals involved in police investigations.[67] The enlistment of local law enforcement agen-cies in immigration enforcement may prove to be a lasting impact of the post–September 11 "war on terrorism."

Race, Crime, and Removal

Often overlooked in the study of "criminal aliens" is the impact of racially skewed U.S. law enforcement on the deportation of immigrants. The vast majority of today's immigrants are people of color from de-veloping nations. "Since 1965, upwards of seventy-five percent of im-migrants have been from Asia, Africa, or Central or South America."[68] Many immigrate and join family and friends in the United States, often moving to ethnic enclaves with the assistance of family and social net-works. Many are poor and working-class people, one of the complaints of immigration restrictionists who clamor to improve the skill levels of the immigrant stream.[69]

Domestic communities of color, particularly African Americans and Latinas/os, have long complained of racially discriminatory law enforcement. African Americans have been targeted under increasingly onerous drug laws, such as the punitive measures implemented with respect to the sale and use of crack cocaine, and have been subjected to the death penalty in disproportionate numbers.[70] Such glaring racial disparities have provoked the controversial call for jury nullification to fight racial discrimination in the criminal justice system.[71]

Latinas/os, who are overrepresented in the nation's prisons, have also complained of discriminatory law enforcement.[72] Latina/o youth have been demonized as criminals,[73] even though the available empirical data does not support this claim.[74] The well-documented history of discriminatory law enforcement treatment of persons of Mexican descent in the Southwest is common knowledge to Chicanas/os.[75] Persons of Puerto Rican ancestry have similar experiences in the Northeast. Southeast Asians and other Asian immigrants have also suffered from discriminatory law enforcement. Racial profiling in law enforcement has been recognized as a national problem for African Americans, Latinas/os, and Asian Americans.[76] Racial profiling in immigration enforcement, which can have criminal consequences, also plagues minority groups.[77]

The national "war on drugs" has had a racially disproportionate impact on minority communities.[78] The domestic war on drugs and immigration enforcement both focus on race. At the same time, heightened drug enforcement and increasingly onerous criminal deportation grounds have had devastating impacts on the immigrant community. Racially disparate criminal law enforcement almost certainly affects rates of removal, much of which results from narcotics crimes.

Similarly, the criminalization of certain immigration grounds has had disparate impacts on immigrants of color. As we have seen, the criminalization of illegal reentry has had a significant effect on citizens of Mexico. Document fraud can also subject an immigrant to deportation. With more than one-half of undocumented immigrants from Mexico, these removal grounds cannot help but result in disproportionate consequences.

Little attention has been paid to the link between race-based law enforcement in the United States and the racially disparate impacts of the criminal deportation provisions of the immigration laws. This is true despite the fact that some of the most egregious recent incidents of police brutality (such as the torture of Haitian immigrant Abner Louima by New York City police officers) have involved immigrants of color.[79] It seems that the likelihood that immigrant communities will be subjected to law enforcement measures while in the United States increases the likelihood that they will be subjected to removal from the country. In sum, discriminatory criminal law enforcement may well contribute to disparate removal and other immigration consequences.

Conclusion

The U.S. government's long history of discriminating against "criminal aliens" in the immigration laws has often stemmed from dubious theories of the criminal propensity of certain racial groups. In the past, the national debate expressly used race to explain immigrant criminality. Today's more subtle racial bias requires careful scrutiny.

The public and politicians condemn "criminal aliens," who have few supporters in the political process. Meanwhile, race-based law enforcement leads to racially disparate deportation rates. As the United States has progressively moved toward a "tough on crime" stance, it has implemented even tougher measures on immigrants convicted of crimes. Once again, the relationship between the treatment of domestic and immigrant minorities becomes clear. When the law cracks down on citizen criminals, even harsher treatment is meted out to "criminal aliens," who lack precious legal protections and can be banished from the country.

Perhaps "criminal aliens" do not deserve our sympathy. If we have borders, why not keep criminals out for the common good? If we deport immigrants, should criminals not be near the top of the deportation list? The political process has responded in the affirmative to both questions. At the same time, as Congress has embraced harsh, hard-line rules, such as mandatory detention and removal without judicial review, individual equities in immigrant cases have often fallen by the wayside. The virtual nonexistence of legal restraints on Congress's treatment of immigrants has resulted in particularly severe treatment of "criminal aliens."

6

The Marginalization of Women Under the Immigration and Nationality Laws

The treatment of women throughout the history of the U.S. immigration laws parallels the place of women in the United States. For much of U.S. history, the law, including the immigration and nationality laws, treated women as extensions of their spouses, with no independent legal identity. The notion of coverture—that women are subordinate to and under the control of men—substantially shaped the laws and had severely negative consequences for women. As the status of women evolved in the United States, their treatment under the immigration laws evolved as well.

The treatment of immigrant women differed in important ways from the treatment of other groups studied herein. Unlike racial minorities, political dissidents, the poor, and others, for example, women in certain circumstances have shared the immigration privileges of the men they married. At the same time, however, women's marriages to immigrant men, particularly immigrant men of color, have disadvantaged them legally.

The immigration law's exclusion and deportation grounds, although seemingly gender neutral, often disparately impact women. In the early days of federal immigration regulation, the focus on exclusion and deportation of immigrant prostitutes adversely affected noncitizen women. With the limited number of job opportunities in the U.S. labor market, the same can be said of the public charge exclusion and deportation grounds discussed in Chapter 4. Single immigrant women have often been presumed to be likely to become public charges. Under these circumstances, women's ability to immigrate has often turned almost exclusively on their spouses' income, skills, and ability to immigrate.

The nationality laws took the treatment of women as the property of their husbands to the extreme. Perhaps the most shocking policy (at least to modern sensibilities), which was in place for a time early in the twentieth century, was the practice of stripping a woman of her U.S. citizenship upon her marriage to an immigrant, since the woman's citizenship was considered identical to that of her spouse. This was particularly problematic for women who married immigrants who were ineligible to naturalize (such as virtually all racial minorities), since these women lost not only their citizenship but also their eligibility to regain it.

In the modern era, women have constituted an increasing segment of the overall immigrant population of the United States. As discrimination against women in U.S. society has declined, the immigration laws have followed suit. As social awareness of domestic violence grew, Congress amended the immigration laws—although perhaps not quickly or decisively enough—in an attempt to reduce the likelihood that women would be subjected to domestic abuse. Again the immigration laws' treatment of a historically subordinated group mirrored changes in society's views of that group domestically.

Coverture pervaded the history of the immigration laws, just as it did in the domestic laws.[1] This chapter examines the influence of coverture on the treatment of women under the immigration laws. During the twentieth century, the immigration laws improved with the dramatic change in the status of women in the United States. But the disadvantaging of immigrant women—particularly immigrant women of color—and their exploitation in the low-wage domestic labor market highlight the need for further reforms.

Excluding and Deporting Prostitutes

Prostitutes were one of the first groups of criminals targeted by the federal immigration laws. In the late 1800s, many Chinese women were allegedly brought to the United States to engage in the sex trade. The state of California required shipowners to provide a bond for "lewd and debauched women" (although the U.S. Supreme Court refused to enforce this requirement in the case of a Chinese woman named Chy Lung).[2]

In 1885, Congress passed the first of a series of laws that addressed immigrant prostitution. The Alien Prostitution Importation Act of 1875 outlawed the importation of immigrant women for prostitution.[3] The first major federal immigration statute, this act focused on the exclusion of prostitutes, particularly Chinese prostitutes, who were generally viewed as the problem of the day.[4] Known as the Page Law for its California sponsor, Congressman Horace F. Page, the statute expressly provided that "women imported for the purposes of prostitution" could be excluded from the country.[5] The 1875 act reflected a national consensus on "the need for legislation to curb the twin evils of Chinese immigration: the coolie trade and the importation of women for prostitution."[6] "For 70 years after the 1875 Page Law excluding prostitutes, Chinese women [were] systematically barred from entering and joining Chinese men to form families" in the United States.[7] The exclusion of Chinese women all but eliminated the possibility of marrying and forming nuclear families for Chinese immigrant men in the United States; marriage with white women was, after all, prohibited by the antimiscegenation laws in most of the Western states.

Related to the prostitution exclusion grounds were the public charge provisions of the immigration laws (see Chapter 4). A number of early public charge cases involved women from Japan, who came in the wave of immigrants after the Chinese. In both *The Japanese Immigrant Case* (1903)[8] and *Nishimura Ekiu v. United States* (1892),[9] the Supreme Court upheld the exclusion of Japanese women on the grounds that they were likely to become public charges. Unmarried immigrant women were presumed to be either prostitutes or paupers and were particularly susceptible to exclusion and deportation on public charge grounds.[10]

In 1907, Congress broadened the prostitution provisions of the immigration laws to apply to any woman seeking to enter the United States for "immoral purposes" and to persons responsible for bringing these women into the country.[11] The Immigration Act of 1907 further stated that "any alien woman or girl who shall be found an inmate of a house of prostitution or practicing prostitution, at any time within three years after she shall have entered the United States, shall be deemed to be unlawfully within the United States and *shall be deported*."[12] Supreme Court Justice John Marshall Harlan explained, "There can be no doubt as to what class was aimed at by the clause forbidding the importation of alien women for purposes of 'prostitution.' It refers to women who for hire or without hire offer their bodies to indiscriminate intercourse with men. The lives and example of such persons are in hostility to 'the idea of the family, as consisting in and springing from the union for life of one man and one woman in the holy estate of matrimony; the sure foundation of all that is stable and noble in our civilization; the best guaranty of that reverent morality which is the source of all beneficent progress in social and political improvement.'"[13] As illustrated repeatedly in the debates over immigration throughout U.S. history, policy makers often saw immigrants as a threat to the core of U.S. society; thus, the restriction of their entry into the country was deemed necessary to protect the nation.

Prostitution remained a pressing social concern during the Progressive era. The federal government successfully pursued the deportation of prostitutes.[14] In 1910, Congress passed the Mann Act, also known as the White Slave Traffic Act,[15] to stop the interstate transportation of women, including immigrant women, for purposes of prostitution. In 1911, the Dillingham Commission, whose investigation of immigration at the direction of Congress greatly influenced the development of the immigration laws of that era, issued a report titled "Importation and Harboring of Women for Immoral Purposes." The report observed that "[t]he importation and harboring of alien women and girls for immoral purposes and the practice of prostitution by them—the so-called 'white slave traffic'—is the most pitiful and most revolting phase of the immigration question. . . . This business had assumed such large proportions and was exerting so evil an influence upon our country that the Immigration Commission felt compelled to make it the subject of a thorough investigation."[16]

At the time, immigration from Europe, where prostitution was tolerated to a greater extent than in the United States, was the focal point of concern. However, the particular immigrant group considered suspect changed over time, with the latest wave of immigrants invariably targeted. This period of U.S. immigration history has been described as follows:

> As increasing waves of foreign immigrants and southern blacks settled in major northern cities, xenophobia and racism came to dominate the discussion of prostitution [in the early twentieth century]. Contradicting the data they had collected, Progressive reformers continually depicted the villainous ringleaders of "prostitution syndicates" as foreigners. Depending on the year and the writer, the procurer or white slaver was depicted as a "sleazy French maquereau, in black velvet trouser and silkcap," an avaricious "Russian or Hungarian Jew with a white face and long beard," or a "devious Chinese merchant who, because of his peculiar and elastic code of morals," posed a special threat to the community.
>
> *Prostitutes were also typically portrayed as foreign, even though reformers' own records show the majority to have been the native-born daughters of immigrant parents.*[17]

Later immigration laws continued the exclusion of prostitutes. Section 3 of the Immigration Act of 1917 provided that "prostitutes, or persons coming into the United States for the purpose of prostitution or for any other immoral purpose" could be excluded.[18] The courts aggressively enforced the prostitution provisions of the immigration laws.[19]

The Immigration and Nationality Act of 1952 (INA), which, as amended, continues to regulate immigration to the United States, allows for the exclusion and deportation of prostitutes. An alien is inadmissible who "com[es] to the United States solely, principally, or incidentally to engage in prostitution, or has engaged in prostitution within 10 years of the date of application for a visa, admission, or adjustment of status."[20] These grounds continue to be enforced.[21] In the 1966 case of *Woodby v. INS*, the INS sought to deport an immigrant woman who had engaged in prostitution to pay for medical care for her sick infant. In a move that was, in all probability, motivated by sympathy, the Supreme Court set aside the order on the basis of a legal technicality.[22]

The modern incarnation of the prostitution problem is the smuggling of immigrant women into the country to engage in the sex trade. "Congress has estimated that at least 700,000 people are trafficked within or across international borders each year, with 45,000 to 50,000 victims brought into the United States. . . . Prostitution, pornography, sex tourism, and other commercial sexual services account for much of the human trafficking in the United States."[23] In the year 2000, Congress passed a law designed to address problems in human trafficking.[24] The new law aims to protect exploited immigrant women and punish the traffickers. The justification is, at least in part, the fact that smugglers often defraud immigrant women about the work that awaits them in the United States. Changing social mores about women and prostitution also may well have influenced U.S. government policy.

In sum, the regulation of prostitution in the immigration laws had an acute effect on women who sought to immigrate to the United States. There are clear racial overtones in the debates over the exclusion and deportation of prostitutes. The bar on the immigration of prostitutes in the late nineteenth century was, for example, a precursor to the Chinese exclusion laws. The victims of modern-day human sex traffickers, in contrast, have received more sympathetic treatment from the federal government.

Immigration Law and Domestic Violence

Family reunification is one of the central themes of U.S. immigration law, and marriage to a U.S. citizen has been perhaps the easiest way to obtain an immigrant visa. Many men who are U.S. citizens marry immigrant women, but marriage to a U.S. citizen has not always guaranteed citizenship to all racial groups. For example, for decades, male citizens of Chinese ancestry found it difficult to bring spouses from China.[25]

U.S. immigration law has also addressed the problem of "sham marriages"—marriages contracted solely to secure immigration benefits. In 1953, in *Lutwak v. United States*,[26] the Supreme Court held that persons who married for monetary compensation exclusively for immigration purposes could be subject to criminal sanction. To qualify as a marriage under immigration law, the marriage must be recognized by the law of a state and "the bride and groom [must have] intend[ed] to establish a life together at the time they were married."[27] This perhaps arbitrary definition governs the definition of marriage for the purposes of the immigration laws.

In the 1980s, the belief that sham marriages were rampant resulted in a crackdown by way of the immigration laws. In 1985, Alan Nelson, commissioner of the INS, testified before a congressional committee that the agency estimated that 30 percent of marriage relationships claimed for immigration purposes were fraudulent. This figure, as it turned out, was based on a survey that the drafter later admitted to be "statistically invalid and lack[ing] any probative value."[28] Nonetheless, the testimony impressed Congress.[29] The policy solution was the Immigration Marriage Fraud Amendments of 1986 (IMFA),[30] which created a series of rigorous procedures designed to uncover sham marriages. Unfortunately, the law also created the incentive for battered immigrant women to remain with their batterers to avoid losing their lawful immigration status.[31]

It is important to note that it does not appear that Congress intended to harm immigrant women in the way that it did. Consideration of the law's potential impact on women seems to have simply slipped through the legislative cracks. Under the IMFA, the spouse of a citizen or lawful permanent resident who sought to immigrate to the United States was afforded conditional lawful permanent resident status for two years. After that time, both husband and wife were required to petition jointly for permanent status for the immigrant spouse.[32] "[U]nder these circumstances, many immigrant women were reluctant to leave even the most abusive of partners for fear of being deported. When faced with the choice between protection from their batterers and protection against deportation, many immigrant women chose the latter."[33]

Attempting to ameliorate this negative consequence, Congress passed the Immigration Act of 1990, which allowed for a waiver of the IMFA's requirements for hardship caused by domestic violence.[34] Some observers nonetheless criticized the waiver provisions as too onerous for many abused immigrant women to put to use.[35] Congress further relaxed the requirements for battered immigrant women in the Violence

Against Women Act of 1994,[36] whose provisions have also been criticized as disproportionately onerous for immigrant women of color who face cultural and other barriers to leaving their batterers.[37] In the year 2000, Congress passed the Battered Immigrant Women Protection Act, providing even greater protections for abused immigrant women.[38] Thus, it took three acts of Congress passed over a period of nearly fifteen years to ameliorate the harsh impacts of a single effort to put an end to marriage fraud.

Provisions designed to protect battered immigrant women were also included in the 1996 immigration reforms.[39] For example, the law authorized the deportation of perpetrators of domestic violence. However, a battered immigrant woman, who faces the prospect of having her spouse deported and thus being left with no means of financial support for her family might well refrain from reporting her batterer.

The series of laws designed to address the problems of battered immigrant women clearly reflect sympathy toward victims of domestic violence. As one commentator explained, "Battered immigrant women fall into a severely marginalized category of American society. Language, culture, and a lack of legal resources often prevent battered immigrants from leaving an abusive relationship. In addition, these women often have trouble finding shelter and employment due to language barriers, lack of income, and ineligibility for public assistance. Finally, the battered immigrant woman is often faced with an unenviable choice. She must decide to suffer in silence with her abusive husband or risk deportation to her country of origin. This combination of factors often leads the woman to stay with her batterer rather than face unknown consequences."[40] Unfortunately, efforts to protect battered immigrant women can also arise from racial stereotypes of the criminal, barbaric, battering man of color.

An offshoot of spouse-based immigration is the mail-order bride industry, which has provoked growing public concern. In this age of low-cost Internet access, increasing numbers of the country's male citizens have arranged for mail-order brides—frequently immigrant women of color—to come to the United States. The marriages have been criticized as inconsistent with the traditional understanding of matrimony and an abuse of the immigration laws. Moreover, U.S. men who pursue sexualized gender stereotypes have married women of color, including many from Asia, in order to dominate them. In these situations and others, mail-order brides have sometimes been subjected to domestic violence and other forms of abuse. Many of these women, who are vulnerable to economic and other coercion, fear ending the abusive relationships.[41]

Some might compare the modern mail-order bride industry with the twentieth-century practice of selecting Japanese brides from pictures.[42] The picture-bride practice, however, involved the selection of Japanese brides by Japanese men, who were, in many states, prohibited by law from marrying white women. These racial and other power issues differed significantly from those associated with today's mail-order bride industry.

Clearly, the spouse-based immigration laws and efforts to prevent fraud have had dramatic negative effects on immigrant women. The mail-order bride industry, which was in part spawned by these laws, has created further problems for noncitizen women. At the same time, efforts to police the marriage relationship in the name of preventing marriage fraud bring complex issues of privacy into play and raise broader questions of the nature of relationships that the law should sanction.

Gender-Based Asylum

The U.S. immigration laws provide relief from deportation for noncitizens who face possible persecution on account of race, political opinion, religion, nationality, and membership in a particular social group, if returned to their native country.[43] Borrowed from international law, they do not, however, provide relief from persecution on account of gender.[44] Because the requirements for asylum tend to focus on the public sphere, generally dominated by males throughout the world, rather than the private sphere, where gender-based persecution is prevalent, it has historically been more difficult for women who are fleeing persecution to satisfy the requirements for asylum.[45]

At the close of the twentieth century, however, the courts began to expand the circumstances under which women might qualify for asylum on one of the five grounds. Early cases focused on women who fled alleged persecution in the Muslim world[46] and rape as a form of persecution.[47] These were followed by cases of genital mutilation of young women, a practice found in some African nations. In *Matter of Kasinga*,[48] the Board of Immigration Appeals held that a woman from Togo who feared that she would be subjected to genital mutilation if she returned to her country might be eligible for relief. More recently, women who flee domestic violence in their native land, at least when local police are unwilling to intervene, are more frequently being considered eligible for asylum.[49]

The general trend in the law has been favorable for immigrant women. However, at times improvements have been founded on stereotypes about conditions and men in developing countries. The general view that Islamic nations are barbaric, for example, has affected the treatment of women from these nations.[50] Stereotypes about domineering men of color in the developing world may also affect evolution of the laws in favor of women asylum seekers.

Changes in the immigration law have mirrored increased sensitivity toward women in U.S. law in general. As the U.S. government has eschewed gender stereotypes and moved to enforce the laws that prohibit domestic violence, Congress has offered greater protections to immigrant women as well. The growing consciousness about the treatment of women in the United States is evident in the treatment of immigrant women.

Gendered Citizenship Laws

From 1790 until the emancipation of African American slaves after the Civil War, immigrant naturalization was reserved for white people; from the end of the Civil War until 1952, only persons of African ancestry were added to those who were eligible for naturalization. These requirements barred from citizenship Asian immigrants, even those groups that scientists of the day classified as biologically "white"; the Supreme Court held that Asian immigrants were not eligible to naturalize and become U.S. citizens.[51] Once again, the immigration and nationality laws revealed the social construction of race.

The nationality laws have, in the past, linked women's eligibility for citizenship, even in the case of women who were already U.S. citizens, with the eligibility of the men they married. At one time,

> eligibility for naturalization . . . depended on a woman's marital status. Congress in 1855 declared that a foreign woman automatically acquired citizenship upon marriage to a U.S. citizen, or upon the naturalization of her alien husband. . . . A wife's acquisition of citizenship, however, remained subject to her individual qualification for naturalization—that is, on whether she was a "white person." Thus, the Supreme Court held in 1868 that only "white women" could gain citizenship by marrying a citizen. Racial restrictions further complicated matters for noncitizen women in that naturalization was denied to those married to a man racially ineligible for citizenship, irrespective of the woman's own qualifications, racial or otherwise. The automatic naturalization of a woman upon her marriage to a citizen or upon the naturalization of her husband ended in 1922.[52]

In 1907, Congress passed a law (which was not completely repealed until 1931)[53] that terminated a woman's U.S. citizenship upon her marriage to a noncitizen.[54] The law was partially repealed in 1922 to alleviate the expatriation of women married to German nationals who were denied naturalization as "alien enemies" during World War I,[55] but the law "continued to require the expatriation of any woman who married a foreigner *racially barred* from citizenship."[56] At one time, nonwhite immigrant women who married U.S. citizens were barred from citizenship on racial grounds.[57] The gender-linked citizenship laws reflected the now-antiquated view that women were legally inseparable from their husbands; therefore, except for those who were barred on racial grounds, a woman's citizenship rights depended on those of her husband.

The operation of these gender discriminatory laws had its own racial components and impacts: "These legal penalties for marriage to racially barred aliens made such unions far less likely, and thus skewed the procreative choices that determined the appearance of the U.S. population."[58] In other words, the laws provided disincentives for women to marry nonwhite or nonblack noncitizens. In addition, other social and legal forces, such as the antimiscegenation laws,[59] inhibited interracial marriages, especially between black and white persons.[60]

Like the race-based naturalization requirements, the citizenship laws' gender classifications jar modern sensibilities. They enforced a social order that categorized women as the property of their husbands and discouraged interracial marriage.[61] Female citizens and lawful permanent residents had much to lose by transcending racial boundaries. The laws for women contrasted sharply with the long-standing laws that made the (white or nonwhite) wives of male citizens eligible to immigrate (although perhaps not naturalize).[62]

The Supreme Court refused to disturb the blatant gender discrimination in the citizenship laws. In the landmark case of *Mackenzie v. Hare*, the Court upheld Congress's authority, as an inherent power of sovereignty, to expatriate under the 1907 law a female U.S. citizen who married a foreign national. The Court explained, "The identity of husband and wife is an ancient principle of our jurisprudence. It was neither accidental nor arbitrary and worked in many instances for her protection. . . . *It is determined by their intimate relation and unity of interests, and this relation and unity may make it of public concern in many instances to merge their identity, and give dominance to the husband.*"[63] Despite the harsh treatment of female citizens under the law upheld by the Court, this case is frequently recalled more for the extraordinary power that the decision gives to Congress with respect to expatriation than for its impact on women.[64]

Gender discrimination has been found in not only the content but also the application of the law's naturalization requirements. Historically, the INS employed a double standard in determining whether the personal lives of men and women satisfied the "good moral character" requirement for naturalization.[65] For example, although the decision was rejected by a reviewing court on appeal, the INS found that an immigrant woman lacked "good moral character" because she had an ongoing sexual relationship with a man to whom she was not married.[66] It is difficult to imagine similar reasoning being applied to a man; in at least one case, it was not.[67]

Discrimination against women is not an ancient relic of the immigration and nationality laws. The proposals for limiting birthright citizenship, for example, are based on stereotypes about immigrant women, particularly immigrant women of color, and a desire to maintain the racial status quo.[68] In California, the restrictionist claim has been that women from Mexico enter the state to give birth—and the benefit of U.S. citizenship—to their children.

Another important aspect of the modern immigration laws involves gender stereotypes. Under the current immigration laws, it is easier for the mother than for the father of an "illegitimate" noncitizen child to sponsor the child's immigration into the United States.[69] In the 2001 case of *Nguyen v. INS*, the Supreme Court upheld the discrimination saying that the gender classification was justified because giving birth to the child makes a woman more likely to have a relationship with the child.[70] Four Supreme Court justices, including the two women justices (Sandra Day O'Connor and Ruth Bader Ginsburg), dissented, protesting that the majority relied on gender stereotypes. This law has racial impacts as well, since many U.S. military personnel of color stationed in various parts of the world father racially mixed children out of wedlock. Under the current immigration laws, it is more difficult for the fathers of these children to bring them to the United States than it would be for citizen mothers to do so.[71]

Modern Trends in Immigration Law for Women

Until recently, people have persisted in stereotyping the immigrant as male despite women's long history of immigration to the United States. Academics are now beginning to study the unique experiences of immigrant women and the impact of immigration law on them.[72] In the 1990s, women accounted for about 50 percent of all immigrants, refugees, and naturalized citizens.[73]

The increase in the migration of women to the United States belies the bias that has endured in the U.S. immigration laws. For example, "[f]emale primary beneficiaries consume only a paltry number of employment-based immigrant visas to the United States. While a substantial number of women immigrate in the employment-based categories, they do so largely by means of derivative status based on a family relationship with a male primary beneficiary. Employment-based immigration increasingly favors those with advanced education, scientific or technical renown, prominent managerial position, or wealth, a shift in valued attributes that is likely to impede rather than to enhance the ability of women to qualify independently for employment-based immigration."[74]

This is not to suggest that work traditionally relegated to women—"women's work"—is not needed. However, it is difficult to secure employment immigrant visas based on such low-wage, unskilled labor as child care, a service needed by most working mothers. It is no surprise, then, that President Clinton withdrew his first two nominees for attorney general, Zoe Baird and Kimba Wood (who were also the first two women ever nominated to serve as attorney general), because they had employed undocumented child care providers.[75] (Interestingly, the woman who got the job, Attorney General Janet Reno, had no children.) The difficulty of securing child care is one of the indirect impacts of immigration law on the nation's female citizens.

Immigrant women in the United States are vulnerable to exploitation in the workplace. Employer sanctions are intended to enforce the prohibition against hiring undocumented immigrants but fail to offer a realistic deterrent.[76] The uncertain immigration status of undocumented workers affords employers great leverage in establishing the terms and conditions of employment.[77] Language, cultural, and other differences further facilitate exploitation. Undocumented women have proved to be particularly exploitable. Garment sweat shops in major urban centers employ immigrant women from Latin America and Asia.[78] The much-publicized discovery of a group of mostly female undocumented workers from Thailand who had been held in slavelike conditions in California offers a stark example.[79] As we saw earlier in this chapter, the modern sex trade also exploits immigrant women.

Domestic service workers, often poor immigrant women, are paid low wages and work under poor conditions in middle- and upper-class homes across the country. Both legal and undocumented modes of immigration facilitate the exploitation. "In addition to low wages, long hours, the lack of both privacy and benefits that are common among live-in conditions, immigrant women experience other abuses. They include passport confiscation, limited freedom of movement and ability to communicate with others, employer threats of deportation, assault and battery, rape, servitude, torture, and trafficking."[80]

The typical "illegal alien" stereotype fails to incorporate women despite their long-term and increasing (lawful and unlawful) immigration to the United States.[81] Undocumented women may well be even more vulnerable to exploitation in the labor market than are undocumented men.[82] The law, however, generally offers no special protections for undocumented women, and we have little understanding of how undocumented women live and work in U.S. society.[83]

Modern Public Benefits and the Impact on Women

As we saw in Chapter 4, the close of the twentieth century was frought with great concern about immigrants' receipt of public benefits. The proportion of women and families (many of whom are in need of but ineligible for health and other benefits) in the undocumented Mexican population has increased.[84] Because there is evidence that undocumented women who migrate to the United States tend to remain longer than men, women may constitute a greater proportion of the undocumented population than simple migration patterns suggest.[85]

Despite the fact that women use some public benefits (e.g., prenatal care) more than men, the political debate over the reduction of public assistance to immigrants generally fails to weigh the disproportionate impact of such measures on immigrant women. The elimination of public education for undocumented children, one of the goals of California's Proposition 187, would have disparately affected women, who (in both single- and two-parent households) are often responsible for child care.[86] The same can be said with respect to such public benefits as general assistance and social services, including battered women's shelters.

Gender-based political attacks on immigrant women include critiques of high fertility rates and allegations that they seek free medical assistance in childbirth and automatic U.S. citizenship for their children. For example, in 1993, Governor Pete Wilson of California stated, "We give people a reward for violating the law and successfully entering the country illegally. . . . If you come to this country illegally and have a baby, the reward is your baby will become a citizen, entitled to all the rights and perquisites of any American citizen."[87] On a 1994 television talk show broadcast, a California assemblyman and drafter of Proposition 187 stated that undocumented mothers "come here for that birth certificate. They come here to get on the California dole."[88] Mexican women are thus characterized as hyperfertile breeders.[89]

In short, immigrant women have been the subject of gender-specific attacks in the political process, and the concerns have influenced the political debate over immigration and welfare reform. Immigrants, especially immigrant women have been used as sacrificial lambs.

Conclusion

Over the course of U.S. history, the immigration and nationality laws have discriminated against women in many ways. The biases in these laws typically mirror general stereotypes about women in the United States. Historically, women have been treated as appendages of their husbands. Thus, domestic violence often went unknown or unexposed. As the women's movement transformed notions of the appropriate treatment of women, the immigration laws began (albeit slowly) to change as well. In recent years, the concerted efforts of immigrants' rights advocates and women's groups have done much to move the laws concerning women in a favorable direction.

7

Exclusion and Deportation of Lesbians and Gay Men

ike other historically unpopular groups in the United States, lesbians and gay men have suffered the wrath of the immigration laws. Interestingly, homosexual immigrants, much like homosexuals generally, were virtually invisible until 1952. Reminiscent of Nazism, which included both communists and homosexuals among the "undesirables" sent to concentration camps,[1] McCarthyism equated homosexuals with communists. The immigration laws of the Cold War era were deeply influenced by fear of "the communist threat." At the same time that Congress increased efforts to police communist sympathies, therefore, it also amended the immigration laws to expressly exclude homosexuals from the country.

From 1952 until 1990, the law barred the immigration of homosexuals to the United States as "psychopathic personalities"—and, more specifically, under a 1965 revision to the law—for living a life of "sexual deviation." Reflecting a general lack of concern with the legal rights of lesbians and gay men at that time, the Supreme Court rejected constitutional challenges to the law. As time passed, however, and society's sense of the unfairness of the laws grew, the courts uncovered loopholes to the homosexual exclusion and deportation grounds.

140

In 1990, in response to both political activism and a growing recognition of the rights of lesbians and gay men generally, Congress repealed the homosexual exclusion. In ways that are not always readily apparent, however, homosexuals have remained disadvantaged by other aspects of the immigration laws. Certain exclusion grounds based on either "criminal" activity or HIV infection continue to impact gay men disparately. Moreover, same-sex partnerships do not qualify homosexuals for the most common immigrant visa—legal residency based on marriage to a citizen. Consequently, although heterosexual citizens are generally entitled to bring a noncitizen spouse into the United States, homosexual citizens do not have that right. In the long run, change appears unlikely unless same-sex partnerships become recognized under U.S. law. Finally, how the courts and the executive branch treat homosexual asylum seekers who flee persecution on account of their sexual orientation, now and in the future, is inextricably linked to how lesbians and gay men are treated generally.

A History of Exclusion of Homosexual Immigrants

Not until well into the twentieth century did the U.S. immigration laws begin to address homosexuality directly.[2] During the first part of the century, prostitution, targeted as the primary threat to sexual morality, was the subject of extensive legal regulation (see Chapter 6). Unlike with other groups of immigrants—whose potential mass migration to the United States sparked the fear that contributed, for example, to the early federal efforts to exclude the Chinese (see Chapter 2) and the poor (see Chapter 4)—for the most part, the public at large has not had to concern itself with a mass migration of homosexuals to the United States. As a result, homosexuals generally have not been the focal point of the immigration laws or their enforcement.

Some individual cases have been notable, however. Consider, for instance, the 1912 example of Nicholas P., who had engaged in homosexual relations and was deported on the ground that he was likely to become a public charge.[3] In this case, the all-purpose public charge exclusion served as the means to remove a noncitizen who was deemed undesirable because of his sexual orientation.

What evolved into the homosexual exclusion was originally part of the Immigration Act of 1917, which provided "[t]hat the following classes of aliens shall be excluded from admission into the United States: All idiots, imbeciles, feeble-minded persons, epileptics, insane persons, persons who have had one or more attacks of insanity at any time previously; *persons of constitutional psychopathic inferiority.*"[4]

Placing "persons of constitutional psychopathic inferiority" in the company of "idiots, imbeciles, feeble-minded persons, [and] insane persons" reveals society's attitude toward persons in this general exclusion category. The 1917 exclusion ground went hand in hand with the popular eugenics movement, which promoted the fear that the turn-of-the-century immigrant stream was mentally and physically inferior to the general U.S. population, with the inferiority closely tied to race.[5] Concerns about the racial composition of the immigrants of this era culminated in the national origins quota system in the Immigration Act of 1924. Before 1952, the "constitutional psychopathic inferiority" exclusion ground was not employed to exclude homosexuals with any degree of regularity.

When the "psychopathic inferiority" language in the 1917 Act was folded into the Immigration and Nationality Act of 1952 (INA), however, the use of this exclusion ground changed. The exclusion applied to "aliens afflicted with psychopathic personality, epilepsy or a mental defect."[6] A Senate report expressly stated that the language in this provision was designed to bar "homosexuals and sex perverts" from the United States.[7] During the McCarthy era, when homosexuals were overtly equated with communists, the federal government spied on gay and lesbian organizations as part of the war on communism.[8] In addition to being viewed as subversive in their own right, homosexuals were considered to be vulnerable to extortion by communists, who might threaten to reveal their sexual orientation. Homosexuals were thus seen as a threat to the national security.

The federal government invoked the "psychopathic personality" exclusion of the 1952 act as a means of prohibiting gay men,[9] and occasionally lesbians, from entering the country. In one case, Sara Harb Quiroz, a lawful permanent resident from Mexico, was arrested while seeking to reenter the United States and was ordered removed from the country because she "seemed like" a lesbian to the INS officers. Although she admitted to having engaged in homosexual relations, Quiroz denied that she was a lesbian; in fact, she married a man before her ultimate deportation.[10]

Over time, growing recognition that the harshness of the exclusion ground was inconsistent with emerging social norms weakened the resolve to invoke it with respect to homosexual *status* rather than *conduct*. In *Fleuti v. Rosenberg*,[11] the court of appeals ruled that the wording "psychopathic personality" in the immigration laws was so vague and ambiguous as to be unconstitutional. The Supreme Court sidestepped the constitutional question by creating a legal fiction that the noncitizen in question, George Fleuti, who had lived in the United States for many years and had engaged in homosexual relationships, had never left the country during a weekend trip to Mexico, was therefore not "reentering" the country, and, as a result, was not subject to the exclusion and deportation grounds.[12] In 1965, in response to the lower court's decision in *Fleuti*, Congress added that "persons afflicted with . . . sexual deviation" could be barred from entering the United States.[13]

Two years later, the Supreme Court upheld the application of the homosexual exclusion ground in *Boutilier v. INS*.[14] Clive Boutilier, an immigrant from Canada, had lived quietly in the United States as a lawful permanent resident for more than a decade but was ordered deported on the ground that he had been excludable at the time of his entry into the country. The Court emphasized that "[t]he legislative history indicates beyond a shadow of a doubt that the Congress intended the phrase 'psychopathic personality' to include homosexuals."[15] In his dissent, Justice William Douglas, with the excesses of the 1950s war on communism firmly in mind, recognized that "[t]he term psychopathic personality is a treacherous one like 'communist' or in an earlier day 'Bolshevik.'"[16] Reviewing psychological literature, including the famous study of Dr. Alfred Kinsey finding that 37 percent of the male population reported at least one homosexual experience,[17] Justice Douglas acknowledged that "homosexuals have risen high in our own public service—both in Congress and in the Executive Branch—and have served with distinction. It is therefore not credible that Congress wanted to deport everyone and anyone who was a sexual deviate, no matter how blameless his social conduct had been nor how creative his work nor how valuable his contribution to society."[18]

After *Boutilier*, the courts and the immigration bureaucracy regularly upheld the exclusion and deportation of homosexuals.[19] Issues continued to arise about the technical application of the homosexuality provisions of the immigration laws. In no small part, the controversy stemmed from changing social mores about homosexuality. In 1979, the Public Health Service (which issues health certificates on health exclusion grounds) announced that, because the American Psychiatric Association had dropped homosexuality as a psychiatric disorder, it would no longer issue to suspected homosexuals the Class A medical certificate that warrants exclusion from the country. A split among the lower courts developed on whether a medical certificate was necessary in order to exclude a homosexual from the country.[20]

Change in the immigration laws came slowly. In 1980, the Mariel boatlift brought thousands of alleged homosexuals and criminals, as well as poor Afro-Cubans, to the shores of south Florida. This influx of immigrants no doubt dampened enthusiasm for removal of the homosexual exclusion from the INA. In this unusual instance, the fear of a mass migration of homosexuals and other "undesirables" influenced both public opinion and policy makers.

Gradually, however, popular support grew for the removal of the homosexuality exclusion ground.[21] The Immigration Act of 1990[22] did precisely that. The law changed the relevant language to state that an alien could be excluded from the country if he or she was determined "to have a physical or mental disorder and behavior associated with the disorder that *may pose or has posed, a threat to property, safety, or welfare of the alien or others.*"[23] As amended, the exclusion focuses on potentially dangerous *conduct* rather than mere *status*. The House of Representatives Report explained that the "psychopathic personality" exclusion ground had become "out of step with current notions of privacy and personal dignity [and was] inconsistent with contemporary psychiatric theories. When this provision was adopted, homosexuality was commonly viewed as a form of mental illness. However, the American Psychiatric Association determined that homosexuality in fact is not a mental disorder."[24] The medical profession's changing view of homosexuality thus influenced Congress's repeal of the exclusion.[25]

The American Psychiatric Association's reconsideration of homosexuality was consistent with the dramatic change in U.S. society's view of homosexuality since 1952. By 1990, the immigration law's prohibition of lesbian and gay immigration had become out of step with the growing awareness and acceptance of homosexuals in the United States. The 1969 Stonewall riots in protest of discriminatory law enforcement by police commenced a slow national awakening about homosexuals and homosexuality.[26] Changes in the law followed. Consider that, in 1986, the Supreme Court decision in *Bowers v. Hardwick*[27] upheld a criminal conviction under a Georgia sodomy law, provoking protests and criticism. A decade later, in *Romer v. Evans*, the Court invalidated a Colorado law that discriminated on the basis of sexual orientation.[28] Legalities aside, the turnabout in results aligns with changing views of homosexuality.

By the same token, the lesbian and gay community has begun to wield more political power in domestic politics. Openly homosexual politicians, including several members of the U.S. Congress, decry discrimination on the basis of sexual orientation. In the end, Congress owed its ability to remove the homosexual exclusion from the immigration laws to the country's changing political landscape.

The HIV Exclusion

During the later decades of the twentieth century, acquired immunodeficiency syndrome (AIDS) emerged as a disease of worldwide concern. Initially linked to gay men and Haitians, AIDS threw fear into the nation. After years of controversy, Congress added infection with the human immunodeficiency virus (HIV), which causes AIDS, as a ground for excluding noncitizens from the country. The controversial history of the HIV exclusion should be viewed as separate from but associated with the gay and lesbian exclusion ground.[29] Some commentators who have called for abolition of the homosexual exclusion on equality grounds have supported the HIV exclusion for public health reasons.[30]

The Public Health Service (PHS) has historically been entrusted with identifying "dangerous contagious diseases" that warrant exclusion from the country. In 1987, Congress ordered the president to add HIV to the list of dangerous contagious diseases. After Congress amended the health-related exclusion grounds in 1990, the PHS proposed removing HIV from the list of excludable diseases, based on the conclusion that doing so would not significantly increase the risk of HIV infection in the U.S. population. A public furor followed, fueled by fears of (1) the potential spread of AIDS, (2) health care costs that might be incurred by immigrants who already suffered from the disease and citizens who might become infected with it, and, more subtly, (3) the potential influx of homosexuals and poor, black Haitians, who were viewed by many as the primary carriers of the disease. Congress ultimately intervened, expressly adding the HIV exclusion to the immigration laws, thus making it the only disease specifically identified in the section that covered disease-based exclusion grounds.[31] Although waivers of the exclusion ground are possible, they are extremely difficult to secure.[32]

Both cost and health concerns have influenced the federal government's enforcement of the HIV exclusion. Absent a virtual guarantee that the government will not be required to pay for a noncitizen's medical treatment, the government has refused to grant a waiver.[33] Christopher Arneson, an HIV-positive lawful permanent resident from New Zealand, faced exclusion when he attempted to return to the United States to obtain benefits that he claimed to have earned during almost thirty years of employment in the United States.[34] Similarly, Haitians, who raise fears of mass migration, have been subjected to more rigorous HIV screening procedures than other asylum seekers.[35]

Commentators are quick to criticize the HIV exclusion.[36] As a result of medical advances and education about the modes of AIDS transmission, the hysteria that has surrounded the disease has begun to subside. The change in the public's attitude toward AIDS may allow the federal government to adopt less-severe measures with respect to HIV-infected noncitizens in the future. The INS General Counsel has already called for more humanitarian enforcement of the HIV exclusion.[37] Still, little popular support exists for its repeal at this time. Support for the HIV exclusion is encouraged by the view that the AIDS problem can be equated with people of color and the gay population.

Same-Sex Marriages and the Immigration Laws

In the United States, a debate has raged over domestic partnerships and same-sex marriages.[38] Congress was spurred to act to "protect" traditional marriage after the state of Hawaii considered recognizing same-sex marriages. The Defense of Marriage Act,[39] which was enacted in 1996, defines marriage as heterosexual and authorizes states to ignore same-sex marriages that are recognized by sister states.

Homosexuals are ineligible for immigrant visas that are the centerpiece of the U.S. immigration laws: visas that are founded on the promotion of family unity.[40] Homosexual partners are ineligible for immigration opportunities that heterosexual married couples enjoy. In *Adams v. Howerton*,[41] for example, Richard Adams, a U.S. citizen, filed a visa petition for his Australian partner, Tony Sullivan. In denying the petition, the INS wrote to Adams: "Upon consideration, it is ordered that your visa petition filed on April 28, 1975 for classification of Anthony Corbett Sullivan as the spouse of a United States citizen be denied for the following reasons: '*You have failed to establish that a bona fide marital relationship can exist between two faggots.*'"[42]

Although it avoided the use of epithets, the court of appeals upheld the INS decision, ruling that a gay man could not qualify as the "spouse" of a U.S. citizen and therefore Sullivan was ineligible to immigrate to the United States. Because Congress acted to exclude homosexuals from immigrating, the court concluded, it could not have been the intention of Congress to give homosexual spouses preferential immigration treatment. In addition to denying lawful immigrant status to Sullivan, the INS sought to deport him, and the courts later denied him relief from deportation.[43]

Criticism by commentators has not prompted Congress to demonstrate any significant willingness to intervene on behalf of the rights of same-sex couples.[44] Although bills have been introduced that would allow for the recognition of same-sex partnerships under the U.S. immigration laws as under the immigration laws of some other countries,[45] they have received no groundswell of political or public support. Meanwhile, the issue remains of special importance to gay and lesbian citizens who seek to bring immigrant partners into the United States.[46]

Whether homosexual relationships deserve legal recognition, of course, is at the center of the controversy over same-sex partnerships in the United States. Immigration law, like domestic law generally, has traditionally defined "family" as "heterosexual nuclear family." Changing the family-based immigration provisions to permit the immigration of partners of persons of the same sex requires a reconceptualization of "family" for the purposes of the immigration laws.[47] This issue affects more than simply same-sex relationships. Extended family networks, much more commonly recognized in other countries than in the United States, receive far less solicitude under the immigration laws, and under U.S. laws generally, than do nuclear families.

Resistance to recognition of same-sex partnerships under U.S. immigration law, as under U.S. domestic law, is inevitable. The current immigrant visa system has been criticized as contributing to "chain migration" of family members. In 1995, in response to that criticism, the U.S. Commission on Immigration Reform suggested tightening, rather than expanding, the family immigrant visa categories and the relatives of U.S. citizens and immigrants who are eligible for immigration to this country.[48] Although this action does not directly address same-sex partnerships, the thrust of the recommendations bodes ill for liberalization of family immigrant visas.

The recognition of same-sex partnerships under domestic law and under immigration law are linked. Recognition under immigration law without recognition under domestic law would be anomalous. That being the case, acceptance of same-sex partnerships for immigration purposes is not likely to precede acceptance of same-sex partnerships between citizens.

Homosexuals, Crime, and Good Moral Character

Even with the removal of the homosexual exclusion in 1990, various features of the U.S. immigration laws disparately impact homosexuals. "[L]esbians and gay men convicted of sodomy or of a public morality offense are at risk of exclusion or deportation under the 'crimes involving moral turpitude' exclusion, and may be denied citizenship under the 'good moral character' requirement" for naturalization.[49] Certain criminal laws and their enforcement clearly target homosexuals.

The courts have considered consensual sodomy to be a crime of moral turpitude. In 1972, one court of appeals emphasized that "[s]odomy is a crime of moral turpitude in Virginia . . . , and is still a crime considered a felony in the District of Columbia. . . . Similarly, the Board [of Immigration Appeals] has held that the crime of solicitation to commit sodomy was a crime involving moral turpitude as early as 1949."[50] The general definition of a "crime of moral turpitude" suggests the harsh view of sodomy: "an act of baseness, vileness, or depravity in the private and social duties which a man owes to his fellow men, or to society in general, contrary to the accepted and customary rule of right and duty between man and man."[51]

Courts have found solicitation of homosexual acts in a public place and related offenses to be crimes of moral turpitude that warranted exclusion or deportation from the country.[52] Naturalization petitions by homosexuals have been denied on the ground that the petitioners' sexual orientation indicated that they lacked the good moral character required for naturalization.[53] In 1968, one court found that a lesbian who had "never been convicted of a crime or offense, never discharged from any employment by reason of sexual deviation and [for whom] a character investigation revealed that although she is known and reputed to be a lesbian, nothing else of a derogatory nature was disclosed," lacked the "good moral character" necessary for citizenship.[54] In so ruling, the court stated that "few behavioral deviations are more offensive to American mores than is homosexuality."[55]

Gradually, the courts have allowed more homosexuals to naturalize absent criminal convictions.[56] But the criminal law exclusions continue to provide avenues for discrimination against lesbians and gay men.

Sexual Orientation and Asylum

Interestingly, some doors have opened for lesbians and gay men in another area of immigration law. A noncitizen who faces a well-founded fear of persecution as a result of membership in a particular social group may be eligible for asylum in the United States.[57] As the homosexual exclusion was removed from the immigration laws, the immigration agencies and the courts began to recognize that, like those persecuted on account of political opinion, race, religion, and nationality, lesbians and gay men may be persecuted because of their sexual orientation. Homosexuals have suffered human rights abuses in many countries. Indeed, much-publicized hate crimes against homosexuals in the United States, such as the cold-blooded 1998 murder of Matthew Shepard in Wyoming, gave the issue national attention. Commentators rallied to endorse the extension of the asylum laws to protect gay men and lesbians.[58]

In *Matter of Toboso-Alfonso*,[59] the Board of Immigration Appeals (BIA) recognized eligibility of relief for a homosexual who suffered persecution by the Cuban government because of his homosexual status alone. The BIA initially decided the case during the first Bush administration. It was decided as a nonprecedent case; that is, it was limited to its facts and was not binding for the immigration courts and the BIA. After the election of President Bill Clinton, Attorney General Janet Reno—partly in response to political pressure from Barney Frank,[60] a gay congressman—certified the decision as precedent binding on the entire executive branch. The history of *Toboso* demonstrates the role of politics—and the growing recognition of the rights and political influence of homosexuals—affecting law.

In *Pitcherskaia v. INS*,[61] the court of appeals granted Alla Konstantinova Pitcherskaia's asylum claim based on the Russian government's efforts to subject her, as a "suspected" lesbian, to forced medical treatment that was egregious enough to qualify as "persecution." Similarly, in *Hernández-Montiel v. INS*,[62] the court found that a gay man from Mexico who had been beaten and raped by police had established persecution on the basis of his membership in a group of gay men who dressed as women.

After removal of the homosexual exclusion in 1990, the enforcement of the U.S. immigration laws saw a liberalization in the treatment of homosexuals who petition for asylum. As the public gained awareness of hate crimes against gays and lesbians, tolerance of homosexuality grew, and the immigration laws began to follow suit.

Conclusion

This history of the inhospitality of the immigration laws toward lesbians and gay men exemplifies the link between immigration law and domestic views toward particular groups. The treatment of lesbian and gay *immigrants*, in turn, is bound to the efforts of lesbian and gay *citizens* to secure full and equal citizenship in the United States.[63] Until 1990, gay men and lesbians were treated as "psychopaths" by law. As domestic sensibilities changed, the political influence of homosexuals grew, and the trajectory of the law began to change.

In addition to the exclusion and deportation of homosexuals per se, HIV and criminal exclusion and deportation grounds and marriage, asylum, and naturalization provisions have all impacted lesbians and gay men. The treatment of homosexuals under the immigration laws is closely tied to their treatment under domestic law. The fact that gay and lesbian immigration does not, for the most part, raise fears of mass migration may facilitate future relaxation of the immigration laws that affect homosexuals. At the same time, however, the stigma of homosexuality, and its ability to ignite a spontaneous firestorm of controversy, could provide a formidable barrier to change.

8

The Future of Immigration and Civil Rights in the United States

As we have seen, exclusion and deportation of minorities have been part and parcel of the U.S. immigration laws. People of color, political dissidents, the poor and the working class, criminals, women, and homosexuals have all suffered the wrath of immigration law and enforcement at various times in U.S. history. The nation's harsh treatment of its immigrants runs counter to the devotion to equality and the commitment to the "huddled masses" on which our country was built.

Because noncitizens are afforded precious few legal and civil rights, they possess few of the protections that citizens enjoy in the current U.S. constitutional order. This differentiation is rationalized in part by classifying noncitizens as "aliens." This chapter considers the impact of terminology on the treatment of immigrants, examines the need for a new conception of civil rights in an increasingly multiracial United States, and sketches a few alternatives for reform.

The "Alien" Problem

Both large and small factors have contributed to the severe treatment of immigrants throughout U.S. history.[1] The artful use of the word "alien" in legal discussions that address the rights of noncitizens in the United States facilitates rationalization of the harsh treatment of immigrants. By definition, "aliens" are outsiders to the national community. Even if they have lived in this country for many years, have native-born U.S. citizen children, and have worked and developed deep community ties in the United States, noncitizens remain "aliens"—institutionalized "others," different and apart from "us."

The classification of persons as "aliens," as opposed to citizens, has legal, social, and political significance. Citizens are afforded a large number of political and civil rights, many of which are guaranteed by the U.S. Constitution; noncitizens are afforded considerably fewer constitutional and statutory protections. Immigrants, for example (as we saw in Chapter 3), risk deportation if they engage in certain political activities that citizens have the constitutional right to pursue. The crux of the matter, in fact, is just that: Immigrants can be deported from the country, whereas citizens cannot.

The concept of the "alien" has more subtle social consequences as well. Most important, it helps to strengthen nativist sentiment toward members of new immigrant groups, in turn influencing U.S. responses to immigration. Immigrants have long been disfavored in the United States, with targeted subgroups varying over time. In the late 1790s, the Federalists pressed for passage of the now infamous Alien and Sedition Acts in an effort to halt the importation of "radical" ideas from France and to cut off the burgeoning immigrant support for the Republican Party.[2] In the 1800s, Irish immigrants, who were considered at the time to be members of a distinct and inferior race of people, were the subject of hostility.[3] Near the end of the nineteenth century, Chinese immigrants suffered violent attacks and bore the brunt of a wave of draconian federal immigration laws.[4] Animosity directed at Japanese immigrants and citizens of Japanese ancestry culminated in their internment during World War II.[5]

As this history suggests, race and perceived racial difference have influenced the social and legal construction of the "alien." Some restrictionist laws, such as the laws passed by Congress in the late 1800s that barred virtually all Chinese immigration, have been expressly race based. Before 1952, the law prohibited most nonwhite immigrants from naturalizing,[6] thereby forever relegating noncitizens of color to "alien" status and effectively defining them as permanent outsiders to the national community. In modern times, the word "aliens," around which U.S. immigration laws are based and which permeates public debate, is often code for "immigrants of color."

Commentators have expressed general concerns about the terminology in immigration law.[7] Despite such concerns, the term "alien" is regularly used, often with some reluctance or at least the perceived need for explanation, in academic analysis of immigration. This is the almost inevitable result of the fact that the "alien" is the nucleus around which the comprehensive immigration law, the Immigration and Nationality Act of 1952 (INA),[8] is built. At the same time, "aliens" and "illegal aliens" are terms invoked with enthusiasm by restrictionists who decry the current levels of immigration to the United States.

Race as a social construction has been thoroughly analyzed.[9] The "alien" is socially constructed as well. Fabricated out of whole cloth, the "alien" represents a body of rules passed by Congress and reinforced by popular culture. It is society, with the assistance of the law, that defines who is an "alien," an institutionalized "other," and who is not. It is society, through Congress and the courts, that determines which rights to afford "aliens." There is no inherent requirement, however, that society create or maintain a category of "aliens." We could, following the general operation of the public education and tax systems in the United States, dole out political rights and obligations depending on residence in the community. Indeed, a few scholars have advocated extending the franchise to noncitizen residents of this country, as did a number of states and localities early in the twentieth century.[10]

Like the social construction of race, which helps to legitimize racial subordination, the construction of the "alien" has helped justify the limitation on noncitizen rights imposed by our legal system. "Alien" terminology helps rationalize harsh, perhaps inhumane, treatment of persons from other countries.[11] Consider the terms of the public debate: Faceless "illegal aliens" invade the nation, and we must stop them or be destroyed. Such images help animate, invigorate, and reinforce the move to bolster immigration enforcement efforts and seal the borders.

The images that "alien" terminology creates have more far-reaching, often subtle, racial consequences. Federal and state laws regularly, and lawfully, discriminate against "aliens."[12] This discrimination is sanctioned by the Constitution, which stipulates, for example, that the president must be a "natural born citizen."[13] In contrast, governmental reliance on racial classifications is generally subjected to strict scrutiny and is, under most circumstances, considered unconstitutional.[14] Because a majority of immigrants are people of color,[15] "alienage" classifications may be employed as a convenient proxy for race. Discrimination against immigrants allows people of color to be disproportionately disadvantaged.

The value of citizenship is nothing new to U.S. law. On the eve of the Civil War, for example, the Supreme Court held that Dred Scott, a black man suing for his freedom, was not a "citizen" and therefore could not invoke the diversity of citizenship jurisdiction of the federal courts.[16] By denying Scott citizenship and thus the right of access to the federal courts, the Court, in effect, ruled that freed blacks, like slaves, were not full members of the national community. Thus, manipulation of citizenship status based on race has a lengthy, if not illustrious, history in U.S. law.

The comprehensive immigration statute, the INA, defines an "alien" as "any person not a citizen or national of the United States."[17] Although the definition is bland on the whole, the word "alien" alone brings forth rich imagery. The word evokes the image of space invaders[18] as depicted on television and in film. Popular culture reinforces the idea that "aliens" may be killed with impunity; in fact, if not, "they" will destroy the world as we know it. Synonyms for "alien" include "stranger, intruder, interloper, . . . outsider, [and] barbarian,"[19] all terms that justify severe measures in the name of self-protection. In effect, the term "alien" serves to dehumanize persons. We have few, if any, legal obligations to "alien" outsiders to the community; we have obligations only to persons. Persons have rights, whereas "aliens" do not.

Consider this phenomenon in concrete terms. If we think that people who come to the United States from another nation are hardworking and "good," it is difficult to treat them harshly. If we consider them to be foreign criminals who sap finite public resources and damage the environment, it is far easier to rationalize their harsh treatment. Understanding these different images is important to our understanding of the ongoing political debate about undocumented immigration. In 1989, while he served as western regional commissioner of the INS in charge of border enforcement in the West, Harold Ezell (who was later a sponsor of California Proposition 187) had this to say about "illegal aliens": "If you catch 'em, you ought to clean 'em and fry 'em."[20] This dehumanizing characterization leaves no room for consideration of the human toll on undocumented immigrants who migrate to the United States: the often difficult decision to leave family, friends, and community, the arduous journey replete with dangers, and the uncertain status awaiting immigrants upon their arrival in this country.

The "Illegal Alien"

The most damning terminology for noncitizens is "illegal aliens," unquestionably an unpopular group in U.S. society. Although "alien" is found repeatedly in the INA, "illegal alien" is not.[21] "Illegal alien" is a pejorative term that implies criminality and suggests that punishment, not legal protection, under the law is due.[22] Nevertheless, it is common, if not standard, terminology in the modern public debate about undocumented immigration.

The "illegal alien" label is inaccurate and inadequate at several levels. Many nuances of immigration law make it extremely difficult to distinguish between an "illegal alien" and a "legal alien." For example, a person who has lived without documents in this country for a number of years may be eligible for relief from deportation and lawful permanent resident status. The individual may have children who were born in this country and are thus U.S. citizens; he or she may have a job and community ties here. It would be difficult to contend that this person, as an "illegal alien," is indistinguishable from a person who entered without inspection yesterday.

The vaguely defined but emotionally charged "illegal alien" terminology also fails to distinguish between types of undocumented persons in the United States. About half the undocumented immigrants in this country are people who crossed the border without inspection; about half are noncitizens who entered lawfully but overstayed their business, tourist, student, or other visas. The "illegal alien" in public discussion often refers not only generally to a person who enters the country without inspection but also specifically to a national of Mexico. The furor over "illegal aliens," especially in the Southwest, often constitutes a veiled attack on undocumented Mexicans, if not lawful Mexican immigrants and Mexican American citizens.

History teaches us that it is difficult to confine anti-"alien" sentiment to any one segment of the immigrant community (such as to undocumented immigrants only).[23] This is evidenced by the reduction of public benefits to all categories of noncitizens that took place in the 1990s (see Chapter 4). In 1996, on the heels of the passage of Proposition 187, which focused on reducing benefits to undocumented persons, Congress enacted welfare reform legislation that greatly limited legal immigrants' eligibility for public benefit programs. Nativist outbursts have consistently failed to make the fine legal distinctions among members of outsider groups that are the craft of lawyers and policy makers.

"Aliens," Race, and Mexicans

Immigrant status has not always been linked to race. Today, however, "aliens" are increasingly equated with racial minorities. As one commentator succinctly observed, "[T]he discourse of legal [immigration] status permits coded discussion in which listeners will understand that reference is being made, not to aliens in the abstract, but to the particular foreign group that is the principal focus of current hostility."[24]

An important first association between "aliens" and racial minorities can be seen in the foundational immigration cases that allowed for the exclusion and deportation of Chinese persons in the late 1800s. In the early part of the twentieth century, some states, including California and Washington, passed laws known as the "alien land laws" that barred "aliens ineligible to citizenship" from owning certain real property. This facially neutral phrase was borrowed from the immigration and naturalization laws, which prohibited most nonwhite persons from becoming citizens. The borrowed terminology resulted in the states' effective exclusion of certain nonwhites from eligibility to own real property. These laws were undisputedly directed at persons of Japanese ancestry.[25]

Since 1965, when Congress repealed the national origins quota system, there has been a sharp increase in the proportion of racial minorities in the immigrant stream to the United States. Not coincidentally, the "alien" has increasingly become associated with racial minorities in the modern debate over immigration. The words "alien" and "illegal alien" today carry subtle racial connotations. The dominant image of the "alien" is often an undocumented Mexican or some other person of color, perhaps a Haitian, Chinese, Cuban, or Arab or Muslim person from a developing nation. Treating racial minorities unfavorably on the ground that they are "aliens" or "illegal aliens" allows us to insulate ourselves from certain groups of persons that we view as racially or otherwise different without perceiving ourselves as racist.[26]

Concern about "illegal aliens" in the United States has long dominated debate over immigration reform. "The illegal alien is said to sneak into the United States, insinuate himself into our midst, hide, remain without asking permission. The introjection language, language of overstepping, is both literal and unmistakable."[27] Although the term "illegal alien" is seemingly race neutral, we have no difficulty discerning which noncitizens provoke concern. Examination of the use of the terminology in context reveals that, particularly in the Southwest, the term refers to undocumented Mexicans, playing into stereotypes of Mexicans as criminals[28]—although it better masks nativist sympathies than "wetbacks," the popular vernacular that it replaced.[29] The link between "illegal aliens" and Mexican citizens is often an unstated assumption. The courts, with little explanation, have frequently approached the "illegal immigration situation" as an exclusively Mexican problem.[30]

According to the best estimate of the INS, however, only 50 to 60 percent of the undocumented population in the United States is of Mexican origin.[31] Still, all too often, the public debate treats undocumented immigrants as exclusively Mexican. Conversely, there is no acknowledgment of the existence of undocumented *white* "aliens." In recent years, the INS has estimated that three of the top ten nations of origin for undocumented immigrants are Canada, Poland, and Ireland.[32] A 1993 study by the state of New York estimated that, contrary to images of predominantly Chinese and Central American undocumented immigrants in New York, the state's three largest undocumented groups were from Ecuador, Italy, and Poland.[33]

U.S. Supreme Court decisions, still focusing on the "illegal alien" as a Mexican immigrant, are replete with negative imagery about undocumented immigration from Mexico.[34] Such immigration, in the Court's view, is a "colossal problem"[35] posing "enormous difficulties"[36] and "formidable law enforcement problems."[37] One justice observed that immigration from Mexico is "virtually uncontrollable."[38] In 1975, Chief Justice Warren Burger stated that the nation "is powerless to stop the tide of illegal aliens—and dangerous drugs—that daily and freely crosses our 2000-mile southern boundary."[39] Even Justice William Brennan, a well-known liberal jurist, made the following statement in his analysis of the lawfulness of a workplace raid in southern California: "No one doubts that the presence of large numbers of undocumented aliens in the country creates law enforcement problems of titanic proportions."[40]

Ignoring the heated debate among social scientists about the contribution of undocumented immigrants to the economy,[41] the Supreme Court has stated unequivocally that undocumented Mexicans "create significant economic and social problems, competing with citizens and legal resident aliens for jobs, and generating extra demand for social services."[42] Such perceptions inspired Chief Justice Burger to add an extraordinary appendix to a Supreme Court opinion that described in detail "the illegal alien problem"[43]; the appendix focused exclusively on unauthorized migration from Mexico.

Given the intractable nature of the "problem," the Supreme Court permits exceptions to the law to allow efforts to reduce undocumented immigration from Mexico to proceed unimpeded. For example, the Court recognized that special Fourth Amendment rules apply to efforts "to intercept illegal aliens" and acknowledged the formidable law enforcement difficulties "posed by the northbound tide of illegal entrants into the United States."[44] This recognition by the Court permits the racial profiling in immigration enforcement analyzed in Chapter 2. In

2002, the Court held that, although an employer violated the federal labor laws in firing an employee for union organizing activities, the law barred the National Labor Relations Board from awarding back pay to the undocumented worker; thus, when employers violate federal labor law, "illegal aliens" are not eligible for the compensation to which a U.S. citizen or lawful immigrant would be entitled.[45]

Concerns about "illegal aliens" from Mexico and other developing nations influence policy makers. For example, in arguing for an overhaul of immigration enforcement in 1981, Attorney General William French Smith proclaimed, "We have lost control of our borders."[46] Around that time, the Reagan administration began to interdict Haitians who fled political turmoil and to detain all Central Americans who sought asylum from political persecution.[47] The public perception that illegal immigration was "out of control" motivated President Bill Clinton to use high-tech military-style operations to increase enforcement efforts along the U.S.-Mexican border.[48] This perception also prompted congressional action designed to bolster border enforcement. As the government fortified the southern border with Mexico, reports of undocumented immigrants being smuggled across the northern border with Canada did little to provoke public concern—at least until it was learned that terrorists had used the northern border to gain entry into the United States.[49]

The use of "illegal alien" as code for "Mexicans" was evident in the debate over California's Proposition 187, which has been discussed throughout this book. Consider the following argument in favor of the measure that appeared in the pamphlet distributed to registered voters:

WE CAN STOP ILLEGAL ALIENS. . . .
Proposition 187 will be the first giant stride in ultimately ending the ILLEGAL ALIEN invasion. . . .
It has been estimated that ILLEGAL ALIENS are costing taxpayers in excess of 5 billion dollars a year. . . .
Welfare, medical and educational benefits are the magnets that draw these ILLEGAL ALIENS across our borders. . . .
Should our Senior Citizens be denied full service under Medi-Cal to subsidize the cost of ILLEGAL ALIENS? . . .
We are American, by birth or naturalization. . . .
[A]s a final slap on the face, they voted to continue free prenatal care for ILLEGAL ALIENS!
Vote YES ON PROPOSITION 187. ENOUGH IS ENOUGH![50]

Natives of Mexico constitute the largest immigrant group in California and the nation and have long faced discrimination in the state. The disfavored status of Mexican immigrants therefore comes as no surprise, and there is no uncertainty as to which group of "illegal aliens" was targeted by the proponents of Proposition 187.

Policy makers and the courts rely heavily on "alien" terminology as a rhetorical tool to rationalize harsh treatment of noncitizens. The deplorable treatment of Haitians who were fleeing political violence in their homeland in 1992 demonstrates the powerful legal impact of "alien" terminology on racial minorities. In May 1992, President George H. Bush issued an executive order titled Interdiction of Illegal Aliens, which—flouting international law[51]—authorized the repatriation of Haitians without inquiry into the grounds for their fear of persecution if returned to their homeland.[52] Although the order referred generally to "illegal aliens," President Bush, and later President Clinton, implemented the repatriation policies exclusively against persons who fled Haiti.[53] The Supreme Court decision upholding this radical policy is no less sterile than the executive order; it emphasized at the outset that only the rights of "aliens" were at stake.

It has become standard for the Supreme Court to uphold discrimination against "aliens" by stressing that "Congress regularly makes rules that would be unacceptable if applied to citizens."[54] The federal government's decision to detain some Cubans for an indefinite period of time is an extreme example. In the 1980 Mariel boatlift, Fidel Castro allowed numerous Cuban citizens to leave for the United States. When Cuba refused to accept the return of some Cuban citizens convicted of crimes, the United States held the noncitizens in indefinite detention, often in maximum-security federal penitentiaries. In one case that challenged the detention, the court emphasized in the very first line of its opinion, "Alexis Barrera-Echavarria is an alien."[55] In the end, the court upheld the indefinite detention.[56]

Because the modern immigration laws do not manifestly discriminate on the basis of race, they can be defended as "color blind." By the same token, most restrictionists today deny that racial concerns motivate their objections to immigration. They complicate the debate by pointing to other alleged impacts of immigration. They contend, for example, that "aliens" take jobs from U.S. citizens, contribute to overpopulation that damages the environment, overconsume public benefits, and commit crimes.[57]

Unlike in anti-immigrant eras of the past, discrimination on the basis of race runs counter to modern sensibilities and the current state of the law.[58] Consequently, race is ordinarily submerged in the public discourse about immigration. The persistent surfacing of racist statements in the immigration debate, however, clearly demonstrates that, at some level, racial concerns influence restrictionist sentiments.[59]

The Impact of "Alien" Terminology

Legal construction of the "alien" has facilitated the rationalization of harsh treatment of noncitizens of color. In modern times, "alien" imagery is often merely code for racial minority status. For too long, the racial impacts of legal rules and fictions have been obscured and ignored. We must remain vigilant of the use of language that masks the human impacts of the immigration laws and their enforcement. The difficult choices that we face must be made with the full realization that those who are affected by them in fundamental ways are people, not faceless, inhuman, demon "aliens."

In analyzing the term "alien," we have seen how it can obscure invidious racial discrimination. In addition, however, foreign radicals and terrorists are detained and deported as "aliens" who threaten the national interest. Impoverished "aliens" are not allowed to enter the country and may be deported if they suffer economic setbacks while living in the United States. "Criminal aliens," perhaps the most disfavored group, targeted both by those who are hostile toward criminals and those who are hostile toward immigrants, have lost such cherished rights as judicial review through acts of Congress. Immigrant women, often invisible to the public eye, have been not only disadvantaged by the immigration laws but also left open to exploitation once in the United States. Lesbian and gay immigrants, like lesbians and gay men in U.S. society in general, have suffered the effects of homophobia, including classification as "psychopathic personalities" and "sexual deviants." "Aliens," as the terminology intends, can be stripped of rights as the U.S. government sees fit.

The Latina/o Diaspora

The term "alien" obscures but cannot hide the issue of race in immigration. The changing demographics of immigration in the United States since 1965 have contributed to new civil rights challenges. Increasingly diverse communities of color live in this country, adding to the modern civil rights agenda in new and complex ways and transforming old civil rights concerns.[60] It is likely that two particular demographic changes tied to immigration will forever change the future of civil rights law: the growing Latina/o population in the United States, fueled in large part by immigration, and, more generally, the increasing overlap between "immigrants" and "racial minorities."

Migration from Mexico to the United States was a fact of life for the entire twentieth century, with the flow of migrants accelerating as the new millennium approached. Mexicans currently constitute about one-fifth of the legal immigrants each year and more than one-half of the undocumented immigrant population in the United States.[61] The civil rights of Mexican and other Latin American immigrants and of the established Latina/o community in this country have been affected by the efforts to regulate migration from Mexico. At this point, the full ramifications of the Mexican diaspora with respect to civil rights in the United States have not yet been fully appreciated or realized.

Mexican migration today affects the entire United States, not just one particular region. Many Mexican migrants now journey far beyond the Southwest, a territory once part of Mexico and the traditional home to many Mexican Americans. The demand for cheap labor and emerging social networks and family ties have pulled Mexican migrants to locations across the country. Burgeoning migrant communities can be found throughout the South, Midwest, and East—as far as Siler City, North Carolina; Rogers, Arkansas; Atlanta, Georgia; and Farmingville, New York. Over the 1990s, Memphis, Tennessee, saw nearly 300 percent growth in its Latina/o population. Latinas/os now constitute 12 percent of the population of Milwaukee, Wisconsin, and 26 percent of the population of Chicago. In the nation's heartland, Mexican immigrants have swelled the ranks of poultry and meatpacking workers.[62]

Today's Mexican migrants do not fit the stereotype of the poor, rural Mexican citizen who comes to the United States to work in agriculture. Many migrants come from urban areas, and once they are in the United States, they are more likely to find jobs in commercial service industries than in agriculture. About half of the migrants from Mexico have a high school diploma or a college degree.[63] Mexican migrants have thus changed the nature of the labor and employment issues in the United States.

Moreover, by moving back and forth between nations, many Mexican migrants have developed transnational identities, maintaining old ties with their native country as they develop new ties in the United States. The geographic proximity of their homeland, which permits relatively inexpensive and easy movement between nations, differentiates this group of migrants from their European and Asian predecessors. Social networks facilitate migration from towns in Mexico to particular cities in the United States.[64] "Hometown clubs" composed of natives of Mexican towns who live in the United States provide resources to fund hometown improvements and to assist hometown residents who seek to journey north.[65] The law acknowledges and facilitates the development of transnational allegiances; dual nationality is now recognized by both the U.S. and Mexican governments.[66]

When the border enforcement craze of the 1990s hit new levels after September 11, the flow between nations temporarily diminished to some degree, later returning to pre–September 11 levels.[67] An unforseen consequence of the implementation of heightened border enforcement may well have been an increase in the undocumented population, with migrants viewing the return to Mexico as too risky and opting instead to stay put in the United States.[68]

The long-range impacts of the emergence of transnational identities are far from certain. Some may result in a diminished commitment to the United States on the part of long-term residents from Mexico who maintain allegiances to their homeland.[69] This diminished commitment may, in turn, limit their integration into the mainstream and inhibit their feeling of "belonging to America."[70] At the same time, however, many persons of Mexican ancestry in the United States have long held deep cultural and other affiliations with their homeland and have long felt alienated from the U.S. mainstream. Consequently, the future impacts of the changing transnational identities of many Mexican migrants are as yet unclear.

New Enforcement Measures

Despite the fact that migrants respond to the demand for labor by U.S. employers, immigration enforcement efforts have pursued Mexican immigrants to all corners of the United States. These immigration measures are consistent with the view expressed by influential Harvard professor Samuel Huntington that immigration from Mexico is the real immigration problem. In Huntington's words, "Mexican immigration is a unique, disturbing, and looming challenge to our cultural integrity, our national identity, and potentially to our future as a country."[71]

INS operations designed to remove undocumented workers (many of them Mexican) from the workplace and the country have provoked controversy in Nebraska.[72] Local police in the interior of the country have cooperated with the INS to enforce the immigration laws in ways that have discriminated against Latinas/os.[73] Alleged racial profiling of Latinas/os in Ohio resulted in a lawsuit,[74] while police roadblocks to enforce motor vehicle laws against undocumented Mexican workers in Kentucky sparked controversy.[75] Anti-immigrant sentiment has also grown in cities as they have experienced the emergence of Mexican migrant communities.[76] Upstate New York, for example, has seen hate crimes directed at Mexican immigrants.[77] African Americans have joined whites in expressing concern about the impacts of immigration.[78] Vigilante groups have used force against undocumented Mexican immigrants, frequently with tragic results.

In the midst of expanded Mexican migration combined with new enforcement efforts, the Mexican government has advocated the "regularization" of the immigration status of undocumented Mexican migrants in the United States; the United States, in turn, has considered a new

"guest worker" program.[79] In the last large-scale guest worker program
—the Bracero Program, which lasted from the 1940s to the early 1960s—
wage and condition protections for temporary workers were honored
more in the breach than in the observance.[80] Indeed, in 2001, decades
after the program formally ended, Mexican *braceros* sued banks and the
U.S. government for 10 percent of the workers' wages that employers
withheld as mandatory savings but never provided to the workers.[81]

Practically speaking, absent the enforcement of formal labor protections, a new guest worker program may differ from the current "system"
(in which undocumented workers lack full labor and employment law
protections) only in providing employers with easier access to an inexpensive, government-sponsored labor supply.[82] Moreover, a guest
worker arrangement raises the serious moral concern that migrant workers would offer their labor when needed but could be returned to their
homelands when their labor was no longer needed; they would, in effect, constitute a disposable labor force enforced by law. As in the current limited temporary worker programs, most of the workers probably
would be people of color from developing nations.[83] Consequently, any
new guest worker program that allowed for disposable labor would almost certainly possess racial caste qualities.

If history is an accurate guide, immigration and immigration enforcement will remain a civil rights trouble spot in the United States. Various regions will continue to grapple with the long-standing conflict between employers' demand for cheaper labor, local residents' negative
reaction to the social change brought by immigrants, and immigrants' demand for fair treatment. The civil rights fallout from the clash is likely
to remain with us for the indefinite future.

It is important to note that the Mexican diaspora is only part of a
larger demographic shift in the U.S. population. The focus on Mexican
immigration results in large part from the fact that persons of Mexican
ancestry constitute the nation's largest immigrant population. Early in
the twenty-first century, Latinas/os will become, if they have not become already, the nation's largest minority group. Census 2000 revealed
that Hispanics currently constitute over 12.5 percent of the total U.S.
population, or almost 35 million people, roughly approximating the num-

ber of African Americans in this country.[84] Moreover, the migration of persons from Asia, which has increased dramatically since 1965, as well as from other regions of the world (such as Africa, the Caribbean, and Central and South America), has also deeply affected the civil rights agenda. As it has in the past, the very notion of what constitutes a "civil rights" issue promises to change.[85]

The "New" Civil Rights

Changing demographics arguably impact everything from education[86] to voting rights litigation and electoral reapportionment[87] to employment opportunities[88] to law enforcement.[89] As various communities adjust, this change will almost inevitably cause tensions. The 2001 Los Angeles mayoral election, in which 80 percent of Latina/o voters chose a Latino candidate and 80 percent of African American voters chose a white candidate, exemplifies the stark political divisions that can exist between minority communities.[90] African Americans, Latinas/os, Asian Americans, Native Americans, and other racial minorities have histories of treating each other as competition.[91] Although coalitions on political issues are possible (in fact, at times necessary), they require careful development and great sensitivity.

This latest era of immigration fits into a long history of Mexican immigration and the resulting Mexican civil rights issues in the United States (see Chapter 2). Immigrants from Mexico have historically been subjected to civil rights abuses and economic exploitation. The question is whether the law in the future can serve to ameliorate this discrimination.

An increase in the percentage of racial minorities in the nation's population, as well as an increase in the sheer number of minority groups, will unquestionably impact the civil rights agenda. Civil rights activists have begun to appreciate the relevance of immigrants to the struggle for racial and economic justice.[92] Despite a long history of restrictionist stances dating at least as far back as the Chinese exclusion laws of the late 1800s, labor unions now wage campaigns to organize immigrant, particularly Latina/o, workers.[93] In a dramatic change in its position on immigration, the American Federation of Labor and Congress of Industrial Workers (AFL-CIO) has endorsed an amnesty for undocumented immigrants. The move reflected the view that the future of organized labor lies in organizing all workers rather than seeking to bar immigrant laborers from entering the country.[94] Civil rights organizations fight for the rights of day laborers (many of them undocumented immigrants) to seek work[95] and to foster humane conditions in the garment industry.[96] Even regulation of the use of leaf blowers implicates social justice concerns for immigrant gardeners.[97] Similarly, Latina/o street vendors have engaged in struggles for their economic rights.[98]

The overlap of race and class concerns for immigrants, as well as for people of color generally, suggests that race scholars should "make common cause with the incipient movement for economic democracy."[99] Social and economic class concerns have long played prominent roles in the Latina/o struggle for justice.[100] With a growing immigrant population of color concentrated in low-wage jobs, we might expect that class and race will prove central to future efforts toward social change.

Demographic changes also have brought other civil rights issues to the forefront. Because language overlaps with race and national origin, the regulation of language has increasingly been considered a civil rights matter.[101] Moreover, new civil rights issues arise from immigrants' cultural differences. For example, Mexican immigrants have been gouged with deceptively high charges for wiring money to family and friends in Mexico.[102] Poor and working-class Mexican immigrants in need of legal services, often for immigration matters, have been easy prey for fraudulent *notarios*, who are the equivalent of lawyers in Mexico but lack that status and authority in the United States.[103] With respect to certain criminal charges, recognition of the "cultural defense"—and other efforts at cultural sensitivity in the law—for immigrants has generated public controversy.[104] The abuse of mail-order brides (see Chapter 6), usually immigrant women of color from the developing world, has also grown as a civil rights concern.

Matters routine to most U.S. citizens may amount to serious civil rights grievances for certain immigrant communities. For example, the denial of drivers' licenses to undocumented Mexicans exacerbates fears of arrest and deportation, limits access to jobs, and generally increases immigrant vulnerability to exploitation in the workplace.[105] In 2001, without acknowledging these impacts, the Supreme Court rejected a class-action suit brought by Martha Sandoval. Sandoval, a lawful permanent resident from Mexico who speaks primarily Spanish, challenged Alabama's English-language requirement for testing for a driver's license,[106] which disproportionately impacted minority communities. The state made no provisions for Spanish speakers but provided testing accommodations for illiterate and disabled English speakers.[107]

A fundamental change to the conception of civil rights flows directly from the demographic shift in the U.S. population. The immigrant population's large percentage of people of color increases the overlap between minorities and immigrants. It is important to note that the courts have failed to acknowledge this overlap, with significant practical consequences. Although the law tolerates discrimination against immigrants within limits,[108] it generally prohibits discrimination on the basis of race.[109] For example, although a citizenship requirement for a job as a police officer might withstand legal scrutiny, a racial requirement would not. Because of the overlap of immigrant status and racial minority status in the modern United States, discrimination based on immigrant status may in fact mask unlawful racial discrimination.

To date, the courts have failed to give careful consideration to the immigrant/racial minority overlap in the interpretation and application of the antidiscrimination laws. For example, in *Espinoza* v. *Farah Manufacturing Co.*,[110] the Supreme Court held that Title VII of the Civil Rights Act of 1964, which bars discrimination in employment on the basis of race, color, religion, sex, or national origin, did not prohibit discrimination based on citizenship status. A lawful immigrant residing in San Antonio, Texas, who had immigrated from Mexico, was thus lawfully denied a job because she was not a U.S. citizen.[111] In Texas and much of the Southwest, immigrants from Mexico—by far the largest immigrant group in a state that borders that nation—are (as employers who have adopted the citizenship rule could clearly foresee) most directly affected by this decision. As we have noted, citizenship in certain circumstances may serve as a proxy for race. To ensure that the law does not invite invidious racial or national origin discrimination,[112] greater sensitivity and more careful analysis than those offered by the Supreme Court in *Espinoza* are clearly required.

Similarly, the courts are split on whether private discrimination based on immigration status is covered by Section 1981, which provides, in relevant part, that "[a]ll persons within the jurisdiction of the United States shall have the same right . . . to make and enforce contracts, to sue, be parties, give evidence, and to the full and equal benefit of all laws and proceedings for the security of persons and property as is enjoyed by white citizens."[113] Not coincidentally, the leading cases on the question involve noncitizens of color.[114] Noticeably absent from the judicial analysis is recognition of the overlap between race and immigrant status. Courts called on to apply Section 1981 should be sensitive to the fact that immigrant status may, in certain circumstances, substitute for race.

In sum, antidiscrimination law must come to grips with the changes in the racial demographics of the United States. Because "immigrants" today most often means "immigrants of color," the law—if it truly remains committed to eradicating racial discrimination—must look more carefully at immigration classifications to discern whether they mask discriminatory motives. The current "race" issues in immigration are simply the latest chapter in the long saga of U.S. immigration history. Race and racial difference of immigrants have influenced many of the exclusions in the U.S. immigration laws. (See Chapter 2.) Race and class of Chinese immigrants resulted in their exclusion under the immigration laws beginning in the nineteenth century. Southern and eastern European immigration culminated in the Immigration Act of 1924 and the national origins quota system, which responded to overlapping concerns about race, political extremism, poverty, and criminality. These "new" immigrants of the early twentieth century were viewed as racially different (and inferior); poor; and inclined toward anarchism, communism, and other anti-American political ideologies. Similarly, the modern Arab and Muslim deportation and exclusion efforts focus on many of these differences.

The immigration laws affect the civil rights of other groups as well. Immigrant women have historically been penalized as presumptive public charges or prostitutes or for sharing the undesirable racial, political, and class qualities of their husbands. The exclusions have often been enforced with racial intents and impacts. Immigrant women—many of whom are women of color—have been liberally admitted as spouses of white U.S. citizens. However, the legal conditions for this admission, such as the marriage fraud amendments of 1986, have at times enhanced the possibilities for domestic violence and abuse. Immigrant women— particularly immigrant women of color from developing nations—have frequently been ignored, facilitating exploitation in the garment industry and other jobs, the burgeoning mail-order bride industry, and the trafficking of women for the sex trade.

Lesbians and gay men were first marked for exclusion and deportation in the INA, passed by Congress in 1952, at the height of the Cold War, when homosexuals were viewed under the law as deviants prone to communism. The immigration laws exemplify the potential double penalization of socially unpopular groups; gay and lesbian immigrants, for example, were penalized as both homosexuals and immigrants. As the social attitude toward lesbians and gay men changed in the United States, the desire to exclude and deport them changed as well.

Future Possibilities

This book has studied the relationship between the immigration laws and the civil rights of various minority groups in the United States. Throughout U.S. history, the exclusion and deportation provisions of the U.S. immigration laws have acted as a "magic mirror" into the domestic prejudices and biases in the nation's heart and soul. The immigration laws reflect, and at the same time help shape, national identity. These laws have created the modern racial demography of the United States.

U.S. citizens who are racial minorities, political dissidents, poor and working-class people, criminals, women, and lesbians and gay men have historically been disfavored under the law. Although the law has offered protections to U.S. citizens of many different minority groups, throughout U.S. history, noncitizen minorities have been sporadically attacked and punished, often mercilessly. Deportation, detention, and penalization of particular disfavored groups of noncitizens have commonly occurred. The nation looks back on these eras with regret, but regularly repeats the same mistakes.

Many of the disadvantaged groups intersect and overlap. In the late nineteenth century, the United States excluded Chinese immigrants from the country for reasons of race, class, gender, and alleged criminality. Many immigrants today, such as Mexicans, Haitians, and Chinese, face similar stereotypes, now refined to avoid jarring modern sensibilities. Because legitimate social concerns may obscure racial animus, immigration laws can be used as a tool to discriminate on grounds that are generally considered impermissible. It is a difficult, if not impossible, task to separate the legitimate from the invidious.

U.S. immigration law represents a national Rorschach test of the nation's civil rights sensibilities. With few legal constraints, Congress can act with impunity toward the groups that are most politically unpopular. Sadly, U.S. generosity toward citizens of the world belies the harsh underside to the nation's immigration history. This history suggests the need for circumspection in considering current immigration policies.

What can we do in the future to avoid repeating the unfortunate treatment of immigrants that plagues our national memory? "Open borders," embraced by some scholars, would prevent pitfalls ordinarily associated with immigration regulation.[115] However, this liberal approach appears unlikely to garner popular political support in the United States in the foreseeable future.

Fears of mass migration of poor people of color have always shaped U.S. immigration law and policy. Opposition to liberalization of the immigration laws is likely to continue because of the post–September 11 terrorism concerns that have produced a number of immigration restrictions. Absent a change in the conventional wisdom, a significant opening of the U.S. borders seems unlikely.

The European Union Model

Europe has experimented with a regional labor migration program, a kind of limited open border, which commentators have viewed as a possible model for the United States.[116] Following liberalization of trade between European Union (EU) nations, the EU created a system of labor migration between member countries. The movement of labor revolutionized migration in Europe.

Still, the EU is not without its own migration and civil rights problems. "Fortress Europe" has emerged to limit entry into the new EU.[117] As a condition to joining the EU, for example, Spain introduced an immigration law designed to bar North Africans from entry to allay northern European fears of a mass migration. Undocumented migration and accompanying deaths on the Mediterranean Sea have resulted. Enhanced border enforcement has been aimed at keeping unwanted migrants—poor, unskilled, Muslims, for example—out of the EU. Moreover, civil rights of immigrants, particularly North Africans, have frequently been violated. Xenophobic violence has occurred with regularity, and anti-immigrant politicians have gained worldwide attention.

The United States could conceivably move in a direction similar to that of the EU. The North American Free Trade Agreement (NAFTA), which went into effect in 1994, liberalized trade between the United Sates, Canada, and Mexico. However, because the United States had insisted that migration between the member nations be kept off the bargaining table, the trade partners studiously avoided addressing the issue. Still, as occurred with the EU, NAFTA may lead to discussion of possible labor migration between member nations at some point in the future.

However, relatively minor efforts in the direction of freer migration between the United States and Mexico have gone nowhere to date. Although economic considerations arguably militate in favor of freer migration between nations,[118] race, culture, and class serve as powerful social counterweights to movements toward integration. The United States as a nation has not shown a willingness to consider freer labor migration within the nations covered by NAFTA.[119] Samuel Huntington has offered a bleak assessment of labor migration between the United States and Mexico: "If over one million Mexican soldiers crossed the border Americans would treat it as a major threat to their national security and react accordingly. The invasion of over one million Mexican civilians . . . would be a comparable threat to American societal security, and Americans should react against it with comparable vigor."[120]

Before September 11, 2001, the United States and Mexico appeared to be approaching serious discussions of a migration agreement. Mexico's newly elected president, Vicente Fox, and President George W. Bush were engaged in talks about a temporary worker program, regularizing the status of undocumented Mexican immigrants in the United States, and related migration matters. September 11 ended those discussions. Since that fateful day, U.S. immigration policy has moved away from loosening restrictions to enhance labor mobility but instead has focused its efforts on tightening the borders in the name of fighting terrorism.

Short-term crisis management in the wake of September 11 aside, a long-term solution to migration with Mexico must be pursued. Because of the proximity of the nations, the economic opportunities in the United States, and the family and social networks created by generations of migration from Mexico, migration pressures—and actual migration—are likely continue for the indefinite future. Policy options must take into consideration the fact that, in light of these powerful social forces, militarization of the border is not likely to end undocumented migration to the United States. In the current system, undocumented immigrants risk life and limb to evade border checkpoints and simply exist below the radar screen once in the United States. A system that tracks and regularizes the stream of migrants seems more likely to enhance border security and ensure orderly administration of the laws.

Expansion of Legal Protections for Immigrants

Historically, U.S. immigration policy has moved from crisis to crisis. Immigration law has reflected biases toward and stereotypes of immigrants who were unpopular during particular eras. The courts and law have been largely irrelevant. With few legal constraints, the president and Congress have been permitted to act with impunity in the treatment of noncitizens. Any far-reaching immigration reform would require both visionary leadership and skillful political maneuvering.

As many influential commentators have contended, one limited possible legal solution would be to make the law more relevant to noncitizens and immigrants by subjecting both immigration law and the conduct of the U.S. government to constitutional scrutiny. This would require that the U.S. government keep its conduct consistent with the Constitution and, concomitantly, recognize legal rights for noncitizens. Current moves toward greater respect for the rights of noncitizens must be expanded to include recognition of full legal rights for noncitizens and a full review of the immigration laws for substantive fairness and equality.

Judicial review of the constitutionality of executive branch treatment of noncitizens would contribute toward a much-needed dialogue between Congress and the courts on the fair and proper treatment of noncitizens, like the dialogue that exists with respect to the rights of minority groups in the United States. Currently, the political branches are encouraged to pursue the popular prejudice of the day, with noncitizens serving as vulnerable scapegoats for the current problems facing the nation. Lack of judicial oversight promotes extreme policies, which are particularly extreme during times of national crisis.

Of course, judicial review is not a fail-safe device for protecting legal rights. History is replete with examples of hate-motivated conduct toward minority citizens that has been left unchecked by the courts. Without judicial review, however, noncitizens, particularly those who share characteristics with disadvantaged members of U.S. society, are left to the whimsy of the political branches. The checks and balances that are a cornerstone of the government established by our nation's founders simply do not currently exist for noncitizens.

In sum, internal political pressures facilitate the penalization of unpopular outsiders whose citizen counterparts we cannot attack with impunity. Law—or, more accurately, the lack of law—permits U.S. society to act out its aggressions toward noncitizens. Law and judicial review could moderate this aggression, but they cannot replace the vigilance needed to protect the rights of the most unpopular noncitizens. Political awareness and action are essential to any effort to put a stop to the U.S. government's harsh treatment of its immigrants.

Racial discrimination, witch-hunts for political dissidents, marginalization of the poor, penalization of the "criminal alien," marginalization of women, and discrimination on the basis of sexual orientation are all part of U.S. immigration history. Years pass before we begin to see the errors of our ways. By then, it is too late for the noncitizens who have already been caught in harm's way. We must strive to replace harsh, punitive, and invidiously discriminatory policies with policies that foster fair and equal treatment of noncitizens. We must create an immigration history that reflects the egalitarian principles on which our great nation is based.

Rather than repeat the mistakes of past history, we should learn from them and strive to remove the racism, political censorship, classism, sexism, and homophobia from the U.S. immigration laws. One way to begin that project would be to experiment with allowing labor migration within North America, already a region that sees considerable migration. A more daring test of the U.S. commitment to equality and freedom would be to abolish the immigration laws in their entirety (with narrow exceptions for immigrants who present a clear and present danger to the national security).[121] Only then will the United States even begin to approximate the promise to the world inscribed on the Statue of Liberty.

Notes

Chapter 1: Immigration and Civil Rights in the United States

1. Emma Lazarus, "The New Colossus" (1883), *reprinted in* EMMA LAZARUS: SELECTIONS FROM HER POETRY AND PROSE 48 (Morris Schappes ed., 1967).

2. *See* Juan F. Perea, *The Statue of Liberty: Notes from Behind the Gilded Door, in* IMMIGRANTS OUT! THE NEW NATIVISM AND THE ANTI-IMMIGRANT IMPULSE IN THE UNITED STATES 44 (Juan F. Perea ed., 1997).

3. *See* U.S. DEPARTMENT OF JUSTICE, 2001 STATISTICAL YEARBOOK OF THE IMMIGRATION AND NATURALIZATION SERVICE 16 (tbl 1) (2003).

4. 347 U.S. 483 (1954). *See generally* RICHARD KLUGER, SIMPLE JUSTICE: THE HISTORY OF BROWN V. BOARD OF EDUCATION AND BLACK AMERICA'S STRUGGLE FOR EQUALITY (1975).

5. *See* George A. Martínez, Race, Immigration Law and the "State of Nature" (Mar. 2002) (unpublished manuscript, on file with the author). *See generally* T. ALEXANDER ALEINIKOFF, SEMBLANCES OF SOVEREIGNTY: THE CONSTITUTION, THE STATE AND AMERICAN CITIZENSHIP (2002) (analyzing Supreme Court rulings that federal government had "plenary power" over immigration, Native American tribes, and territories); Sarah H. Cleveland, *Powers Inherent in Sovereignty: Indians, Aliens, Territories, and the Nineteenth Century Origins of Plenary Power over Foreign Affairs*, 81 TEXAS LAW REVIEW 1 (2002) (to the same effect); Natsu Taylor Saito, *Asserting Plenary Power over the "Other": Indians, Immigrants, Colonial Subjects, and Why U.S. Jurisprudence Needs to Incorporate International Law*, 20 YALE LAW AND POLICY REVIEW 427 (2002) (to the same effect).

6. *See generally* EDWIN J. ESCOBAR, RACE, POLICE, AND THE MAKING OF A POLITICAL IDENTITY: MEXICAN AMERICANS AND THE LOS ANGELES POLICE DEPARTMENT, 1900–1945 (1999).

7. *See* IZUMI HIROBE, JAPANESE PRIDE, AMERICAN PREJUDICE (2001) (discussing the negative impact in Japan of the 1924 law barring Japanese immigration to the United States).

8. *See* Mary Dudziak, *Desegregation as a Cold War Imperative*, 46 STANFORD LAW REVIEW 61 (1988).

9. *See* Sale v. Haitian Centers Council, Inc., 509 U.S. 918 (1993).

10. *See, for example,* MICHAEL OMI & HOWARD WINANT, RACIAL FORMATION IN THE UNITED STATES: FROM THE 1960s TO THE 1980s (2d ed. 1994); IAN F. HANEY LÓPEZ, WHITE BY LAW: THE LEGAL CONSTRUCTION OF RACE (1996).

11. *See generally* NOEL IGNATIEV, HOW THE IRISH BECAME WHITE (1995); Karen Brodkin Sacks, *How Did Jews Become White Folks? in* RACE 78 (Steven Gregory & Roger Sanjek eds., 1994); CRITICAL WHITE STUDIES: LOOKING BEHIND THE MIRROR (Richard Delgado & Jean Stefancic eds., 1997).

12. *See generally* JOHN HIGHAM, STRANGERS IN THE LAND: PATTERNS OF AMERICAN NATIVISM, 1860–1925 (3d ed. 1992).

13. *See generally* ANDREW HACKER, TWO NATIONS: BLACK AND WHITE, SEPARATE, HOSTILE, UNEQUAL (rev. ed. 1995).

14. *See* Padilla v. Bush, 233 F. Supp. 2d 564 (S.D.N.Y. 2002); *see also* Hamdi v. Rumsfeld, 316 F.3d 450 (4th Cir.2003) (reviewing claims of native-born U.S. citizen, Yaser Esam Hamdi, held as an "enemy combatant").

Chapter 2: Exclusion and Deportation of Racial Minorities

1. PETER BRIMELOW, ALIEN NATION: COMMON SENSE ABOUT AMERICA'S IMMIGRATION DISASTER (1995).

2. *See, for example,* Fiallo v. Bell, 430 U.S. 787, 792 (1977) (upholding gender and legitimacy classifications in immigration laws); Kleindienst v. Mandel, 408 U.S. 753, 765–67 (1972) (rejecting, on ideological grounds, a constitutional challenge to the denial of a nonimmigrant visa to a Marxist academic); Boutilier v. INS, 387 U.S. 118, 122–23 (1967) (allowing the exclusion of homosexuals). For debate about whether the doctrine has been abrogated *sub silentio*, compare Cornelia T.L. Pillard & T. Alexander Aleinikoff, *Skeptical Scrutiny of Plenary Power: Judicial and Executive Branch Decision Making in* Miller v. Albright, 1998 SUPREME COURT REVIEW 1 (contending that the latest Supreme Court decision requires revisitation of the plenary power doctrine); Peter J. Spiro, *Explaining the End of Plenary Power,* 16 GEORGETOWN IMMIGRATION LAW JOURNAL 339 (2002) (pointing to signs of the plenary power doctrine's demise) *and* Gabriel J. Chin, *Is There a Plenary Power Doctrine? A Tentative Apology and Prediction for Our Strange but Unexceptional Constitutional Immigration Law,* 14 GEORGETOWN IMMIGRATION LAW JOURNAL 257 (2000) (questioning the existence of the doctrine), *with* Gabriel J. Chin, *Segregation's Last Stronghold: Race Discrimination and the Constitutional Law of Immigration,* 46 UCLA LAW REVIEW 1 (1998) (advocating elimination of the plenary power doctrine) *and* Kevin R. Johnson, *Race and Immigration Law and Enforcement: A Response to* Is There a Plenary Power Doctrine? 14 GEORGETOWN IMMIGRATION LAW JOURNAL 289 (2000) (disputing the contention of the doctrine's demise).

3. *See, for example,* Mathews v. Diaz, 426 U.S. 67, 78–84 (1976) (upholding discrimination against lawful permanent residents in a federal medical benefits program).

4. *See, for example,* Brown v. Board of Education, 347 U.S. 483, 493 (1954).

5. Public Law No. 88-352, 78 Statutes at Large 241 (1964).

6. *See, for example,* Adarand Constructors, Inc. v. Peña, 515 U.S. 200, 225 (1995) (holding that all racial classifications, including those in a federal program designed

to foster minority enterprise, are subject to strict scrutiny); City of Richmond v. J.A. Croson Co., 488 U.S. 469, 498 (1989) (invalidating the city's minority business program as a violation of equal protection).

7. *See* United States v. Carolene Products Co., 304 U.S. 144, 152–53 n.4 (1938) (recognizing that "prejudice against discrete and insular minorities may be a special condition, which tends seriously to curtail the operation of those political processes ordinarily to be relied upon to protect minorities, and which may call for a correspondingly more searching judicial inquiry"). *See generally* JOHN HART ELY, DEMOCRACY AND DISTRUST (1980).

8. *See, for example,* DINESH D'SOUZA, THE END OF RACISM: PRINCIPLES FOR A MULTIRACIAL SOCIETY 3, 22–24 (1995); Peter H. Schuck, *Alien Rumination,* 105 YALE LAW JOURNAL 1963, 1966 (1996) (book review).

9. *See, for example,* Coalition for Economic Equity v. Wilson, 122 F.3d 692, 701 (9th Cir.) (rejecting constitutional challenges to California's Proposition 209, which prohibits consideration of race and gender in any state program), *cert. denied,* 522 U.S. 963 (1997); Hopwood v. Texas, 78 F.3d 932, 934 (5th Cir.) (holding that affirmative action by the University of Texas in law school admissions violated the Fourteenth Amendment), *cert. denied sub nom.,* 518 U.S. 1033 (1996). As this book went to press, the Supreme Court upheld the constitutionality of narrowly tailored affirmative action programs in two cases involving the University of Michigan. *See* Grutter v. Bollinger, 123 S. Ct. 2325 (2003); Gratz v. Bollinger, 123 S. Ct. 2411 (2003).

10. *See, for example,* ARTHUR M. SCHLESINGER JR., THE DISUNITING OF AMERICA (1992) (contending that multiculturalism is a destructive force in the United States); J. HARVIE WILKINSON III, ONE NATION INDIVISIBLE: HOW ETHNIC SEPARATISM THREATENS AMERICA (1997) (contending that ethnic separatism threatens the nation).

11. *See, for example,* Uniting and Strengthening America by Providing Appropriate Tools Required to Intercept and Obstruct Terrorism (USA PATRIOT) Act of 2001, Pubic Law No. 107-56, 115 Statutes at Large 272 (2001); Illegal Immigration Reform and Immigrant Responsibility Act of 1996, Public Law No. 104-208, 110 Statutes at Large 3009; Personal Responsibility and Work Opportunity Reconciliation Act of 1996, Public Law No. 104-193, 110 Statutes at Large 2105; Antiterrorism and Effective Death Penalty Act of 1996, Public Law No. 104-132, 110 Statutes at Large 1214.

12. *See generally* MICHAEL OMI & HOWARD WINANT, RACIAL FORMATION IN THE UNITED STATES: FROM THE 1960s TO THE 1980s (2d ed. 1994) (analyzing racial formation).

13. Dred Scott v. Sandford, 60 U.S. (19 How.) 393, 407 (1856).

14. KENNETH M. STAMPP, THE PECULIAR INSTITUTION, at vii (1956).

15. 347 U.S. 483 (1954).

16. *See generally* RODOLFO F. ACUÑA, OCCUPIED AMERICA: A HISTORY OF CHICANOS (3d ed., 1988); TOMAS ALMAGUER, RACIAL FAULT LINES: THE HISTORICAL ORIGINS OF WHITE SUPREMACY IN CALIFORNIA (1994); REGINALD HORSMAN, RACE AND MANIFEST DESTINY: THE ORIGINS OF AMERICAN ANGLO-SAXONISM (1981).

17. JOHN HIGHAM, STRANGERS IN THE LAND: PATTERNS OF AMERICAN NATIVISM 1860–1925, at 4 (3d ed. 1992).

18. *See generally* LAURENCE H. TRIBE, AMERICAN CONSTITUTIONAL LAW § 16-14, at 1466–74 (2d ed. 1988).

19. *See The Chinese Exclusion Case* (Chae Chan Ping v. United States), 130 U.S. 581 (1889).

20. Although the U.S. Supreme Court has held it impermissible to discriminate against minority immigrants in the country on the basis of race—*see* Yick Wo v. Hopkins, 118 U.S. 356 (1886)—the formidable burden of proof that the state actor intentionally used immigrant status as a proxy for race falls to the plaintiff. *See* Washington v. Davis, 426 U.S. 229 (1976). *See generally* Theodore Eisenberg & Sheri Lynn Johnson, *The Effects of Intent: Do We Know How Legal Standards Work?* 76 CORNELL LAW REVIEW 1151 (1991).

21. *See* Mathews v. Diaz, 426 U.S. 67, 84–87 (1976). *But see* Hampton v. Mow Sun Wong, 426 U.S. 88 (1976) (invalidating federal civil service rule that barred employment of lawful permanent residents).

22. *See generally* Kevin R. Johnson, *Los Olvidados: Images of the Immigrant, Political Power of Noncitizens, and Immigration Law and Enforcement,* 1993 BRIGHAM YOUNG UNIVERSITY LAW REVIEW 1139.

23. *See generally* RONALD TAKAKI, STRANGERS FROM A DIFFERENT SHORE: A HISTORY OF ASIAN AMERICANS 79–130 (1989). Unwilling to be passive victims, the Chinese community aggressively challenged the various forms of discrimination employed by federal, state, and local governments. *See generally* CHARLES J. MCCLAIN, IN SEARCH OF EQUALITY: THE CHINESE STRUGGLE AGAINST DISCRIMINATION IN NINETEENTH-CENTURY AMERICA (1994).

24. *See generally* GERALD L. NEUMAN, STRANGERS TO THE CONSTITUTION: IMMIGRANTS, BORDERS, AND FUNDAMENTAL LAW 19–43 (1996).

25. *See, for example,* Wong Wing v. United States, 163 U.S. 228, 233 (1896) (invalidating law that provided that a Chinese immigrant unlawfully in the country "shall be imprisoned [without a jury trial] at hard labor").

26. *See generally* ROGER DANIELS, ASIAN AMERICA: CHINESE AND JAPANESE IN THE UNITED STATES SINCE 1850, at 9–99 (1988); ELMER CLARENCE SANDMEYER, THE ANTI-CHINESE MOVEMENT IN CALIFORNIA (2d ed. 1991). In 1871, for example, mob violence against people of Chinese ancestry in Los Angeles resulted in the deaths of at least eighteen people. *See* SANDMEYER, *supra,* at 48; *see also* DANIELS, *supra,* at 58–66 (describing anti-Chinese violence on the West Coast during this period).

27. Fong Yue Ting v. United States, 149 U.S. 698, 743 (1893) (Brewer, J., dissenting); *see* Frank H. Wu, *The Limits of Borders: A Moderate Proposal for Immigration Reform,* 7 STANFORD LAW AND POLICY REVIEW 35, 43–45 (1996) (summarizing U.S. Supreme Court decisions, denominated as the "anti-Asian cases," that upheld the Chinese exclusion laws).

28. *The Chinese Exclusion Case* (Chae Chan Ping v. United States), 130 U.S. 581, 609 (1889) (alteration added).

29. 149 U.S. at 698, 707.

30. For an analysis of the impact of the immigration laws on the evolution of the Asian American community in the United States, see BILL ONG HING, MAKING AND REMAKING ASIAN AMERICA THROUGH IMMIGRATION POLICY, 1850–1990 (1993).

31. *See* DANIELS, *supra* note 26, at 123–28.

32. Immigration Act of 1917, ch. 29, § 3, 39 Statutes at Large 874, 875–76 (1917) (repealed 1952); *see* HING, *supra* note 30, at 32.

33. Immigration Act of 1924, ch. 190, § 11(d), 43 Statutes at Large 153, 159 (1924); *see* TAKAKI, *supra* note 23, at 209–10 (observing the impact of this restrictive exclusion ground on immigration from Japan).

34. DANIELS, *supra* note 26, at 65 (citing BARBARA MILLER SOLOMON, ANCESTORS AND IMMIGRANTS (2d ed. 1972)); *see* MALDWYN ALLEN JONES, AMERICAN IMMIGRATION 227 (2d ed. 1992).

35. *See generally* IAN F. HANEY LÓPEZ, WHITE BY LAW: THE LEGAL CONSTRUCTION OF RACE (1996). The impact of the racial prerequisite to the naturalization laws was ameliorated to some extent by the birthright-citizenship rule, which bestows citizenship on virtually all persons born in the United States. *See* United States v. Wong Kim Ark, 169 U.S. 649 (1898).

36. 261 U.S. 204 (1923).

37. 260 U.S. 178 (1922).

38. 60 U.S. (19 How.) 393 (1856).

39. *See* Cockrill v. California, 268 U.S. 258 (1925); Terrace v. Thompson, 263 U.S. 197 (1923). For analysis of the alien land laws of California and other states, see Keith Aoki, *No Right To Own? The Early Twentieth Century "Alien Law" as a Prelude to Internment*, 40 BOSTON COLLEGE LAW REVIEW 37, 19 BOSTON COLLEGE THIRD WORLD LAW JOURNAL 37 (1998); Gabriel J. Chin, *Citizenship and Exclusion: Wyoming's Anti-Japanese Alien Land Law in Context*, 1 WYOMING LAW REVIEW 497 (2001); Edwin E. Ferguson, *The California Alien Land Law and the Fourteenth Amendment*, 35 CALIFORNIA LAW REVIEW 61 (1947); Dudley O. McGovney, *The Anti-Japanese Land Laws of California and Ten Other States*, 35 CALIFORNIA LAW REVIEW 7 (1947).

40. *See* Oyama v. California, 332 U.S. 633, 658–59 (1948) (Murphy, J., concurring); Ferguson, *supra* note 39, at 62–73.

41. CONGRESSIONAL GLOBE, 39th Congress, 1st Session 1056 (1866) (comments of Representative William Higby).

42. *See* NEUMAN, *supra* note 24, at 39–40.

43. *See* MILTON R. KONVITZ, THE ALIEN AND THE ASIATIC IN AMERICAN LAW 10–12 (1946).

44. STUART CREIGHTON MILLER, THE UNWELCOME IMMIGRANT: THE AMERICAN IMAGE OF THE CHINESE, 1785–1882, at 151 (1969).

45. ALEXANDER SAXTON, THE INDISPENSABLE ENEMY: A STUDY OF THE ANTI-CHINESE MOVEMENT IN CALIFORNIA 260 (2d ed. 1995).

46. Plessy v. Ferguson, 163 U.S. 537, 559, 561 (1896) (Harlan, J., dissenting).

47. Yick Wo v. Hopkins, 118 U.S. 356, 368 (1886).

48. *See, for example,* TRIBE, *supra* note 18, at 1483.

49. *See* Thomas Wuil Joo, *New "Conspiracy Theory" of the Fourteenth Amendment: Nineteenth Century Chinese Civil Rights Cases and the Development of Substantive Due Process Jurisprudence*, 29 UNIVERSITY OF SAN FRANCISCO LAW REVIEW 353, 356 (1995); Lochner v. New York, 198 U.S. 45 (1905) (invalidating state maximum hour law).

50. 323 U.S. 214 (1944). *See generally* Symposium, *The Long Shadow of* Korematsu, 40 BOSTON COLLEGE LAW REVIEW 1, 19 BOSTON COLLEGE THIRD WORLD LAW JOURNAL 1 (1998).

51. *See* Manning Marable, Race, Reform and Rebellion: The Second Reconstruction in Black America, 1945–1982, at 12–15 (1984).

52. 347 U.S. 483 (1954). In 1948, only three years after the decision in *Korematsu,* President Harry Truman ordered the desegregation of the armed forces in response to pressures from African American activists. *See generally* Richard M. Dalfiume, Desegregation of the U.S. Armed Forces 148–74 (1969); Morris J. MacGregor Jr., Integration of the Armed Forces, 1940–1965, at 291–314 (1981).

53. *See* Eugene V. Rostow, *The Japanese American Cases—a Disaster,* 54 Yale Law Journal 489 (1945).

54. *See* Daniels, *supra* note 26, at 186–98.

55. *See* Act of December 17, 1943, ch. 344, 57 Statutes at Large 600 (1943) (amended 1946).

56. *See* Mary L. Dudziak, *Desegregation as a Cold War Imperative,* 41 Stanford Law Review 61 (1988).

57. *See, for example,* United States v. Piche, 981 F.2d 706, 710 (4th Cir. 1992) (affirming the conviction of the murderer of an Asian American who told his victim that he hated the Vietnamese because his brother had been killed in Vietnam and the Vietnamese should not have come to the United States), *cert. denied,* 508 U.S. 916 (1993); Vietnamese Fishermen Ass'n v. Knights of Ku Klux Klan, 518 F. Supp. 993 (S.D. Tex. 1981) (enjoining the Ku Klux Klan and affiliates from harassing and intimidating Vietnamese fishermen).

58. *See* Marable, *supra* note 51, at 111–16.

59. *See* Robert S. Chang, Disoriented: Asian Americans, Law, and the Nation State (1999); Frank Wu, Yellow: Race in America Beyond Black and White (2002); Keith Aoki, *"Foreign-ness" and Asian American Identities: Yellowface, World War II Propaganda, and Bifurcated Racial Stereotypes,* 4 UCLA Asian Pacific American Law Journal 1 (1996); Natsu Taylor Saito, *Alien and Non-alien Alike: Citizenship, "Foreignness" and Racial Hierarchy in American Law,* 76 Oregon Law Review 261 (1997).

60. *See* Jan C. Ting, *"Other Than a Chinaman": How U.S. Immigration Law Resulted from and Still Reflects a Policy of Excluding and Restricting Asian Immigration,* 4 Temple Political and Civil Rights Law Review 301 (1995).

61. *See, for example,* Hirabayashi v. United States, 320 U.S. 81, 96–97 (1943) (observing in this Japanese internment case that many factors "prevented [Japanese] assimilation as an integral part of the white population"); *The Chinese Exclusion Case* (Chae Chan Ping v. United States), 130 U.S. 581, 595 (1889) (justifying the law that barred Chinese immigration by stating, "It seem[s] impossible for [the Chinese] to assimilate with our people") (alterations added).

62. *See* Robert S. Chang, *Toward an Asian American Legal Scholarship: Critical Race Theory, Post-Structuralism, and Narrative Space,* 81 California Law Review 1241, 1300–03 (1993).

63. *See* Immigration Act of 1924, *supra* note 33, ch. 190, § 11(a), 43 Statutes at Large at 159.

64. *See id.* The 1924 act was a successor to the Immigration Act of 1921, which had a more liberal quota of 3 percent of the number of persons from a particular country in the United States as determined by the 1910 census. *See* Act of May 19, 1921,

ch. 8, § 2(a), 42 Statutes at Large 5, 5 (1921). *See generally* MATTHEW FRYE JACOBSON, WHITENESS OF A DIFFERENT COLOR: EUROPEAN IMMIGRANTS AND THE ALCHEMY OF RACE (1998); DESMOND KING, MAKING AMERICANS: IMMIGRATION, RACE, AND THE ORIGINS OF A DIVERSE AMERICA (2000).

65. Hiroshi Motomura, *Whose Alien Nation? Two Models of Constitutional Immigration Law*, 94 MICHIGAN LAW REVIEW 1927, 1933 (1996) (book review) (footnote omitted).

66. Immigration Act of Feb. 5, 1917, *supra* note 32, § 3, 39 Statutes at Large at 877.

67. *See* HIGHAM, *supra* note 17, at 300–30; EDWARD P. HUTCHINSON, LEGISLATIVE HISTORY OF AMERICAN IMMIGRATION POLICY, 1798–1965, at 465–68, 481–83 (1981).

68. HUTCHINSON, *supra* note 67, at 484–85 (emphasis added) (quoting STAFF OF HOUSE COMMITTEE ON IMMIGRATION AND NATURALIZATION, REPORT ON RESTRICTION OF IMMIGRATION, HOUSE OF REPRESENTATIVES REPORT NO. 68-350, pt. 1, at 13–14, 16 (1924)).

69. A. Warner Parker, *The Quota Provisions of the Immigration Act of 1924*, 18 AMERICAN JOURNAL OF INTERNATIONAL LAW 737, 740 (1924).

70. *Id.*

71. *See* HIGHAM, *supra* note 17, at 149–57. An influential book in this regard is MADISON GRANT, THE PASSING OF THE GREAT RACE (4th rev. ed. 1923).

72. *See generally* JOHN HIGHAM, SEND THESE TO ME: IMMIGRANTS IN URBAN AMERICA 81–174 (rev. ed. 1984).

73. *See* NATHAN GLAZER & DANIEL PATRICK MOYNIHAN, BEYOND THE MELTING POT 137–85 (1963). *See generally* ROBERT S. WISTRICH, ANTISEMITISM (1991).

74. *See generally* HENRY L. FEINGOLD, THE POLITICS OF RESCUE (1970); SAUL S. FRIEDMAN, NO HAVEN FOR THE OPPRESSED (1973); GORDON THOMAS & MAX MORGAN WITTS, VOYAGE OF THE DAMNED (1974).

75. *See* Bill Ong Hing, *Immigration Policies: Messages of Exclusion to African Americans*, 37 HOWARD LAW JOURNAL 237, 240 (1994).

76. *See* PRESIDENT'S COMMISSION ON IMMIGRATION AND NATURALIZATION, WHOM SHALL WE WELCOME? 52–56 (1953).

77. *See* Immigration and Nationality Act of 1952, § 201(a), Public Law No. 82-414, 66 Statutes at Large 163, 175 (1952) [hereinafter INA] (providing nations with quotas equal to one-sixth of 1 percent of the number of current U.S. inhabitants who traced their ancestry to that country in 1920).

78. *See* PUBLIC PAPERS OF THE PRESIDENTS OF THE UNITED STATES: HARRY S. TRUMAN 441 (1952–1953) [hereinafter TRUMAN PAPERS] (explaining his veto of the INA because it perpetuated the discriminatory national origins quota system and emphasizing that "immigration policy is . . . important to the conduct of our foreign relations and to our responsibilities of moral leadership in the struggle for world peace").

79. *See* Robert C. Alexander, *A Defense of the McCarren-Walter Act*, 21 LAW AND CONTEMPORARY PROBLEMS 382, 385–86 (1956). Some observers, however, claimed that the public at large opposed the INA, especially the national origins quota system. *See* Harry N. Rosenfield, *The Prospects for Immigration Amendments*, 21 LAW AND CONTEMPORARY PROBLEMS 401, 411 (1956).

80. Staff of Senate Committee on the Judiciary, Report on the Immigration and Naturalization Systems of the United States, Senate Report No. 81-1515, at 455 (1951).

81. *See* Glazer & Moynihan, *supra* note 73, at 181–218 (documenting the Italian immigrant experience in New York City).

82. Public Law No. 88-352, *supra* note 5, 78 Statutes at Large at 241 (codified as amended in scattered sections of 28 and 42 U.S.C.).

83. Immigration Act of 1965, Public Law No. 89-236, 79 Statutes at Large 911 (1965) (codified as amended in scattered sections of 8 U.S.C.).

84. *See id.* § 1, 79 Statutes at Large at 911 (codified as amended at INA § 201, 8 U.S.C. § 1151 (1998).

85. *See id.* § 2, 79 Statutes at Large at 911–12 (codified as amended at INA § 202, 8 U.S.C. § 1152).

86. *See id.* § 21(e), 79 Statutes at Large at 921 (repealed 1976).

87. *See* Motomura, *supra* note 65, at 1934; *see, for example,* House of Representatives Report No. 89-745, at 48 (1965) (noting that the "most compelling reason" for imposing the Western Hemisphere quota was fear of increased immigration from Latin America resulting from projected population growth); Senate Report No. 89-748, at 17–18, *reprinted in* 1965 U.S. Code Congressional & Administrative News 3328, 3336 (expressing concern about the level of immigration from the Western Hemisphere).

88. U.S. Select Commission on Immigration and Refugee Policy, Staff Report: U.S. Immigration Policy and the National Interest 208 (1981) (emphasis added) (footnote omitted).

89. *See* U.S. Department of Justice, 1995 Statistical Yearbook of the Immigration and Naturalization Service 23 tbl.D (1997) [hereinafter 1995 INS Statistical Yearbook] (presenting statistical data showing that the top five countries of birth for immigrants in fiscal year 1995 were Mexico, the Philippines, Vietnam, the Dominican Republic, and the People's Republic of China).

90. *See, for example,* Brimelow, *supra* note 1, at 11 (expressing concern about increased immigration of racial minorities because "[r]ace and ethnicity are destiny in American politics") (emphasis omitted); Richard D. Lamm & Gary Imhoff, The Immigration Time Bomb: The Fragmenting of America 76–98 (1985) (expressing fear of immigration of non-Anglo-Saxon immigrants who fail to assimilate).

91. *See* Immigration Act of 1965, Public Law No. 89-236, *supra* note 83, § 2, 79 Statutes at Large at 911, 911–12 (codified as amended at INA § 202(a), 8 U.S.C § 1152(a)). The per-country limits were not extended to nations in the Western Hemisphere until 1976. *See* INA Amendments of 1976, Public Law No. 94-571, § 2, 90 Statutes at Large 2703, 2703 (1976) (codified as amended at INA § 201(a), 8 U.S.C. §1151(a)).

92. *See* INA, *supra* note 77, § 203(a)(4), 8 U.S.C. §1153(a)(4).

93. *See* U.S. Department of State, Bureau of Consular Affairs, Immigrant Numbers for March 1998, Visa Bulletin, Mar. 1998 at 1, 2.

94. *See* INA, *supra* note 77, § 203(a)(3), 8 U.S.C. § 1153(a)(3).

95. *See* U.S. Department of State, *supra* note 93, at 2.

96. *See* Stephen H. Legomsky, *Immigration, Equality and Diversity*, 31 COLUMBIA JOURNAL OF TRANSNATIONAL LAW 319, 333 (1993); Ting, *supra* note 60, at 308; Bernard Trujillo, *Immigrant Visa Distribution: The Case of Mexico*, 2000 WISCONSIN LAW REVIEW 713.

97. Public Law No. 96-212, 94 Statutes at Large 102 (1980) (codified in scattered sections of 8, 22, and 42 U.S.C.).

98. *See, for example,* 126 CONGRESSIONAL RECORD 4501 (1980) (comments of Representative Peter Rodino) (characterizing this law as "one of the most important pieces of humanitarian legislation ever enacted"); Deborah E. Anker & Michael H. Posner, *The Forty Year Crisis: A Legislative History of the Refugee Act of 1980*, 19 SAN DIEGO LAW REVIEW 9 (1981).

99. *See* HING, *supra* note 30, at 121–38; GIL LOESCHER & JOHN A. SCANLAN, CALCULATED KINDNESS: REFUGEES AND AMERICA'S HALF-OPEN DOOR, 1945 TO THE PRESENT 102–69 (1986); Harvey Gee, *The Refugee Burden: A Closer Look at the Refugee Act of 1980*, NORTH CAROLINA JOURNAL OF INTERNATIONAL LAW AND COMMERCIAL REGULATION 559 (2001).

100. *See* Legal Assistance for Vietnamese Asylum Seekers v. Department of State, 104 F.3d 1349 (D.C. Cir. 1997) (dismissing claims on jurisdictional grounds).

101. *See* INA, *supra* note 77, § 212(a)(4)(A), 8 U.S.C. § 1182(a)(4)(A) ("Any alien . . . likely at any time to become a public charge is inadmissible").

102. Public Law No. 101-649, 104 Statutes at Large 4978 (1990) (codified as amended primarily in scattered sections of 8 U.S.C.).

103. *See id.* § 131, 104 Statutes at Large at 4997–99 (codified as amended at INA § 203(c), 8 U.S.C. § 1153(c)).

104. *See* STEPHEN H. LEGOMSKY, IMMIGRATION AND REFUGEE LAW AND POLICY 238–41 (3d ed. 2002) (explaining the genesis and operation of the diversity visa program). "Since many more Americans already trace their ancestry to Europe than to Asia or Latin America, the statutory 'diversity' program is in truth an *'anti-diversity'* program; it causes the resulting population mix to be *less* diverse than it would otherwise be." *Id.* at 241 (emphasis in original).

105. *See* 1995 INS STATISTICAL YEARBOOK, *supra* note 89, at 21.

106. *See* U.S. DEPARTMENT OF JUSTICE, 1999 STATISTICAL YEARBOOK OF THE IMMIGRATION AND NATURALIZATION SERVICE 44, 45 tbl.8 (2002).

107. Howard F. Chang, *Immigration Policy, Liberal Principles, and the Republican Tradition*, 85 GEORGETOWN LAW JOURNAL 2105, 2115 (1997) (emphasis omitted).

108. *See generally* CAREY MCWILLIAMS, NORTH FROM MEXICO: THE SPANISH-SPEAKING PEOPLE OF THE UNITED STATES (rev. ed. 1990); MARIO BARRERA, RACE AND CLASS IN THE SOUTHWEST: A THEORY OF RACIAL INEQUALITY (1979).

109. *See generally* FRANCISCO E. BALDERRAMA & RAYMOND RODRIGUEZ, DECADE OF BETRAYAL: MEXICAN REPATRIATION IN THE 1930S (1995); CAMILLE GUERÍN-GONZALES, MEXICAN WORKERS AND AMERICAN DREAMS: IMMIGRATION, REPATRIATION AND CALIFORNIA FARM LABOR, 1900–1939 (1994); ABRAHAM HOFFMAN, UNWANTED MEXICAN AMERICANS IN THE GREAT DEPRESSION: REPATRIATION PRESSURES, 1929–1939 (1974).

110. *See* KITTY CALAVITA, INSIDE THE STATE: THE BRACERO PROGRAM, IMMIGRATION, AND THE I.N.S. 218 (1992).

111. Eleanor M. Hadley, *A Critical Analysis of the Wetback Problem*, 21 LAW AND CONTEMPORARY PROBLEMS 334, 344 (1956); *see, for example,* Henry M. Hart Jr., *The Power of Congress to Limit the Jurisdiction of the Federal Courts: An Exercise in Dialectic,* 66 HARVARD LAW REVIEW 1362, 1395 (1953) (lamenting a Supreme Court dictum "say[ing], in effect, that a Mexican wetback who sneaks successfully across the Rio Grande is entitled to the full panoply of due process in his deportation") (alteration added) (footnote omitted). *See generally* Jorge A. Bustamante, *The "Wetback" as Deviant: An Application of Labeling Theory,* 77 AMERICAN JOURNAL OF SOCIOLOGY 706 (1972).

112. *See, for example,* Brimelow, *supra* note 1, at 262–63.

113. *See* 1995 INS STATISTICAL YEARBOOK, *supra* note 89, at 185–86 (estimating that, as of October 1996, about 54 percent of the undocumented population was of Mexican origin and that fifteen countries contributed fifty thousand or more persons to the undocumented population in the United States). *See generally* LEO R. CHAVEZ, COVERING IMMIGRATION: POPULAR IMAGES AND THE POLITICS OF THE NATION (2001).

114. *See generally* U.S. COMMISSION ON IMMIGRATION REFORM, U.S. IMMIGRATION POLICY: RESTORING CREDIBILITY 10–19 (1994); TIMOTHY J. DUNN, THE MILITARIZATION OF THE U.S.-MEXICO BORDER, 1978–1992: LOW-INTENSITY CONFLICT COMES HOME (1996); Bill Ong Hing, *The Dark Side of Operation Gatekeeper,* 7 UNIVERSITY OF CALIFORNIA AT DAVIS JOURNAL OF INTERNATIONAL LAW AND POLICY 121 (2001).

115. *See* H.G. Reza, *Military Silently Patrols U.S. Border,* LOS ANGELES TIMES, June 29, 1997, at A3. In March 2003, the functions of the Immigration and Naturalization Service were split into several agencies and placed in the new Department of Homeland Security.

116. *See* U.S. COMMISSION ON CIVIL RIGHTS, FEDERAL IMMIGRATION LAW ENFORCEMENT IN THE SOUTHWEST 80 (1997); AMNESTY INTERNATIONAL, UNITED STATES OF AMERICA: HUMAN RIGHTS CONCERNS IN THE BORDER REGION WITH MEXICO (1998); AMERICAN FRIENDS SERVICE COMMITTEE, HUMAN AND CIVIL RIGHTS VIOLATIONS ON THE U.S. MEXICO BORDER 1995–97 (1998); HUMAN RIGHTS WATCH, CROSSING THE LINE: HUMAN RIGHTS ABUSES ALONG THE U.S. BORDER WITH MEXICO PERSIST AMID CLIMATE OF IMPUNITY (1995), *available at* http://www.hrw.org/reports/1995/Us1.htm.

117. *See* U.S. GENERAL ACCOUNTING OFFICE, INS' SOUTHWEST BORDER STRATEGY: RESOURCE AND IMPACT ISSUES REMAIN AFTER SEVEN YEARS (2001); U.S. GENERAL ACCOUNTING OFFICE, ILLEGAL IMMIGRATION: SOUTHWEST BORDER STRATEGY RESULTS INCONCLUSIVE; MORE EVALUATION NEEDED (1997).

118. BELINDA I. REYES ET AL., HOLDING THE LINE? THE EFFECT OF THE RECENT BORDER BUILD-UP ON UNAUTHORIZED IMMIGRATION, at viii, xii (Public Policy Institute of California, 2002) (emphasis added).

119. *See* FREDRIC C. GEY ET AL., CALIFORNIA LATINA/LATINO DEMOGRAPHIC DATA BOOK 8–9 tbls.1-2 to 1-3 (1993) (examining data showing that the population of California was 19 percent Latina/o in 1980 and 25 percent Latina/o in 1990, with 80 percent of the Latinas/os in 1990 identifying themselves as of Mexican ancestry).

120. *See generally* Rachel F. Moran, *Bilingual Education as a Status Conflict,* 75 CALIFORNIA LAW REVIEW 321 (1987); Kevin R. Johnson & George A. Martínez, *Discrimination by Proxy: The Case of Proposition 227 and the Ban on Bilingual Education,* 33 UNIVERSITY OF CALIFORNIA AT DAVIS LAW REVIEW 1227 (2000).

121. *See* Kevin R. Johnson, *Some Thoughts on the Future of Latino Legal Scholarship*, 2 HARVARD LATINO LAW REVIEW 101, 117–29 (1997).

122. JUAN RAMON GARCÍA, OPERATION WETBACK 230–31 (1980); *see* JULIAN SAMORA, LOS MOJADOS: THE WETBACK STORY 52 (1971).

123. U.S. GENERAL ACCOUNTING OFFICE, IMMIGRATION REFORM: EMPLOYER SANCTIONS AND THE QUESTION OF DISCRIMINATION 5–6 (1990); *see* U.S. COMMISSION ON CIVIL RIGHTS, THE IMMIGRATION REFORM AND CONTROL ACT, at iv (1989). Such discrimination occurs despite the existence of provisions that prohibit it. *See* INA, *supra* note 77, § 274B, 8 U.S.C. § 1324b.

124. *See* WILLIAM C. BERMAN, THE POLITICS OF CIVIL RIGHTS IN THE TRUMAN ADMINISTRATION 4 (1970) ("Negroes voted for Roosevelt in 1936 and 1940 largely because their economic deprivation, stemming from unemployment and discrimination, had been lessened through the work of [the] . . . New Deal agencies.").

125. 347 U.S. 483 (1954).

126. *See* Hernández v. Texas, 347 U.S. 475 (1954) (reversing the finding that Mexican Americans failed to constitute a cognizable class for equal protection purposes); *see also* Ian F. Haney López, *Race, Ethnicity, Erasure: The Salience of Race to LatCrit Theory*, 85 CALIFORNIA LAW REVIEW 1143 (1997) (analyzing *Hernández* in terms of racialization of Mexican Americans in Texas); George A. Martínez, *The Legal Construction of Race: Mexican-Americans and Whiteness*, 2 HARVARD LATINO LAW REVIEW 321, 328 (1997) (analyzing the lower court decision in *Hernández* and the treatment of Mexican Americans under the law as "white" as to their disadvantage).

127. United States v. Brignoni-Ponce, 422 U.S. 873, 886–87 (1975) (emphasis added).

128. *See id.* at 879 (footnote omitted). To support this proposition, the Court cited United States v. Baca, 368 F. Supp. 398, 402 (S.D. Cal. 1973), which relied on a 1974 Justice Department report and reinforced its reasoning by stating that a high proportion of the deportable immigrants came from Mexico. *See Brignoni-Ponce*, 422 U.S. at 979 & n.5. For analysis of the misleading use of statistics to support policy choices, see JOEL BEST, DAMNED LIES AND STATISTICS: UNTANGLING NUMBERS FROM THE MEDIA, POLITICIANS, AND ACTIVISTS (2001). For in-depth criticism of racial profiles in immigration enforcement, see Kevin R. Johnson, *The Case Against Race Profiling in Immigration Enforcement*, 78 WASHINGTON UNIVERSITY LAW QUARTERLY 675 (2000).

129. *Brignoni-Ponce*, 422 U.S. at 886 (footnote omitted).

130. United States v. Martinez-Fuerte, 428 U.S. 543, 563 (1976).

131. Gonzalez-Rivera v. INS, 22 F.3d 1441, 1450 (9th Cir. 1994) (citation omitted); *see* United States v. Garcia-Camacho, 53 F.3d 244, 248 n.7 (9th Cir. 1995).

132. *See, for example,* United States v. Cruz-Hernandez, 62 F.3d 1353, 1355–56 (11th Cir. 1995); United States v. Rodriguez, 976 F.2d 592, 594 (9th Cir. 1992), *amended*, 997 F.2d 1306 (9th Cir. 1993); United States v. Franco-Munoz, 952 F.2d 1055, 1056 (9th Cir. 1991); United States v. Magana, 797 F.2d 777, 781 (9th Cir. 1986); United States v. Pulido-Santoyo, 580 F.2d 352, 354 (9th Cir.), *cert. denied*, 439 U.S. 915 (1978).

133. Nicacio v. INS, 797 F.2d 700, 704 (9th Cir. 1999).

134. *See* United States v. Jones, 149 F.3d 364, 369 (5th Cir. 1998); United States v. Rubio-Hernandez, 39 F. Supp. 2d 808, 835 (W.D. Tex. 1998).

135. *See, for example, Garcia-Camacho*, 53 F.3d at 244, 247–48; *Rodriguez*, 976 F.2d at 592, 595–96; United States v. Ortega-Serrano, 788 F.2d 299, 302 (5th Cir. 1986).

136. *See* United States v. Magana, 797 F.2d 777, 781 (9th Cir. 1986) (stating that Border Patrol officers observed, among other factors, that automobile passengers "appeared to be farm workers, one of whom wore a hat which the officers emphasized was indicative of someone who came from the Mexican state of Jalisco"); United States v. Garcia, 732 F.2d 1221, 1228 (5th Cir. 1984) (Tate, J., dissenting) (contending "that, stripped to its essence, the stop was based upon no more than the Border Patrol's speculation that poor and dirty Hispanic appearing persons might possibly be Mexican aliens"); United States v. Hernandez-Lopez, 538 F.2d 284, 285–86 (9th Cir.) (stating that Border Patrol officers observed that the person stopped "did not look like he had lived in the United States, but rather looked like a 'Mexican cowboy'") (footnote omitted), *cert. denied*, 429 U.S. 981 (1976).

137. *See* Jim Yardley, *Some Texans Say Border Patrol Singles Out Too Many Blameless Hispanics*, NEW YORK TIMES, Jan. 26, 2000, at A17.

138. Lee Romney, *Over the Line? Citing Questioning of Mayor, Activists Say Border Patrol Targets All Latinos*, LOS ANGELES TIMES, Sept. 2, 1993, at J1 (quoting mayor).

139. *See, for example*, Hodgers-Durgin v. de la Vina, 199 F.3d 1037 (9th Cir. 1999) (en banc); Nicacio v. INS, 797 F.2d 700 (9th Cir. 1985); LaDuke v. Nelson, 762 F.2d 1318 (9th Cir. 1985), *modified*, 796 F.2d 309 (9th Cir. 1986).

140. *See* Murillo v. Musegades, 809 F. Supp. 487 (W.D. Tex. 1992).

141. 199 F.3d 1037 (9th Cir. 1999) (en banc) (affirming dismissal on justiciability grounds).

142. *See, for example*, *Nicacio*, 797 F.2d at 700; *LaDuke*, 762 F.2d at 1318, *modified*, 796 F.2d at 309; Cervantes-Cuevas v. INS, 797 F.2d 707 (9th Cir. 1985); United States v. Gonzalez-Vargas, 496 F. Supp. 1296 (N.D. Ga. 1980).

143. *See, for example*, Ramirez v. Webb, 787 F.2d 592 (6th Cir. 1986); Illinois Migrant Council v. Pilliod, 540 F.2d 1062 (7th Cir. 1976), *modified*, 548 F.2d 715 (7th Cir. 1977) (en banc).

144. *See* Farm Labor Organizing Committee v. Ohio State Highway Patrol, 308 F.3d 523 (6th Cir. 2002).

145. *See* Anne-Marie O'Connor, *Rampart Set Up Latinos to Be Deported, INS Says*, LOS ANGELES TIMES, Feb. 24, 2000, at A1 (reporting that the Los Angeles Police Department gang task force indiscriminately rounded up Latinas/os and turned over those with questionable immigration status to the INS). *See generally* Theodore W. Maya, Comment, *To Serve and Protect or to Betray and Neglect? The LAPD and Undocumented Immigrants*, 49 UCLA LAW REVIEW 1611 (2002) (analyzing the long history of the Los Angeles Police Department's abuse of the civil rights of undocumented immigrants and the need for reform).

146. *See* MANUEL PASTOR JR. ET AL., LATINOS AND THE LOS ANGELES UPRISING: THE ECONOMIC CONTEXT 11–13 (1993).

147. OFFICE OF THE ATTORNEY GENERAL OF ARIZONA, RESULTS OF THE CHANDLER SURVEY 31 (1997).

148. Edwin Harwood, *Arrests Without Warrant: The Legal and Organizational Environment of Immigration Law Enforcement*, 17 UNIVERSITY OF CALIFORNIA AT DAVIS

LAW REVIEW 505, 531 (1984) (emphasis added); *see* EDWIN HARWOOD, IN LIBERTY'S SHADOW: ILLEGAL ALIENS AND IMMIGRATION LAW ENFORCEMENT 59 (1986) ("INS officers can easily circumvent the constitutional requirements. To justify a stop, officers can easily claim that they thought the individual was wearing Mexican clothing, behaved furtively, or closely resembled a person they had processed before"); *Developments in the Law—Immigration Policy and the Rights of Aliens*, 96 HARVARD LAW REVIEW 1286, 1374 (1983) (stating that the Supreme Court has "grant[ed] INS agents the freedom to select individuals for interrogation on the basis of ethnicity, as long as the agents can meet the minimal burden of devising plausible post hoc rationalizations for their actions") (footnote omitted).

149. *See* Harwood, *supra* note 148, at 532 n.105 (noting that officers he observed believed that they identified undocumented persons correctly over 90 percent of the time and that they had a "'sixth sense' for distinguishing an illegal alien," when, in fact, their accuracy was in the 20 to 25 percent range).

150. *See* United States v. Zapata-Ibarra, 212 F.3d 877, 885 (5th Cir.) (Wiener, J., dissenting) (footnotes omitted), *cert. denied*, 531 U.S. 972 (2000).

151. *See, for example*, International Ladies Garment Workers' Union v. Sureck, 681 F.2d 624, 627 n.5 (9th Cir. 1982) (stating that the INS acknowledged that it considered the "'apparent Latin descent'" of workers in deciding to raid a factory), *rev'd sub nom.*, INS v. Delgado, 466 U.S. 210 (1984); Blackie's House of Beef, Inc. v. Castillo, 659 F.2d 1211, 1226 n.17 (D.C. Cir. 1981) (condoning INS consideration of "'foreign appearances'" of employees in deciding to embark on an enforcement operation), *cert. denied*, 455 U.S. 940 (1982); Pearl Meadows Mushroom Farm, Inc. v. Nelson, 723 F. Supp 432, 442 (N.D. Cal. 1989) (recounting the testimony of INS agents that "when questioned as to the justification for entering [a workplace] without a warrant, [they] answered that they did not need one 'if they could see Mexicans in plain view of the street'") (footnote omitted) (alteration added).

152. *See Delgado*, 466 U.S. at 210.

153. *See* International Molders' and Allied Workers' Local Union No. 164 v. Nelson, 674 F. Supp. 294, 295 (N.D. Cal. 1987).

154. *See* Hoffman Plastic Compounds, Inc. v. NLRB, 535 U.S. 137 (2002) (holding that the National Labor Relations Board could not order an employer who violated federal labor law to pay back wages to undocumented immigrant workers).

155. *See, for example*, Hodgers-Durgin v. de la Vina, 199 F.3d 1037 (9th Cir. 1999) (en banc) (dismissing an action that claimed a pattern and practice of INS discrimination against Latina/o motorists on justiciability grounds).

156. *See* Bill Ong Hing, *Border Patrol Abuse: Evaluating Complaint Procedures Available to Victims*, 9 GEORGETOWN IMMIGRATION LAW JOURNAL 757 (1995); Stephen A. Rosenbaum, *Keeping an Eye on the INS: A Case for Civilian Review of Uncivil Conduct*, 7 LA RAZA LAW JOURNAL 1 (1994).

157. *See* INS v. Lopez-Mendoza, 468 U.S. 1032 (1984).

158. *Id.* at 1050–51 (citation omitted) (footnote omitted).

159. *See, for example*, Gonzales-Rivera v. INS, 22 F.3d 1441, 1448–52 (9th Cir. 1994) (finding that the Border Patrol's conduct in making a race-based stop was "egregious," thereby justifying application of the exclusionary rule); Orhorhaghe v.

INS, 38 F.3d 488, 498 (9th Cir. 1994) (finding that a person's "Nigerian-sounding name," which the court reasoned might serve as a proxy for race, was insufficient to justify an INS stop).

160. ELIZABETH HULL, WITHOUT JUSTICE FOR ALL: THE CONSTITUTIONAL RIGHTS OF ALIENS 100 (1985).

161. *See* Arthur F. Corwin, *The Numbers Game: Estimates of Illegal Aliens in the United States, 1970–1981,* 45 LAW AND CONTEMPORARY PROBLEMS 223, 246, 259 (1982) (reviewing estimates of undocumented immigrants in the United States and concluding that the best estimate at the time was that only 50 to 60 percent of the undocumented population was of Mexican origin).

162. U.S. SELECT COMMISSION ON IMMIGRATION AND REFUGEE POLICY, FINAL REPORT AND RECOMMENDATIONS: U.S. POLICY AND THE NATIONAL INTEREST 36 (1981) (emphasis added).

163. *See* U.S. DEPARTMENT OF JUSTICE, 1997 STATISTICAL YEARBOOK OF THE IMMIGRATION AND NATURALIZATION SERVICE 200 tbl.N (1999) [hereinafter 1997 INS STATISTICAL YEARBOOK]. Other estimates are considerably lower. *See* Frank Sharry, *Myths, Realities and Solutions; Facts About Illegal Immigrants,* 67 SPECTRUM: THE JOURNAL OF STATE GOVERNMENT 20 (1994) (contending that data show that Mexican nationals constitute only 30 percent of the undocumented immigrant population in the United States).

164. See 1997 INS STATISTICAL YEARBOOK, *supra* note 163, at 199.

165. *Id.*

166. Declining to follow the Court's 1975 ruling in *Brignoni-Ponce* that race could be considered as one factor in an immigration stop, one court of appeals emphasized the dramatic growth of the Latina/o population since the 1970s. *See* United States v. Montero-Camargo, 208 F.3d 1122, 1132–34 (9th Cir.) (en banc), *cert. denied sub nom.,* 531 U.S. 889 (2000).

167. *See* U.S. BUREAU OF THE CENSUS, CURRENT POPULATION REPORTS P20-511, THE HISPANIC POPULATION IN THE UNITED STATES: MARCH 1997 (UPDATE) (1998).

168. *See* U.S. DEPARTMENT OF COMMERCE, STATISTICAL ABSTRACT OF THE UNITED STATES 19 tbl.19 (119th ed., 1999).

169. *See* 1997 INS STATISTICAL YEARBOOK, *supra* note 163, at 200 tbl.N.

170. *See* U.S. BUREAU OF THE CENSUS, CURRENT POPULATION REPORTS—POPULATION PROJECTIONS OF THE UNITED STATES BY AGE, SEX, RACE, AND HISPANIC ORIGIN: 1995 TO 2050, at 13 tbl.J (1996).

171. *See* 1997 INS STATISTICAL YEARBOOK, *supra* note 163, at 21 tbl.C.

172. *See id.* at 26 tbl.2.

173. *See id.* at 148 tbl.47.

174. *See* JON STILES ET AL., CALIFORNIA LATINO DEMOGRAPHIC DATABOOK 2–5 tbl.2.1 (1998 ed.) [hereinafter LATINO DEMOGRAPHIC DATABOOK].

175. *See* U.S. Bureau of the Census, ST-98-45, States Ranked by Hispanic Population 1998, *available at* http://www.census.gov/population/estimates/state/rank/strnktb.5.1.

176. *See* LATINO DEMOGRAPHIC DATABOOK, *supra* note 174, at 2-32, 2-34 (Maps 2.22, 2.24).

177. *See* U.S. BUREAU OF THE CENSUS, POPULATION ESTIMATES FOR COUNTIES BY RACE AND HISPANIC ORIGIN: JULY 1, 1999 (1999).

178. Joseph Tussman & Jacobus tenBroek, *The Equal Protection of the Laws*, 37 CALIFORNIA LAW REVIEW 341, 351–52 (1949).

179. María Pabón López, *The Phoenix Rises from El Cenizo: A Community Creates and Affirms a Latino/a Border Cultural Citizenship Through Its Language and Safe Haven Ordinances*, 78 DENVER UNIVERSITY LAW REVIEW 1017 (2001).

180. Rachel F. Moran, *Neither Black Nor White*, 2 HARVARD LATINO LAW REVIEW 61, 96 (1997) (footnote omitted).

181. United States v. Zapata-Ibarra, 212 F.3d 877, 885 (5th Cir.) (Weiner, J., dissenting), *cert. denied*, 531 U.S. 972 (2000).

182. *See* U.S. DEPARTMENT OF JUSTICE, IMMIGRATION AND NATURALIZATION SERVICE, INS SETS NEW REMOVALS RECORD, Nov. 12, 1999. There are important limits to this comparison, since immigrants may be removed from the country on many grounds other than entering without inspection or violating the terms of a visa. *See* INA, *supra* note 77, § 237, 8 U.S.C. § 1227 (listing many different grounds for removal). At a minimum, however, the gross disparity suggests the possibility of racially disparate enforcement and warrants further inquiry.

183. *See, for example,* Diaz v. Reno, 40 F. Supp. 2d 984 (N.D. Ill. 1999) (addressing motions in action in which the INS was accused of wrongfully deporting a U.S. citizen); Suzanne Espinosa, *Snafu Underscores Civil Rights Issues*, SAN FRANCISCO CHRONICLE, Oct. 22, 1993, at A1 (recounting the story of a U.S. citizen arrested by Border Patrol while repairing his parents' roof near Santa Barbara, California, and deported to Mexico).

184. *See* Kevin R. Johnson, *"Melting Pot" or "Ring of Fire"? Assimilation and the Mexican-American Experience*, 85 CALIFORNIA LAW REVIEW 1259, 1291–93 (1997).

185. JULIAN SAMORA & PATRICIA VANDEL SIMON, A HISTORY OF THE MEXICAN-AMERICAN PEOPLE 8 (rev. ed. 1993) (emphasis added).

186. *See* Jane E. Larson, *Free Markets Deep in the Heart of Texas*, 84 GEORGETOWN LAW JOURNAL 179, 225 (1995) ("[A] persistent expression of anti-Mexican prejudice in Texas has been the belief that the skin and bodies of Mexicans are dirty, and by extension so too are their habits and morals") (footnote omitted).

187. *See* Johnson, *supra* note 184, at 1269–79, 1305–09. *See generally* KEVIN R. JOHNSON, HOW DID YOU GET TO BE MEXICAN? A WHITE/BROWN MAN'S SEARCH FOR IDENTITY (1999).

188. *See* 1997 INS STATISTICAL YEARBOOK, *supra* note 163, at 140 tbl.K (showing that 32.2 percent of Mexican immigrants admitted to the United States in fiscal year 1997 naturalized, compared with 52.7 percent of immigrants from all countries).

189. *See generally* LOESCHER & SCANLAN, *supra* note 99, at 6–84.

190. *See* Kevin R. Johnson, *A "Hard Look" at the Executive Branch's Asylum Decisions*, 1991 UTAH LAW REVIEW 279, 343–48.

191. *See* Guo Chin Di v. Carroll, 842 F. Supp. 858, 866–67 (E.D. Va. 1994) (tracing inconsistency in the U.S. government's treatment of Chinese persons who fled the one-child rule), *rev'd without opinion*, 66 F.3d 315 (4th Cir. 1995). In 1996, Congress changed the law, which now expressly makes persons who fled such policies

eligible for asylum. *See* INA, *supra* note 77, § 101(a)(42), 8 U.S.C. § 1101(a)(42) (as amended by the Illegal Immigration Reform and Immigrant Responsibility Act of 1996, Public Law No. 104-208, *supra* note 11, § 601(a)(1), 110 Statutes at Large at 3009, 3689).

192. *See, for example, In re* Chen, 20 Immigration and Nationality Decisions 16 (Board of Immigration Appeals 1989) (granting asylum to a Chinese refugee based on past persecution during the Cultural Revolution despite the minimal threat of future persecution).

193. *See* Ting, *supra* note 60, at 310–11; *see, for example,* Xin-Chang Zhang v. Slattery, 55 F.3d 732 (2d Cir. 1995), *cert. denied,* 515 U.S. 1176 (1996); Chen Zhou Chai v. Carroll, 48 F.3d 1331 (4th Cir. 1995).

194. *See* Orantes-Hernández v. Thornburgh, 919 F.2d 549 (9th Cir. 1990); ROBERT S. KAHN, OTHER PEOPLE'S BLOOD 209–19 (1996).

195. Motomura, *supra* note 65, at 1950 (emphasis omitted); *see* Charles J. Ogletree Jr., *America's Schizophrenic Immigration Policy: Race, Class, and Reason,* 41 BOSTON COLLEGE LAW REVIEW 755 (2000).

196. *See* THOMAS CAROTHERS, IN THE NAME OF DEMOCRACY 183 (1991).

197. *See* Kevin R. Johnson, *Judicial Acquiescence to the Executive Branch's Pursuit of Foreign Policy and Domestic Agendas in Immigration Matters: The Case of the Haitian Asylum-Seekers,* 7 GEORGETOWN IMMIGRATION LAW JOURNAL 1, 12–14 (1993); Kevin R. Johnson, *Comparative Racialization: Culture and National Origin in the Latina/o Communities,* 78 DENVER UNIVERSITY LAW REVIEW 633, 650–51 (2001).

198. *See* Sale v. Haitian Centers Council, Inc., 509 U.S. 155, 160–62 (1993) (describing the evolution in the U.S. government's treatment of Haitians during the 1980s and early 1990s).

199. *Id.* (quoting the district court's "uncontested finding of fact").

200. *See* Executive Order No. 12,807, 3 C.F.R. 303 (1993), *reprinted in* 8 U.S.C. 1182 (1994).

201. *See* Elaine Sciolino, *Clinton Says U.S. Will Continue Ban on Haitian Exodus,* NEW YORK TIMES, Jan. 15, 1993, at A1.

202. *See Sale,* 509 U.S. at 188.

203. *See* Brief of the National Association for the Advancement of Colored People, TransAfrica, and the Congressional Black Caucus as Amici Curiae in Support of Respondents, Sale v. Haitian Centers Council, Inc., 509 U.S. 155 (No. 92-344) (1993).

204. *See* Joyce A. Hughes & Linda R. Crane, *Haitians: Seeking Refuge in the United States,* 7 GEORGETOWN IMMIGRATION LAW JOURNAL 747, 749 & n.12 (1993); Malissia Lennox, Note, *Refugees, Racism, and Reparations: A Critique of the United States' Haitian Immigration Policy,* 45 STANFORD LAW REVIEW 687, 688 (1993); *see also* Haitian Refugee Center v. Civiletti, 503 F. Supp. 442, 451 (S.D. Fla. 1980) (stating that a "possible underlying reason" that Haitians were treated differently from other refugees fleeing repressive regimes is that they are black), *aff'd as modified sub nom.,* Haitian Refugee Center v. Smith, 676 F.2d 1023 (5th Cir. 1982).

205. James Harney, *Critics of U.S. Policy See Racist Overtones,* USA TODAY, Feb. 3, 1992, at 2A (quoting Legomsky).

206. *See* Janice D. Villiers, *Closed Borders, Closed Ports: The Plight of Haitians Seeking Political Asylum in the United States*, 60 BROOKLYN LAW REVIEW 841, 904–15 (1994); *see also* Peter Margulies, *Difference and Distrust in Asylum Law: Haitian and Holocaust Refugee Narratives*, 6 ST. THOMAS LAW REVIEW 135 (1993) (analyzing difficulties faced by Haitian refugees and comparing their plight to that of Jews who fled Nazi Germany).

207. *See* John Marelius, *Wilson Ad Out to Ease Prop. 187 Drumbeat*, SAN DIEGO UNION-TRIBUNE, Oct. 25, 1994, at A3. *See generally* KENT A. ONO & JOHN M. SLOOP, SHIFTING BORDERS: RHETORIC, IMMIGRATION, AND CALIFORNIA'S PROPOSITION 187 (2002)

208. *See, for example*, TONY MILLER, ACTING SECRETARY OF STATE, CALIFORNIA BALLOT PAMPHLET: GENERAL ELECTION, NOVEMBER 8, 1994, at 54 (1994) [hereinafter CALIFORNIA BALLOT PAMPHLET] ("It has been estimated that ILLEGAL ALIENS are costing taxpayers in excess of 5 billion dollars a year. While our own citizens and legal residents go wanting, those who choose to enter our country ILLEGALLY get royal treatment at the expense of the California taxpayer. IT IS TIME THIS STOPS!") (capitals in original) (argument in favor of Proposition 187).

209. *See id.* at 50–53.

210. *Id.* at 54 (capitals in original).

211. *See* Linda R. Hayes, *Letter to the Editor*, NEW YORK TIMES, Oct. 15, 1994, at § 1, 18 (expressing concern that "a Mexico-controlled California could vote to establish Spanish as the sole language of California, 10 million more English-speaking Californians could flee, and there could be a statewide vote to leave the Union and annex California to Mexico"). For similar themes, see PATRICK J. BUCHANAN, THE DEATH OF THE WEST: HOW DYING POPULATIONS AND IMMIGRANT INVASIONS PERIL OUR COUNTRY AND CIVILIZATION 97–149 (2002).

212. George Ramos, *Prop. 187 Debate: No Tolerance but Abundant Anger*, LOS ANGELES TIMES, Oct. 10, 1994, at B3 (quoting Ron Prince).

213. Marc Cooper, *The War Against Illegal Immigrants Heats Up*, VILLAGE VOICE, Oct. 4, 1994, at 28 (quoting Prince).

214. *See* Olga Briseno, *Mister Migra Harold Ezell*, SAN DIEGO UNION-TRIBUNE, Aug. 23, 1989, at F1 (recounting Ezell's "most famous quote" in which "he said illegal aliens should be 'caught, skinned and fried'").

215. Daniel B. Wood, *Ballot Vote on Illegal Immigrants Set for Fall in California*, CHRISTIAN SCIENCE MONITOR, June 1, 1994, at 1, 18 (quoting Ezell).

216. *See, for example*, Assembly Bill 24, California 1995–1996 Reg. Sess. (1994) (Mountjoy) (proposing to implement English as the official language provision of the state constitution by requiring state and local governments to take steps to preserve, protect, and enhance the role of English); Assembly Joint Resolution 46, California 1993–1994 Reg. Sess. (Mountjoy) (1994) (resolving that the U.S. government should negotiate agreements with countries that receive U.S. foreign aid that would allow nationals of those countries convicted of crimes in the United States to serve sentences in their countries of origin); Assembly Joint Resolution 49, California 1993–1994 Reg. Sess. (Mountjoy) (1993) (resolving that Congress should propose amendments to the U.S. Constitution limiting citizenship to persons who are born

in the United States to mothers who are citizens or lawful permanent residents); Assembly Bill 131a, California 1993–1994 Spec. Sess. "A" (Mountjoy) (1994) (proposing measures to facilitate the deportation of immigrant felons); Assembly Bill 149, California 1993–1994 Reg. Sess. (1993) (Mountjoy) (proposing the prohibition of the expenditure of state funds for the education of undocumented immigrants); Assembly Bill 151, California 1993–1994 Reg. Sess. (1993) (Mountjoy) (proposing that undocumented immigrants be ineligible for workers' compensation); Assembly Bill 2171, California 1993–1994 Reg. Sess. (1993) (Mountjoy) (requiring that an undocumented immigrant be ineligible for issuance or renewal of a driver's license); Assembly Bill 2228, California 1993–1994 Reg. Sess. (1993) (Mountjoy) (proposing that undocumented immigrants be prohibited from enrolling in any public post-secondary institution).

217. *Sonya Live* (CNN television broadcast, Feb. 16, 1994) (talk show interview with Mountjoy) [hereinafter *Sonya Live*].

218. Major Garrett, *Economic Plan Includes Aliens' Medical Funds*, WASHINGTON TIMES, July 14, 1993, at A1 (quoting Mountjoy) (emphasis added).

219. *Sonya Live, supra* note 217.

220. Elizabeth Kadetsky, *"Save Our State" Initiative: Bashing Illegals in California*, 259 NATION 416, 418 (1994) (quoting Barbara Kiley).

221. Margot Hornblower Lamont, *Making and Breaking Law*, TIME, Nov. 21, 1994, at 68, 73 (quoting Richard Kiley).

222. Sara Catania, *County Report: A Message Hits Home*, LOS ANGELES TIMES, Nov. 20, 1994, at B1 (alteration added) (quoting Richard Kiley).

223. Carol Byrne, *Proposition 187's Uproar*, STAR TRIBUNE (Minneapolis), Oct. 20, 1994, at 7A (quoting Coe).

224. Pamela J. Podger & Michael Doyle, *War of Words*, FRESNO BEE, Jan. 9, 1994, at A1 (quoting Coe).

225. *See* Kevin R. Johnson, *Public Benefits and Immigration: The Intersection of Immigration Status, Ethnicity, Gender, and Class*, 42 UCLA LAW REVIEW 1509, 1571–72 (1995); Kevin R. Johnson, *An Essay on Immigration Politics, Popular Democracy, and California's Proposition 187: The Political Relevance and Legal Irrelevance of Race*, 70 WASHINGTON LAW REVIEW 629 (1995).

226. *See Times Poll: A Look at the Electorate*, LOS ANGELES TIMES, Nov. 10, 1994, at B2 (describing exit poll results). Polls taken immediately before the election suggested that the vote would be much closer. *See* Ed Mendel, *"The Door Is Open" If Voters Kill 187, Co-author Warns*, SAN DIEGO UNION-TRIBUNE, Nov. 4, 1994, at A1 (reporting that the polls showed that the Proposition 187 vote was a dead heat). A disjunction between polls and election results is common in racially polarized elections.

227. *See, for example*, Paul Feldman & Jon Garcia, *California Elections/Proposition 187*, LOS ANGELES TIMES, Nov. 8, 1994, at A3 (reporting that at southern California high schools stickers bearing a swastika and stating "stop non-white immigration" were posted throughout the campuses).

228. *See, for example*, Thomas D. Elias, *Fear, Insults Increase After Prop. 187 Vote*, ARIZONA REPUBLIC, Dec. 10, 1994, at A31; *187's Vigilante "Enforcers,"* CHRISTIAN SCIENCE MONITOR, Dec. 27, 1994, at 19.

229. *Morning Edition: Prop. 187 Causing Problems Despite Court Restraint* (National Public Radio broadcast, Nov. 29, 1994).

230. Maria Puente, *States Setting Stage for Their Own Prop. 187s*, USA TODAY, Nov. 18, 1994, at 3A (emphasis added) (quoting Don Barrington).

231. CALIFORNIA SENATE OFFICE OF RESEARCH, ANALYSIS OF STATE PROPOSITIONS ON THE NOVEMBER 1994 BALLOT 93–94 (1994) (alteration added) (quoting Bill Hemby, lobbyist for the California Organization of Police and Sheriffs).

232. *See, for example*, Orhorhaghe v. INS, 38 F.3d 488 (9th Cir. 1994) (finding that the INS violated the Fourth Amendment by searching and seizing and later seeking to deport a noncitizen in part because of his Nigerian-sounding name); Gonzalez-Rivera v. INS, 22 F.3d 1441, 1446–47 (9th Cir. 1994) (finding that Border Patrol officers stopped a noncitizen exclusively because of Hispanic appearance).

233. *See* CALIFORNIA SENATE OFFICE OF RESEARCH, *supra* note 231, at 75–78; CALIFORNIA BALLOT PAMPHLET, *supra* note 208, at 51 (analysis of the legislative analyst).

234. *See, for example*, Rich Connell, *Prop 187's Support Shows No Boundaries*, LOS ANGELES TIMES, Sept. 25, 1994, at A1 (reporting that critics claimed that Proposition 187 would throw suspicion on minorities who speak with accents).

235. *See* League of United Latin American Citizens v. Wilson, 908 F. Supp. 755 (C.D. Cal. 1995).

236. *See* Peter H. Schuck, *The Message of 187*, AMERICAN PROSPECT, Spring 1995, at 85.

237. *See, for example*, Yniguez v. Arizonans for Official English, 69 F.3d 920, 947 (9th Cir. 1995) (en banc) ("[T]he adverse impact of . . . the overbreadth [of Arizona's English-only law] is especially egregious because it is not uniformly spread over the population, but falls almost entirely upon Hispanics and other national origin minorities.") (citation omitted) (alterations added), *vacated as moot*, 520 U.S. 43 (1997).

238. *See, for example*, Fiallo v. Bell, 430 U.S. 787, 792 (1977) (upholding gender and legitimacy classifications in immigration laws and recognizing the "limited scope of judicial inquiry into immigration legislation"); Kleindienst v. Mandel, 408 U.S. 753, 770 (1972) (holding "that when Executive exercises . . . power . . . on the basis of a facially neutral and bona fide reason, the courts will neither look behind the exercise of that discretion, nor test it by balancing its justification against the First Amendment interests of those who seek personal communication with the applicant").

239. *See* Peter H. Schuck, *The Transformation of Immigration Law*, 84 COLUMBIA LAW REVIEW 1, 1 (1984).

240. *See, for example*, GERALD L. NEUMAN, STRANGERS TO THE CONSTITUTION: IMMIGRANTS, BORDERS, AND FUNDAMENTAL LAW (1996); Gabriel J. Chin, *Segregation's Last Stronghold: Race Discrimination and the Constitutional Law of Immigration*, 46 UCLA LAW REVIEW 1 (1998); Linda Kelly, *Preserving the Fundamental Right to Family Unity: Championing Notions of Social Contract and Community Ties in the Battle of Plenary Power Versus Aliens' Rights*, 41 VILLANOVA LAW REVIEW 725, 771–82 (1996); Stephen H. Legomsky, *Immigration Law and the Principle of Plenary Congressional Power*, 1984 SUPREME COURT REVIEW 255; Michael Scaperlanda, *Partial Membership and the Constitutional Community*, 81 IOWA LAW REVIEW 707 (1996); Margaret H. Taylor, *Detained Aliens Challenging Conditions of Confinement and the Porous Border of the*

Plenary Power Doctrine, 22 HASTINGS CONSTITUTIONAL LAW JOURNAL 1087, 1155–56 (1995).

241. Graham v. Richardson, 403 U.S. 365, 372 (1971) (quoting United States v. Carolene Products Co., 304 U.S. 144, 153 n.4 (1938)); *see* Sugarman v. Dougall, 413 U.S. 634 (1973) (invalidating the prohibition of noncitizens from the state civil service system).

242. *See* Gerald M. Rosberg, *The Protection of Aliens from Discriminatory Treatment by the National Government,* 1977 SUPREME COURT REVIEW 275, 294 ("[I]f alienage is a suspect classification when made the basis of state regulation, should it not remain suspect when it is used by the federal government?").

243. 426 U.S. 67 (1976).

244. 347 U.S. 483 (1954).

245. *See, for example,* Kleindienst v. Mandel, 408 U.S. 753, 762–65 (1972) (refusing, because the attorney general offered legitimate and bona fide non-speech-related reason not to waive exclusion grounds, to consider First Amendment interests of citizens who would have communicated with a noncitizen denied entry into the United States); Adams v. Baker, 909 F.2d 643, 647 n.1 (1st Cir. 1990) ("[I]t is important to recognize that the only issue that may be addressed by this court is the possibility of impairment of United States citizens' First Amendment rights through the exclusion of the alien") (*citing Mandel,* 408 U.S. at 762); Allende v. Schultz, 605 F. Supp. 1220, 1224 (D. Mass. 1985) ("The lower federal courts have interpreted *Mandel* to require the Government to provide a justification for an alien's exclusion when that exclusion is challenged by United States citizens asserting constitutional claims.") (emphasis added), *aff'd,* 845 F.2d 1111 (1st Cir. 1988).

246. Rosberg, *supra* note 242, at 327.

247. TRUMAN PAPERS, *supra* note 78, at 443.

248. Gabriel J. Chin, *The Civil Rights Revolution Comes to Immigration Law: A New Look at the Immigration and Nationality Act of 1965,* 75 NORTH CAROLINA LAW REVIEW 273, 302 (1996) (quoting *Immigration: Hearings Before Subcommittee No. 1 of the House Committee on the Judiciary on H.R. 7700 and 55 Identical Bills,* 88th Cong. 390 (1964)); *see* Louis L. Jaffe, *The Philosophy of Our Immigration Law,* 21 LAW AND CONTEMPORARY PROBLEMS 358, 358 (1956) ("[National origin] quota provisions were born in racial prejudice. They give needless offense to many of our citizens and to the people of other countries; they bedevil the conduct of our foreign relations and add nothing to our public welfare.").

249. Brown v. Board of Education, 347 U.S. 483, 494 (1954).

250. *See generally* DAVID G. GUTIÉRREZ, WALLS AND MIRRORS: MEXICAN AMERICANS, MEXICAN IMMIGRANTS, AND THE POLITICS OF ETHNICITY (1995); Kevin R. Johnson, *Immigration and Latino Identity,* 19 UCLA CHICANO-LATINO LAW REVIEW 197 (1998).

251. *See* PETER SKERRY, MEXICAN AMERICANS: THE AMBIVALENT MINORITY 304–08 (1993).

252. *See* Patricia W. Linville et al., *Stereotyping and Perceived Distributions of Social Characteristics: An Application to Ingroup-Outgroup Perception, in* PREJUDICE, DISCRIMINATION, AND RACISM 165 (John F. Dovidio & Samuel L. Gaertner eds., 1986).

253. See Henri Tajfel, *Cognitive Aspects of Prejudice*, 25 JOURNAL OF SOCIOLOGICAL ISSUES 79, 82 (1969).

254. *See* Harry H.L. Kitano, *Asian-Americans: The Chinese, Japanese, Koreans, Pilipinos, and Southeast Asians*, 454 ANNALS 125, 126 (1981).

255. Korematsu v. United States, 323 U.S. 214 (1944).

256. *See, for example,* Peggy C. Davis, *Law as Microaggression*, 98 YALE LAW JOURNAL 1559 (1989); Richard Delgado, *Words That Wound: A Tort Action for Racial Insults, Epithets, and Name-Calling*, 17 HARVARD CIVIL RIGHTS–CIVIL LIBERTIES LAW REVIEW 133, 135–49 (1982); Charles R. Lawrence III, *The Id, the Ego, and Equal Protection: Reckoning with Unconscious Racism*, 39 STANFORD LAW REVIEW 317 (1987).

257. Thomas L. Shaffer, *Undue Influence, Confidential Relationship, and the Psychology of Transference*, 45 NOTRE DAME LAWYER 197, 205 (1970).

258. *See* Elizabeth F. Loftus, *Unconscious Transference in Eyewitness Identification*, 2 LAW AND PSYCHOLOGY LAW REVIEW 93 (1976); *see also* Francis A. Gilligan et al., *The Theory of "Unconscious Transference": The Latest Threat to the Shield Laws Protecting the Privacy of Sex Offenses*, 38 BOSTON COLLEGE LAW REVIEW 107, 111–17 (1996).

259. As Gordon Allport observed in a different context, "No single theory of prejudice is adequate." GORDON W. ALLPORT, THE NATURE OF PREJUDICE 352 (1954). The psychological literature makes clear that a complex interplay of factors contributes to the development of anti-immigrant sentiment. *See, for example,* Gregory R. Maio et al., *Ambivalence and Persuasion: The Processing of Messages About Immigrant Groups*, 32 JOURNAL OF EXPERIMENTAL SOCIAL PSYCHOLOGY 513 (1996); Gregory R. Maio et al., *The Formation of Attitudes Toward New Immigrant Groups*, 24 JOURNAL OF APPLIED SOCIAL PSYCHOLOGY 1762 (1994).

260. DAVID KRECH ET AL., ELEMENTS OF PSYCHOLOGY 768 (2d ed. 1969).

261. *See* ALLPORT, *supra* note 259, at 343–53.

262. *See* Neal E. Miller & Richard Bugelski, *Minor Studies of Aggression: II. The Influence of Frustrations Imposed by the In-Group on Attitudes Expressed Toward Out-Groups*, 25 JOURNAL OF PSYCHOLOGY 437 (1948).

263. *See* ALLPORT, *supra* note 259, at 243–59.

264. *Id.* at 352.

265. *See generally* LEON FESTINGER, A THEORY OF COGNITIVE DISSONANCE (1957).

266. Cass R. Sunstein, *Three Civil Rights Fallacies*, 79 CALIFORNIA LAW REVIEW 751, 759–60 (1991) (footnote omitted).

267. GRANT, *supra* note 71, at 17; *see also* ROY L. GARIS, IMMIGRATION RESTRICTION: A STUDY OF THE OPPOSITION TO AND REGULATION OF IMMIGRATION INTO THE UNITED STATES, at vii (1927) (expressing similar views and emphasizing that "our capacity to maintain our cherished institutions stands diluted by a stream of alien blood, with all its inherited misconceptions respecting the relationships of the governing power to the governed").

268. *See* Kimberlé Crenshaw, *Demarginalizing the Intersection of Race and Sex: A Feminist Critique of Antidiscrimination Doctrine, Feminist Theory and Antiracist Politics*, 1989 UNIVERSITY OF CHICAGO LEGAL FORUM 139; Angela P. Harris, *Race and Essentialism in Feminist Legal Theory*, 42 STANFORD LAW REVIEW 58 (1990).

Chapter 3: Exclusion and Deportation
of Political Undesirables

1. *See generally* JAMES MORTON SMITH, FREEDOM'S FETTERS: THE ALIEN AND SEDITION LAWS AND AMERICAN CIVIL LIBERTIES (1956).

2. *See* Viet D. Dinh, *Foreword: Freedom and Security After September 11*, 25 HARVARD JOURNAL OF LAW AND PUBLIC POLICY 399, 401–06 (2002); *The Aftermath of September 11: A Chronology*, 79 INTERPRETER RELEASES app. I, at 1359 (2002); Margaret Graham, *The Closing Door: U.S. Policies Leave Immigrants Separate and Unequal*, ABA JOURNAL, Sept. 2002, at 43; *see also* Michele R. Pistone, *A Time Sensitive Response to Professor Aleinikoff's Detaining Plenary Power*, 16 GEORGETOWN IMMIGRATION LAW JOURNAL 391, 399–400 (2002) (observing that, after September 11, 2001, the nation had moved from contemplating more open borders to considering policy options and controls that would enhance security). For criticism of the various measures, see Susan M. Akram & Kevin R. Johnson, *Race, Civil Rights, and Immigration Law After September 11, 2001: The Targeting of Arabs and Muslims*, 58 NEW YORK UNIVERSITY ANNUAL SURVEY OF AMERICAN LAW 295 (2002); Raquel Aldana-Pindell, *The 9/11 "National Security" Cases: Three Principles Guiding Judges' Decision-Making*, OREGON LAW REVIEW (forthcoming 2003); Sameer M. Ashar, *Immigration Enforcement and Subordination: The Consequences of Racial Profiling After September 11*, 34 CONNECTICUT LAW REVIEW 1185 (2002); David Cole, *Enemy Aliens*, 54 STANFORD LAW REVIEW 853 (2002); Bill Ong Hing, *Vigilante Racism: The De-Americanization of Immigrant America*, 7 MICHIGAN JOURNAL OF RACE AND LAW 441 (2002); Thomas W. Joo, *Presumed Disloyal: Wen Ho Lee, War on Terrorism and Construction of Race*, 34 COLUMBIA HUMAN RIGHTS LAW REVIEW 1 (2002); Leti Volpp, *The Citizen and the Terrorist*, 49 UCLA LAW REVIEW 1575 (2002).

3. John A. Scanlan, *Aliens in the Marketplace of Ideas: The Government, the Academy, and the McCarran-Walter Act*, 66 TEXAS LAW REVIEW 1481, 1518 (1988).

4. *See* SMITH, *supra* note 1, at 23.

5. *See* JOHN HIGHAM, STRANGERS IN THE LAND: PATTERNS OF AMERICAN NATIVISM 1860–1925, at 55 (3d ed. 1992).

6. *See generally* MARTY JEZER, THE DARK AGES: LIFE IN THE UNITED STATES 1945–1960, at 77–106 (1982); STEPHEN J. WHITFIELD, THE CULTURE OF THE COLD WAR (1991).

7. *See, for example,* Jay v. Boyd, 351 U.S. 345 (1956) (permitting the attorney general to deport a sixty-five-year-old noncitizen who had entered the United States in 1921); Galvan v. Press, 347 U.S. 522 (1954) (upholding the deportation of a man who had lived in the United States since 1918); Shaughnessy v. United States *ex rel.* Mezei, 345 U.S. 206, 208 (1953) (refusing reentry into the country to a lawful permanent resident who had lived in the United States for twenty-five years).

8. *See* Public Law No. 107-56, 115 Statutes at Large 272 (2001) (Uniting and Strengthening America by Providing Appropriate Tools Required to Intercept and Obstruct Terrorism (USA PATRIOT) Act of 2001) [hereinafter USA PATRIOT Act].

9. Scanlan, *supra* note 3, at 1504–05 (footnotes omitted).

10. *See* HIGHAM, *supra* note 5, at 75 (discussing nationalistic tendencies in the United States during the 1890s).

11. *See* Narenji v. Civiletti, 617 F.2d 745, 746–47 (D.C. Cir. 1979) (upholding requirements), *cert. denied sub nom.*, 446 U.S. 957 (1980).

12. *See* KEITH FITZGERALD, THE FACE OF THE NATION: IMMIGRATION, THE STATE, AND THE NATIONAL IDENTITY 77–95 (1996).

13. *See* Kevin R. Johnson, *Responding to the "Litigation Explosion": The Plain Meaning of Executive Branch Primacy over Immigration*, 71 NORTH CAROLINA LAW REVIEW 413, 455–56 (1993); Michael G. Heyman, *Judicial Review of Discretionary Immigration Decisionmaking*, 31 SAN DIEGO LAW REVIEW 861, 866–71 (1994); Daniel Kanstroom, *Surrounding the Hole in the Doughnut: Discretion and Deference in U.S. Immigration Law*, 71 TULANE LAW REVIEW 703, 801–06 (1997).

14. *See* Antiterrorism and Effective Death Penalty Act of 1996, Public Law No. 104-132, 110 Statutes at Large 1214 (1996) [hereinafter AEDPA].

15. *See* Illegal Immigration Reform and Immigrant Responsibility Act of 1996, Public Law No. 104-208, 110 Statutes at Large 3009 (1996) [hereinafter IIRIRA].

16. *See, for example*, Emily M. Berstein, *Islam in Oklahoma: Fear About Retaliation Among Muslim Groups: Arab-American Groups Condemn Act*, NEW YORK TIMES, Apr. 21, 1995, at A26; Walter Goodman, *Wary Network Anchors Battle Dubious Scoops*, NEW YORK TIMES, Apr. 20, 1995, at B12.

17. *See* United States v. Rahman, 854 F. Supp. 254, 258 (S.D.N.Y. 1994); Joseph P. Fried, *Sheik and Nine Followers Guilty of Conspiracy of Terrorism*, NEW YORK TIMES, Oct. 2, 1995, at A1.

18. *See* Statement on Signing the Antiterrorism and Effective Death Penalty Act of 1996, 17 WEEKLY COMPILATION OF PRESIDENTIAL DOCUMENTS 719, 721 (Apr. 24, 1996).

19. *See* Note, *Blown Away? The Bill of Rights After Oklahoma City*, 109 HARVARD LAW REVIEW 2074, 2074–75 & nn.3–4 (1996) (summarizing the roots of the AEDPA in the Oklahoma City bombing).

20. *See* U.S. CONST, amend. I (guaranteeing freedom of speech and press); *see, for example*, R.A.V. v. City of St. Paul, 505 U.S. 377, 395–96 (1992) (invalidating the hate crime statute in a case in which the defendant was convicted of burning a cross on the lawn of an African American family); Texas v. Johnson, 491 U.S. 397, 420 (1989) (holding that the First Amendment protects the expression of unpopular political views by citizens and explaining that burning the U.S. flag is a form of political expression); Brandenberg v. Ohio, 395 U.S. 444, 447 (1969) (holding, in a case involving the Ku Klux Klan, that the government may criminalize speech only when the speaker intended to incite "imminent lawless action" and the speech has the clear and present danger of producing that result); *see also* MICHAEL WELCH, FLAG BURNING: MORAL PANIC AND THE CRIMINALIZATION OF PROTEST (2000) (analyzing the U.S. government's efforts to regulate political speech in the form of flag burning).

21. Whitney v. California, 274 U.S. 357, 375 (1927) (Brandeis, J., concurring) (footnote omitted).

22. Abrams v. United States, 250 U.S. 616, 630 (1919) (Holmes, J., dissenting).

23. *See* Robert H. Bork, *Neutral Principles and Some First Amendment Problems*, 47 INDIANA LAW JOURNAL 1, 20 (1971).

24. *See* 2 CHARLES GORDON ET AL., IMMIGRATION LAW AND PROCEDURE § 61.04[2], at 61-58 to 61-63 (1996); EDWARD P. HUTCHINSON, LEGISLATIVE HISTORY OF AMERICAN IMMIGRATION POLICY 1798–1965, at 443–46 (1981); Mitchell C. Tilner, *Ideological Exclusion of Aliens: The Evolution of a Policy*, 2 GEORGETOWN IMMIGRATION LAW JOURNAL 1, 53–57 (1987).

25. Alien Enemy Act of July 14, 1798, ch. 66, § 1, 1 Statutes at Large 577 (1798) (current version at 50 U.S.C. §§ 21–23 (1994)).

26. Alien Act of June 25, 1798, ch. 58, § 1, 1 Statutes at Large 570, 571 (1798) (expired 1800); *see* CLEMENT L. BOUVÉ, A TREATISE ON THE LAWS GOVERNING THE EXCLUSION AND EXPULSION OF ALIENS IN THE UNITED STATES 51–55 (1912) (summarizing the provisions of the act and the fact that "Jefferson, Madison and other jurists and statesmen . . . denounced the act, not only as being unconstitutional, but as opposed to recognized precepts of international law adopted and cherished by civilized nations").

27. SMITH, *supra* note 1, at 175.

28. *See* Louis Henkin, *The Constitution and United States Sovereignty: A Century of Chinese Exclusion and Its Progeny*, 100 HARVARD LAW REVIEW 853, 859 (1987) (stating that "[t]he *Chinese Exclusion* doctrine and its extensions have permitted, and perhaps encouraged, paranoia, xenophobia, and racism, particularly during periods of international tension").

29. *See* PAUL AVRICH, THE HAYMARKET TRAGEDY 181–96 (1984); HENRY DAVID, THE HISTORY OF THE HAYMARKET AFFAIR 194, 198–204 (2d ed. 1958).

30. Spies v. Illinois, 123 U.S. 131, 182 (1887).

31. *See* HIGHAM, *supra* note 5, at 54–63 (analyzing the rise of nativist sentiment during this period).

32. *See* U.S. SELECT COMMISSION ON IMMIGRATION AND REFUGEE POLICY, STAFF REPORT: U.S. IMMIGRATION POLICY AND THE NATIONAL INTEREST 732 (1981).

33. Immigration Act of March 3, 1903, ch. 1012, § 2, 32 Statutes at Large 1213, 1214 (1903). The Immigration Act of February 20, 1907, for the most part carried forward the ideological exclusions of the 1903 law. *See* Immigration Act of February 20, 1907, ch. 1138, § 43, 34 Statutes at Large 898, 899 (1907).

34. Scanlan, *supra* note 3, at 1493.

35. 194 U.S. 279, 283 (1904).

36. *Id.* at 283 (quoting one of Turner's addresses).

37. *Id.* at 294; *see* Scanlan, *supra* note 3, at 1499–1505. *But see* Berta Esperanza Hernández-Truyol, *Natives, Newcomers and Nativism: A Human Rights Model for the Twenty-first Century*, 23 FORDHAM URBAN LAW JOURNAL 1096 (1996) (stating that human rights considerations place limits on sovereign power to exclude immigrants); James A.R. Nafziger, *The General Admission of Aliens Under International Law*, 77 AMERICAN JOURNAL OF INTERNATIONAL LAW 804, 804–05 (1983) (challenging the notion that sovereign powers of nations allow unlimited power to exclude); Michael Scaperlanda, *Polishing the Tarnished Golden Door*, 1993 WISCONSIN LAW REVIEW 965, 1002–31 (arguing that the conception that the nation had absolute sovereignty over immigration has lost intellectual force because of growing respect for human rights under international law).

38. *See* 4 PHILIP S. FONER, HISTORY OF THE LABOR MOVEMENT IN THE UNITED STATES: THE INDUSTRIAL WORKERS OF THE WORLD, 1905–07, at 23–24 (1965).

39. JOHN CLENDENIN TOWNSEND, RUNNING THE GAUNTLET: CULTURAL SOURCES OF VIOLENCE AGAINST THE I.W.W. 3 (1986).

40. *See* WILLIAM PRESTON JR., ALIENS AND DISSENTERS: FEDERAL SUPPRESSION OF RADICALS, 1903–1933, at 5–8 (2d ed. 1994).

41. ELDRIDGE FOSTER DOWELL, A HISTORY OF CRIMINAL SYNDICALISM LEGISLATION IN THE UNITED STATES 22–23 (1939) (footnotes omitted).

42. *See generally* PAUL AVRICH, SACCO AND VANZETTI: THE ANARCHIST BACKGROUND (1991); FRANCIS RUSSELL, SACCO AND VANZETTI: THE CASE RESOLVED (1986).

43. Anarchist Act of October 16, 1918, ch. 186, 40 Statutes at Large 1012 (1918).

44. *Id.* § 1 (emphasis added).

45. HOUSE OF REPRESENTATIVES REPORT NO. 65-645, at 1 (1918).

46. *See generally* EDWIN P. HOYT, THE PALMER RAIDS 1919–1920: AN ATTEMPT TO SUPPRESS DISSENT (1969); Robert D. Warth, *The Palmer Raids,* 48 SOUTH ATLANTIC QUARTERLY 1 (1949).

47. *See, for example,* United States *ex rel.* Diamond v. Uhl, 266 F. 34, 39–40 (2d Cir. 1920); United States *ex rel.* Rakics v. Uhl, 266 F. 646, 648, 652 (2d Cir. 1920); Guiney v. Bonham, 261 F. 582, 583, 586 (9th Cir. 1919). A refreshing exception to this pattern is *Ex parte* Jackson, 263 F. 110, 112 (D. Mont.), *appeal dismissed,* 267 F. 1022 (9th Cir. 1920), in which Judge George M. Bourquin granted a writ of habeas corpus and decried the unlawful conduct of the government raiders who "perpetrated a reign of terror, violence, and *crime against citizen and alien alike*" (emphasis added).

48. *See* RICHARD DRINNON, REBEL IN PARADISE: A BIOGRAPHY OF EMMA GOLDMAN 222 (1961); HOYT, *supra* note 46, at 73–82.

49. *See* MICHAEL R. BELKNAP, COLD WAR POLITICAL JUSTICE: THE SMITH ACT, THE COMMUNIST PARTY, AND AMERICAN CIVIL LIBERTIES 16, 134 (1977); MILTON R. KONVITZ, CIVIL RIGHTS IN IMMIGRATION 123 (Greenwood Press, 1977) (1953).

50. R.G. BROWN ET AL., REPORT UPON THE ILLEGAL PRACTICES OF THE UNITED STATES DEPARTMENT OF JUSTICE 4 (1920) (emphasis added).

51. *Id.* at 7 (emphasis added).

52. *See* Anarchist Act of June 5, 1920, ch. 251, 41 Statutes at Large 1008 (1920).

53. *See* HOUSE OF REPRESENTATIVES REPORT NO. 66-504, at 7 (1919) (concluding that "the joining of an organization such as the Industrial Workers of the World by an alien is of itself the overt act sufficient to warrant deportation").

54. 264 U.S. 131 (1924); *see also* United States *ex rel.* Vajtauer v. Commissioner of Immigration, 273 U.S. 103, 113 (1927) (affirming a deportation order based on the Anarchist Act of 1918, as amended in 1920, for a Czechoslovakian newspaper editor who advocated the overthrow of the U.S. government by violence).

55. *See* Jamin B. Raskin, *Legal Aliens, Local Citizens: The Historical, Constitutional and Theoretical Meanings of Alien Suffrage,* 141 UNIVERSITY OF PENNSYLVANIA LAW REVIEW 1391, 1415–16 (1993).

56. *See* U.S. DEPARTMENT OF JUSTICE, IMMIGRATION AND NATURALIZATION SERVICE, 1994 STATISTICAL YEARBOOK OF THE IMMIGRATION AND NATURALIZATION SERVICE

166 tbl.66 (Aliens Deported by Cause Fiscal Years 1908–80) (1996) [hereinafter 1994 INS STATISTICAL YEARBOOK].

57. *See id.* at 162 tbl.61 (Aliens Excluded by Cause Fiscal Years 1892–1984).

58. *See* U.S. DEPARTMENT OF STATE, REPORT OF THE VISA OFFICE 76 tbl. XXII (Immigrant and Nonimmigrant Visas Refused) (1974) (reporting statistical data showing that, in final consular decisions, more than 200 immigrant visas and more than 350 nonimmigrant visas were denied on ideological grounds in fiscal year 1974).

59. 307 U.S. 22 (1939).

60. *See* U.S. SELECT COMMISSION ON IMMIGRATION AND REFUGEE POLICY, STAFF REPORT, *supra* note 32, at 737.

61. *See* Alien Registration Act of 1940, ch. 439, §§ 1–4, 54 Stat. 670, 670–76 (1940).

62. *See, for example,* Galvan v. Press, 347 U.S. 522, 529–30 (1954) (permitting the deportation of a noncitizen because of past membership in the Communist Party), *cert. denied,* 355 U.S. 905 (1957); Carlson v. Landon, 342 U.S. 524, 544–46 (1952) (allowing the detention of a noncitizen without bail in order to prevent potential inculcation of "doctrines of force and violence into the political philosophy of the American people"); Ocon v. Guercio, 237 F.2d 177, 179–80 (9th Cir. 1956) (concluding that the law making membership in the Communist Party a ground for deportation did not violate the Constitution); United States *ex rel.* Avramovich v. Lehmann, 235 F.2d 260, 262–63 (6th Cir. 1956) (recognizing the authority of the attorney general to label organizations as communist and recognizing that membership in such organizations may be grounds for deportation), *cert. denied,* 355 U.S. 905 (1957); *see also* Steven R. Shapiro, *Ideological Exclusions: Closing the Border to Political Dissidents,* 100 HARVARD LAW REVIEW 930, 939–42 (1987) (discussing the government's justification of ideological exclusions during the McCarthy era).

63. 338 U.S. 537 (1950).

64. 345 U.S. 206 (1953). For a discussion of the life stories behind *Knauff* and *Mezei,* see Charles D. Weisselberg, *The Exclusion and Detention of Aliens: Lessons from the Lives of Ellen Knauff and Ignatz Mezei,* 143 UNIVERSITY OF PENNSYLVANIA LAW REVIEW 933, 954–85 (1995).

65. *See* Knauff v. Shaughnessy, 338 U.S. 537, 546–47 (1950).

66. *Id.* at 542 (citing United States v. Curtiss-Wright Export Corp., 299 U.S. 304 (1936)).

67. Shaughnessy v. United States *ex rel.* Mezei, 345 U.S. 208 (1953).

68. *Id.* at 210 (citing, *inter alia, The Chinese Exclusion Case* (Chae Chan Ping v. United States), 130 U.S. 581 (1889)); *see Knauff,* 338 U.S. at 537; Harisiades v. Shaughnessy, 342 U.S. 580 (1952)). *But see* Henry M. Hart Jr., *The Power of Congress to Limit the Jurisdiction of Federal Courts: An Exercise in Dialectic,* 66 HARVARD LAW REVIEW 1362, 1391–96 (1953) (criticizing the "brutal conclusions" of *Knauff* and *Mezei*).

69. *See* T. Alexander Aleinikoff, *Aliens, Due Process and "Community Ties": A Response to Martin,* 44 UNIVERSITY OF PITTSBURGH LAW REVIEW 237, 237 (1983).

70. *See* ELIZABETH HULL, WITHOUT JUSTICE FOR ALL: THE CONSTITUTIONAL RIGHTS OF ALIENS 56–57 (1985); KONVITZ, *supra* note 49, at 49.

71. *See* Weisselberg, *supra* note 64, at 963–64.

72. *Id.* at 971–75, 983–84. The U.S. government had previously ordered some members of the International Workers Order (IWO) to be deported. *See In re* D, 4

Immigration and Nationality Decisions 578, 579, 588 (Board of Immigration Appeals 1951) (sustaining the deportation of a Ukrainian immigrant who was a member of the IWO national committee); *In re* L, 1 Immigration and Nationality Decisions 450, 458 (Board of Immigration Appeals 1943) (finding that a noncitizen was inadmissible because of IWO membership).

73. 342 U.S. 580 (1952).

74. *Id.* at 590; *see* Scaperlanda, *supra* note 37, at 988 & n.102 (describing the extreme hardships of deportation faced by former Communist Party members in *Harisiades*). In *Harisiades*, the Court arguably applied the same narrow interpretation of First Amendment protections then applicable to citizens. *See* Harisiades v. Shaughnessy, 342 U.S. 591–92 (1952).

75. *Harisiades*, 342 U.S. at 597 (Frankfurter, J., concurring).

76. Internal Security Act of 1950, Public Law No. 81-831, § 22, 64 Statutes at Large 987, 1006–07 (1950); *see* Carlson v. Landon, 342 U.S. 524, 537–47 (1952) (upholding various portions of the act in the face of constitutional challenge). *See generally* Charles Gordon, *The Immigration Process and National Security*, 24 TEMPLE LAW QUARTERLY 302 (1950).

77. Internal Security Act of 1950, Public Law No. 81-831, *supra* note 76, § 2(12)–(14), 64 Statutes at Large at 987, 988–89 (emphasis added); *see* HOUSE OF REPRESENTATIVES REPORT NO. 81-2980 (1950), *reprinted in* 1950 U.S. CODE CONGRESSIONAL & ADMINISTRATIVE NEWS 3886, 3886–90 (echoing similar concerns about communist infiltration by foreigners in describing the necessity for legislation).

78. 347 U.S. 522 (1954).

79. *Id.* at 524. Neither the Court's decision nor the record is clear on the precise nature of the Spanish Speaking Club. The organization was possibly a mutual aid society (*mutualista*) organized by Mexican-Americans and Mexican immigrants, common in the Southwest during this era. *See* JULIAN SAMORA & PATRICIA VANDEL SIMON, A HISTORY OF THE MEXICAN-AMERICAN PEOPLE 173–75 (1993). Some *mutualistas* that were designed to improve working conditions—the precise type of activity targeted for inquisition during the Cold War—bore names similar to the Spanish Speaking Club. See RODOLFO F. ACUÑA, OCCUPIED AMERICA: THE CHICANO'S STRUGGLE TOWARD LIBERATION 216–18 (1972).

80. *Galvan v. Press*, 347 U.S. at 531.

81. *Id.* at 532–33 (Black, J., dissenting) (citation omitted).

82. Immigration and Nationality Act of 1952, Public Law No. 82-414, 66 Statutes at Large 163 (1952) (codified as amended in scattered sections of 8 U.S.C.) [hereinafter INA]. *See generally* Jack Wasserman, *The Immigration and Nationality Act of 1952: Our New Alien and Sedition Act*, 27 TEMPLE LAW QUARTERLY 62, 77–89 (1953) (criticizing various provisions of the INA).

83. 351 U.S. 345, 360–61 (1956).

84. *Jay*, 351 U.S. at 362 (Black, J., dissenting). Justice Black criticized the majority for upholding Jay's deportation based on his Communist Party membership; ten years *after* Jay left the party, membership was made a ground for deportation. *See id.* at 362–63.

85. *See* 1994 INS STATISTICAL YEARBOOK, *supra* note 56, at 166 tbl.66 (Aliens Deported by Cause Fiscal Years 1908–80).

86. *Id.* at 162 tbl.61 (Aliens Excluded by Cause Fiscal Years 1892–1984).

87. *See generally* STANLEY I. KUTLER, THE AMERICAN INQUISITION: JUSTICE AND IN-JUSTICE IN THE COLD WAR (1982).

88. *See* Norman Dorsen, *Foreign Affairs and Civil Liberties*, 83 AMERICAN JOURNAL OF INTERNATIONAL LAW 840, 841 (1989).

89. Scanlan, *supra* note 3, at 1504.

90. KUTLER, *supra* note 87, at 149. *See generally* CHARLES P. LARROWE, HARRY BRIDGES: THE RISE AND FALL OF RADICAL LABOR IN THE UNITED STATES (1972).

91. *See* Peter Irons, *Politics and Principle: An Assessment of the Roosevelt Record on Civil Rights and Liberties*, 59 WASHINGTON LAW REVIEW 693, 711–16 (1984).

92. *See* U.S. DEPARTMENT OF LABOR, IN THE MATTER OF HARRY R. BRIDGES, FIND-INGS AND CONCLUSIONS OF THE TRIAL EXAMINER 132–34 (1939).

93. *See* Bridges v. Wixon, 326 U.S. 135, 140–41 (1945) (detailing Bridges's participation in unions and his dealings with the Communist Party).

94. *Id.* at 147.

95. *Id.* at 148 (citation omitted) (emphasis added).

96. *Id.* at 157 (Murphy, J., concurring) (emphasis added).

97. *See* United States v. Bridges, 87 F. Supp. 14 (N.D. Cal. 1949).

98. *See* Bridges v. United States, 199 F.2d 811, 815 (9th Cir. 1952), *rev'd and remanded*, 346 U.S. 209 (1953).

99. *See* United States v. Bridges, 133 F. Supp. 638, 643 (N.D. Cal. 1955). A chronology of the U.S. government's many efforts to rid the country of Bridges can be found in *id.* app. A, at 638, 644.

100. *See* Michael Scaperlanda, *Partial Membership: Aliens and the Constitutional Community*, 81 IOWA LAW REVIEW 707, 726 (1996) (stating that "[d]uring the 'red scare' of McCarthyism, Congress wielded [plenary] power to deport long time resident aliens for their thoughts and associations. Today it continues to stand as a sentry at our gates, allowing the political branches to formulate immigration policy without the restrictions that would otherwise be required by our constitutional traditions") (footnotes omitted).

101. *See* Foreign Relations Authorization Act, Public Law No. 100-204 § 901(a)(d), 101 Statutes at Large 1331, 1399–1400 (1987) (suspending Congress's ability to deny visa petitions because of political beliefs that would be constitutionally protected if held by a U.S. citizen).

102. *See* Arthur C. Helton, *Reconciling the Power to Bar or Expel Aliens on Political Grounds with Fairness and the Freedoms of Speech and Association: An Analysis of Recent Legislative Proposals*, 11 FORDHAM INTERNATIONAL LAW JOURNAL 467, 467 (1988) (offering examples); Burt Neuborne & Steven R. Shapiro, *The Nylon Curtain: America's National Border and the Free Flow of Ideas*, 26 WILLIAM AND MARY LAW REVIEW 719, 749–51 (1985) (same); Shapiro, *supra* note 62, at 935–36 (same); *see also* Randall v. Meese, 854 F.2d 472, 472–73 (D.C. Cir. 1988) (reviewing the procedural history in a case in which the INS sought to bar the award of lawful permanent resident status to noted writer and photographer Margaret Randall on the ground that her work reflected communist beliefs).

103. *See* Allende v. Shultz, 605 F. Supp. 1220, 1226–27 (D. Mass. 1985).

104. *See* Harvard Law School Forum v. Shultz, 633 F. Supp. 525, 531–32 (D. Mass. 1986) (enjoining the secretary of state from refusing to grant a visa that would

permit a Palestine Liberation Organization member to participate in a political debate on Middle Eastern politics), *vacated without opinion,* 852 F.2d 563 (1st Cir. 1980); *see also* Allende v. Shultz, 845 F.2d 1111 (1st Cir. 1988) (affirming the summary judgment for the plaintiffs in the case).

105. *See* Abourezk v. Reagan, 592 F. Supp. 880, 888 (D.D.C. 1984) (deciding a challenge to the denial of a visa to Interior Minister of Nicaragua Tomas Borge), *vacated and remanded without opinion,* 785 F.2d 1043 (D.C. Cir. 1986).

106. Neuborne & Shapiro, *supra* note 102, at 723 (footnote omitted).

107. 408 U.S. 753 (1972).

108. *See* 1994 INS STATISTICAL YEARBOOK, *supra* note 56, at 162 tbl.61 (Aliens Excluded by Cause Fiscal Years 1892–1984) and tbl.62 (Aliens Excluded by Cause Fiscal Years 1985–1994).

109. *See id.* at 166.

110. *See, for example,* Scanlan, *supra* note 3, at 1490 (stating that the McCarran-Walter Act allowed for the exclusion of noncitizens who merely belonged to subversive organizations); Shapiro, *supra* note 62, at 939 (stating that Congress showed little enthusiasm for reaffirming the McCarran-Walter Act's ideological exclusion provisions); *see also* U.S. SELECT COMMISSION ON IMMIGRATION AND REFUGEE POLICY, STAFF REPORT, *supra* note 32, at 751 (mentioning criticism of the ideological exclusions heard by the Select Commission).

111. Immigration Act of 1990, Public Law 101-649, 104 Statutes at Large 4978 (1990) (codified as amended in scattered sections of 8 U.S.C.).

112. *See* INA, *supra* note 82, § 212(a)(3)(D)(iii), 8 U.S.C. § 1182 (a)(3)(D)(iii).

113. *Id.* § 212(a)(3)(C)(iii), 8 U.S.C. § 1182(a)(3)(C)(iii).

114. *Id.*; *see* HOUSE CONFERENCE REPORT NO. 101-955, at 129 (1990), *reprinted in* 1990 U.S. CODE CONGRESSIONAL & ADMINISTRATIVE NEWS 6784, 6794 (explaining the "intent of the conference committee that [the secretary of state's] authority [be] used sparingly and not merely because there is a likelihood that an alien will make critical remarks about the United States or its policies").

115. INA, *supra* note 82, § 212(a)(3)(A), 8 U.S.C. § 1182(a)(3)(A).

116. *See id.* § 212(a)(3)(B)(iii), 8 U.S.C. § 1182(a)(3)(B)(ii).

117. *Id.* § 212(a)(3)(C)(i), 8 U.S.C. § 1182(a)(3)(C)(i); *see* Massieu v. Reno, 915 F. Supp. 681, 710–11 (D.N.J. 1996) (holding that the provision could not constitutionally be applied to deport the former attorney general of Mexico), *rev'd on other grounds,* 91 F.3d 416 (3d Cir. 1996).

118. INA, *supra* note 82, § 212(a)(3)(E), 8 U.S.C. § 1182(a)(3)(E).

119. AEDPA, *supra* note 14, § 411, 110 Statutes at Large at 1268 (amending section 212(a)(3)(B)(iii), (iv) of INA, 8 U.S.C. § 1182(a)(3)(B)(iii), (iv)). Congress had previously provided that "[a]n alien who is an officer, official representative, or spokesman of the Palestinian Liberation Organization is considered . . . to be engaged in a terrorist activity." INA, *supra* note 82, § 212(a)(3)(B)(i)(II), 8 U.S.C. § 1182(a)(3)(B)(i)(II).

120. AEDPA, *supra* note 14, § 302, 110 Statutes at Large at 1250 (adding section 219 of INA, 8 U.S.C. § 1189). In adding the provision, Congress found that "the power of the United States over immigration and naturalization permits the exclusion from the United States of persons belonging to international terrorist organizations." *Id.* § 301, 110 Statutes at Large at 1247.

121. *See* David L. Marcus, *Many Thorny Questions Arise as U.S. Compiles Terrorist List,* BOSTON GLOBE, Feb. 4, 1997, at A1 (quoting State Department official).

122. INA, *supra* note 82, § 241(a)(4)(D), 8 U.S.C. § 1251(a)(4).

123. Gerald L. Neuman, *Justifying U.S. Naturalization Policies,* 35 VIRGINIA JOURNAL OF INTERNATIONAL LAW 237, 255 (1994) (footnote omitted).

124. INA, *supra* note 82, § 316(a), 8 U.S.C. § 1427(a); *see, for example,* United States v. Schwimmer, 279 U.S. 644, 652–53 (1929) (finding that a conscientious objector was not attached to constitutional principles). *But see* Girouard v. United States, 328 U.S. 61, 70 (1946) (holding that a noncitizen whose conscientious objection is based on religious reasons may be sufficiently attached to constitutional principles). *See generally* Neuman, *supra* note 123, at 253–63 (analyzing ideological qualifications for naturalization).

125. *See, for example, In re* Clavijo de Bellis, 493 F. Supp. 534, 536 (E.D. Pa. 1980) (denying a naturalization petition because the petitioner failed to take the prescribed oath of allegiance for religious reasons); *In re* Williams, 474 F. Supp. 384, 387 (D. Ariz. 1979) (denying a naturalization petition because of the petitioner's refusal to vote, participate actively in politics, serve on juries, bear arms, or participate in the service for religious reasons); *In re* Matz, 296 F. Supp. 927, 933 (E.D. Cal. 1969) (refusing petitions for naturalization by two lawful permanent residents who, as Jehovah's Witnesses, refused to take the portion of the allegiance oath regarding bearing arms and engaging in noncombatant service in times of war). *But see In re* Del Olmo, 682 F. Supp. 489, 491 (D. Or. 1988) (holding that similar religious objections failed to demonstrate a lack of attachment to constitutional principles); *In re* Battle, 379 F. Supp. 334, 337 (E.D.N.Y. 1974) (reasoning that the petitioner demonstrated "awareness and an appreciation" of her First Amendment rights to free exercise of speech and religion); *In re* Pisciattano, 308 F. Supp. 818, 821 (D. Conn. 1970) (granting a naturalization petition even though the petitioner refused to vote, engage in politics, or serve on a jury).

126. *See* INA, *supra* note 82, §§ 313(a)(1)–(6), 8 U.S.C. §§ 1424(a)(1)–(6).

127. *See* Stasiukevich v. Nicolls, 168 F.2d 474, 480 (1st Cir. 1948); *In re* Thompson, 209 F. Supp. 494, 499 (N.D. Ill. 1962), *appeal dismissed,* 318 F.2d 681 (7th Cir. 1963).

128. *See* Philip Monrad, Comment, *Ideological Exclusion, Plenary Power, and the PLO,* 77 CALIFORNIA LAW REVIEW 831, 833–36 (1989) (reviewing various efforts aimed at excluding members of the Palestine Liberation Organization). The differential treatment afforded to citizens and lawful permanent residents who attended a conference in Syria sponsored by the Palestine Youth Organization is illuminating. *See* Rafeedie v. INS, 688 F. Supp. 729 (D.D.C. 1988) (distinguishing the constitutional protection afforded to citizens and lawful permanent residents from the protection afforded to immigrants without lawful permanent residence), *aff'd in part, rev'd in part,* 880 F.2d 506 (D.C. Cir. 1989). In 1986, a citizen was permitted to return to the United States after the conference, but two lawful permanent residents were placed in exclusion proceedings. *See Rafeedie,* 688 F. Supp. at 744, 752.

129. *See* American-Arab Anti-discrimination Committee v. Meese, 714 F. Supp. 1060, 1063 (C.D. Cal. 1989), *aff'd in part and rev'd in part on other grounds,* American-Arab Anti-discrimination Committee v. Thornburgh, 970 F.2d 501 (9th Cir.

1991); *see also* Linda S. Bosniak, *Membership, Equality, and the Difference That Alienage Makes,* 69 NEW YORK UNIVERSITY LAW REVIEW 1047, 1133–34 (1994) (discussing arguments of parties in a case that included the government's assertion that immigrants do not have First Amendment rights).

130. *See* American-Arab Anti-discrimination Committee v. Reno, 70 F.3d 1045, 1052–53 (9th Cir. 1995) (chronicling the history of charges filed against members of the PFLP).

131. *See Nomination of William H. Webster: Hearings on Nomination of William H. Webster to Be Director of Central Intelligence Before the Select Committee on Intelligence,* 100th Cong. 94–95 (1987) (statement of William H. Webster); *see also American-Arab Anti-discrimination Committee,* 70 F.3d at 1053 (referring to Webster's testimony).

132. INA, *supra* note 82, § 241(a)(4)(B), 8 U.S.C. § 1251(a)(4)(B).

133. *Id.* § 212(a)(3)(B)(iii), 8 U.S.C. § 1182(a)(3)(B)(iii) (emphasis added).

134. Bosniak, *supra* note 129, at 1131 n.347 (quoting a letter from immigration law professors to Attorney General Janet Reno and the U.S. Department of Justice (Sept. 20, 1993)).

135. *See American-Arab Anti-discrimination Committee,* 70 F.3d at 1063.

136. *Id.* at 1054.

137. *See* Reno v. American-Arab Anti-discrimination Committee, 525 U.S. 471 (1999).

138. *See* Benjamin Wittes, *Will "Removal Court" Remove Due Process? Anti-terrorism Bill Creates Secretive Deportation Tribunal,* LEGAL TIMES, Apr. 22, 1996, at 1, 16.

139. HOUSE OF REPRESENTATIVES CONFERENCE REPORT NO. 104-518, at 116 (1996), *reprinted in* 1996 U.S. CODE CONGRESSIONAL & ADMINISTRATIVE NEWS 944, 949.

140. *Id.* at 115, *reprinted in* 1996 U.S. CODE CONGRESSIONAL & ADMINISTRATIVE NEWS at 948.

141. *See* AEDPA, *supra* note 14, § 401, 110 Statutes at Large at 1258 (adding Title V to the INA at sections 501–07); *see also* Michael Scaperlanda, *Are We That Far Gone? Due Process and Secret Deportation Proceedings,* 7 STANFORD LAW AND POLICY REVIEW 23, 25–27 (1996) (analyzing special removal procedures in the predecessor bill).

142. *See* AEDPA, *supra* note 14, § 401, 110 Statutes at Large at 1259–60 (adding sections 502 and 503 to the INA).

143. *See id.* § 401, 110 Statutes at Large at 1262–63 (adding section 504(e)(3) to the INA).

144. *See* Susan M. Akram, *Scheherezade Meets Kafka: Two Dozen Sordid Tales of Ideological Exclusion,* 14 GEORGETOWN IMMIGRATION LAW JOURNAL 51, 52 n.4 (1999).

145. *See* Rafeedie v. INS, 795 F. Supp. 13, 15–22 (D.D.C. 1992).

146. *See, for example,* INS v. Doherty, 502 U.S. 314 (1992); *In re* McMullen, 989 F.2d 603 (2d Cir.), *cert. denied,* 510 U.S. 913 (1993); *see* James T. Kelly, *The Empire Strikes Back: The Taking of Joe Doherty,* 61 FORDHAM LAW REVIEW 317, 319–29 (1992); *see also In re* Doherty, 599 F. Supp. 270, 277 (S.D.N.Y. 1984) (refusing to extradite a PIRA member to the United Kingdom because the crime on which extradition was requested was a "political offense" that, under applicable treaty, was an exception to extradition).

147. *See Guard for Bush Isn't Allowed Aboard Flight,* NEW YORK TIMES, Dec. 27, 2001, at B5; Ken Ellingwood & Nicholas Riccardi, *Arab Americans Enduring Hard*

Stares of Other Fliers, Los Angeles Times, Sept. 20, 2001, at A1; Phillip Morris, *Racial Profiling Has a New Target*, Plain Dealer, Sept. 25, 2001, at B9.

148. *See* Akram & Johnson, *supra* note 2.

149. *See* Laurie Goodstein & Tamar Lewin, *Victims of Mistaken Identity, Sikhs Pay a Price for Turbans*, New York Times, Sept. 19, 2001, at A1.

150. *See* Korematsu v. United States, 323 U.S. 214 (1944) (upholding the internment of persons of Japanese ancestry during World War II). *See generally* Symposium, *The Long Shadow of* Korematsu, 40 Boston College Law Review 1, 19 Boston College Third World Law Journal 1 (1998).

151. *See* Natsu Taylor Saito, *Symbolism Under Siege: Japanese American Redress and the "Racing" of Arab Americans as Terrorists*, 8 Asian Law Journal 1, 11–26 (2001). *See generally* Michael Omi & Howard Winant, Racial Formation in the United States: From the 1960s to the 1980s (2d ed. 1994) (analyzing process of racial formation).

152. *See* Adrien Katherine Wing, Reno v. American-Arab Anti-discrimination Committee: *A Critical Race Critique*, 21 Columbia Human Rights Law Review 561, 571–94 (2000).

153. *See* U.S. Department of Justice, Office of the Inspector General, The September 11 Detainees: A Review of the Treatment of Aliens Held on Immigration Charges in Connection with the Investigation of the September 11 Attacks (2003).

154. *See* USA PATRIOT Act, *supra* note 8.

155. *See* Military Order of November 13, 2001, 66 Federal Register 57833 (Nov. 16, 2001). For assessment of the legality of the military tribunals, see Kenneth Anderson, *What to Do with Bin Laden and Al Qaeda Terrorists? A Qualified Defense of Military Commissions and United States Policy on Detainees at Guantanamo Bay Naval Base*, 25 Harvard Journal of Law and Public Policy 591 (2002); Curtis A. Bradley & Jack L. Goldsmith, *The Constitutional Validity of Military Commissions*, 5 Green Bag 2d 249 (2002); Mark A. Drumbl, *Judging the 11 September Terrorist Attack*, 24 Human Rights Quarterly 323 (2002); George P. Fletcher, *On Justice and War: Contradictions in the Proposed Military Tribunals*, 25 Harvard Journal of Law and Public Policy 635 (2002); Neal K. Katyal & Laurence H. Tribe, *Waging War, Deciding Guilt: Trying the Military Tribunals*, 11 Yale Law Journal 1259 (2002); Jordan J. Paust, *Antiterrorism Military Commissions: Courting Illegality*, 23 Michigan Journal of International Law 1 (2001).

156. *See* David E. Rovella, *Clock Ticks on 9/11 Detentions*, National Law Journal, Nov. 5, 2001, at A1; *A Deliberate Strategy of Disruption*, Washington Post, Nov. 4, 2001, at A1; Lois Romano & David S. Fallis, *Questions Swirl Around Men Held in Terror Probe*, Washington Post, Oct. 15, 2001, at A1.

157. *See DOJ Orders Incentives, "Voluntary" Interviews of Aliens to Obtain Info on Terrorists*, 78 Interpreter Releases 1816, 1817 (2001); Josh Meyer, *The Investigation: The Dragnet Produces Few Terrorist Ties*, Los Angeles Times, Nov. 28, 2001, at A1; *see also* Greg Smith & Joe Calderone, *No Big Fish in 9/11 Dragnet*, Daily News (New York), Nov. 30, 2001, at 6. The first person indicted for conspiracy in the hijackings was Zacarias Moussaoui, who was in federal custody for immigration violations on September 11. *See* David Johnston & Philip Shenon, *Man Held in Custody Since Au-*

gust Is Charged with a Role in Sept. 11 Terror Plot, NEW YORK TIMES, Dec. 12, 2001, at A1.

158. *See* Evan Thomas & Michael Isikoff, *Justice Kept in the Dark,* NEWSWEEK, Dec. 10, 2001, at 37.

159. *See id.* at 42.

160. *See* Susan Milligan, *Fighting Terror/The Detainees Testimony; Yemeni Immigrant Says He Was Abused,* BOSTON GLOBE, Dec. 5, 2001, at A13.

161. *See* Thomas & Isikoff, *supra* note 158, at 39–40.

162. *See* June Fritsch, *Grateful Egyptian Is Freed as U.S. Terror Case Fizzles,* NEW YORK TIMES, Jan. 18, 2002, at A1.

163. *See Excerpts from Attorney General's Testimony Before Senate Judiciary Committee,* NEW YORK TIMES, Dec. 7, 2002, at B6.

164. *See* Thomas & Isikoff, *supra* note 158, at 43; *DOJ Orders Incentives, "Voluntary" Interviews of Aliens to Obtain Info on Terrorists, supra* note 157, at 1816, 1817.

165. *See Al Najjar Again in INS Detention Due to Alleged Terrorist Ties,* 78 INTERPRETER RELEASES 1859 (2001); Anthony Lewis, *Abroad at Home; It Can Happen Here,* NEW YORK TIMES, Dec. 1, 2001, at A27.

166. *See Office of the Deputy Attorney General, Guidelines for the Interviews Regarding International Terrorism,* 78 INTERPRETER RELEASES 1829, app. I (2001).

167. According to one informed observer, the federal government detained Arabs and Muslims who were being held for immigration violations pending deportation as a "symbolic" gesture to show that the U.S. government was "getting tough" on immigration enforcement. *See Testimony of Margaret H. Taylor, Professor of Wake Forest, University School of Law, Hearing Before the Subcommittee on Immigration and Claims, Judiciary Committee, House of Representatives,* FEDERAL DOCUMENT CLEARINGHOUSE, Dec. 19, 2001.

168. *See, for example,* United States v. Sokolow, 490 U.S. 1, 7 (1989); Terry v. Ohio, 392 U.S. 1, 27 (1968)

169. *See* R. Richard Banks, *Race-Based Suspect Selection and Colorblind Equal Protection Doctrine,* 48 UCLA LAW REVIEW 1075 (2001).

170. *See* U.S. Bureau of the Census, Profile of Selected Social Characteristics: 2000, *available at* http://factfinder.census.gov/servlet/TTable?ds_name=ACS_C2SS_EST_G00_ (last visited Dec. 10, 2001).

171. *See* United States v. Carolene Products, 304 U.S. 144, 152 n.4 (1938) (holding that a heightened level of scrutiny of classifications that affect "discrete and insular minorities" might be justified because of deficiencies of the political process).

172. *See* Frank Wu, YELLOW: RACE IN AMERICA BEYOND BLACK AND WHITE 79–129 (2002); Keith Aoki *"Foreign-ness" and Asian American Identities: Yellowface, Wold War II Propaganda, and Bifurcated Racial Stereotype,"* 4 UCLA ASIAN PACIFIC AMERICAN LAW JOURNAL 1 (1997).

173. 617 F.2d 745 (1979), *cert. denied sub nom.,* 446 U.S. 957 (1980); *see* Hiroshi Motomura, *Immigration Law After a Century of Plenary Power: Phantom Constitutional Norms and Statutory Interpretation,* 100 YALE LAW JOURNAL 545, 587–88 (1990) (discussing how the district court had sought to invalidate the president's action because it constituted discrimination on the basis of nationality); Sale v. Haitian Cen-

ters Council, Inc., 509 U.S. 155 (1993) (upholding the interdiction and repatriation policy directed exclusively at Haitians).

174. *Narenji*, 617 F.2d at 748.

175. *See, for example*, Ghaelian v. INS, 717 F.2d 950 (6th Cir. 1983) (holding that the court lacked jurisdiction to review an equal protection challenge to a regulation in a deportation action); Dastmalchi v. INS, 660 F.2d 880 (3d Cir. 1981) (same); Nademi v. INS, 679 F.2d 811 (10th Cir.) (upholding a regulation that allowed Iranian citizens only fifteen days before voluntarily departing the country), *cert. denied*, 459 U.S. 872 (1982); Malek-Marzban v. INS, 653 F.2d 113 (4th Cir. 1981) (same).

176. *See* Reno v. American-Arab Anti-discrimination Committee, 525 U.S. 471 (1999) (holding that, as amended in 1996, the INA barred review of a selective enforcement claim by members of the PFLP).

177. *Id.* at 491.

178. *Id.*

179. The courts have expressed a willingness to invalidate an immigration stop under the Fourth Amendment if based exclusively on race. *See* Brignoni-Ponce v. United States, 422 U.S. 873 (1975) (invalidating an immigration stop near the U.S.-Mexican border based exclusively on race); INS v. Lopez-Mendoza, 468 U.S. 1032, 1050–51 (1984) (stating that the exclusionary rule might apply to deportation proceedings in cases of "egregious violations of Fourth Amendment or other liberties that might transgress notions of fundamental fairness and undermine the probative value of the evidence obtained") (citation omitted); *see, for example*, Orhorhaghe v. INS, 38 F.3d 488, 497 (9th Cir. 1994) (finding that the sole basis for seizure by the INS was the person's racial background or national origin, thus constituting an egregious violation of the Fourth Amendment); Judy C. Wong, Note, *Egregious Fourth Amendment Violations and the Use of the Exclusionary Rule in Deportation Hearings: The Need for Substantive Equal Protection Rights for Undocumented Immigrants*, 28 COLUMBIA HUMAN RIGHTS LAW REVIEW 431, 455–60 (1997) (summarizing lower court decisions finding that an immigration stop based exclusively on race was an egregious Fourth Amendment violation that justified application of the exclusionary rule).

180. Peter E. Quint, *The Separation of Powers Under Carter*, 62 TEXAS LAW REVIEW 785, 856 (1984) (emphasis added) (footnotes omitted). *See generally* PETER ANDREAS, BORDER GAMES: POLICING THE U.S.-MEXICO DIVIDE (2000)(analyzing how the U.S. government has pursued increased border enforcement for the resulting political and symbolic impacts despite its overall lack of effectiveness); DOUGLAS S. MASSEY ET AL., BEYOND SMOKE AND MIRRORS: MEXICAN IMMIGRATION IN AN ERA OF ECONOMIC INTEGRATION (2002) (to the same effect).

181. *See, for example*, St. Francis College v. Al-Khazraji, 481 U.S. 604 (1987); Amini v. Oberlin College, 259 F.3d 493 (6th Cir. 2001).

182. *See* David A. Harris, *The Stories, the Statistics, and the Law: Why "Driving While Black" Matters*, 84 MINNESOTA LAW REVIEW 265, 298–300 (1999).

183. *See* James Sterngold with Diana Jean Schemo, *10 Arrested in Visa Cases in San Diego*, NEW YORK TIMES, Dec. 13, 2001, at B1.

184. *See DOJ Focusing on Removal of Six Thousand Men from Al Qaeda Haven Countries*, 79 INTERPRETER RELEASES 115, 115 (2002); Dan Eggen & Cheryl W. Thompson, *U.S. Seeks Thousands of Fugitive Deportees; Middle Eastern Men Are Focus of Search*,

WASHINGTON POST, Jan. 8, 2002, at A1; *Deputy Attorney General Releases Internal Guidance for "Absconder" Apprehensions,* 79 INTERPRETER RELEASES 261 (2002); Dan Eggen, *Deportee Sweep Will Start with Mideast Focus,* WASHINGTON POST, Feb. 8, 2002.

185. Public Law No. 107-173, 116 Statutes at Large 543 (2002).

186. *See* Eric Lichtblau, *Strict New Visa Rules Outlined Amid Protests,* LOS ANGELES TIMES, June 6, 2002, at A1; Eric Schmitt, *U.S. Will Seek to Fingerprint Visa Holders,* NEW YORK TIMES, June 4, 2002, at A1; *Groups Voice Concerns over Plan to Fingerprint, Track U.S. Visitors,* 70 UNITED STATES LAW WEEK, June 18, 2002, at 2793.

187. *See* 67 Federal Register 40581 (June 13, 2002); U.S. Department of Justice, National Security Entry-Exit Tracking System Fact Sheet (June 5, 2002), *available at* http://www.usdoj.gov/ag/speeches/2002/natlsecentryexittracjingsys.htm (last visited June 7, 2002).

188. *See* Jonathan Alter, *Time to Think About Torture,* NEWSWEEK, Nov. 5, 2001, at 45 (quoting Professor Alan Dershowitz of Harvard Law School to the effect that, if torture is to be used, judicial approval should be required).

189. *See* Linda S. Bosniak, *Opposing Prop. 187: Undocumented Immigrants and the National Imagination,* 28 CONNECTICUT LAW REVIEW 555, 576–77 (1996) ("While [the undocumented] formally are afforded the minimum rights of personhood under the law, they lie entirely outside the law's protections for many purposes, and they live subject[ed] to the fear of deportation at virtually all times.") (citations omitted) (alteration added); Lori A. Nessel, *Undocumented Immigrants in the Workplace: The Fallacy of Labor Protection and the Need for Reform,* 36 HARVARD CIVIL RIGHTS–CIVIL LIBERTIES LAW REVIEW 345, 348 (2001) (contending that federal labor laws fail to protect undocumented workers adequately, leaving them "without meaningful remedies and vulnerable to deportation if they assert their protected rights"); Maria L. Ontiveros, *To Help Those Most in Need: Undocumented Workers' Rights and Remedies Under Title VII,* 20 NEW YORK UNIVERSITY REVIEW OF LAW AND SOCIAL CHANGE 607 (1994) (arguing that employers exploit undocumented workers, including many Latinas/os, who have few legal remedies); *see also* Jorge A. Vargas, *U.S. Border Patrol Abuses, Undocumented Mexican Workers, and International Human Rights,* 2 SAN DIEGO INTERNATIONAL LAW JOURNAL 1 (2001) (discussing human rights abuses suffered by undocumented Mexican workers in the United States).

190. *See* Richard Morin & Claudia Deane, *Most Americans Back U.S. Tactics: Poll Finds Little Worry over Rights,* WASHINGTON POST, Nov. 29, 2001, at A1 (reporting poll results that show broad support for Bush administration measures to combat terrorism with little concern for loss of civil rights); USA Today/CNN/Gallup Poll Results, Sept. 16, 2001 (showing that almost 50 percent of persons polled supported a special identification card for Arabs, including U.S. citizens, and that almost 60 percent favored more intensive security checks before Arabs are allowed to board airplanes).

191. *See* USA PATRIOT Act, *supra* note 8, at § 411 (amending §§ 212(a)(3) (inadmissibility grounds) and 237(a)(4)(B) (removal grounds) of the INA).

192. *See id.* § 411 (amending § 212(a)(3) of the INA).

193. *See id.* (alteration added).

194. *See id.* § 411 (amending §§ 212(a)(3) (inadmissibility grounds) and 237(a)(4)(B) (removal grounds) of the INA).

195. *See id.* § 402 (authorizing appropriations necessary to triple the Border Patrol personnel along the northern border). This provision responds to fears that terrorists might seek to enter the United States from Canada, in the wake of the arrest of an Algerian man with bomb-making materials who tried to enter the United States from Canada on the eve of the new millennium. *See* Sam Howe Verhovek with Tim Weiner, *Man Seized with Bomb Parts at Border Spurs U.S. Inquiry,* NEW YORK TIMES, Dec. 19, 1999, at A1. The act's emphasis on northern border enforcement may shift the myopic focus from the southern border with Mexico, which was the primary site of heightened border enforcement in the 1990s. *See* Bill Ong Hing, *The Dark Side of Operation Gatekeeper,* 7 UNIVERSITY OF CALIFORNIA AT DAVIS JOURNAL OF INTERNATIONAL LAW AND POLICY 121 (2001) (analyzing the human impacts of greatly increased border enforcement operations along the U.S.-Mexican border); Vargas, *supra* note 189 (same).

196. Public Law No. 107-71 § 111(a)(2)(A)(ii), 115 Statutes at Large 597, 617 (2001).

197. *See, for example,* Cabell v. Chavez-Salido, 454 U.S. 432 (1982) (finding that California law requiring a probation officer to be a citizen was constitutional); Ambach v. Norwick, 441 U.S. 68 (1979) (refusing to find unconstitutional a state that law barred immigrants from employment as public school teachers); Foley v. Connelie, 435 U.S. 291 (1978) (upholding a state law that made U.S. citizenship a qualification for police officers).

198. *See* Steven Greenhouse, *Groups Seek to Lift Ban on Foreign Screeners,* NEW YORK TIMES, Dec. 12, 2001, at B10 (reporting that 80 percent of the security screeners at San Francisco International Airport and 40 percent of those at Los Angeles International Airport are immigrants who faced the loss of their jobs); *see also* Sam Skolnik, *INS Checking Sea-Tac Workers,* SEATTLE POST-INTELLIGENCER, Nov. 28, 2001, at A1 (stating that the INS was reviewing the immigration status of Seattle Airport's eighteen thousand workers because of security concerns).

199. *See* 50 U.S.C. app. § 453 (1994); *see also* Charles E. Roh Jr. & Frank K. Upham, *The Status of Aliens Under United States Draft Laws,* 13 HARVARD JOURNAL OF INTERNATIONAL LAW 501 (1972).

200. GERALD L. NEUMAN, STRANGERS TO THE CONSTITUTION: IMMIGRANTS, BORDERS, AND FUNDAMENTAL LAW (1996).

201. *See, for example,* Gabriel J. Chin, *Segregation's Last Stronghold: Race Discrimination and the Constitutional Law of Immigration,* 46 UCLA LAW REVIEW 1 (1998); Stephen H. Legomsky, *Immigration Law and the Principle of Plenary Congressional Power,* 1984 SUPREME COURT REVIEW 255, 255 (1985); Stephen H. Legomsky, *Ten More Years of Plenary Power: Immigration, Congress, and the Courts,* 22 HASTINGS CONSTITUTIONAL LAW QUARTERLY 925, 930–37 (1995); Hiroshi Motomura, *The Curious Evolution of Immigration Law: Procedural Surrogates for Substantive Constitutional Rights,* 92 COLUMBIA LAW REVIEW 1625, 1631 (1992); Hiroshi Motomura, *Immigration Law After a Century of Plenary Power: Phantom Constitutional Norms and Statutory Interpretation,* 100 YALE LAW JOURNAL 545, 549 (1990); Scaperlanda, *supra* note 37, at 1028; Peter H. Schuck, *The Transformation of Immigration Law,* 84 COLUMBIA LAW REVIEW 1, 81–85 (1984).

202. *See, for example,* Nguyen v. INS, 533 U.S. 53 (2001) (upholding gender discrimination in immigration and nationality laws); Fiallo v. Bell, 430 U.S. 787, 792 (1977) (rejecting a constitutional challenge to the provision of the immigration laws that discriminates against the father of an illegitimate child); Mathews v. Diaz, 426 U.S. 67, 80 (1976) (upholding discrimination against lawful permanent residents in a federal public benefit program); Galvan v. Press, 347 U.S. 522, 530 (1954) (discussing congressional power over the admission of immigrants).

203. *See* Duldulao v. INS, 90 F.3d 396, 399 (9th Cir. 1996) (rejecting a constitutional challenge to § 440(c) of AEDPA, which bars judicial review of the final orders of deportation of noncitizens convicted of certain criminal offenses); Rahman v. McElroy, 884 F. Supp. 782, 785 (S.D.N.Y. 1995) (dismissing a constitutional challenge to diversity visa lottery provisions and citing Harisiades v. Shaughnessy, 342 U.S. 580 (1952), for the principle of limited judicial review).

204. 509 U.S. 155, 188 (1993) (refusing to disturb the president's Haitian interdiction and repatriation policy and emphasizing that "we are construing treaty and statutory provisions that may involve foreign and military affairs for which the President has unique responsibility") (citing United States v. Curtis-Wright Export Co., 299 U.S. 304 (1936)).

205. Reno v. Flores, 507 U.S. 292, 305–06 (1993) (citing, *inter alia, Fiallo,* 430 U.S. at 787, 792) (emphasis added).

206. *See, for example,* Kolster v. INS, 101 F.3d 785, 790–91 (1st Cir. 1996) (citing *Flores* and upholding the AEDPA limitation on judicial review); Ali v. Reno, 22 F.3d 442, 448 (2d Cir. 1994) (citing *Flores* and upholding the rescission of a noncitizen's permanent resident status); Chan v. Reno, 916 F. Supp. 1289, 1296 (S.D.N.Y. 1996) (citing *Flores* for the proposition that "judicial review in immigration matters is narrowly circumscribed").

207. *See* Demore v. Kim, 123 S. Ct. 1708, 1716 (2003).

208. *See* Scaperlanda, *supra* note 100, at 758–59 (employing this partial membership analysis).

209. *See, for example,* Kleindienst v. Mandel, 408 U.S. 753 (1972) (permitting the denial of a nonimmigrant visa to a noncitizen because of his Marxist beliefs); Galvan v. Press, 347 U.S. 523, 532 (1954) (upholding as constitutional a statute that provided for the deportation of resident immigrants who were members of the Communist Party); Shaughnessy v. United States *ex rel.* Mezei, 345 U.S. 206, 210–11 (1953) (granting the attorney general permission to detain a noncitizen indefinitely based on confidential information); United States *ex rel.* Knauff v. Shaughnessy, 338 U.S. 537, 541 (1950) (holding that the attorney general may exclude a noncitizen from entry if "such entry would be prejudicial to the interests of the United States").

210. *See* Kevin R. Johnson, *Los Olvidados: Images of the Immigrant, Political Power of Noncitizens, and Immigration Law and Enforcement,* 1993 BRIGHAM YOUNG UNIVERSITY LAW REVIEW 1139, 1162–63.

211. *See* T. Alexander Aleinikoff, *Non-judicial Checks on Agency Actions,* 49 ADMINISTRATIVE LAW REVIEW 193, 194 (1997) (stating that "[t]raditionally, the courts have been wary of stepping into the immigration area. Congress, well aware of such judicial hesitance, appears willing to make the most of it") (footnote omitted).

212. *See* IIRIRA, *supra* note 15, § 306(a)(2), 110 Statutes at Large at 1666–75 (limiting judicial review of certain immigration decisions). In addition, the Immigration Reform Act provides for summary exclusion of certain noncitizens who seek to apply for asylum, with limited administrative and no judicial review. *See id.* § 302, 110 Statutes at Large at 1620–29 (amending section 235 of the INA).

213. *See* INS v. St. Cyr, 533 U.S. 289 (2001).

214. *See* AEDPA, *supra* note 14, § 440(d), 110 Statutes at Large at 1277 (barring relief from deportation to noncitizens convicted of certain crimes). Similarly, section 304 of the IIRIRA narrowed relief from deportation by repealing section 212(c); section 240A of the IIRIRA replaced section 212(c) relief with a new and narrower form of relief called "cancellation of removal." IIRIRA, *supra* note 15, §§ 240A, 304, 110 Statutes at Large at 1644, 1650.

215. Statement on Signing the Antiterrorism and Effective Death Penalty Act of 1996, 32 WEEKLY COMPILATION OF PRESIDENTIAL DOCUMENTS 721 (Apr. 24, 1996) (emphasis added).

216. Public Law No. 104-134, 110 Statutes at Large 1321 (1996); Mark Tushnet & Larry Yackle, *Symbolic Statutes and Real Law: The Pathologies of the Antiterrorism and Effective Death Penalty Act and the Prison Litigation Reform Act,* 47 DUKE LAW JOURNAL 1 (1997); Ira Bloom, *Prisons, Prisoners, and Pine Forests: Congress Breaches the Wall Separating Legislative from Judicial Power,* 40 ARIZONA LAW REVIEW 389 (1998).

Chapter 4: Exclusion and Deportation of the Poor

1. *See* Immigration and Nationality Act of 1952, Public Law No. 82-414, 66 Statutes at Large 163 (1952), § 203(a)(5), 8 U.S.C. § 1153(a)(5) [hereinafter INA].

2. *See, for example,* GEORGE J. BORJAS, HEAVEN'S DOOR: IMMIGRATION POLICY AND THE AMERICAN ECONOMY (1999); VERNON M. BRIGGS JR., MASS IMMIGRATION AND THE NATIONAL INTEREST (1992).

3. *See* Ann Devroy, *President Insists Congress Enact Reforms in Welfare, Health Care,* WASHINGTON POST, Jan. 26, 1994, at A1, A4 (quoting President Clinton).

4. *See, for example,* Mayor of the City of New York v. Miln, 36 U.S. (11 Pet.) 102, 133 (1837) (upholding a New York law designed "to prevent New York from being burdened by an influx of persons . . . either from foreign countries, or from any other of the states . . . and to prevent them from becoming chargeable as paupers"); *The Passenger Cases* (Smith v. Turner), 48 U.S. (7 How.) 283 (1849) (invalidating New York and Massachusetts laws designed to deter migration of "paupers" by imposing taxes on immigrant passengers arriving in ports of those states).

5. Gerald L. Neuman, *The Lost Century of American Immigration Law (1776–1875),* 93 COLUMBIA LAW REVIEW 1833, 1847–48 (1993) (footnotes omitted); *see* MALDWYN ALLEN JONES, AMERICAN IMMIGRATION 36–43, 68–69, 90–91, 114–16, 130–31, 204–05, 212–21 (2d ed. 1992); BENJAMIN JOSEPH KLEBANER, PUBLIC POOR RELIEF IN AMERICA 1790–1860, ch. 5 (1976).

6. *See* Henderson v. Mayor of New York, 92 U.S. 259 (1876); *The Passenger Cases,* 49 U.S. 283 (1849); Mayor of New York v. Miln, 36 U.S. 102 (1837); Chy Lung v. Freeman, 92 U.S. 275 (1876).

7. Immigration Act of August 3, 1882, ch. 376, § 2, 22 Statutes at Large 214, 214 (1882).

8. Act of Congress of March 3, 1891, ch. 551 (emphasis added); *see, for example,* Nishimura Ekiu v. United States, 142 U.S. 651 (1891) (upholding the exclusion of a Japanese woman as a public charge).

9. *See* WILLIAM C. VAN VLECK, THE ADMINISTRATIVE CONTROL OF ALIENS 3–60, 116–27 (1932).

10. *See* JOHN HIGHAM, STRANGERS IN THE LAND: PATTERNS OF AMERICAN NATIVISM 1860–1925, at 35–45, 68–105 (3d ed. 1992).

11. *See* BILL ONG HING, MAKING AND REMAKING ASIAN AMERICA THROUGH IMMIGRATION POLICY, 1850–1990, at 19–26 (1993); JONES, *supra* note 5, at 212–16.

12. *See* KITTY CALAVITA, U.S. IMMIGRATION LAW AND THE CONTROL OF LABOR: 1820–1924, at 86–88 (1984).

13. Act of February 20, 1907, Public Law No. 96, ch. 1134, § 20, 34 Statutes at Large 898, 904–05 (1907).

14. Act of February 5, 1917, Public Law No. 301, ch. 29, § 19, 39 Statutes at Large 874, 889 (1917).

15. *See, for example, Ex parte* Wong Nung, 30 F.2d 766 (9th Cir. 1929); Gabriel v. Johnson, 29 F.2d 347 (1st Cir. 1928).

16. *See, for example,* Yamataya v. Fisher (*The Japanese Immigrant Case*), 189 U.S. 86 (1903); Nishimura Ekiu v. United States, 142 U.S. 651 (1892); Lam Fung Yen v. Frick, 233 F. 393 (6th Cir.), *cert. denied,* 242 U.S. 642 (1916).

17. *Yamataya,* 189 U.S. at 86.

18. *Nishimura,* 142 U.S. at 651.

19. LUCY E. SALYER, LAWS HARSH AS TIGERS: CHINESE IMMIGRANTS AND THE SHAPING OF MODERN IMMIGRATION LAW 200 (1995) (emphasis added).

20. *See In re* Rhagat Singh, 209 F. 700 (N.D. Cal. 1913).

21. *See* Gegiow v. Uhl, 239 U.S. 3 (1915).

22. *See generally* FRANCISCO E. BALDERRAMA & RAYMOND RODRÍGUEZ, DECADE OF BETRAYAL: MEXICAN REPATRIATION IN THE 1930S (1995); CAMILLE GUERNÍN-GONZALES, MEXICAN WORKERS AND AMERICAN DREAMS: IMMIGRATION, REPATRIATION AND CALIFORNIA FARM LABOR, 1900–1939 (1994); ABRAHAM HOFFMAN, UNWANTED MEXICAN AMERICANS IN THE GREAT DEPRESSION: REPATRIATION PRESSURES, 1929–1939 (1974).

23. *See* FRANCES FOX PIVEN & RICHARD A. CLOWARD, REGULATING THE POOR: THE FUNCTIONS OF PUBLIC WELFARE 80–119 (2d ed. 1993).

24. *See In re* Nunez, 18 F. Supp. 1007 (S.D. Cal. 1937).

25. *See Ex parte* Nunez, 93 F.2d 41 (9th Cir. 1937).

26. *See* Bill Piatt, *Born as Second Class Citizens in the U.S.A.: Children of Undocumented Parents,* 63 NOTRE DAME LAW REVIEW 35 (1988).

27. *See* INA, *supra* note 1, § 212(a)(4), 8 U.S.C. § 1182(a)(4).

28. *See* Will Maslow, Recasting *Our Deportation Law: Proposals for Reform,* 56 COLUMBIA LAW REVIEW 309, 340–41 (1956).

29. *See* INA, *supra* note 1, § 212(a)(4)(B), 8 U.S.C. § 1182(a)(4)(B).

30. *See* STEPHEN H. LEGOMSKY, IMMIGRATION AND REFUGEE LAW AND POLICY 409 (3d ed. 2002) ("Over the years, the public charge provision has become the single

most common affirmative substantive basis for denials of immigrant visas.") (foot-notes omitted).

31. *See* U.S. DEPARTMENT OF STATE, REPORT OF THE VISA OFFICE FOR 1998, at 147–48 tbl.XX (2001).

32. *See* HING, *supra* note 11, at 113–15.

33. INA, *supra* note 1, § 241(a)(5), 8 U.S.C. § 1251(a)(5).

34. *See* UNITED STATES DEPARTMENT OF JUSTICE, 1992 STATISTICAL YEARBOOK OF THE IMMIGRATION AND NATURALIZATION SERVICE 162 (1992) [hereinafter INS 1992 STATISTICAL YEARBOOK] (compiling statistics that show fewer than six deportations on the public charge ground for each year from 1971 to 1980, two in 1981, and none in 1982 and omitting this information for the years from 1983 to 1992).

35. *See, for example,* Matter of Vindman, 16 Immigration and Nationality Deci-sions 131 (Regional Commissioner 1977) (ruling that refugee parolees were ineligi-ble for adjustment of status because they had not been employed and had received benefit payments); Matter of Harutunian, 14 I. & N. Dec. 583 (Regional Commis-sioner 1974) (same).

36. *See, for example,* GARRETT HARDIN, THE IMMIGRATION DILEMMA: AVOIDING THE TRAGEDY OF THE COMMONS (1995).

37. *See* ROY BECK, THE CASE AGAINST IMMIGRATION: THE MORAL, ECONOMIC, SO-CIAL, AND ENVIRONMENTAL REASONS FOR REDUCING U.S. IMMIGRATION BACK TO TRA-DITIONAL LEVELS 60–66 (1996); MICHAEL LIND, THE NEXT AMERICAN NATION: THE NEW NATIONALISM AND THE FOURTH AMERICAN REVOLUTION 181–216 (1995).

38. *See* PETER BRIMELOW, ALIEN NATION: COMMON SENSE ABOUT AMERICA'S IM-MIGRATION DISASTER 146–50 (1995).

39. *See* Olsen v. Albright, 990 F. Supp. 31 (D.D.C. 1997).

40. *Compare* Robert Rubin, *Walking a Gray Line: The "Color of Law" Test Govern-ing Noncitizen Eligibility for Public Benefits*, 24 SAN DIEGO LAW REVIEW 411 (1987) (ar-guing for an expansive definition) *with* Daniel Stein & Steven Zanowic, *Permanent Resident Alien Under Color of Law: The Opening Door to Alien Entitlement Eligibility*, 1 GEORGETOWN IMMIGRATION LAW JOURNAL 231 (1986) (arguing for a restrictive defi-nition).

41. *See, for example,* 7 U.S.C. § 2014(i) (food stamp program) (amended); 42 U.S.C. § 615(a) (Aid to Families with Dependent Children) (amended); 42 U.S.C. § 1382j(a) (Supplemental Security Income) (amended).

42. *See* INA, *supra* note 1, § 244A, 8 U.S.C. § 1254a (as amended by Immigra-tion Act of 1990).

43. *See id.* § 245A(h), 8 U.S.C. § 1255a(h) (as amended by Immigration Reform and Control Act of 1986).

44. *Id.* § 245A(d)(2)(B)(iii), 8 U.S.C. § 1255a(d)(2)(B)(iii) (emphasis added).

45. *See* Carol Sanger, *Immigration Reform and Control of the Undocumented Family*, 2 GEORGETOWN IMMIGRATION LAW JOURNAL 295, 324–28 (1987); *see, for example,* Con-stanza Montana, *Final Countdown for Amnesty: Aliens Urged to Seize Chance by Wednes-day*, CHICAGO TRIBUNE, May 3, 1988, at 7 (reporting that some immigrants had not applied for amnesty because they believed that accepting benefits for citizen chil-dren disqualified them from immigration legalization based on the public charge ground); Antonio Rodriguez & Gloria J. Romero, *Where's the Amnesty for Women? Bar-riers to Legalization Fall Most Heavily on Them*, LOS ANGELES TIMES, Feb. 2, 1988, pt.

2, at p. 7 (contending that, although women constitute approximately one-half of the undocumented population, a relatively small proportion applied for amnesty because they believed that they would become ineligible for immigration legalization if they had received public assistance).

46. *See* ERIC COHEN ET AL., NATURALIZATION: A GUIDE FOR LEGAL PRACTITIONERS AND OTHER COMMUNITY ADVOCATES 6–10 (1994) (Immigrant Legal Resource Center publication).

47. *See, for example,* Rady v. Ashcroft, 193 F. Supp. 2d 454, 455 (D. Conn. 2002); Webb v. Weiss, 69 F. Supp. 2d 335, 339 (D. Conn. 1999).

48. *See, for example,* Lewis v. Grinker, 965 F.2d 1206 (2d Cir. 1992) (affirming a permanent injunction that barred the secretary of health and human services from denying undocumented women Medicaid coverage for prenatal care); Doe v. Reivitz, 830 F.2d 1441, *as amended,* 842 F.2d 194 (7th Cir. 1987) (invalidating a state decision to deny benefits to citizen children and eligible noncitizen children of undocumented parents under the Aid to Families with Dependent Children—Unemployed Parents program).

49. Mathews v. Diaz, 426 U.S. 67, 80 (1976) (emphasis added); *see, for example,* Smart v. Shalala, 9 F.3d 921 (11th Cir. 1993) (per curiam).

50. *See* Sudomir v. McMahon, 767 F.2d 1456 (9th Cir. 1985); Zurmati v. McMahon, 180 Cal. App. 3d 164, 225 Cal. Rptr. 374 (1986); Joudah v. Ohio Department of Human Services, 94 Ohio App. 3d 614, 641 N.E.2d 288 (1994). *But see* Department of Health Department of Rehabilitative Services v. Solis, 580 So.2d 146 (Fla. 1991) (reaching a contrary conclusion).

51. *See* Stephen H. Legomsky, *Immigration Law and the Principle of Plenary Congressional Power,* 1984 SUPREME COURT REVIEW 255, 261–69; Gerald M. Rosberg, *The Protection of Aliens from Discriminatory Treatment by the National Government,* 1977 SUPREME COURT REVIEW 275, 328.

52. *See* Hiroshi Motomura, *Immigration Law After a Century of Plenary Power: Phantom Constitutional Norms and Statutory Interpretations,* 100 YALE LAW JOURNAL 545, 607–13 (1990).

53. 403 U.S. 365 (1971).

54. *See* League of United Latin American Citizens v. Wilson, 997 F. Supp. 1244 (C.D. Cal 1997).

55. *See* WAYNE A. CORNELIUS, AMERICA IN THE ERA OF LIMITS: NATIVIST REACTIONS TO THE "NEW" IMMIGRATION 21–24 (1982).

56. *See* JANET CALVO, IMMIGRANT STATUS AND LEGAL ACCESS TO HEALTH CARE 50–52 (1993); Sana Loue, *Access to Health Care and the Undocumented Alien,* 13 JOURNAL OF LEGAL MEDICINE 271, 272–78 (1992).

57. MICHAEL FIX & JEFFREY S. PASSEL, IMMIGRATION AND IMMIGRANTS: SETTING THE RECORD STRAIGHT 6 (1994) (emphasis in original). This finding is consistent with previous studies. *See, for example,* JULIAN L. SIMON, THE ECONOMIC CONSEQUENCES OF IMMIGRATION 105–42 (1989); Marta Tienda & Leif Jensen, *Immigration and Public Assistance Participation: Dispelling the Myth of Dependency,* 15 SOCIAL SCIENCE RESEARCH 372 (1986).

58. INA, *supra* note 1, § 101(a)(42)(A), 8 U.S.C. § 1101(a)(42(A) (alteration added).

59. *See* § 207, 8 U.S.C. § 1157.

60. *See* 8 C.F.R. § 208.7 (2003).

61. *See* LEGOMSKY, *supra* note 30, at 852–71 (overseas refugee admissions); Kevin R. Johnson, *A "Hard Look" at the Executive Branch's Asylum Decisions*, 1991 UTAH LAW REVIEW 279, 335–50 (same).

62. Refugees from Laos, for example, have exhibited what some characterize as a "pattern of welfare dependency." MICHAEL PETER SMITH & BERNADETTE TARALLO, CALIFORNIA'S CHANGING FACES: NEW IMMIGRANT SURVIVAL STRATEGIES AND STATE POLICY, at ix (1993); *see* Shur Vang Vangyi, *Hmong Employment and Welfare Dependency in* THE HMONG IN TRANSITION 192, 196 (Glenn L. Hendricks et al. eds., 1986) (discussing welfare dependency among Hmong refugees).

63. *See, for example*, Harold W. Ezell, *Enough Is More Than Enough*, LOS ANGELES TIMES, Oct. 23, 1994, at M5 (referring to a potential $15 billion loss in federal funds as a result of Proposition 187 as "baloney" because the Clinton administration would not take money from the state); TONY MILLER, ACTING SECRETARY OF STATE, CALIFORNIA BALLOT PAMPHLET: GENERAL ELECTION, NOVEMBER 8, 1994, at 55 (1994) [hereinafter CALIFORNIA BALLOT PAMPHLET] (Rebuttal to Argument Against 187) (responding to the argument based on the potential loss of federal funds saying, "NONSENSE. HOW CAN GETTING RID OF THE PRESENT COSTS END UP COSTING MORE?") (capitals in original).

64. *See* CALIFORNIA BALLOT PAMPHLET, *supra* note 63, at 52.

65. *Id.* at 52.

66. *See id.* at 53.

67. *See* Mark Gladstone, *Firms Lower Ratings of State's Long-Term Bonds*, LOS ANGELES TIMES, July 16, 1994, at A1.

68. *See* CALIFORNIA BALLOT PAMPHLET, *supra* note 63, at 52–53.

69. *See id.* at 52 ("[E]liminating prenatal services to illegal immigrant women could result in higher Medi-Cal costs for their infants, who would be citizens. In addition, failure to treat and control serious contagious diseases, such as tuberculosis, among illegal immigrants could increase future costs to treat the disease in the general population.").

70. *See* Lewis v. Grinker, 965 F.2d 1206, 1219 (2d Cir. 1992) ("Studies have shown that every dollar spent on prenatal care saves between two and ten dollars in future medical care costs.") (citation omitted).

71. *See* CALIFORNIA BALLOT PAMPHLET, *supra* note 63, at 50–53.

72. *See, for example, 187: It's a Risky Proposition; Hazards of Immigration Measure Dwarf Potential Benefits*, LOS ANGELES TIMES (Valley ed.), Oct. 16, 1994, at B18.

73. Ronald Brownstein & Patrick J. McDonnell, *Kemp, Bennett and INS Chief Decry Prop. 197*, LOS ANGELES TIMES, Oct. 19, 1994, at A1 (quoting Bennett and Kemp).

74. *See* United States v. Wong Kim Ark, 169 U.S. 649 (1898). *But see* PETER H. SCHUCK & ROGERS M. SMITH, CITIZENSHIP WITHOUT CONSENT: ILLEGAL ALIENS IN THE AMERICAN POLITY (1985) (questioning this interpretation of the Fourteenth Amendment and calling for "consensualist-based" interpretation that bars bestowing citizenship on children of persons unlawfully in this country).

75. Public Law No. 104-193, 110 Statutes at Large 2105 (1996); *see* Public Law No. 171 § 4401, 116 Statutes at Large 134, 333 (2000) (restoring immigrant eligibility for food stamps).

76. Recent Legislation, *Welfare Reform—Treatment of Legal Immigrants*, 110 HARVARD LAW REVIEW 1191, 1192 (1997) (footnotes omitted) (alteration added). A number of states declined to deny benefits to lawful permanent residents. *See* Michael J. Wishnie, *Laboratories of Bigotry? Devolution of the Immigration Power, Equal Protection, and Federalism*, 76 NEW YORK UNIVERSITY LAW REVIEW 493, 511–18 (2001).

77. *See, for example*, Sheryll D. Cashin, *Federalism, Welfare Reform, and the Minority Poor: Accounting for the Tyranny of State Majorities*, 99 COLUMBIA LAW REVIEW 552 (1999); Berta Esperanza Hernández-Truyol & Kimberly A. Johns, *Global Rights, Local Wrongs, and Legal Fixes: An International Human Rights Critique of Immigration and Welfare "Reform,"* 71 SOUTHERN CALIFORNIA LAW REVIEW 547 (1998); Elizabeth Hull, *The Unkindest Cuts: The 1996 Welfare Reform Act's Impact on Resident Aliens*, 33 GONZAGA LAW REVIEW 471 (1997–1998); Michael Scaperlanda, *Who Is My Neighbor? An Essay on Immigrants, Welfare Reform, and the Constitution*, 29 CONNECTICUT LAW REVIEW 1587 (1997); Nancy A. Wright, *Welfare Reform Under the Personal Responsibility Act: Ending Welfare as We Know It or Governmental Child Abuse*, 25 HASTINGS CONSTITUTIONAL LAW QUARTERLY 357 (1998); Connie Chang, Comment, *Immigrants Under the New Welfare Law: A Call for Uniformity, a Call for Justice*, 45 UCLA LAW REVIEW 205 (1997); Symposium, *Closing the Door on the Immigrant Poor*, 9 STANFORD LAW AND POLICY REVIEW 141 (1998); Lauren E. Moynihan, Note, *Welfare Reform and the Meaning of Membership: Constitutional Challenges and State Reactions*, 12 GEORGETOWN IMMIGRATION LAW JOURNAL 657 (1998); Lanelle E. Polen, Note, *Salvaging a Safety Net: Modifying the Bar to Supplemental Security Income for Legal Aliens*, 76 WASHINGTON UNIVERSITY LAW QUARTERLY 1455 (1998).

78. *See* R. KENT WEAVER, ENDING WELFARE AS WE KNOW IT 264 (2000); Kenneth D. Heath, *The Symmetries of Citizenship: Welfare, Expatriate Taxation, and Stakeholding*, 13 GEORGETOWN IMMIGRATION LAW JOURNAL 533, 552–58 (1999).

79. *See* Linda Burnham, *Welfare Reform, Family Hardship, and Women of Color*, 577 ANNALS 38, 42–46 (2001).

80. For review of the data on the economic impacts of immigration, see BILL ONG HING, TO BE AN AMERICAN 44–145 (1997).

81. *See* Bill Ong Hing, *Don't Give Me Your Tired, Your Poor: Conflicted Immigrant Stories and Welfare Reform*, 33 HARVARD CIVIL RIGHTS–CIVIL LIBERTIES LAW REVIEW 159 (1998).

82. *See, for example*, ON UNDERSTANDING POVERTY (Daniel P. Moynihan ed., 1987); JOEL F. HANDLER & YEHESKEL HASENFELD, WE THE POOR PEOPLE: WORK, POVERTY, AND WELFARE 201 (1997); Dorothy E. Roberts, *Welfare and the Problem of Black Citizenship*, 105 YALE LAW JOURNAL 1563 (1996); Sylvia A. Law, *Ending Welfare as We Know It*, 49 STANFORD LAW REVIEW 471 (1997).

83. INA, *supra* note 1, § 213A(a)(1)(A), 8 U.S.C. § 1183a(A)(1)(A); *see* Michael J. Sheridan, *The New Affidavit of Support and Other 1996 Amendments to Immigration and Welfare Provisions Designed to Prevent Aliens from Becoming Public Charges*, 31 CREIGHTON LAW REVIEW 741 (1998).

84. *See Prepared Testimony of Norman Matloff, University of California at Davis, Before the Senate Judiciary Committee, Subcommittee on Immigration, Welfare Use Among Elderly Chinese Immigrants*, FEDERAL NEWS SERVICE, Feb. 6, 1996; *Testimony March 1, 1994 Norman Matloff, Professor, Department of Computer Science, University of Califor-*

nia at Davis, House Ways and Means/Human Resources Supplemental Security Income Modernization, FEDERAL DOCUMENT CLEARING HOUSE CONGRESSIONAL TESTIMONY, Mar. 1, 1994; *see also* Norman Matloff, *Loopholes Let Affluent Immigrants Put Parents on Welfare,* SAN FRANCISCO EXAMINER, July 8, 1994, at A23.

85. *See* Lewis v. Thompson, 252 F.3d 567 (2d Cir. 2001); Aleman v. Glickman, 217 F.3d 1191 (9th Cir. 2000); Alvarez v. Shalala, 189 F.3d 598 (7th Cir. 1999); City of New York v. United States, 179 F.3d 29 (2d Cir. 1999), *cert. denied,* 528 U.S. 1115 (2000); Rodriguez v. United States, 169 F.3d 1342 (11th Cir. 1999).

86. *See generally* CHARLES J. McCLAIN, IN SEARCH OF EQUALITY: THE CHINESE STRUGGLE AGAINST DISCRIMINATION IN NINETEENTH-CENTURY AMERICA (1994).

87. *See* John F. Stanton, Note, *The Immigration Laws from a Disability Perspective: Where We Were, Where We Are, Where We Should Be,* 10 GEORGETOWN IMMIGRATION LAW JOURNAL 441 (1996).

88. *See generally* CLAIRE H. LIACHOWITZ, DISABILITY AS A SOCIAL CONSTRUCT (1988).

89. *See* Neuman, *supra* note 5, at 1846–59.

90. *Id.* at 1847–48 (footnote omitted).

91. *The Passenger Cases,* 48 U.S. 283, 285 (1849).

92. *See* Oceanic Steam Navigation Co. v. Stranahan, 214 U.S. 320, 330 (1909); *see also* Lloyd Sabaudo Societa Anonima Per Azioni v. Elting, 287 U.S. 329 (1932).

93. *See, for example,* United States *ex rel.* Johnson v. Shaughnessy, 336 U.S. 806 (1949) (classification as "mentally defective"); United States *ex rel.* Leon v. Murff, 250 F.2d 436 (2d Cir. 1957) ("constitutional psychopathic inferiority"); United States *ex rel.* Casimano v. Commissioner of Immigration, 15 F.2d 555 (2d Cir. 1926) (mental illness); United States *ex rel.* Patton v. Tod, 297 F. 385 (2d Cir. 1923) (classification as "imbecile"), *cert. dismissed,* 267 U.S. 607 (1925); United States *ex rel.* Haft v. Tod, 300 F. 918 (2d Cir. 1924) (mental breakdown found to be a symptom of a "constitutional psychopathic personality"); United States *ex rel.* De Rienzo, 185 F. 334 (3d Cir. 1911) (idiocy); *Ex parte* Joyce, 212 F. 285 (D. Mass. 1913) (feeble-mindedness).

94. Act of August 3, 1882, *supra* note 7, § 2, ch. 376, 22 Statutes at Large at 214, 214.

95. *See, for example,* Maniglia v. Tillinghast, 24 F.2d 489 (1st Cir. 1925) (deafness and muteness); United States *ex rel.* Markin v. Curran, 9 F.2d 900 (2d Cir. 1925) (blindness in one eye); Tambara v. Weedin, 299 F. 299 (9th Cir. 1924) (deafness); United States *ex rel.* Barlin v. Rodgers, 191 F. 970 (3d Cir. 1911) (congenital hand deformity); United States *ex rel.* Chanin v. Williams, 177 F. 689 (2d Cir. 1910) (heart defect).

96. *See* HIGHAM, *supra* note 10, at 202–04, 270–77.

97. Act of February 5, 1917, *supra* note 14, § 3, ch. 29, 39 Statutes at Large at 874, 875.

98. *See* Public Law No. 68-139, 43 Statutes at Large 153 (1924) (repealed 1965). As Stephen Jay Gould acknowledged, with respect to the 1924 law, "Eugenicists lobbied not only for limits on immigration, but for changing its character by imposing harsh quotas against nations of inferior stock—a feature of the 1924 act that might never have been implemented, or even considered, without . . . eugenicist

propaganda." STEPHEN JAY GOULD, THE MISMEASURE OF MAN 262 (1996 ed.); *see* HIGHAM, *supra* note 10, at 270–77.

99. Act of February 5, 1917, *supra* note 14, 39 Statutes at Large at 874; *see* HIGHAM, *supra* note 10, at 202–03; JONES, *supra* note 5, 212–38.

100. For critical analysis of Goddard's work, see GOULD, *supra* note 98, at 188–204; LEON J. KAMIN, THE SCIENCE AND POLITICS OF I.Q. 15–32 (1974); LEILA ZENDERLAND, MEASURING MINDS: HENRY HERBERT GODDARD AND THE ORIGINS OF AMERICAN INTELLIGENCE TESTING 263–81 (1998).

101. *See* INA, *supra* note 1, § 212(a)(4), 8 U.S.C. § 1182(a)(4) (amended in 1990).

102. Public Law No. 101-336, 104 Statutes at Large 327 (1990); *see, for example,* PGA Tour, Inc. v. Martin, 532 U.S. 661 (2001).

103. *See* INA, *supra* note 1, § 212(a)(1)(A), 8 U.S.C. § 1182(a)(1)(A); *see* Jennifer Blakeman, Comment, *The Exclusion of Mentally Ill Aliens Who May Pose a Danger to Others: Where Does the Real Threat Lie?* 31 UNIVERSITY OF MIAMI INTER-AMERICAN LAW REVIEW 287 (2000).

104. *See* Immigration and Nationality Technical Corrections Act of 1994, Public Law No. 103-416, § 108(a), 108 Statutes at Large 4305, 4309–10 (1994) (codified at INS § 312(b)(1), 8 U.S.C. § 1423(b)(1)). It has been claimed, however, that the INS's interpretation of the oath of allegiance requirement for naturalization adversely affects naturalization applicants with severe mental disabilities. *See* Joren Lyons, Comment, *Mentally Disabled Citizenship Applicants and the Meaningful Oath Requirement for Naturalization,* 87 CALIFORNIA LAW REVIEW 1017 (1999).

105. *See* Arlene Kanter & Kristin Dadey, *The Right to Asylum for People with Disabilities,* 73 TEMPLE LAW REVIEW 1117 (2000).

106. *See* Jonathan C. Drimmer, Comment, *Cripples, Overcomers, and Civil Rights: Tracing the Evolution of Federal Legislation and Social Policy for People with Disabilities,* 40 UCLA LAW REVIEW 1341 (1993).

107. *See* Personal Responsibility and Work Opportunity Reconciliation Act of 1996, Public Law No. 104-193, *supra* note 75, 110 Statutes at Large at 2105.

108. Nora V. Demleitner, *The Fallacy of Social "Citizenship," or the Threat of Exclusion,* 12 GEORGETOWN IMMIGRATION LAW JOURNAL 35, 46 (1997).

Chapter 5: Exclusion and Deportation of Criminals

1. Bridges v. Wixon, 326 U.S. 135, 147 (1945) (citations omitted).

2. *See* U.S. DEPARTMENT OF JUSTICE, 1998 STATISTICAL YEARBOOK OF THE IMMIGRATION AND NATURALIZATION SERVICE 203 (2000) [hereinafter 1998 INS STATISTICAL YEARBOOK].

3. *See* A.G.L. SHAW, CONVICTS AND THE COLONIES 21–37 (1966).

4. *See* Benjamin Franklin, *Felons and Rattlesnakes, in* 4 PAPERS OF BENJAMIN FRANKLIN 130 (Leonard W. Labaree ed., 1961) (reprinting a letter published in the *Pennsylvania Gazette,* May 9, 1751).

5. *See* WILLIAM J. BROMWELL, HISTORY OF IMMIGRATION TO THE UNITED STATES 199–205 (1856); Gerald L. Neuman, *The Lost Century of American Immigration Law (1776–1875),* 93 COLUMBIA LAW REVIEW 1833, 1841–46 (1993).

6. See GERALD L. NEUMAN, STRANGERS TO THE CONSTITUTION: IMMIGRANTS, BOR-
DERS, AND FUNDAMENTAL LAW 22–23 (1996); Daniel Kanstroom, *Deportation, Social
Control, and Punishment: Some Thoughts About Why Hard Laws Make Bad Cases*, 113
HARVARD LAW REVIEW 1889, 1908 (2000).

7. Act of March 3, 1875, ch. 141, 18 Statutes at Large 477 (1875).

8. Act of August 3, 1882, ch. 376, 22 Statutes at Large 214 (1882); *see* U.S. SE-
LECT COMMISSION ON IMMIGRATION AND REFUGEE POLICY, U.S. IMMIGRATION POLICY
AND THE NATIONAL INTEREST 180 (1981); BILL ONG HING, MAKING AND REMAKING
ASIAN AMERICA THROUGH IMMIGRATION POLICY 23 (1993).

9. *See, for example,* Bugajewitz v. Adams, 228 U.S. 585 (1913); Zakonaite v. Wolf,
226 U.S. 272 (1912); United States v. Bitty, 208 U.S. 393 (1908).

10. Act of February 5, 1917, Public Law No. 301, ch. 29, § 19, 39 Statutes at
Large 874, 889 (1917).

11. *See, for example,* Jordan v. DeGeorge, 341 U.S. 223 (1951) (conspiracy to defraud on taxes on distilled spirits is considered a crime of moral turpitude); United
States *ex rel.* Volpe v. Smith, 289 U.S. 422 (1933) (counterfeiting is considered a crime
of moral turpitude); United States *ex rel.* Claussen v. Day, 279 U.S. 398 (1929)
(manslaughter is considered a crime of moral turpitude).

12. *See* Brian C. Harms, *Redefining "Crimes of Moral Turpitude": A Proposal to Congress,* 15 GEORGETOWN IMMIGRATION LAW JOURNAL 259 (2001) (reviewing cases that
attempt to define the contours of "crimes of moral turpitude").

13. *See* JOHN HIGHAM, STRANGERS IN THE LAND: PATTERNS OF AMERICAN NATIVISM,
1860–1925, at 90, 160, 267–68 (3d ed. 1992).

14. *See* REPORT OF THE UNITED STATES IMMIGRATION COMMISSION (1911); MALD-
WYN ALLEN JONES, AMERICAN IMMIGRATION 152–56 (2d ed. 1992).

15. DAVID A. OREBAUGH, CRIME, DEGENERACY AND IMMIGRATION: THEIR INTER-
RELATIONS AND INTERACTIONS 225 (1929).

16. *See* David R. Wade, *The Conclusion That a Sinister Conspiracy of Foreign Origin
Controls Organized Crime: The Influence of Nativism in the Kefauver Committee Investigation,* 16 NORTHERN ILLINOIS LAW REVIEW 371 (1976); *see, for example, Third Interim Report of the Special Committee to Investigate Organized Crime in Interstate Commerce,* SEN-
ATE REPORT NO. 307, 82d Cong., 1st Sess. (1951).

17. See HOUSE OF REPRESENTATIVES REPORT NO. 565, 87th Cong., 1st Sess. 6–7,
11 (1961); HOUSE OF REPRESENTATIVES REPORT NO. 1086, 87th Cong., 1st Sess. (1961),
1961 U.S. CODE CONGRESSIONAL & ADMINISTRATIVE NEWS 2950, 2967.

18. *See* Immigration and Nationality Act of 1952, Public Law No. 82-414, 66 Stat-
ues at Large 163 (1952), § 106, 8 U.S.C. § 1105a (added by act of September 26, 1961,
Public Law No. 87-301 § 5, 75 Statutes at Large 649, 651–53 (1961) (repealed))
[hereinafter INA].

19. STEPHEN H. LEGOMSKY, IMMIGRATION AND REFUGEE LAW AND POLICY 722 (3d
ed. 2002) (citation omitted); *see* Lenni B. Benson, *Back to the Future: Congress Attacks
the Right to Judicial Review of Immigration Proceedings,* 29 CONNECTICUT LAW REVIEW
1411, 1431 & n.101 (1997); Mark A. Mancini, *The Carlos Marcello Case,* 1999(2) IM-
MIGRATION AND NATIONALITY LAW at 2–10.

20. *See* Immigration and Nationality Act, *supra* note 18, §§ 212(a)(2), 237(a)(2),
8 U.S.C. §§ 1182(a)(2), 1227(a)(2).

21. Public Law No. 100-690, 102 Statutes at Large 4181 (1988).

22. *See* Kevin R. Johnson, *Public Benefits and Immigration: The Intersection of Immigration Status, Ethnicity, Gender, and Class*, 42 UCLA LAW REVIEW 1509, 1531–34, 1561 (1995).

23. *See, for example,* U.S. COMMISSION ON IMMIGRATION REFORM, U.S. IMMIGRATION POLICY: RESTORING CREDIBILITY, at xxvii–xxviii, 152–62 (1994) (recommending various policy reforms to expedite the detention and removal of criminal immigrants from the country).

24. Barbara Coe, *Keep Illegals Out of State*, USA TODAY, Oct. 12, 1994, at 12A.

25. *See, for example,* Federation of Immigration Reform, Issue Brief: Criminal Aliens, *available at* http://www.fairus.org/html/04110608.htm (last visited July 17, 2002).

26. Peter H. Schuck, *Alien Rumination*, 105 YALE LAW JOURNAL 1963, 1988 (1996) (book review) (footnote omitted).

27. *See, for example,* James Bornemeir & Patrick J. McDonnell, *U.S. Panel Issues Sweeping Immigration Reform Plan*, LOS ANGELES TIMES, Oct. 1, 1994, at A1 (quoting Barbara Jordan, chair of the U.S. Commission on Immigration Reform, on why undocumented persons should be denied public benefits: "Illegal aliens don't have the right to be here. . . . They broke the law to get here.").

28. *See* Mary B.W. Tabor, *Specter of Terror; U.S. Indicts Egyptian Cleric as Head of Group Plotting "War of Urban Terrorism,"* NEW YORK TIMES, Aug. 26, 1993, at A1; *Hearing of the Senate Judiciary Committee, Nomination of Janet Reno to Be Attorney General*, FEDERAL NEWS SERVICE, Mar. 9, 1993.

29. Public Law No. 101-649, 104 Statutes at Large 4778 (1990).

30. Public Law No. 103-322, 108 Statutes at Large 1796 (1994).

31. *See* ACCEPTING THE IMMIGRATION CHALLENGE: THE PRESIDENT'S REPORT ON IMMIGRATION 27–34 (1994); *Statement of Janet Reno, Attorney General, Before the Committee on the Judiciary, United States Senate, Concerning Proposals to Reduce Illegal Immigration and to Control Financial Costs to Taxpayers*, FEDERAL DOCUMENT CLEARING HOUSE CONGRESSIONAL TESTIMONY, Mar. 14, 1995; *Testimony of T. Alexander Aleinikoff, General Counsel, Immigration and Naturalization Service, Department of Justice, Regarding Identification of Criminal Aliens and Removal of Criminal Aliens Before the House Judiciary Committee, Subcommittee on Immigration*, FEDERAL DOCUMENT CLEARING HOUSE CONGRESSIONAL TESTIMONY, Mar. 23, 1995.

32. *See* Peter H. Schuck & John Williams, *Removing Criminal Aliens: The Pitfalls and Promises of Federalism*, 22 HARVARD JOURNAL OF LAW AND PUBLIC POLICY 367, 376–82 (1999).

33. *See* URBAN INSTITUTE FISCAL IMPACT OF UNDOCUMENTED ALIENS: SELECTED ESTIMATES FOR SEVEN STATES at ii (1994) (summarizing the conclusion of a study estimating that the annual cost of incarcerating undocumented persons is $368 million in California and $45 million in New York).

34. Marc Sandalow, *Mexican Envoy Berates State on Immigration*, SAN FRANCISCO CHRONICLE, July 6, 1994, at A1 (quoting the Mexican ambassador to the United States); *see* Mark Fineman, *California Elections; Mexico Assails State's Passage of Prop. 187*, LOS ANGELES TIMES, Nov. 10, 1994, at A28 (quoting the Mexican president as stating that Proposition 187 was "racist" and "a disgrace for U.S.-Mexico relations").

35. *See generally* Kevin R. Johnson, *Los Olvidados: Images of the Immigrant, Political Power of Noncitizens, and Immigration Law and Enforcement*, 1993 BRIGHAM YOUNG UNIVERSITY LAW REVIEW 1139 (analyzing how images of the immigrant affect the development of immigration law and policy).

36. *See* ACCEPTING THE IMMIGRATION CHALLENGE, *supra* note 31.

37. *See* Antiterrorism and Effective Death Penalty Act, Public Law No. 104-132, 110 Statutes at Large 1214 (1996); Illegal Immigration Reform and Immigrant Responsibility Act, Public Law No. 104-208, 110 Statutes at Large 3009 (1996).

38. Schuck & Williams, *supra* note 32, at 371.

39. *See* Bill Ong Hing, *The Immigrant as Criminal: Punishing Dreamers*, 9 HASTINGS WOMEN'S LAW JOURNAL 79 (1998); Maria Isabel Medina, *The Criminalization of Immigration Law: Employer Sanctions and Marriage Fraud*, 5 GEORGE MASON LAW REVIEW 669 (1997).

40. *See* PETER BRIMELOW, ALIEN NATION: COMMON SENSE ABOUT AMERICA'S IMMIGRATION DISASTER 184 (1995).

41. *See generally* MINORITIES, MIGRANTS, AND CRIME: DIVERSITY AND SIMILARITY ACROSS EUROPE AND THE UNITED STATES (Ineke Haen Marshall ed., 1997).

42. For analysis of crime among immigrants to the United States, see John Hagan & Alberto Palloni, *Immigration and Crime in the United States, in* THE IMMIGRATION DEBATE: STUDIES ON THE ECONOMIC, DEMOGRAPHIC, AND FISCAL EFFECTS OF IMMIGRATION (James P. Smith & Barry Edmonston eds., 1998); DAVID M. REIMERS, UNWELCOME STRANGERS: AMERICAN IDENTITY AND THE TURN AGAINST IMMIGRATION 79–84 (1998); TONY WATERS, CRIME AND IMMIGRANT YOUTH (1999).

43. *See* INA, *supra* note 18, § 237(a)(2), 8 U.S.C. § 1227(a)(2).

44. *See id.* § 101(a)(43), 8 U.S.C. § 1101(a)(43).

45. *See, for example*, United States v. Alejo-Alejo, 286 F.3d 711 (4th Cir. 2002) (holding that a misdemeanor conviction was an "aggravated felony"). For an analysis of the various collateral consequences, including important immigration consequences, of criminal convictions, see Nora V. Demleitner, *"Collateral Damage": No Re-entry for Drug Offenders*, 47 VILLANOVA LAW REVIEW 1027 (2002).

46. Nancy Morawetz, *Understanding the Impact of the 1996 Deportation Laws and the Limited Scope of Proposed Reforms*, 113 HARVARD LAW REVIEW 1936, 1948, 1949–50 (2000) (emphasis added) (footnotes omitted).

47. *See* Julie Anne Rah, Note, *The Removal of Aliens Who Drink and Drive: Felony DWI as a Crime of Violence Under 18 U.S.C. § 16(b)*, 70 FORDHAM LAW REVIEW 2109 (2002).

48. *See* Morawetz, *supra* note 46, at 1949.

49. *See, for example, In re* Yanez-Garcia, 23 Immigration and Nationality Decisions 39 (Board of Immigration Appeals 2002); *In re* Salazar-Regino, 23 Immigration and Nationality Decisions 223 (Board of Immigration Appeals 2002).

50. *See, for example*, Ramirez-Castro v. INS, 287 F.3d 1172 (9th Cir. 2002); Jean-Baptiste v. Reno, 144 F.3d 212 (2d Cir. 1998); Kolster v. INS, 101 F.3d 785 (1st Cir. 1996); Drax v. Ashcroft, 178 F. Supp.2d 296 (E.D.N.Y. 2001).

51. *See* Bill Ong Hing, *Deport Winona?* SAN FRANCISCO CHRONICLE, Dec. 10, 2002.

52. *See, for example*, Iris Bennett, Note, *The Unconstitutionality of Nonuniform Immigration Consequences of "Aggravated Felony" Convictions*, 74 N. Y. U. LAW REVIEW

1696 (1999); Alison Holland, Note, *Across the Border and over the Line: Congress's Attack on Criminal Aliens and the Judiciary Under the Antiterrorism and Effective Death Penalty Act of 1996*, 27 AMERICAN JOURNAL OF CRIMINAL LAW 385 (2000); Christina LaBrie, *Lack of Uniformity in the Deportation of Criminal Aliens*, 25 NEW YORK UNIVERSITY REVIEW OF LAW AND SOCIAL CHANGE 357 (1999); Jacqueline P. Ulin, Note, *A Common Sense Reconstruction of the INA's Crime-Related Removal System: Eliminating the Caveats from the Statue of Liberty's Welcoming Words*, 78 WASHINGTON UNIVERSITY LAW QUARTERLY 1549 (2000).

53. *See* Nancy Morawetz, *Rethinking Retroactive Deportation Laws and the Due Process Clause*, 73 NEW YORK UNIVERSITY LAW REVIEW 97, 115–16 (1998).

54. *See* Anthony Lewis, *Punishing the Past*, NEW YORK TIMES, Mar. 30, 1998, at A17; Anthony Lewis, *When It Is Unjust*, NEW YORK TIMES, Dec. 26, 1997, at A39; Anthony Lewis, *Abroad at Home; A Generous Country*, NEW YORK TIMES, Dec. 22, 1997, at A27; Anthony Lewis, *"Accent the Positive,"* NEW YORK TIMES, Oct. 10, 1997, at A23.

55. *See* 1998 INS STATISTICAL YEARBOOK, *supra* note 2, at 203.

56. *See* Lenni B. Benson, *The New World of Judicial Review of Removal Orders*, 12 GEORGETOWN IMMIGRATION LAW JOURNAL 233 (1998).

57. *See* Peter H. Schuck & Theodore Wang, *Continuity and Change: Patterns of Immigration Litigation in the Courts, 1979–1990*, 45 STANFORD LAW REVIEW 115 (1992).

58. *See* INS v. St. Cyr, 533 U.S. 289 (2001). *See generally* Gerald L. Neuman, *Habeas Corpus, Executive Detention, and the Removal of Aliens*, 98 COLUMBIA LAW REVIEW 961 (1998).

59. *See* INA, *supra* note 18, § 236(c), 8 U.S.C. § 1226(c); Ellis M. Johnston, Note, *Once a Criminal, Always a Criminal? Constitutional Presumptions for Mandatory Detention of Criminal Aliens*, 89 GEORGETOWN LAW JOURNAL 2593 (2001); Amy Langenfeld, Comment, *Living in Limbo: Mandatory Detention of Immigrants Under the Illegal Immigration Reform and Responsibility Act of 1996*, 31 ARIZONA STATE LAW JOURNAL 1041 (1999). For a critique of the retroactive application of the mandatory detention provisions of the IIRIRA, see Debra Lyn Bassett, *In the Wake of Schooner Peggy: Deconstructing Legislative Retroactivity Analysis*, 69 UNIVERSITY OF CINCINNATI LAW REVIEW 453 (2001).

60. *See* Demore v. Kim 123 S. Ct. 1708 (2003).

61. 44 F.3d 1441 (9th Cir.) (en banc), *cert. denied*, 516 U.S. 976 (1995).

62. *See* Laurie Joyce, *INS Detention Practices Post–Zadvydas v. Davis*, 79 INTERPRETER RELEASES 809, 811 (2002); Elizabeth Larson Beyer, Comment, *A Right or a Privilege: Constitutional Protection for Detained Deportable Aliens Refused Access or Return to Their Native Countries*, 35 WAKE FOREST LAW REVIEW 1029, 1029–30 (2000); Lourdes M. Guiribitey, Comment, *Criminal Aliens Facing Indefinite Detention Under INS: An Analysis of the Review Process*, 55 UNIVERSITY OF MIAMI LAW REVIEW 275 (2001).

63. *See* Zadvydas v. Davis, 533 U.S. 678 (2001); *see* Margaret H. Taylor, *Behind the Scenes of* St. Cyr *and* Zadvydas: *Making Policy in the Midst of Litigation*, 16 GEORGETOWN IMMIGRATION LAW JOURNAL 271, 288–95 (2002); *Developments in the Law—the Law of Prisons*, 115 HARVARD LAW REVIEW 1838, 1915–39 (2002).

64. *See* 8 U.S.C. § 1326(a).

65. *See, for example,* Almendarez-Torres v. United States, 523 U.S. 224 (1998); United States v. Mendoza-Lopez, 481 U.S. 828 (1987); United States v. Maria-

Gonzalez, 268 F.3d 664 (9th Cir. 2001), *cert. denied*, 535 U.S. 965 (2002); United States v. Martinez-Garcia, 268 F.3d 460 (7th Cir. 2001), *cert. denied*, 534 U.S. 1149 (2002); Pamela A. MacLean, *Study Suggests Hispanic Men Face Excessive Prosecution*, DAILY RECORDER (Sacramento), Oct. 11, 2001, at 1.

66. 163 U.S. 228 (1896).

67. The Los Angeles Police Department, however, has often violated this policy, repeatedly depriving U.S. citizens and immigrants of Mexican ancestry of their civil rights. *See* Theodore W. Maya, Comment, *To Serve and Protect or to Betray and Neglect? The LAPD and Undocumented Immigrants*, 49 UCLA LAW REVIEW 1611 (2002).

68. Gabriel J. Chin, *The Civil Rights Revolution Comes to Immigration Law: A New Look at the Immigration and Nationality Act of 1965*, 75 NORTH CAROLINA LAW REVIEW 273, 276 (1996) (footnote omitted).

69. *See, for example*, GEORGE J. BORJAS, HEAVEN'S DOOR: IMMIGRATION POLICY AND THE AMERICAN ECONOMY (1999).

70. *See* McCleskey v. Kemp, 481 U.S. 279 (1987); David A. Sklansky, *Cocaine, Race, and Equal Protection*, 47 STANFORD LAW REVIEW 1283 (1995).

71. *See* Paul Butler, *Racially Based Jury Nullification: Black Power in the Criminal Justice System*, 105 YALE LAW JOURNAL 677 (1995).

72. *See* EDWARD J. ESCOBAR, RACE, POLICE, AND THE MAKING OF A POLITICAL IDENTITY: MEXICAN AMERICANS AND THE LOS ANGELES POLICE DEPARTMENT, 1900–1945 (1999); Cruz Reynoso, *Hispanics and the Criminal Justice System*, *in* HISPANICS IN THE UNITED STATES: AN AGENDA FOR THE TWENTY-FIRST CENTURY 277 (Pastora San Juan Cafferty & David W. Engstrom eds., 2000); FRANCISCO A. VILLARRUEL, ET AL. ¿DÓNDE ESTÁ LA JUSTICIA? A CALL TO ACTION ON BEHALF OF LATINO AND LATINA YOUTH IN THE U.S. JUSTICE SYSTEM (2002).

73. *See* Mary Romero, *State Violence, and the Social and Legal Construction of Latino Criminality: From El Bandido to Gang Member*, 78 DENVER UNIVERSITY LAW REVIEW 1081 (2001).

74. *See* RAMIRO MARTINEZ JR., LATINO HOMICIDE: IMMIGRATION, VIOLENCE, AND COMMUNITY (2002) (reviewing homicide data in major cities with large Latina/o populations and finding that rates were lower than would be expected).

75. *See generally* RODOLFO F. ACUÑA, OCCUPIED AMERICA: A HISTORY OF CHICANOS (3d ed. 1988); TOMÁS ALMAGUER, RACIAL FAULT LINES: THE HISTORICAL ORIGINS OF WHITE SUPREMACY IN CALIFORNIA (1994).

76. *See, for example*, Angela J. Davis, *Race, Cops, and Traffic Stops*, 51 UNIVERSITY OF MIAMI LAW REVIEW 425 (1997); David A. Harris, *The Stories, the Statistics, and the Law: Why "Driving While Black" Matters*, 84 MINNESOTA LAW REVIEW 265 (1999); Anthony C. Thompson, *Stopping the Usual Suspects: Race and the Fourth Amendment*, 74 NEW YORK UNIVERSITY LAW REVIEW 956 (1999).

77. *See* Kevin R. Johnson, *The Case Against Race Profiling in Immigration Enforcement*, 78 WASHINGTON UNIVERSITY LAW QUARTERLY 675 (2000). *See generally* ALFREDO MIRANDÉ, GRINGO JUSTICE (1987).

78. *See* Ira Glasser, *American Drug Laws: The New Jim Crow*, 63 ALBANY LAW REVIEW 703 (2000); Kenneth B. Nunn, *The "Darden Dilemma": Should African Americans Prosecute Crimes?* 68 FORDHAM LAW REVIEW 1473, 1484–85 (2000); David Rudovsky, *The Impact of the War on Drugs on Procedural Fairness and Racial Equality*, 1994 UNI-

VERSITY OF CHICAGO LEGAL FORUM 237 (1994); Michael Tonry, *Race and the War on Drugs*, 1994 UNIVERSITY OF CHICAGO LEGAL FORUM 25 (1994).

79. *See* Blaine Harden & Devon Spurgeon, *Marching New Yorkers Protest Police Brutality*, WASHINGTON POST, Aug. 30, 1997, at A4.

Chapter 6: The Marginalization of Women Under the Immigration and Nationality Laws

1. *See* Janet M. Calvo, *Spouse-Based Immigration Laws: The Legacies of Coverture*, 28 SAN DIEGO LAW REVIEW 593, 600–06 (1991).

2. *See* Chy Lung v. Freeman, 92 U.S. 275 (1875).

3. Act of March 3, 1875, ch. 141, 18 Statutes at Large 477 (1875).

4. *See* Sucheng Chan, *The Exclusion of Chinese Women, 1870–1943*, at 105–09, *in* ENTRY DENIED: EXCLUSION AND THE CHINESE COMMUNITY IN AMERICA, 1882–1943 (Sucheng Chan ed., 1991).

5. Act of March 3, 1875, *supra* note 3, ch. 141, § 5, 18 Statutes at Large at 477, 477.

6. EDWARD P. HUTCHINSON, LEGISLATIVE HISTORY OF AMERICAN IMMIGRATION POL-ICY 1798–1965, at 65 (1981).

7. BILL ONG HING, MAKING AND REMAKING ASIAN AMERICA THROUGH IMMIGRA-TION POLICY 1850–1990, at 36 (1993). *See generally* GEORGE ANTHONY PEFFER, IF THEY DON'T BRING THEIR WOMEN HERE: CHINESE FEMALE IMMIGRATION BEFORE EXCLU-SION (1999).

8. 189 U.S. 86 (1903).

9. 142 U.S. 651 (1892).

10. *See, for example*, Zurbrick v. Woodhead, 90 F.2d 991 (6th Cir. 1937); United States *ex rel*. Minuto v. Reimer, 83 F.2d 166 (2d Cir. 1936); United States *ex rel*. Shaw v. Van De Mark, 3 F. Supp. 101 (W.D.N.Y. 1933); United States *ex rel*. Mantler v. Commissioner of Immigration, 3 F.2d 234 (2d Cir. 1924); *Ex parte* Hosaye Sakaguchi, 277 F. 913 (9th Cir. 1922): *Ex parte* Mitchell, 256 F. 229 (N.D.N.Y. 1919); *In re* Ah Fong, 1 F. Cases 213 (C.C.D. Cal. 1874); Matter of Kowalski, 10 Immigration and Nationality Decisions 159 (Board of Immigration Appeals 1963); Matter of S, 5 Im-migration and Nationality Decisions 682 (Board of Immigration Appeals 1954); Mat-ter of F, 5 Immigration and Nationality Decisions 209 (Board of Immigration Ap-peals 1953); Matter of M, 2 Immigration and Nationality Decisions 694 (Board of Immigration Appeals 1946).

11. *See* Immigration Act of 1907 § 2, 34 Statutes at Large 898, 899 (1907).

12. *Id.* § 3, 34 Statutes at Large at 900 (emphasis added).

13. United States v. Bitty, 208 U.S. 393, 401 (1908) (citation omitted).

14. *See, for example*, Lapina v. Williams, 232 U.S. 78 (1914); Zakonaite v. Wolf, 226 U.S. 272 (1912); Low Wah Suey v. Backus, 225 U.S. 460 (1912); Toku Sakai v. United States. 239 F. 492 (9th Cir. 1917); Choy Gum v. Backus, 223 F. 487 (9th Cir. 1915), *cert. denied*, 239 U.S. 649 (1916); Haw Moy v. North, 183 F. 89 (9th Cir. 1910), *cert. denied*, 223 U.S. 717 (1911); Chu Tai Ngan v. Backus, 226 F. 446 (9th Cir. 1915), *cert. dismissed*, 241 U.S. 684 (1916); Looe Shee v. North, 170 F. 566 (9th Cir. 1909); *Ex parte* Petterson, 166 F. 536 (D. Minn. 1908).

15. Ch. 395, 36 Statutes at Large 825 (1910) (codified as amended at 18 U.S.C. §§ 2421–24); *see* Marlene D. Beckman, Note, *The White Slave Traffic Act: The Historical Impact of a Criminal Law Policy on Women*, 72 GEORGETOWN LAW JOURNAL 1111 (1984). *See generally* FRANCESCO CORDASCO & THOMAS MONROE PITKIN, THE WHITE SLAVE TRADE AND THE IMMIGRANTS (1981).

16. UNITED STATES IMMIGRATION COMMISSION, REPORT OF THE IMMIGRATION COMMISSION, vol. 37, at 3 (1910).

17. RUTH ROSEN, THE LOST SISTERHOOD: PROSTITUTION IN AMERICA, 1900–1918, at 44 (1982) (emphasis added) (footnotes omitted); *see* Nancy K. Ota, *Flying Buttresses*, 49 DEPAUL LAW REVIEW 693 (2000).

18. Act of February 5, 1917, ch. 29, § 3, 39 Statutes at Large 874, 876 (1917).

19. *See, for example,* Hansen v. Haff, 291 U.S. 559 (1934); Sohaiby v. Savoretti, 195 F.2d 139 (5th Cir. 1952); United States *ex rel.* Ng Wing v. Brough, 15 F.2d 377 (2d Cir. 1926); Chan Wong v. Nagle, 17 F.2d 987 (9th Cir. 1927).

20. Immigration and Nationality Act of 1952, Public Law No. 82-414, 66 Statutes at Large 163 (1952), § 212(a)(2)(D)(i), 8 U.S.C. § 1182 (a)(2)(D)(i) (alteration added) [hereinafter INA].

21. *See, for example,* Greene v. INS, 313 F.2d 148 (9th Cir.), *cert. denied*, 374 U.S. 828 (1963); Gilles v. Del Guercio, 150 F. Supp. 864 (C.D. Cal. 1957).

22. 385 U.S. 276 (1966); *see* Woodby v. INS, 370 F.2d 989 (6th Cir. 1965).

23. Lisa Raffonelli, *INS Final Rule to Assist Victims of Trafficking*, 23 REFUGEE REPORTS, Apr. 2002, at 2.

24. *See* Victims of Trafficking and Violence Protection Act of 2000, Public Law No. 106-386, 114 Statutes at Large 1464 (2000) (codified and amended in scattered sections of 8, 18, 22 U.S. Code); Jacqueline Bhabha, *Lone Travelers: Rights, Criminalization, and the Transnational Migration of Unaccompanied Children*, 7 UNIVERSITY OF CHICAGO LAW SCHOOL ROUNDTABLE 269 (2000); Kelly E. Hyland, *Protecting Human Victims of Trafficking: An American Framework*, 16 BERKELEY WOMEN'S LAW JOURNAL 29 (2001); Michael R. Candes, *The Victims of Trafficking and Violence Protection Act of 2000: Will It Become the Thirteenth Amendment of the Twenty-first Century?* 32 UNIVERSITY OF MIAMI INTER-AMERICAN LAW REVIEW 571 (2001); Tiffany St. Clair King, *The Modern Slave Trade*, 8 UNIVERSITY OF CALIFORNIA AT DAVIS JOURNAL OF INTERNATIONAL LAW AND POLICY 293 (2002); Susan W. Tiefenbrun, *Sex Sells but Drugs Don't Talk: Trafficking of Women Sex Workers*, 23 THOMAS JEFFERSON LAW REVIEW 199 (2001); Michelle O.P. Dunbar, Comment, *The Past, Present, and Future of International Trafficking in Women for Prostitution*, 8 BUFFALO WOMEN'S LAW JOURNAL 103 (1999/2000); Maya Raghu, Note, *Sex Trafficking of Thai Women and the United States Asylum Law Response*, 12 GEORGETOWN IMMIGRATION LAW JOURNAL 145 (1997). *See generally* KO-LIN CHIN, SMUGGLED CHINESE: CLANDESTINE IMMIGRATION TO THE UNITED STATES (1999).

25. *See* Todd Stevens, *Tender Ties: Husbands' Rights and Racial Exclusion in Chinese Marriage Cases, 1882–1924*, 27 LAW AND SOCIAL INQUIRY 271 (2001).

26. 344 U.S. 604 (1953).

27. Bark v. INS, 511 F.2d 1200, 1201 (9th Cir. 1975) (alterations added).

28. STEPHEN H. LEGOMSKY, IMMIGRATION AND REFUGEE LAW AND POLICY 166–67 (3d ed. 2002) (quoting the drafter of the report) (alterations added).

29. *See* HOUSE OF REPRESENTATIVES REPORT NO. 99-906, 99th Cong., 2d Sess. 6 (1986), *reprinted in* 1986 U.S. CODE CONGRESSIONAL & ADMINISTRATIVE NEWS 5978, 5978.

30. Public Law No. 99-639, 100 Statutes at Large 3537 (1986) (codified as amended in scattered sections of 8 U.S.C.).

31. *See* Calvo, *supra* note 1, at 606–11; Kevin R. Johnson, *Public Benefits and Immigration: The Intersection of Immigration Status, Ethnicity, Gender, and Class,* 42 UCLA LAW REVIEW 1509, 1550–52 (1995); Kimberlé Crenshaw, *Mapping the Margins: Intersectionality, Identity Politics, and Violence Against Women of Color,* 43 STANFORD LAW REVIEW 1241, 1246–50 (1991).

32. *See* INA, *supra* note 20, § 216A, 8 U.S.C. § 1186a.

33. Crenshaw, *supra* note 31, at 1247 (footnotes omitted); *see* Calvo, *supra* note 1, at 613–22; Anna Y. Park, *The Marriage Fraud Act Revised: The Continuing Subordination of Asian and Pacific Islander Women,* 1 UCLA ASIAN AMERICAN PACIFIC ISLANDS LAW JOURNAL 29 (1993); Colleen Sheppard, *Women as Wives: Immigration Law and Domestic Violence,* 26 QUEEN'S LAW JOURNAL 1 (2000).

34. *See* INA, *supra* note 20, § 216A(c)(4)(C), 8 U.S.C. § 1186a(c)(4)(C) (as amended by Immigration Act of 1990, Public Law No. 101-649, 104 Statutes at Large 4978 (1990).

35. *See, for example,* Calvo, *supra* note 1, at 612–13; Crenshaw, *supra* note 31, at 1247–50; *see also* Michelle J. Anderson, Note, *A License to Abuse: The Impact of Conditional Status on Female Immigrants,* 102 YALE LAW JOURNAL 1401, 1416–20 (1993) (arguing that the law, as implemented, exacerbated dependence of immigrant women on spouses, placed unreasonable evidentiary burden on women, and ignored cultural and other fears of bureaucracy).

36. *See* Violent Crime Control and Law Enforcement Act of 1994, Public Law No. 103-322, § 40,701, 108 Statutes at Large 1796, 1953 (1994) (amending INA, *supra* note 20, § 204(a)(1), 8 U.S.C. § 1154(a)(1)).

37. *See* Cecelia M. Espenoza, *No Relief for the Weary: VAWA Relief Denied for Battered Immigrants Lost in the Intersections,* 83 MARQUETTE LAW REVIEW 163 (1999); Linda Kelly, *Stories from the Front: Seeking Refuge for Battered Immigrants in the Violence Against Women Act,* 92 NORTHWESTERN UNIVERSITY LAW REVIEW 665 (1998); Lee J. Teran, *Barriers to Protection at Home and Abroad: Mexican Victims of Domestic Violence and the Violence Against Women Act,* 17 BOSTON UNIVERSITY INTERNATIONAL LAW JOURNAL 1 (1999); Ryan Lilienthal, Note, *Old Hurdles Hamper New Options for Battered Immigrant Women,* 62 BROOKLYN LAW REVIEW 1595 (1996).

38. Public Law No. 106-386, *supra* note 24, 114 Statutes at Large at 1464.

39. *See* Juan P. Osuna, *The 1996 Immigration Act: Adjustment of Status, Battered Spouses, Legalization and Related Issues,* 74 INTERPRETER RELEASES 137 (1997); Linda Kelly, *Domestic Violence Survivors: Surviving the Beatings of 1996,* 11 GEORGETOWN IMMIGRATION LAW JOURNAL 303 (1997).

40. Lori Romeyn Sitowski, *Congress Giveth, Congress Taketh Away, Congress Fixeth Its Mistake? Assessing the Potential Impact of the Battered Immigrant Women Protection Act of 2000,* 19 LAW AND INEQUALITY 259, 259–60 (2001) (footnotes omitted).

41. *See, for example,* Linda Kelly, *Marriage for Sale: The Mail-Order Bride Industry and the Changing Value of Marriage,* 5 IOWA JOURNAL OF GENDER, RACE, AND JUSTICE

175 (2001); Ryiah Lilith, *Buying a Wife but Saving a Child: A Deconstruction of Popular Rhetoric and Legal Analysis of Mail-Order Brides and Intercountry Adoptions*, 9 BUFFALO WOMEN'S LAW JOURNAL 225 (2000–2001); Christine S.Y. Chun, Comment, *The Mail-Order Bride Industry: The Perpetuation of Transnational Economic Inequalities and Stereotypes*, 17 UNIVERSITY OF PENNSYLVANIA JOURNAL OF INTERNATIONAL AND ECONOMIC LAW 1155 (1996); Donna R. Lee, Comment, *Mail Fantasy: Global Sexual Exploitation in the Mail-Order Bride Industry and Proposed Legal Solutions*, 5 ASIAN LAW JOURNAL 139 (1998); Kathryn A. Lloyd, Comment, *Wives for Sale: The Modern International Mail-Order Bride Industry*, 20 NORTHWESTERN JOURNAL OF INTERNATIONAL LAW AND BUSINESS 341 (2000); Vanessa B.M. Vergara, Comment, *Abusive Mail-Order Bride Marriage and the Thirteenth Amendment*, 94 NORTHWESTERN UNIVERSITY LAW REVIEW 1547 (2000); Note, *Mail-Order Brides: Gilded Prostitution and the Legal Response*, 28 UNIVERSITY OF MICHIGAN JOURNAL OF LAW REFORM 197 (1994).

42. *See* Yuji Ichioka, *Amerika Nadeshiko: Japanese Immigrant Women in the United States, 1900–1924*, 49 PACIFIC HISTORICAL REVIEW 339 (1980).

43. *See* INA, *supra* note 20, § 101(a)(42), 8 U.S.C. § 1101(a)(42).

44. *See* United Nations Convention Relating to the Status of Refugees, Article 33.1, 189 U.N.T.S. 137 (1951); United Nations Protocol Relating to the Status of Refugees, Article I, 606 U.N.T.S. 267, 19 U.S.T. 6223, T.I.A.S. No. 6577 (1967).

45. *See generally* Jacqueline Greatbatch, *The Gender Difference: Feminist Critiques of Refugee Discourse*, 1 INTERNATIONAL JOURNAL OF REFUGEE LAW 518 (1989); Nancy Kelly, *Gender-Related Persecution: Assessing the Asylum Claims of Women*, 26 CORNELL INTERNATIONAL LAW JOURNAL 625 (1993).

46. *See, for example,* Fisher v. INS, 79 F.3d 955 (9th Cir. 1996) (en banc); Fatin v. INS, 12 F.3d 1233 (3d Cir. 1993).

47. *See* Matter of D-V-, 21 Immigration and Nationality Decision 77 (Board of Immigration Appeals 1993).

48. 21 Immigration and Nationality Decision 357 (Board of Immigration Appeals 1996); *see* Karen Musalo, In Re Kasinga*: A Big Step Forward for Gender-Based Asylum Claims*, 73 INTERPRETER RELEASES 853 (1996). This was a much-publicized, ground-breaking case. *See, for example,* Celia W. Dugger, *A Refugee's Body Is Intact but Her Family Is Torn*, NEW YORK TIMES, Sept. 11, 1996, at A1: Celia W. Dugger, *In Pursuit of Freedom, Only to Find Prison Bars*, NEW YORK TIMES, July 8, 1996, at B1; Celia W. Dugger, *U.S. Grants Asylum to Woman Fleeing Genital Mutilation*, NEW YORK TIMES, June 14, 1996, at A1. For analyses of the difficult legal issues involved, see Jacqueline Bhabha, *Embodied Rights: Gender Persecution, State Sovereignty, and Refugees*, 9 PUBLIC CULTURE 3 (1996); Isabelle R. Gunning, *Arrogant Perception, World-Travelling and Multicultural Feminism: The Case of Female Genital Surgery*, 23 COLUMBIA HUMAN RIGHTS LAW REVIEW 189 (1992); Hope Lewis, *Between Irua and "Female Genital Mutilation": Feminist Human Rights Discourse and the Cultural Divide*, 8 HARVARD HUMAN RIGHTS JOURNAL 1 (1995).

49. See, *for example,* Aguirre-Cervantes v. INS 242 F.3d 1169 (9th Cir.) (holding that a female native of Mexico subjected to extreme abuse by her father was eligible for asylum), *vacated and remanded,* 273 F.3d 1220 (9th Cir. 2001); Pamela Goldberg, *Anyplace but Home: Asylum in the United States for Women Fleeing Intimate Violence,*

26 CORNELL INTERNATIONAL LAW JOURNAL 565 (1993); Haley Schaffer, Note, *Domestic Violence and Asylum in the United States:* In Re R-A-, 95 NORTHWESTERN UNIVERSITY LAW REVIEW 779 (2001); Anita Sinha, Note, *Domestic Violence and U.S. Asylum Law: Eliminating the "Cultural Hook" for Claims Involving Gender-Related Persecution,* 76 NEW YORK UNIVERSITY LAW REVIEW 1562 (2001).

50. *See* SHERENE RAZACK, LOOKING WHITE PEOPLE IN THE EYE: GENDER, RACE AND CULTURE IN COURTROOMS AND CLASSROOMS (1998); Susan Musarrat Akram, *Orientalism Revisited in Asylum and Refugee Claims,* 12 INTERNATIONAL JOURNAL OF REFUGEE LAW 7 (2000); Leti Volpp, *Feminism Versus Multiculturalism,* 101 COLUMBIA LAW REVIEW 1181 (2001); Leti Volpp, *Blaming Culture for Bad Behavior,* 12 YALE JOURNAL OF LAW AND HUMANITIES 89 (2000).

51. *See* United States v. Bhagat Singh Thind, 261 U.S. 204 (1923); Takao Ozawa v. United States, 260 U.S. 178 (1922).

52. IAN F. HANEY LÓPEZ, WHITE BY LAW: THE LEGAL CONSTRUCTION OF RACE 46–47 (1996) (footnotes omitted); *see* 4 CHARLES GORDON ET AL., IMMIGRATION LAW AND PROCEDURE § 95.03[6], at 95-34, § 97.07[2][a] at 97-53 to 97-54 (1998 2d rev. ed.) (describing gender-based naturalization and expatriation rules); Gary Endelman & Bill Coffman, *The Changing Face of Equal Protection: Gender Bias in U.S. Citizenship Law,* IMMIGRATION BRIEFINGS, Mar. 1995 (analyzing gender discrimination in citizenship law); *see, for example,* Kelly v. Owen, 74 U.S. 496 (1868); *see also* JACQUELINE BHABHA ET AL., WORLDS APART: WOMEN UNDER IMMIGRATION AND NATIONALITY LAW (1985) (criticizing the disparate impact that British immigration and nationality laws have on women).

53. Act of March 3, 1931, ch. 442, § 4(a), 46 Statutes at Large 1511 (1931).

54. Act of March 2, 1907, ch. 2534, § 3, 34 Statutes at Large 1228 (1907) (providing that "any American woman who marries a foreigner shall take the nationality of her husband"); *see* HANEY LÓPEZ, *supra* note 52, at 47. Before this law was passed, there was a split in the courts on the legal impact of the marriage of female citizens to noncitizens. *See* FREDERICK VAN DYNE, CITIZENSHIP OF THE UNITED STATES § 55, at 127–40 (1904).

55. *See* 67 CONGRESSIONAL RECORD 9040–41 (1922) (comments of Representative William Nowell Vaile).

56. HANEY LÓPEZ, *supra* note 52, at 47 (emphasis added); *see* Act of September 22, 1922, ch. 411, § 5 1021–22 (1922).

57. *See, for example,* Chang Chan v. Nagle, 268 U.S. 346, 351–53 (1925); Kelly v. Owen, 74 U.S. 496, 498 (1868).

58. HANEY LÓPEZ, *supra* note 52, at 15.

59. A number of states had such laws until the Supreme Court invalidated Virginia's in 1967. *See* Loving v. Virginia, 388 U.S. 1 (1967).

60. *See generally* MIXED RACE AMERICA AND THE LAW: A READER (Kevin R. Johnson ed., 2002) (collecting readings on this subject).

61. *See* T. Alexander Aleinikoff, *Theories of Loss of Citizenship,* 84 MICHIGAN LAW REVIEW 1471, 1473, 1478–79 (1986).

62. *See* Calvo, *supra* note 1, at 600–03; *see also* John Guendelsberger, *Implementing Family Unification Rights in American Immigration Law: Proposed Amendments,* 25

SAN DIEGO LAW REVIEW 253, 255–58 (1988) (describing the history of gender, race, and class discrimination in the family reunification provisions of the immigration laws).

63. Mackenzie v. Hare, 239 U.S. 299, 311 (1915) (emphasis added); *see also* Pequignot v. City of Detroit, 16 F. 211, 216 (C.C.E.D. Mich. 1883) (stating that "the husband, as the head of the family, is to be considered its political representative, at least for the purposes of citizenship, and that the wife and minor children owe their allegiance to the same sovereign power").

64. *See, for example,* 4 GORDON ET AL., *supra* note 52, § 100.02[2][a]; Donald K. Duvall, *Expatriation Under United States Law*, Perez *to* Afroyim: *The Search for a Philosophy of American Citizenship*, 56 VIRGINIA LAW REVIEW 408, 414–15 (1970).

65. *See* Maurice A. Roberts, *The Tale of the Lady Bartender*, 72 INTERPRETER RELEASES 1533, 1534 (1995) (recounting the 1950s practice of careful scrutinization of whether a single woman was living with anyone in determining whether she satisfied the moral character requirement for naturalization and observing that some immigration examiners seemed to "delv[e] into the intimate details of a female applicant's private life more out of a prurient interest than out of the genuine needs of the case").

66. Petition of Kielbock, 163 F. Supp. 687 (S.D. Cal. 1958); *see, for example,* Landon v. Clarke, 239 F.2d 631 (1st Cir. 1956); Petition of C-C-J-P, 299 F. Supp 767 (E.D. Ill. 1969); United States v. Cloutier, 87 F. Supp. 848 (E.D. Mich. 1949).

67. *See* Petition of Johnson, 292 F. Supp. 381 (E.D.N.Y. 1968).

68. *See* Dorothy E. Roberts, *Who May Give Birth to Citizens? Reproduction, Eugenics, and Immigration, in* IMMIGRANTS OUT! THE NEW NATIVISM AND THE ANTI-IMMIGRANT IMPULSE IN THE UNITED STATES 205 (Juan F. Perea ed., 1997).

69. See INA, *supra* note 20, § 309(a), (c) 8 U.S.C. § 1409(a), (c).

70. Nguyen v. INS, 533 U.S. 53 (2001).

71. *See* Kif Augustine-Adams, *Gendered States: A Comparative Construction of Citizenship and Nation*, 41 VIRGINIA JOURNAL OF INTERNATIONAL LAW 93 (2000).

72. *See, for example,* DONNA GABACCIA, FROM THE OTHER SIDE: WOMEN, GENDER, AND IMMIGRANT LIFE IN THE U.S., 1820–1990 (1994); RITA J. SIMON, RABBIS, LAWYERS, IMMIGRANTS, THIEVES: EXPLORING WOMEN'S ROLES 75–88 (1993); DORIS WEATHERFORD, FOREIGN AND FEMALE: IMMIGRANT WOMEN IN AMERICA, 1840–1930 (rev. ed. 1995); Joan Fitzpatrick, *The Gender Dimension of U.S. Immigration Policy*, 9 YALE JOURNAL OF LAW AND FEMINISM 23 (1997); Joan Fitzpatrick & Katrina R. Kelly, *Gendered Aspects of Migration: Law and the Female Migrant*, 22 HASTINGS INTERNATIONAL AND COMPARATIVE LAW REVIEW 47 (1998); Pierrette Hondagneu-Sotelo, *Feminism and Migration*, 571 ANNALS 107 (2000); Linda Kelly, *Republican Mothers, Bastards' Fathers and Good Victims: Discardiing Citizens and Equal Protection Through the Failures of Legal Images*, 51 HASTINGS LAW JOURNAL 557 (2000); Hope Lewis, *Universal Mother: Transnational Migration and the Human Rights of Black Women in the Americas*, 5 IOWA JOURNAL OF GENDER, RACE AND JUSTICE 197 (2001); Judy Scales-Trent, *Equal Rights Advocates: Addressing the Legal Issues of Women of Color*, 13 BERKELEY WOMEN'S LAW JOURNAL 34 (1998); Bina Kalola, Note, *Immigration Laws and the Immigrant Woman: 1885–1924*, 11 GEORGETOWN IMMIGRATION LAW JOURNAL 553 (1997).

73. *See* U.S. DEPARTMENT OF JUSTICE, 1998 STATISTICAL YEARBOOK OF THE IMMIGRATION AND NATURALIZATION SERVICE 60 tbl.12, 112 tbl.33, 198 tbl.56 (2000).

74. Fitzpatrick, *Gender Dimension, supra* note 72, at 25 (footnotes omitted).

75. *See* M. Isabel Medina, *In Search of Quality Childcare: Closing the Immigration Gate to Childcare Workers*, 8 GEORGETOWN IMMIGRATION LAW JOURNAL 161 (1994); Linda Kelly, *The Fantastic Adventure of Supermom and the Alien: Educating Immigration Policy on the Facts of Life*, 31 CONNECTICUT LAW REVIEW 1045 (1999).

76. *See generally* RHACEL SALAZAR PARREÑAS, SERVANTS OF GLOBALIZATION: WOMEN, MIGRATION, AND DOMESTIC WORK (2001): MARY ROMERO, MAID IN THE U.S.A. (1992); Cecelia M. Espenoza, *The Illusory Provisions of Sanctions: The Immigration Reform and Control Act of 1986*, 8 GEORGETOWN IMMIGRATION LAW JOURNAL 343 (1994).

77. *See* Elvia R. Arriola, *Voices from the Barbed Wires of Despair: Women in the Maquiladoras, Latina Critical Legal Theory, and Gender at the U.S.-Mexico Border*, 49 DEPAUL LAW REVIEW 729 (2000); Maria L. Ontiveros, *To Help Those Most in Need: Undocumented Workers' Rights and Remedies Under Title VII*, 20 NEW YORK UNIVERSITY REVIEW OF LAW AND SOCIAL CHANGE 607 (1993–94); Lora Jo Foo, *The Vulnerable and Exploitable Immigrant Workforce and the Need for Strengthening Worker Protective Legislation*, 103 YALE LAW JOURNAL 2179 (1994); Richard Kamm, *Extending the Progress of the Feminist Movement to Encompass the Rights of Migrant Farmworker Women*, 75 CHICAGO-KENT LAW REVIEW 765 (2000); Lori A. Nessel, *Undocumented Immigrants in the Workplace: The Fallacy of Labor Protection and the Need for Reform*, 36 HARVARD CIVIL RIGHTS–CIVIL LIBERTIES LAW REVIEW 345 (2001); Shruti Rana, *Fulfilling Technology's Promise: Enforcing the Rights of Women Caught in the Global High-Tech Underclass*, 15 BERKELEY WOMEN'S LAW JOURNAL 272 (2000); Leti Volpp, *Migrating Identities: On Labor, Culture, and Law*, 27 NORTH CAROLINA JOURNAL OF INTERNATIONAL LAW AND COMMERCIAL REGULATION 507 (2002). *See generally* GRACE CHANG, DISPOSABLE DOMESTICS, IMMIGRANT WOMEN WORKERS IN THE GLOBAL ECONOMY (2000).

78. *See* Laura Ho, et al., *(Dis)assembling Rights of Women Workers Along the Global Assemby Line: Human Rights and the Garment Industry*, 21 HARVARD CIVIL RIGHTS–CIVIL LIBERTIES LAW REVIEW 383 (1996); William Branigin, *Seventeen-Hour Days, and Collars Sewn for Eleven Cents*, WASHINGTON POST, Sept. 10, 1995, at A12; Patrick J. McDonnell & Paul Feldman, *New Approaches to Sweatshop Problems Urged*, LOS ANGELES TIMES, Aug. 16, 1995, at A1; James Sterngold, *Agency Missteps Put Illegal Aliens at Mercy of Sweatshops*, NEW YORK TIMES, Sept. 21, 1995, at A16.

79. *See* Kenneth B. Noble, *Workers in Sweatshop Raid Start Leaving Detention Sites*, NEW YORK TIMES, Aug. 12, 1995, at 6; *see also* Foo, *supra* note 77, at 2181–88 (describing the exploitation of the undocumented in the sweatshop industry).

80. Mary Romero, *Nanny Diaries and Other Stories: Imaging Immigrant Women's Labor in the Social Reproduction of American Families*, 52 DEPAUL LAW REVIEW 809, 843 (2003) (footnotes omitted); *see* Tauyna Lovell Banks, *Toward a Global Critical Feminist Vision: Domestic Work and the Nanny Tax Debate*, 3 IOWA JOURNAL OF GENDER, RACE, AND JUSTICE 1 (1999). *See generally* MARY ROMERO, MAID IN THE U.S.A. (2002 ed.); PARREÑAS, *supra* note 76.

81. *See* Silvia Pedraza, *Women and Migration: The Social Consequences of Gender*, 17 ANNUAL REVIEW OF SOCIOLOGY 303 (1991) (analyzing relationships among ethnicity,

class, and gender in understanding migration and recognizing that the stereotypical undocumented person is male).

82. *See* Leo R. Chavez, Shadowed Lives: Undocumented Immigrants in American Society 148–49 (1992) (describing the disadvantages that undocumented Mexican and Central American women suffer in domestic work); Ontiveros, *supra* note 77 (arguing that, because of the potential for the exploitation of undocumented women in the labor market, additional legal protections are necessary).

83. *See* Gerald P. Lopez, *The Work We Know So Little About*, 42 Stanford Law Review 1 (1989).

84. *See* Wayne A. Cornelius, *From Sojourners to Settlers: The Changing Profile of Mexican Immigration to the United States*, *in* U.S.-Mexico Relations: Labor Market Interdependence 155, 172–75 (Jorge A. Bustamante et al. eds., 1992). For a study of the experiences of undocumented Mexican women in the United States, see Pierrette Hondagneu-Sotelo, Gendered Transitions: Mexican Experiences of Immigration (1994).

85. *See* Leo R. Chavez, *Settlers and Sojourners: The Case of Mexicans in the United States*, 47 Human Organization 95, 99 (1988); Karen A. Woodrow & Jeffrey S. Passel, *Post-IRCA Undocumented Immigration to the United States: An Assessment Based on the June 1988 CPS*, *in* Undocumented Migration to the United States 33, 66 (Frank D. Bean et al. eds., 1990).

86. *See* Martin H. Malin, *Fathers and Parental Leave*, 72 Texas Law Review 1047–48 (1994) ("Even when both parents are employed outside the home, women tend to carry the predominant responsibility for child-care.") (footnote omitted). *See generally* Mary J. Frug, *Securing Job Equality for Women: Labor Market Hostility to Working Mothers*, 59 Boston University Law Review 55 (1979).

87. Major Garrett, *California Dreaming? Cries for Immigration Relief Shake Nation*, Washington Times, Aug. 15, 1993, at A1 (quoting Governor Wilson of California).

88. *Sonya Live* (CNN television broadcast, Feb. 16, 1994) (talk show with California Assembly member Richard Mountjoy).

89. *See* Kent A. Ono & John M. Sloop, Shifting Borders: Rhetoric, Immigration, and California's Proposition 187, at 39–40 (2002).

Chapter 7: Exclusion and Deportation of Lesbians and Gay Men

1. See generally Richard Plant, The Pink Triangle: The Nazi War Against Homosexuals (1986).

2. *See generally* Robert Foss, *The Demise of the Homosexual Exclusion: New Possibilities for Gay and Lesbian Immigration*, 29 Harvard Civil Rights–Civil Liberties Law Review 439 (1994) (reviewing the history of the treatment of homosexuals under the immigration laws); Rhonda R. Rivera, *Our Straight-Laced Judges: The Legal Position of Homosexual Persons in the United States*, 30 Hastings Law Journal 799, 934–42 (1979) (same).

3. *See* William N. Eskridge Jr., Gaylaw: Challenging the Apartheid of the Closet 35 (1999); William N. Eskridge, *Law and Construction of the Closet: American*

Regulation of Same-Sex Intimacy, 1880–1946, 82 IOWA LAW REVIEW 1007, 1045–46 & n.149 (1997).

4. Act of February 5, 1917, Public Law No. 301, ch. 29, § 3, 39 Statutes at Large 874, 875 (1917) (emphasis added).

5. *See generally* JOHN HIGHAM, STRANGERS TO THE LAND: PATTERNS OF AMERICAN NATIVISM, 1860–1925, at 150–53 (3d ed. 1992). For further discussion of this section as it pertains to the disabled, see Chapter 4.

6. Immigration and Nationality Act of 1952, Public Law No. 82-414, 66 Statutes at Large 163 (1952), § 212(a)(4), 8 U.S.C. § 1182(a)(4) [hereinafter INA].

7. SENATE REPORT NO. 1137, 82d Congress, 2d Session 9 (1952).

8. *See* ESKRIDGE, *supra* note 3, at 67–74; Foss, *supra* note 2, at 449.

9. *See, for example*, Matter of P, 7 I. & N. Dec. 258 (BIA 1956); Matter of S, 8 I. & N. Dec. 409 (BIA 1959).

10. *See* Quiroz v. Neely, 291 F.2d 906 (5th Cir. 1961); Eithne Luibhéid, *"Looking Like a Lesbian": The Organization of Sexual Monitoring at the United States–Mexican Border*, 8 JOURNAL OF THE HISTORY OF SEXUALITY 477 (1998). *See generally* EITHNE LUIBHÉID, ENTRY DENIED—CONTROLLING SEXUALITY AT THE BORDER (2002).

11. 302 F.2d 652 (9th Cir. 1962).

12. *See* Rosenberg v. Fleuti, 374 U.S. 449 (1963). This case, which created an exception from the exclusion grounds for "innocent, brief, and casual" departures from the country, had significant impacts on immigration law generally. *See* Hiroshi Motomura, *Immigration Law After a Century of Plenary Power: Phantom Constitutional Norms and Statutory Interpretation*, 100 YALE LAW JOURNAL 545, 575–78 (1990).

13. *See* Public Law No 89-236, §§ 10, 15, 79 Statutes at Large 917, 919 (1965) (repealed in 1990).

14. 387 U.S. 118 (1967).

15. *Id.* at 120. For an analysis and critique of *Boutilier*'s method of statutory interpretation, see William N. Eskridge Jr., *Gadamer/Statutory Interpretation*, 90 COLUMBIA LAW REVIEW 609 (1990).

16. Boutilier v. INS, 387 U.S. 125 (1967) (Douglas, J., dissenting).

17. *Id.* at 129–30 (citing ALFRED KINSEY ET AL., SEXUAL BEHAVIOR IN THE HUMAN MALE 623 (1948)).

18. *Boutilier*, 387 U.S. at 129.

19. *See, for example*, Lavoie v. INS, 418 F.2d 732 (9th Cir. 1969), *cert. denied*, 400 U.S. 854 (1970); Matter of Caydam, 12 I. & N. Dec. 528 (BIA 1967); Matter of Steele, 12 I. & N. Dec. 302 (1967).

20. *Compare* Hill v. INS, 714 F.2d 1470 (9th Cir. 1983) (requiring a certificate) *with* Matter of Longstaff, 716 F.2d 1439 (5th Cir. 1983) (not requiring a certificate), *cert. denied*, 467 U.S. 1219 (1984).

21. *See, for example*, Jorge L. Carro, *From Constitutional Psychopathic Inferiority to AIDS: What Is in the Future for Homosexual Aliens?* 7 YALE LAW AND POLICY REVIEW 201 (1989); Richard Green, *"Give Me Your Tired, Your Poor, Your Huddled Masses" (of Heterosexuals): An Analysis of American and Canadian Immigration Policy*, 16 ANGLO-AMERICAN LAW REVIEW (1987); Steven M. Silvers, *The Exclusion and Expulsion of Homosexual Aliens*, 15 COLUMBIA HUMAN RIGHTS LAW REVIEW 295 (1984).

22. Public Law No. 101-649 (1990), 104 Statutes at Large 4995 (1990).

23. INA, *supra* note 6, § 212(a)(1)(A)(iii)(I), 8 U.S.C. § 1182(a)(1)(A)(iii)(I) (emphasis added).

24. HOUSE OF REPRESENTATIVES REPORT NO. 101-723(I), at 56 (1990), *reprinted in* 1990 U.S. CODE CONGRESSIONAL & ADMINISTRATIVE NEWS 6710, 6736.

25. *See* Lawrence Lessig, *Understanding Changed Readings: Fidelity and Theory,* 47 STANFORD LAW REVIEW 395, 415–19 (1995).

26. *See* JOHN D'EMILIO, SEXUAL POLITICS, SEXUAL COMMUNITIES: THE MAKING OF A HOMOSEXUAL MINORITY IN THE UNITED STATES 1940–1970, at 231–33 (1983). *See generally* BARRY D. ADAM, THE RISE OF A GAY AND LESBIAN MOVEMENT (rev. ed. 1995); MARTIN DUBERMAN, STONEWALL (1993).

27. 478 U.S. 186 (1986). In 2003, the Court overruled Bowers. *See* Lawrence v. Texas, 123 S. Ct. 2472 (2003).

28. Romer v. Evans, 517 U.S. 620 (1996). The Court, however, upheld the rights of the Boy Scouts of America to discriminate on the basis of sexual orientation. *See* Boy Scouts of America v. Dale, 530 U.S. 640 (2000). *See generally* Madhavi Sunder, *Cultural Dissent,* 54 STANFORD LAW REVIEW 495 (2001).

29. *See* Juan P. Osuna, *The Exclusion from the United States of Aliens Infected with the AIDS Virus: Recent Developments and Prospects for the Future,* 16 HOUSTON JOURNAL OF INTERNATIONAL LAW 1 (1993). *See generally* Margaret A. Somerville & Sarah Wilson, *Crossing Boundaries: Travel, Immigration, Human Rights and AIDS,* 43 McGILL LAW JOURNAL 781 (1998) (comparing the approaches of the United States and Canada toward the immigration of HIV-infected persons).

30. *See* Carro, *supra* note 21.

31. *See* INA, *supra* note 6, § 212(a)(1)(A)(i), 8 U.S.C. § 1182(a)(1)(A)(i) (allowing for the exclusion of any immigrant determined "to have a communicable disease of public health significance, which shall include infection with the etiologic agent for acquired immune deficiency syndrome").

32. *See id.* § 212(g)(1), 8 U.S.C. § 1182(g)(1).

33. *See* Rebecca Kidder, Note, *Administrative Discretion Gone Awry: The Reintroduction of the Public Charge Exclusion for HIV-Positive Refugees and Asylees,* 106 YALE LAW JOURNAL 389 (1996).

34. *See* Mike McKee, *AIDS Patient Enters U.S. Unopposed,* RECORDER (San Francisco) Aug. 5, 1998, at 1.

35. *See* Haitian Centers Council, Inc. v. Sale, 823 F. Supp. 1028 (E.D.N.Y. 1993). For criticism of such policies, see Shayna S. Cook, Note, *The Exclusion of HIV-Positive Immigrants Under the Nicaraguan Adjustment and Central American Relief Act and the Haitian Refugee Immigration Fairness Act,* 99 MICHIGAN LAW REVIEW 452 (2000); Jason A. Pardo, Comment, *Excluding Immigrants on the Basis of Health: The Haitian Centers Council Decision Criticized,* 11 JOURNAL OF CONTEMPORARY HEALTH LAW AND POLICY 523 (1995).

36. *See, for example,* Juan P. Osuna, *The Exclusion from the United States of Aliens Infected with the AIDs Virus: Recent Developments and Prospects for the Future,* 16 HOUSTON JOURNAL OF INTERNATIONAL LAW (1993); Lynn Acker Starr, *The Effectiveness and Impact of the Human Immunodeficiency Virus (HIV) Exclusion in U.S. Immigration Law,* 3 GEORGETOWN IMMIGRATION LAW JOURNAL 87 (1989); Peter A. Barta, Note, *Lamb-*

skin Borders: An Argument for the Abolition of the United States' Exclusion of HIV-Positive Immigrants, 12 GEORGETOWN IMMIGRATION LAW JOURNAL 323 (1998); Lia Macko, Note, *Acquiring Better Global Vision: An Argument Against the United States' Current Exclusion of HIV-Infected Immigrants*, 9 GEORGETOWN IMMIGRATION LAW JOURNAL 545 (1995).

37. *See IJ Grants Asylum to HIV Positive Man, General Counsel Issues HIV Instructions*, 73 INTERPRETER RELEASES 901 (1996); *see also* Peter Margulies, *Asylum, Intersectionality, and AIDS: Women with HIV as a Persecuted Social Group*, 8 GEORGETOWN IMMIGRATION LAW JOURNAL 521 (1994) (analyzing how poor immigrant women of color with HIV face multiple negative stereotypes in seeking asylum).

38. *See generally* WILLIAM N. ESKRIDGE JR., THE CASE FOR SAME-SEX MARRIAGE (1996); Mary Becker, *Family Law in the Secular State and Restrictions on Same-Sex Marriage: Two Are Better Than One*, 2001 UNIVERSITY OF ILLINOIS LAW REVIEW 1. Child custody and adoption by same-sex parents have also sparked controversy. *See* MARK STRASSER, LEGALLY WED 75–99 (1997); William E. Adams Jr., *Whose Family Is It Anyway? The Continuing Struggle for Lesbians and Gay Men Seeking to Adopt Children*, 30 NEW ENGLAND LAW REVIEW 579 (1996).

39. Public Law No. 104-199, 110 Statutes at Large 2419 (1996). For arguments that the law violates the Constitution, see Andrew Koppelman, *Dumb and DOMA: Why the Defense of Marriage Act Is Unconstitutional*, 83 IOWA LAW REVIEW 1 (1997); Larry Kramer, *Same-Sex Marriage, Conflict of Laws, and the Unconstitutional Public Policy Exception*, 106 YALE LAW JOURNAL 1965 (1997).

40. *See* T. ALEXANDER ALEINIKOFF ET AL., IMMIGRATION AND CITIZENSHIP: PROCESS AND POLICY 319 (4th ed. 1998) ("The dominant feature of current arrangements for permanent immigration to the United States is family reunification.").

41. 673 F.2d 1036 (9th Cir.), *cert. denied*, 458 U.S. 1111 (1982).

42. STEPHEN H. LEGOMSKY, IMMIGRATION AND REFUGEE LAW AND POLICY 157 (3d ed. 2002) (quoting letter, emphasis added).

43. *See* Sullivan v. INS, 772 F.2d 609 (9th Cir. 1985).

44. *See* Christopher A. Dueñas, Note, *Coming to America: The Immigration Obstacle Facing Binational Same-Sex Couples*, 73 SOUTHERN CALIFORNIA LAW REVIEW 811 (2000); Cynthia M. Reed, *When Love, Comity, and Justice Conquer Borders: INS Recognition of Same-Sex Marriage*, 20 COLUMBIA HUMAN RIGHTS LAW REVIEW 97 (1996).

45. *See* Sara A. Schubert, *Immigration Rights for Same-Sex Partners Under the Permanent Partners Immigration Act*, 74 TEMPLE LAW REVIEW 541 (2001) (analyzing the proposed Permanent Partners Immigration Act of 2000, HOUSE OF REPRESENTATIVES BILL No. 3650, 105th Congress (2000)); *see, for example*, Permanent Partners Immigration Act of 2003, HOUSE OF REPRESENTATIVES BILL No. 832, 108th Cong., 1st. Sess. (2003); *see also* Wayne van der Meide, *Who Guards the Borders of Canada's "Gay" Community? A Case Study of the Benefits of the Proposed Redefinition of "Spouse" Within the Immigration Act to Include Same-Sex Couples*, 19 WINDSOR YEARBOOK ON ACCESS TO JUSTICE 39 (2001); Desiree Alonso, Note, *Immigration Sponsorship Rights for Gay and Lesbian Couples: Defining Partnerships*, 8 CARDOZO WOMEN'S LAW JOURNAL 207 (2002); Christopher S. Hargis, *Queer Reasoning: Immigration Policy,* Baker v. State of Vermont, *and the (Non)recognition of Same-Gender Relationships*, 10 LAW AND SEXUALITY 211, 238 (2001) (discussing a similar bill proposed in Congress in 2001).

46. *See* Andrew Jacobs, *Gay Couples Divided by '96 Laws: Commitments Have No Legal Standing*, NEW YORK TIMES, Mar. 23, 1999, at B1.

47. A number of commentators have begun this task. *See, for example*, David B. Cruz, *"Just Don't Call It Marriage": The First Amendment and Marriage as an Expressive Resource*, 74 SOUTHERN CALIFORNIA LAW REVIEW 925 (2001); Linda Kelly, *Family Planning, American Style*, 52 ALABAMA LAW REVIEW 943 (2001); Andrew Koppleman, *Same-Sex Marriage, Choice of Law, and Public Policy*, 76 TEXAS LAW REVIEW 921 (1998); David D. Meyer, *Self-definition in the Constitution of Faith and Family*, 86 MINNESOTA LAW REVIEW 791 (2002); Lisa Milot, Note, *Restitching the American Marital Quilt: Untangling Marriage from the Nuclear Family*, 87 VIRGINIA LAW REVIEW 701 (2001); Barbara Stark, *Marriage Proposals: From One-Size-Fits-All to Postmodern Marriage Law*, 89 CALIFORNIA LAW REVIEW 1479 (2001).

48. *See* U.S. COMMISSION ON IMMIGRATION REFORM, LEGAL IMMIGRATION: SETTING PRIORITIES 45–80 (1995) (recommending limiting family immigrant visas to nuclear families). For a review of the historical ambivalence toward family immigration in the U.S. immigration laws, see Lolita Buckner Innis, *Dutch Uncle Sam: Immigration Reform and Notions of Family*, 36 BRANDEIS JOURNAL OF FAMILY LAW 177 (1997–1998).

49. Shannon Minter, Note, *Sodomy and Public Morality Offenses Under U.S. Immigration Law: Penalizing Lesbian and Gay Identity*, 26 CORNELL INTERNATIONAL LAW JOURNAL 771, 772 (1993) (footnotes omitted); *see, for example*, Barbouris v. Esperdy, 269 F.2d 621 (2d Cir. 1959) (disorderly conduct in soliciting men for lewd purposes); Matter of Alfonso-Bermudez, 12 Immigration and Nationality Decision 225 (Board of Immigration Appeals 1967) (public homosexual act).

50. Veles-Lozano v. INS, 463 F.2d 1305, 1307 (D.C. Cir. 1972) (citing Matter of K, 3 Immigration and Nationality Decision 575 (Board of Immigration Appeals (1949)).

51. Marciano v. INS, 450 F.2d 1022, 1025 (8th Cir. 1971) (citations and internal quotations omitted), *cert. denied* 405 U.S. 997 (1972).

52. *See, for example*, Lavoie v. INS, 418 F.2d 732 (9th Cir. 1969), *cert. denied*, 400 U.S. 854 (1970); Wyngaard v. Kennedy, 295 F.2d 184 (D.C. Cir.), *cert. denied*, 368 U.S. 926 (1961); Hudson v. Esperdy, 290 F.2d 879 (2d Cir. 1961), *cert. denied*, 368 U.S. 918 (1961); Babouris v. Esperdy, 269 F.2d 621 (2d Cir. 1959), *cert. denied*, 362 U.S. 913 (1960); United States v. Flores-Rodriguez, 237 F.2d 405 (2d Cir. 1956); Ganduxe y Marino v. Murff, 183 F. Supp. 565 (S.D.N.Y 1959), *aff'd*, 278 F.2d 330 (2d Cir.), *cert. denied*, 364 U.S. 824 (1960).

53. *See* INA, *supra* note 6, § 316(a)(3), 8 U.S.C. § 1427(a)(3).

54. Matter of Schmidt, 58 Misc. 2d 456, 457, 289 N.Y.S. 2d 89, 90 (1968).

55. *Id.* at 459, 92. *See generally* Steven L. Strange, *Private Consensual Conduct and the "Good Moral Character" Requirement of the Immigration and Nationality Act*, 14 COLUMBIA JOURNAL TRANSNATIONAL LAW 357 (1975).

56. *See* ESKRIDGE, *supra* note 38, at 132–33; *see, for example*, Nemetz v. INS, 647 F.2d 432 (4th Cir. 1980); Matter of Brodie, 394 F. Supp. 1208 (D. Or. 1975); Matter of Labady, 326 F. Supp. 924 (S.D.N.Y. 1971). *But see* Matter of Longstaff, 716 F.2d 1439 (5th Cir. 1983) (denying a naturalization petition because of untruthful statements about homosexuality at the time of entry into the country), *cert. denied*, 467 U.S. 219 (1984).

57. *See* INA, *supra* note 6, § 101(a)(42), 8 U.S.C. § 1101(a)(42).

58. *See* Suzanne B. Goldberg, *Give Me Liberty or Give Me Death: Political Asylum and the Global Persecution of Lesbians and Gay Men,* 26 CORNELL INTERNATIONAL LAW JOURNAL 605 (1993); Jin S. Park, Comment, *Pink Asylum: Political Asylum Eligibility of Gay Men and Lesbians Under U.S. Immigration Policy,* 42 UCLA LAW REVIEW 1115 (1995).

59. 20 Immigration and Nationality Decision 819 (Board of Immigration Appeals 1990). Footnote 1 of the decision states, "This case was decided by the Board on March 12, 1990. By Attorney General Order No. 1895-94, dated June 19, 1994, the Attorney General ordered: 'I hereby designate the decision of the Board of Immigration Appeals In re: Fidel Toboso-Alfonso (A-23220644) (March 20, 1990) as precedent in all proceedings involving the same issue or issues.'"

60. *See* Bob Hohler, *U.S. Says That Those Persecuted as Gays Can Get Asylum,* BOSTON GLOBE, June 18, 1994, at 3.

61. 118 F.3d 641 (9th Cir. 1997); *see* Ryan Goodman, Note, *The Incorporation of International Human Rights Standards into Sexual Orientation Asylum Claims: Cases of Involuntary "Medical" Intervention,* 105 YALE LAW JOURNAL 255 (1995). *See generally* David B. Cruz, *Controlling Desires: Sexual Orientation Conversion and the Limits of Knowledge and Law,* 72 SOUTHERN CALIFORNIA LAW REVIEW 1297 (1999).

62. 225 F.3d 1084 (9th Cir. 2000).

63. *See generally* SHANE PHELAN, SEXUAL STRANGERS: GAYS, LESBIANS, AND DILEMMAS OF CITIZENSHIP (2001).

Chapter 8: The Future of Immigration and Civil Rights in the United States

1. For further analysis of the impacts of "alien" terminology in immigration law, see Kevin R. Johnson, *"Aliens" and the Immigration Laws: The Social and Legal Construction of Nonpersons,* 28 UNIVERSITY OF MIAMI INTER-AMERICAN LAW REVIEW 263 (1996–97).

2. *See generally* JAMES MORTON SMITH, FREEDOM'S FETTERS: THE ALIEN AND SEDITION LAWS AND AMERICAN CIVIL LIBERTIES (1956); Chapter 3.

3. *See* JOHN HIGHAM, STRANGERS IN THE LAND: PATTERNS OF AMERICAN NATIVISM 1860–1925, at 26–29 (3d ed. 1992). *See generally* Chapter 2.

4. *See, for example, The Chinese Exclusion Case* (Chae Chan Ping), 130 U.S. 581 (1889). *See generally* Chapter 2.

5. *See* Korematsu v. United States, 323 U.S. 214 (1944). *See generally* Symposium, *The Long Shadow of Korematsu,* 40 BOSTON COLLEGE LAW REVIEW 1, 19 BOSTON COLLEGE THIRD WORLD LAW JOURNAL 1 (1998).

6. *See* Act of March 26, 1790, ch. 3, 1 Statutes at Large 103 (1790) (providing that only a "free white person" could naturalize). *See generally* IAN F. HANEY LÓPEZ, WHITE BY LAW: THE LEGAL CONSTRUCTION OF RACE (1996).

7. *See, for example,* Hiroshi Motomura, *Immigration Law After a Century of Plenary Power: Phantom Constitutional Norms and Statutory Interpretation,* 100 YALE LAW JOURNAL 545, 547 n.4 (1990); Gerald L. Neuman, *Aliens as Outlaws: Government Services, Proposition 187, and the Structure of Equal Protection,* 42 UCLA LAW REVIEW 1425, 1428 (1995); Gerald M. Rosberg, *The Protection of Aliens from Discriminatory Treatment by the National Government,* 1977 SUPREME COURT REVIEW 275, 303.

8. Public Law No. 82-414, 66 Statutes at Large 163 (1952) (codified as amended in scattered sections of 8 U.S.C.) [hereinafter INA].

9. *See, for example,* MICHAEL OMI & HOWARD WINANT, RACIAL FORMATION IN THE UNITED STATES: FROM THE 1960S TO THE 1980S (2d ed. 1994); Ian F. Haney López, *The Social Construction of Race: Some Observations on Illusion, Fabrication, and Choice,* 29 HARVARD CIVIL RIGHTS–CIVIL LIBERTIES LAW REVIEW 1 (1994).

10. *See* Jamin B. Raskin, Legal Aliens, *Local Citizens: The Historical, Constitutional and Theoretical Meanings of Alien Suffrage,* 141 UNIVERSITY OF PENNSYLVANIA LAW REVIEW 1391, 1397–1417 (1993).

11. See ROY L. BROOKS ET AL., CIVIL RIGHTS LITIGATION: CASES AND PERSPECTIVES 976 (1995) (noting that the term "'[i]llegal aliens' seems to dehumanize the 'undocumented alien' and to desensitize the reader"; "'illegal' creates an inference that the person has done something wrong to justify a restriction of rights").

12. *See, for example,* Ambach v. Norwick, 441 U.S. 68 (1979) (upholding the state law that bars immigrants from employment as public school teachers); Foley v. Connelie, 435 U.S. 291 (1978) (upholding the state law that requires that police officers have U.S. citizenship).

13. U.S. CONST. art. II, § 1, cl. 5.

14. *See* Adarand Constructors, Inc. v. Peña, 515 U.S. 200 (1995); City of Richmond v. J.A. Croson Co., 488 U.S. 469 (1989).

15. *See* U.S. DEPARTMENT OF JUSTICE, 1998 STATISTICAL YEARBOOK OF THE IMMIGRATION AND NATURALIZATION SERVICE 44 tbl.8 (2000) [hereinafter INS 1998 STATISTICAL YEARBOOK] (providing a breakdown of immigrants by country of birth for fiscal year 1998).

16. *See* Dred Scott v. Sanford, 60 U.S. 393 (1857).

17. Immigration and Nationality Act of 1952, *supra* note 8, § 101(a)(3), 8 U.S.C. § 1101(a)(3).

18. *See* Hiroshi Motomura, *Whose Alien Nation? Two Models of Constitutional Immigration Law,* 94 MICHIGAN LAW REVIEW 1927, 1929 n.12 (1996) (book review).

19. ROGET'S POCKET THESAURUS 18 (1969 ed.).

20. George Ramos, *Even if Days Are Numbered, Ezell Is Making Them Count,* LOS ANGELES TIMES, May 29, 1989, at 31, col. 2 (quoting Ezell).

21. *See* GERALD L. NEUMAN, STRANGERS TO THE CONSTITUTION: IMMIGRANTS, BORDERS, AND FUNDAMENTAL LAW 177, 270 n.62 (1996).

22. *See* Neuman, *supra* note 7, at 1440–41; *see also* Victor C. Romero, *Equal Protection Held Hostage: Ransoming the Constitutionality of the Hostage Taking Act,* 91 NORTHWESTERN UNIVERSITY LAW REVIEW 573, 573–74 n.4 (1997) (articulating similar concerns about "alien" terminology).

23. *See* T. Alexander Aleinikoff, *The Tightening Circle of Membership,* 22 HASTINGS CONSTITUTIONAL LAW QUARTERLY 915 (1995).

24. Neuman, *supra* note 7, at 1429 (alteration added).

25. *See* Oyama v. California, 332 U.S. 633, 658–59 (1948) (Murphy, J., concurring); Neuman, *supra* note 7, at 1429 n.17. *See generally* Keith Aoki, *No Right to Own? The Early Twentieth Century "Alien Land Laws" as a Prelude to Internment,* 40 BOSTON COLLEGE LAW REVIEW 37, 19 BOSTON THIRD WORLD LAW JOURNAL 37 (1998).

26. *See* Leon Festinger, A Theory of Cognitive Dissonance 7 (1957) (noting how inconsistencies between perceived racial sensibilities and reality generate conflict that persons strive to reconcile).

27. Richard Delgado & Jean Stefancic, *Imposition*, 35 William and Mary Law Review 1025, 1041–42 (1994) (footnote omitted).

28. *See* Richard Delgado & Jean Stefancic, *Images of the Outsider in American Law and Culture: Can Free Expression Remedy Systemic Social Ills?* 77 Cornell Law Review 1258, 1273–75 (1992).

29. *See, for example,* Henry M. Hart Jr., *The Power of Congress to Limit the Jurisdiction of the Federal Courts: An Exercise in Dialectic*, 66 Harvard Law Review 1362, 1395 (1953) (lamenting a Supreme Court decision that said, "in effect, that a Mexican wetback who sneaks successfully across the Rio Grande is entitled to the full panoply of due process in his deportation") (footnote omitted); Eleanor M. Hadley, *A Critical Analysis of the Wetback Problem*, 21 Law and Contemporary Problems 334 (1956). *See generally* Jorge A. Bustamante, *The "Wetback" as Deviant: An Application of Labeling Theory*, 77 American Journal of Sociology 706 (1972).

30. *See generally* Leo R. Chavez, Covering Immigration: Popular Images and the Politics of the Nation (2001).

31. *See* INS 1998 Statistical Yearbook, *supra* note 15, at 239–41.

32. *Id.* at 240 tbl.I.

33. *See* Deborah Sontag, *Study Sees Illegal Aliens in New Light*, New York Times, Sept. 2, 1993, at B1.

34. *See generally* Kevin R. Johnson, *The New Nativism: Something Old, Something New, Something Borrowed, Something Blue, in* Immigrants Out! The New Nativism and the Anti-Immigrant Impulse in the United States 165 (Juan F. Perea ed., 1997).

35. United States v. Valenzuela-Bernal, 458 U.S. 858, 864 n.5 (1982).

36. United States v. Cortez, 449 U.S. 411, 418 (1981).

37. United States v. Martinez-Fuerte, 428 U.S. 543, 552 (1976).

38. Plyler v. Doe, 457 U.S. 202, 237 (1982) (Powell, J., concurring).

39. United States v. Ortiz, 422 U.S. 891, 899 (1975) (Burger, C.J., concurring in judgment) (footnote omitted).

40. INS v. Delgado, 466 U.S. 210, 239 (1984) (Brennan, J., dissenting in part).

41. *See* Bill Ong Hing, To Be an American: Cultural Pluralism and the Rhetoric of Assimilation 44–145 (1997) (summarizing and analyzing conflicting data on the impact of immigration on the U.S. economy).

42. United States v. Brignoni-Ponce, 422 U.S. 873, 878–79 (1975).

43. *Ortiz*, 422 U.S. at 891, 900 (Burger, C.J., concurring in judgment) (excerpting United States v. Baca, 368 F. Supp. 398, 402–08 (S.D. Cal. 1973)).

44. City of Indianapolis v. Edmond, 531 U.S. 32, 37, 38 (2000) (discussing United States v. Martinez-Fuerte, 428 U.S. 543 (1976)). *See generally* Chapter 2 (discussing racial profiling in immigration enforcement).

45. *See* Hoffman Plastic Compounds, Inc. v. NLRB, 535 U.S. 137, 151 (2002).

46. *Immigration Reform and Control Act of 1983: Hearings on H.R. 1510 Before the Subcommittee on Immigration, Refugees, and International Law of the House Committee of the Judiciary*, 98th Congress, 1st Session 1 (1983) (testimony of Attorney General Smith).

47. *See* Orantes-Hernández v. Thornburgh, 919 F.2d 549, 559–67 (9th Cir. 1990) (outlining detention and related policies directed at Central Americans in the early 1980s that were implemented by the INS).

48. *See* U.S. COMMISSION ON IMMIGRATION REFORM, U.S. IMMIGRATION POLICY: RESTORING CREDIBILITY 11–19 (1994). Hundreds of migrants have died as a result of this and other border enforcement measures implemented by the federal government in the 1990s. *See generally* TIMOTHY J. DUNN, THE MILITARIZATION OF THE U.S.–MEXICO BORDER, 1978–1993: LOW-INTENSITY CONFLICT DOCTRINE COMES HOME (1996); JOSEPH NEVINS, OPERATION GATEKEEPER (2002); Bill Ong Hing, *The Dark Side of Operation Gatekeeper,* 7 UNIVERSITY OF CALIFORNIA AT DAVIS JOURNAL OF INTERNATIONAL LAW AND POLICY 121 (2001); Jorge A. Vargas, *U.S. Border Patrol Abuses, Undocumented Mexican Workers, and International Human Rights,* 2 SAN DIEGO INTERNATIONAL LAW JOURNAL 1 (2001).

49. *See* Mark Clayton, *"Refugees" to Canada Slip to US on Mohawk "Trail,"* CHRISTIAN SCIENCE MONITOR, Nov. 13, 1996, at 1.

50. *See* TONY MILLER, ACTING SECRETARY OF STATE, CALIFORNIA BALLOT PAMPHLET: GENERAL ELECTION, NOVEMBER 8, 1994, at 54 (1994) [hereinafter CALIFORNIA BALLOT PAMPHLET] (capitals in original).

51. *See* Brief for the United Nations High Commissioner for Refugees as Amicus Curiae in Support of Respondents, Sale v. Haitian Centers Council, Inc., 509 U.S. 155 (1993).

52. Executive Order No. 12807, 57 Fed. Reg. 23133 (1992).

53. *Sale,* 509 U.S. at 155, 164 n.13.

54. Mathews v. Diaz, 426 U.S. 67, 80 (1976) (upholding the congressional limitation on the eligibility of lawful immigrants for the federal medical insurance program); *see, for example,* Demore v. Kim, 123 S. Ct. 1708, 1716–17 (2003); Fiallo v. Bell, 430 U.S. 787, 792 (1977).

55. Barrera-Echavarria v. Rison, 44 F.3d 1441, 1442 (9th Cir.) (en banc), *cert. denied,* 516 U.S. 976 (1995).

56. *Id.; see also* Fernandez-Roque v. Smith, 734 F.2d 576 (11th Cir. 1984); Garcia-Mir v. Meese, 788 F.2d 1446 (11th Cir. 1986), *cert. denied sub nom.,* 479 U.S. 889 (1986); Gisbert v. U.S. Attorney General, 988 F.2d 1437 (5th Cir. 1993), *amended* 997 F.2d 1112 (5th Cir. 1993). *But see* Rodriquez-Fernandez v. Wilkinson, 654 F.2d 1382 (10th Cir. 1981) (holding that the INA does not permit indefinite detention as an alternative to exclusion). In 2001, the Supreme Court ruled that Congress had not authorized indefinite detention of immigrants in these circumstances (see Chapter 5). *See* Zadvydas v. Davis, 533 U.S. 678 (2001).

57. *See, for example,* FEDERATION FOR AMERICAN IMMIGRATION REFORM, IMMIGRATION 2000: THE CENTURY OF THE NEW AMERICAN SWEATSHOP (1992).

58. *But see* PETER BRIMELOW, ALIEN NATION: COMMON SENSE ABOUT AMERICA'S IMMIGRATION DISASTER (1995) (arguing that immigration should be restricted in part because of its impact on changing racial demographics of United States).

59. *See, for example,* Douglas Jehl, *Buchanan Raises Specter of Intolerance, Critics Say,* LOS ANGELES TIMES, Mar. 17, 1992, at A1 (quoting Patrick Buchanan, Republican presidential candidate: "[I]f we had to take a million immigrants in say, Zulus, next year, or Englishmen, and put them up in Virginia, what group would be easier to assimilate and would cause less problems for the people of Virginia?").

60. *See generally* IMMIGRATION: A CIVIL RIGHTS ISSUE FOR THE AMERICAS (Susanne Jonas & Suzie Dod Thomas eds., 1999); Kevin R. Johnson, *The End of "Civil Rights" as We Know It? Immigration and Civil Rights in the New Millennium*, 49 UCLA LAW REVIEW 1481 (2002).

61. *See* INS 1998 STATISTICAL YEARBOOK, *supra* note 15, at 12, 249 tbl.I.

62. *See* ALEJANDRO PORTES & RUBEN G. RUMBAUT, IMMIGRANT AMERICA: A PORTRAIT 232–35 (1990); Douglas Massey, *The Social and Economic Origins of Immigration*, 510 ANNALS 60, 68–70 (1990); Sergio Bustos, *Small Towns Shaped by Influx of Hispanics*, USA TODAY, May 23, 2001, at 10A; Arian Campo-Flores, *A Town's Two Faces*, NEWSWEEK, June 4, 2001, at 34; Brian Feagans, *Changing Magnolia; Hispanic Population in Duplin Reaches 15 Percent*, MORNING STAR (Wilmington, N.C.), Apr. 4, 2001, at 1A; Jeffrey Gettleman, *Obscure Law Used to Jail Day Laborers in Georgia*, LOS ANGELES TIMES, Aug. 21, 2001, at A1; Patrick J. McDonnell, *Mexicans Changing Face of U.S. Demographics*, LOS ANGELES TIMES, May 10, 2001, Susan Sachs, *A Hue, and a Cry, in the Heartland*, NEW YORK TIMES, Apr. 8, 2001, at sec. 4, p. 5; Hector Tobar, *A Lotta Cultures Goin' On*, LOS ANGELES TIMES, May 16, 2001, at A1; Barry Yeoman, *Hispanic Diaspora*, MOTHER JONES, July 1, 2000, at 34; *see also* Symposium, *Immigration in the Heartland*, 40 BRANDEIS LAW JOURNAL 1 (2002).

63. *See* Mark Fineman, *Mexico Redraws Faces of Migrants*, LOS ANGELES TIMES, July 11, 2001, at A1 (report of the findings of a report of the Mexican National Population Council).

64. *See* Gisele Regatao, *VIVA Poblanos; Mexicans from Puebla Create Mini-version of Home State in New York*, NEWSDAY, May 21, 2001, at C14; Robert S. Leiken, *The Go-Between for Mexico, U.S. Harmony Along the Border*, LOS ANGELES TIMES, Feb. 25, 2001, at M2. *See generally* Roger Rouse, *Migration and the Social Space of Postmodernism*, 1 DIASPORA 8 (1991).

65. *See* Chris Kraul, *Tapping Generosity of Emigrants; Some Mexican Towns Bridge Funding Gap with Help from Clubs in U.S.*, LOS ANGELES TIMES, June 8, 2000, at A1; Nancy Cleeland, *Mexican "Hometown Clubs" Turn Activist*, LOS ANGELES TIMES, June 8, 2000, at A1.

66. *See* T. ALEXANDER ALEINIKOFF, BETWEEN PRINCIPLES AND POLITICS: THE DIRECTION OF U.S. CITIZENSHIP POLICY 31–33 (1998); Peter J. Spiro, *Dual Nationality and the Meaning of Citizenship*, 46 EMORY LAW JOURNAL 1411 (1997); Jorge A. Vargas, *Dual Nationality for Mexicans*, 35 SAN DIEGO LAW REVIEW 823 (1998).

67. *See* Jim Yardley, *Mexicans' Bids to Enter U.S. Rebound to Pre-9/11 Levels*, NEW YORK TIMES, Nov. 24, 2002, at 24 (analyzing INS data).

68. *See* Wayne A. Cornelius, *Death at the Border: Efficiency and Unintended Consequences of U.S. Immigration Control Policy*, 27 POPULATION AND DEVELOPMENT REVIEW 661, 668–69 (2001).

69. *See generally* AIHWA ONG, FLEXIBLE CITIZENSHIP: THE CULTURAL LOGICS OF TRANSNATIONALITY (1999); Anupam Chander, *Diaspora Bonds*, 76 NEW YORK UNIVERSITY LAW REVIEW 1005 (2001).

70. *See* KENNETH L. KARST, BELONGING TO AMERICA: EQUAL CITIZENSHIP AND THE CONSTITUTION (1989) (analyzing the feeling of "belonging to America" of various outsider groups); Peter J. Spiro, *The Citizenship Dilemma*, 51 STANFORD LAW REVIEW 597, 621–25 (1999) (book review) (analyzing the impact of immigrant diasporas on conceptions of citizenship).

71. Samuel P. Huntington, *Reconsidering Immigration: Is Mexico a Special Case,* CENTER FOR IMMIGRATION STUDIES BACKGROUNDER, Nov. 2000, at 5; *see also* PATRICK J. BUCHANAN, THE DEATH OF THE WEST: HOW DYING POPULATIONS AND IMMIGRANT INVASIONS IMPERIL OUR COUNTRY AND CIVILIZATION 97–149 (2002) (voicing similar sentiments); SAMUEL P. HUNTINGTON, THE CLASH OF CIVILIZATIONS AND THE RE-MAKING OF THE WORLD ORDER 204–06 (1996) (expressing concerns about Mexican immigration to the United States and the ability of immigrants from Mexico to as-similate into U.S. society).

72. *See* David LeGesse, *Social Security Officials Halt INS Program in Meatpacking Industry,* DALLAS MORNING NEWS, Aug. 13, 1999, at 5A. INS enforcement efforts di-rected at Mexican immigrants have a long history. *See generally* ALFREDO MIRANDÉ, GRINGO JUSTICE (1985).

73. *See, for example,* OFFICE OF THE ATTORNEY GENERAL OF ARIZONA, RESULTS OF THE CHANDLER SURVEY 31 (1997) (discussing abuses of Latina/o citizens and lawful immigrants in a local police operation in a suburb of Phoenix, Arizona).

74. *See* Farm Labor Organizing Committee v. Ohio State Highway Patrol, 308 F.3d 523 (6th Cir. 2002).

75. *See* Ty Tagami, *INS Arrests Fourteen Hispanics at Courthouse in Monticello,* HER-ALD-LEDGER (Kentucky), Nov. 21, 2000.

76. *See* Sue Anne Pressley, *Hispanic Boom Rattles South,* WASHINGTON POST, Mar. 6, 2000, at A3.

77. *See* Charles LeDuff, *Immigrant Workers Tell of Being Lured and Beaten,* NEW YORK TIMES, Sept. 20, 2000, at B1. *See generally* NATIONAL COUNCIL OF LA RAZA, THE MAINSTREAMING OF HATE (1999) (documenting hate violence against Latinas/os in the 1990s).

78. *See* Jack Miles, *Browns vs. Blacks,* ATLANTIC MONTHLY, Oct. 1992, at 41; Lawrence H. Fuchs, *The Reactions of Black Americans to Immigration, in* IMMIGRATION RECONSIDERED: HISTORY, SOCIOLOGY, AND POLITICS 293 (Virginia Yaks-McLaughlin ed., 1990).

79. *See* Ginger Thompson, *U.S. and Mexico to Open Talks on Freer Migration for Workers,* NEW YORK TIMES, Feb. 16, 2001, at A1.

80. *See* KITTY CALAVITA, INSIDE THE STATE: THE BRACERO PROGRAM, IMMIGRA-TION, AND THE I.N.S. 29, 45–46, 64–66, 70–71 (1992); ERNESTO GALARZA, MERCHANTS OF LABOR: THE MEXICAN BRACERO STORY 183–98 (1964).

81. *See* Shannon Lafferty, *Migrant Workers Aim for Back Pay,* RECORDER (San Fran-cisco), July 18, 2001, at 1.

82. *See* Lori A. Nessel, *Undocumented Immigrants in the Workplace: The Fallacy of Labor Protection and the Need for Reform,* 36 HARVARD CIVIL RIGHTS–CIVIL LIBERTIES LAW REVIEW 345 (2001); Maria L. Ontiveros, *To Help Those Most in Need: Undocu-mented Workers' Rights and Remedies Under Title VII,* 20 NEW YORK UNIVERSITY REVIEW OF LAW AND SOCIAL CHANGE 607 (1993–1994).

83. *See* INS 1998 STATISTICAL YEARBOOK, *supra* note 15, at 123 (Chart G) (show-ing that India and Mexico were leading nations of origin of temporary immigrant workers under current programs).

84. *See* U.S. BUREAU OF THE CENSUS, OVERVIEW OF RACE AND HISPANIC ORIGIN: CENSUS 2000 BRIEF 3 tbl.1, Mar. 2001. Claims have surfaced that the census under-

counted undocumented immigrants, and thus probably the number of Hispanics, in the United States. *See* Aaron Zitner, *Immigrant Tally Doubles in Census,* LOS ANGELES TIMES, Mar. 10, 2001, at A1.

85. *See* Sharon K. Hom & Eric K. Yamamoto, *Collective Memory, History, and Social Justice,* 47 UCLA LAW REVIEW 1747 (2000).

86. *See* Kristi L. Bowman, Note, *The New Face of School Desegregation,* 50 DUKE LAW JOURNAL 1751 (2001) (analyzing distinctive interests of Latinas/os in efforts to desegregate public schools); Gitanjali S. Gutierrez, Note, *Taking Account of Another Race: Reframing Asian-America Challenge to Race-Conscious Admissions in Public Schools,* 86 CORNELL LAW REVIEW 1283 (2001) (analyzing difficulties facing Asian Americans in consideration of race in public school placement).

87. *See* Deborah Ramirez, *Multicultural Empowerment: It's Not Just Black and White Anymore,* 47 STANFORD LAW REVIEW 957, 969–71 (1995). *But see* John O. Calmore, *Race-Conscious Voting Rights and the New Demography in a Multiracing America,* 79 NORTH CAROLINA LAW REVIEW 1252 (2001) (contending that the growing mulitracial population will not undermine the effectiveness of the Voting Rights Act).

88. *See* Ramirez, *supra* note 87, at 972–74.

89. *See* Cruz Reynoso, *Hispanics and the Criminal Justice System, in* HISPANICS IN THE UNITED STATES: AN AGENDA FOR THE TWENTY-FIRST CENTURY 277 (Pastora San Juan Cafferty & David W. Engstrom eds., 2000).

90. *See* Ellis Cose, *A Brownout in Los Angeles,* NEWSWEEK, June 18, 2001, at 32.

91. *See* MIKE DAVIS, MAGICAL URBANISM: LATINOS REINVENT THE U.S. BIG CITY 135–42 (2000); *see, for example,* Orlando Patterson, *Race by the Numbers,* NEW YORK TIMES, May 8, 2001, at A27; Ronald Brownstein, *Latinos Stir Tension in New Brand of Urban Politics,* LOS ANGELES TIMES, Nov. 26, 2001, at A11.

92. *See* Julie Quioroz-Martínez, *Missing Link,* COLORLINES, Summer 2001, at 17; William R. Tamayo, *When the "Coloreds" Are Neither Black Nor Citizens: The United States Civil Rights Movement and Global Migration,* 2 ASIAN LAW JOURNAL 1 (1995).

93. *See* Christopher David Ruiz Cameron, *The Labyrinth of Solidarity: Why the Future of the American Labor Movement Depends on Latino Workers,* 53 UNIVERSITY OF MIAMI LAW REVIEW 1089, 1098–1114 (1999).

94. *See* Nancy Cleeland, *AFL-CIO Calls for Amnesty for Illegal U.S. Workers,* LOS ANGELES TIMES, Feb. 17, 2000, at A1.

95. *See, for example,* Coalition for Humane Immigrant Rights v. Burke, 2000 U.S. Dist. LEXIS 16520 (C.D. Cal. Sept. 12, 2000) (enjoining, on constitutional grounds, the Los Angeles County ordinance that regulated day laborers' ability to seek work in public places); Scott L. Cummings & Ingrid V. Eagly, *A Critical Reflection on Law and Organizing,* 48 UCLA LAW REVIEW 443, 473 (2001) (analyzing the importance of organizing marginalized workers, including undocumented immigrant day laborers).

96. *See* Laura Ho et al., *(Dis)assembling Rights of Women Workers Along the Global Assembly Line: Human Rights and the Garment Industry,* 31 HARVARD CIVIL RIGHTS–CIVIL LIBERTIES LAW REVIEW 383 (1996).

97. *See* Christopher David Ruiz Cameron, *The Rakes of Wrath: Urban Agricultural Workers and the Struggle Against Los Angeles's Ban on Gas-Powered Leaf Blowers,* 33 UNIVERSITY OF CALIFORNIA AT DAVIS LAW REVIEW 1087, 1100 (2000); *see also* Maria L. On-

tiveros, *Forging Our Identity: Transformative Resistance in the Areas of Work, Class, and the Law*, 33 UNIVERSITY OF CALIFORNIA AT DAVIS LAW REVIEW 1057 (2000) (analyzing efforts of Latina/o farmworkers in California to improve unhealthy working conditions).

98. *See* Hispanic Taco Vendors v. City of Pasco, 994 F.2d 676 (9th Cir. 1993) (affirming the dismissal of a challenge to a local ordinance that required the licensing of taco trucks and other itinerant businesses); Patrick J. McDonnell, *Street Vendor Arrests Up Despite Legalization*, LOS ANGELES TIMES, June 1, 1994, at B1 (reporting that local Latina/o street vendors objected to the implementation of a permit scheme).

99. Richard Delgado, *Two Ways to Think About Race: Reflections on the Id, the Ego, and Other Reformist Theories of Equal Protection*, 89 GEORGETOWN LAW JOURNAL 2279, 2281 (2001) (footnote omitted) (alteration added).

100. *See* Rachel F. Moran, *Demography and Distrust: The Latino Challenge to Civil Rights and Immigration Policy in the 1990s and Beyond*, 8 LA RAZA LAW JOURNAL 1, 10–11 (1995). For an analysis of the relationship between race and class in modern Los Angeles, see VICTOR M. VALLE & RODOLFO D. TORRES, LATINO METROPOLIS (2000).

101. *See* Steven W. Bender, *Consumer Protection for Latinos: Overcoming Language Fraud and English-Only in the Marketplace*, 45 AMERICAN UNIVERSITY LAW REVIEW 1027 (1996); Christopher David Ruiz Cameron, *How the García Cousins Lost Their Accents: Understanding the Language of Title VII Decisions Approving English-Only Rules as the Product of Racial Dualism, Latino Invisibility, and Legal Indeterminacy*, 85 CALIFORNIA LAW REVIEW 1347 (1997); Rachel F. Moran, *Bilingual Education as Status Conflict*, 75 CALIFORNIA LAW REVIEW 321 (1987); *see also* Mari J. Matsuda, *Voices of America: Accent, Antidiscrimination Law, and a Jurisprudence for the Last Reconstruction*, 100 YALE LAW JOURNAL 1329 (1991) (analyzing discrimination on the basis of a perceived foreign accent).

102. *See In re* Mexican Money Transfer Litigation, 267 F.3d 743 (7th Cir. 2001), *cert. denied sub nom.*, 535 U.S. 1018 (2002).

103. *See Unlawful Practice Hits Vulnerable Immigrants*, CALIFORNIA BAR JOURNAL, Nov. 2001, at 1; *see, for example*, Varela v. INS, 204 F.3d 1237 (9th Cir. 2000); Lopez v. INS, 184 F.3d 1097 (9th Cir. 1999).

104. *See, for example*, Leti Volpp, *Blaming Culture for Bad Behavior*, 12 YALE JOURNAL OF LAW AND HUMANITIES 89 (2000); *see also* Madhavi Sunder, *Cultural Dissent*, 54 STANFORD LAW REVIEW 495 (2001) (analyzing the dynamic nature of culture and its interaction with the law).

105. *See* David Firestone, *In U.S. Illegally, Immigrants Get License to Drive*, NEW YORK TIMES, Aug. 1, 2001, at A1.

106. *See* Alexander v. Sandoval, 532 U.S. 275 (2001).

107. *See* Sandoval v. Hagan, 197 F.3d 484, 489–91 (11th Cir. 1999); Sandoval v. Hagan, 7 F. Supp. 2d 1234, 1281–83 (M.D. Ala. 1998); *see also* Kevin R. Johnson & George A. Martínez, *Discrimination by Proxy: The Case of Proposition 227 and the Ban on Bilingual Education*, 33 UNIVERSITY OF CALIFORNIA AT DAVIS LAW REVIEW 1227 (2000) (analyzing how language regulation may amount to unlawful race discrimination because language may serve as a proxy for race).

108. *See* Linda S. Bosniak, *Membership, Equality, and the Difference That Alienage Makes*, 69 NEW YORK UNIVERSITY LAW REVIEW 1047, 1055 (1994). *Compare* Mathews v. Diaz, 426 U.S. 67 (1976) (upholding discrimination against lawful immigrants in a federal benefit program) *and* Foley v. Connelie, 435 U.S. 291 (1978) (upholding the citizenship requirement for a local police officer), *with* Plyler v. Doe, 457 U.S. 202 (1982) (invalidating a Texas law that prohibited the enrollment of undocumented immigrant children in public schools).

109. *See, for example*, Adarand Constructors v. Peña, 515 U.S. 200 (1995); City of Richmond v. J.A. Croson Co., 488 U.S. 469 (1989).

110. 414 U.S. 86 (1973).

111. Later, Congress prohibited such discrimination in the Immigration Reform and Control Act of 1986, Public Law No. 99-603, 100 Statutes at Large 3359 (1986). *See* Michael A. Scaperlanda, *The Paradox of a Title: Discrimination Within the Anti-discrimination Provisions of the Immigration Reform and Control Act of 1986*, 1988 WISCONSIN LAW REVIEW 1043. The antidiscrimination provisions, however, have failed to deter employer discrimination against lawful immigrants and citizens of Asian and Latin American ancestry. *See, for example*, U.S. GENERAL ACCOUNTING OFFICE, IMMIGRATION REFORM: EMPLOYER SANCTIONS AND THE QUESTION OF DISCRIMINATION 3–8 (1990) (finding evidence of a "widespread pattern of discrimination" by employers against citizens and lawful immigrants based on national origin).

112. *See* Juan F. Perea, *Ethnicity and Prejudice: Reevaluating "National Origin" Discrimination Under Title VII*, 35 WILLIAM AND MARY LAW REVIEW 805 (1994).

113. 42 U.S.C. §§ 1981. *Compare* Bhandari v. First National Bank, 829 F.2d 1343 (5th Cir. 1987) (en banc) (holding that § 1981 did not extend to "alienage" discrimination), *vacated and remanded*, 492 U.S. 901 (1989), *reaffirmed on remand*, 887 F.2d 609 (5th Cir. 1989), *cert. denied*, 494 U.S. 1061 (1990), *with* Anderson v. Conboy, 156 F.3d 167 (2d Cir. 1998) (holding that § 1981 prohibited private "alienage" discrimination) *and* Duane v. GEICO, 37 F.3d 1036 (4th Cir. 1994) (same), *cert. dismissed*, 515 U.S. 1101 (1995).

114. *See, for example, Anderson*, 156 F.3d at 168 (a lawful permanent resident from Jamaica); *Bhandari*, 829 F.2d at 1343 (India); Guerra v. Manchester Terminal Corp., 498 F.2d 641 (5th Cir. 1974) (Mexico), *overruled by Bhandari*, 829 F.2d at 1343.

115. A growing body of academic commentary has focused on the possibility of open borders. *See, for example*, OPEN BORDERS? CLOSED SOCIETIES THE ETHICAL AND POLITICAL ISSUES (Mark Gibney ed., 1988); Joseph H. Carens, *Aliens and Citizens: The Case for Open Borders*, 49 REVIEW OF POLITICS 251 (1987); NIGEL HARRIS, THINKING THE UNTHINKABLE: THE IMMIGRATION MYTH EXPOSED (2002); TERESA HAYTER, OPEN BORDERS: THE CASE AGAINST IMMIGRATION CONTROLS (2000); R. George Wright, *Federal Immigration Law and the Case for Open Entry*, 27 LOYOLA LOS ANGELES LAW REVIEW 1265 (1994). For an analysis of the case for open borders, see Kevin R. Johnson, *Open Borders?*, 51 UCLA LAW REVIEW (forthcoming 2003).

116. *See generally* John A. Scanlan, *A View from the United States—Social, Economic, and Legal Change, Persistence of the State, and Immigration Policy in the Coming Century*, 2 INDIANA JOURNAL OF GLOBAL LEGAL STUDIES 79 (1994); Kevin R. Johnson, *Free Trade and Closed Borders: NAFTA and Mexican Immigration to the United States*, 27 UNIVERSITY OF CALIFORNIA AT DAVIS LAW REVIEW 937 (1994).

117. *See* Kitty Calavita, *Immigration, Law, and Marginalization in a Global Economy: Notes from Spain*, 32 LAW AND SOCIETY REVIEW 529 (1998); Lydia Esteve González & Richard MacBride, *Fortress Europe: Fear of Immigration? Present and Future Immigration Law and Policy in Spain*, 6 UNIVERSITY OF CALIFORNIA AT DAVIS JOURNAL OF INTERNATIONAL LAW AND POLICY 153 (2000); Kevin R. Johnson, *Regional Integration in North America and Europe: Lessons About Civil Rights and Equal Citizenship*, 9 UNIVERSITY OF MIAMI INTERNATIONAL AND COMPARATIVE LAW REVIEW 33, 40–43 (2000–2001).

118. *See* generally Howard F. Chang, *Liberalized Immigration as Free Trade: Economic Welfare and the Optimal Immigration Policy*, 145 UNIVERSITY OF PENNSYLVANIA LAW REVIEW 1147 (1997).

119. *See* Scanlan, *supra* note 116, at 129.

120. Huntington, *supra* note 71, at 5.

121. *See* Johnson, *supra* note 115.

Index

Act of March 3, 1875, 112. *See also* Crimes, deportation and exclusion of aliens convicted of

Adams v. Howerton (9th Cir. 1982), 147–148

Affirmative Action, 15

African Americans, 13, 15, 19, 20–22, 182n

Aggravated felony, 117–118. *See also* Crimes, deportation and exclusion of aliens convicted of

AIDS (Acquired Immuno-Deficiency Syndrome). *See* HIV exclusion

Al-Hazmi, Dr. Al-Bdr, 79

Al-Muhajir, Abdullah, 12

Al-Najjar, Mazen, case of, 79–80. *See also* Political ideology, regulation of in immigration laws; September 11, 2001, impact on immigration law and enforcement

Al Qaeda, 12

Alien and Sedition Acts, 55, 60–61, 153

"Alien land laws," 18–19

Alien Registration Act of 1940, 65, 67. *See also* Political ideology, regulation of in immigration laws

Aliens, impact of terminology on treatment of immigrants, 152–163

Allende, Hortensia, 71

Allport, Gordon, 51, 197n

American-Arab Anti-discrimination Committee, litigation involving, 77–85. *See also* Political ideology, regulation of in immigration laws

American Federation of Labor, 63

American Psychiatric Association, views on homosexuality, 145

Americans with Disabilities Act, 107. *See also* Disabilities, exclusion of aliens with

Anarchist Acts of 1918 and 1920, 64

Anarchists, exclusion and deportation of, 62–65

Anti-Semitism, influence on immigration laws, 23–24, 25, 40

Antiterrorism and Effective Death Penalty Act of 1996, 58, 75, 88, 90, 117, 119

Arabs and Muslims, treatment by U.S. government, 5, 9, 14, 55, 57, 77–85, 90, 170, 209n. *See also* September 11, 2001, impact on immigration law and enforcement

Ashcroft, John, 79

Assimilation of immigrants, 22, 23. *See also* Mexican immigrants

Asylum, for women, 132–133; for homosexuals, 150–151

Aviation and Transportation Safety Act, 85 September 11, 2001, impact on immigration law and enforcement

Baird, Zoe, 137

Barrera-Echavarria v. Rison (9th Cir. 1955), 120, 161. *See also* Detention of immigrants

Battered Immigrant Women Protection Act, 131. *See also* Domestic violence, against immigrant women

Black, Hugo, 69

Border enforcement, 27–39, 164–65, 165–67, 212n; deaths resulting from, 29, 242n

Border Patrol, 27–39. *See also* Immigration and Naturalization Service